Nineteenth-Century Literary Realism argues for realism as a mode committed to depicting the imperiled ecological system of soul and society. More specifically: realism, Kearns argues, suggests to its readers that social and political and economic reforms are inextricably tied to spiritual well-being. In the process of trying to communicate that suggestion, realism enters into a kind of considerate conversation with its readers that – through the slippage endemic to language – rapidly works to destabilize, even undermine, its own assumptions. Thus realism, in addition to bearing the burden of its own reformist agenda and the duty of character enactment within a restricted environment, is charged with an alternative energy that can be seen at the same time to disrupt and to enrich its generic, formal bounds.

In keeping with the exploration of these conflicting energies, Kearns takes on an assemblage of British and American novels – *Frankenstein, Wuthering Heights, The Blithedale Romance, Hard Times, The Awakening* – whose inclusion in the realist genre deliberately defies critical convention. Fantastic, ambiguous, brokered between the real and surreal, these texts illustrate the complex ways in which realism warred with its own principle of certainty. Kearns's radical revision of realism thus works not just to demonstrate how such unlikely texts fit into the realist world, but conversely to reveal unsounded depths in mainstream realism, to perturb still more profoundly our acceptance of literary genera.

Nineteenth-Century Literary Realism

Nineteenth-Century Literary Realism

Through the Looking-Glass

KATHERINE KEARNS

CAMBRIDGE
UNIVERSITY PRESS

Published by the Press Syndicate of the University of Cambridge
The Pitt Building, Trumpington Street, Cambridge CB2 1RP
40 West 20th Street, New York, NY 10011–4211, USA
10 Stamford Road, Oakleigh, Melbourne 3166, Australia

First published 1996

Printed in the United States of America

Library of Congress Cataloging-in-Publication Data

Kearns, Katherine.
Nineteenth-century literary realism / Katherine Kearns.
p.   cm.
Includes bibliographical references and index.
ISBN 0–521–49606–3
1. English fiction – 19th century – History and criticism.
2. Realism in literature.   3. American fiction – 19th century –
History and criticism.   4. Literature and society – Great Britain –
History – 19th century.   5. Literature and society – United States –
History – 19th century.   6. Social problems in literature.
7. Spiritual life in literature.   8. Fiction – Technique.
PR868.R4K43   1996
823'.80912–dc20   95–8706
                                                                CIP

A catalog record for this book is available from the British Library.

ISBN 0–521–49606–3 hardback

For Nick and Max

The largest elephant in the world except himself
to be seen here.
—Friedrich Nietzsche, *The Use and
Abuse of History* (attributed to
Jonathan Swift)

Contents

Acknowledgments

It may be that only closet nihilists feel compelled to talk about realism, and that they talk about the real in order to bring words back to some testamentary force. To speak of realism is to enforce a conviction of reality's presence through the very medium – language – that has been deprived of its intercessional status as a bridge between materiality and spirit and made instead to stand as evidence of an estrangement from the world of things. The critical and artistic discourses of realism say two truths simultaneously: "There *is* realism," they say, and in so saying they betray a repressed conviction of nothingness. Talking about the real is a way to stay in the world, to keep alive the loved objects whose loss one fears, and to keep at bay the all-too-peremptory externalities that threaten to turn spirit to machinic deadness. Not the least of the benefits of my own engagement with realism has been this chance to script a performance that writes a sort of modest optimism into being. That this recuperation is not an entirely arbitrary or Pollyannaish undertaking is a truth proven to me every day in the goodwill of my friends, colleagues, and family.

I would like to thank the institutions that have facilitated my research and the many friends and colleagues who have encouraged and supported my work. Northwestern State University provided funds to help in my research and enthusiastic support of my year's tenure at the Whitney Humanities Center at Yale University. My reading-group companions in Natchitoches, Louisiana, kept my ideas alive and my thoughts more or less in order: Darrel Colson, Clayton Delery, and most especially Art Williams sustained a conversation long after most others had fallen to heavy course loads and other overwhelming obligations. My other Louisiana friends and colleagues – Gail and Michael Henry, Gwen and Charles Coker, Rodney and Cindy Allen, Art Weiss, Janet Sturman, John Sturman, Karen Cole, Nate Therien, Susan Newton, and Sylvie Magri, to name only a few – have informed my notions of realism and enforced my sense of the generous, flexible parameters of the real. My fellowship at the Whitney Humanities Center has provided invaluable time to work and write, and my affiliation with Yale University has given me access to unparalleled research libraries and unequaled opportunities for formal and informal conversations about matters pertaining to issues of realism. The Gardiner Seminars, the Legal Theory Workshops, the Church and State Seminars, the weekly meetings of the Fellows of the Humanities Center, and the multiple other lectures and discussions at Yale University have provided constant counterpoints, confirmations, and challenges to my versions of the real. My conversations with David Marshall, Sheila Brewer, David Bromwich, Steven Meyer, John Auchard, Candace Waid, Juliet Mitchell, Harold Bloom, Angie Schriever, Richard Rorty, Mark Micale, Michael Riffaterre, and John Coetzee have enriched my thinking and qualified some of my excesses. My old friend Margaret Ketchum Powell, and her family, have made New Haven seem like home.

Lastly, I want to thank my family. Grady Ballenger knows better than most what should count as real and what should not, and he remembers the important things. My children, Nicholas and Max, keep realism in its place, because in a world where everything else shifts and changes, they are as real as real can be.

Introduction

The modern man carries inside him an enormous heap of indigestible
knowledge-stones that occasionally rattle together in his body, as the
fairy tale has it. And the rattle reveals the most striking characteristic
of these modern men – the opposition of something inside them to
which nothing external corresponds, and the reverse.

—Friedrich Nietzsche, *The Use and Abuse of History*

Realism at Zero Degree

I shall acknowledge before the fact the circle within which the argument
at hand is premised: it is the assumption that realism is an essentially pragmatic mode whose predication of character as something enacted, partially
but inevitably, within environmental restrictions is designed to reveal an
imperiled ecological system of soul and society; this assumption is coupled
with the intuition that there is also in realism an alternative energy, perhaps
in direct consequence of its shouldering of ethical and social responsibility,
that is sufficient to destabilize the reformist agenda at hand.[1] Recognizing
that "character" is produced by both intrinsic and extrinsic imperatives,
sensing that these imperatives are brought inevitably into stark relief in a
world moving toward technologization, realism addresses itself with a degree of pragmatic efficiency to the problems at hand. But it does not do
this blithely, because it concedes before the fact that the realist's "duty"
must be felt as a dangerous imperative by all but saints and unregenerately
self-satisfied philanthropists. Those realists in between these extremes will

suffer from their willing engagement with the real, as they apprehend – by virtue of opening their eyes to the world – that their "duty" must make itself manifest at two oppositional levels: as an ideal and unwavering concept and as a constant negotiation within a complex world of work (their own and others') and language (their own and others') and desire (their own and others').

Conducted within the sphere of daily life, duty will come up against desire, because one who turns from generalities to look intimately at people will run the risks and enjoy the pleasures of voyeurism. One who looks is likely to discover that it is not only in ideal forms – beauty, truth, goodness – that pleasure lies; one has but to look to find that love does indeed pitch its mansions in Crazy Jane places, and, recognizing this, one recognizes the erotic in a most basic and non-idealistic way. James speaks directly to the charged field in which the novel performs its obligations: "In the English novel (by which . . . I mean the American as well), more than in any other, there is a traditional difference between that which people know and that which they agree to admit they know, that which they see and that which they speak of, that which they feel to be a part of life and that which they allow to enter into literature."[2] There is, in other words, a subtextual message in realism's songs of experience affirming that duty shares an affiliation with domination, that pain shares an affiliation with pleasure, that both the body and the body of the text are *there* with a sufficiency that exceeds any idealisms or mundanities one might impose to contain them. (It is no wonder that hysteria flourishes, both as illness and as diagnosis, in the latter half of the century, no wonder that Anna O. comes up with the talking cure, for the hysteric is the enriched allegory of this taut multiplicity of desire and control, and of the multiple, and often oppositional, levels of the real.) "Duty" unravels under close inspection into threads of altruism and self-servedness, an intuition regarding itself that realism embodies in an entire series of bogus do-gooders and other hypocrites; though necessary, the realist's duty will also be felt as necessarily suspect, because a non-idealized, non-aestheticized vision of things will also comprehend itself as such.

And thus duty will also come up against language; all semantic equations become increasingly complex under this burden of sightedness, and one cannot but be ambivalent about a disorder that is also, at the same time, an enrichment. As Eliot says, "one word stands for many things, and many words for one thing; the subtle shades of meaning, and still subtler echoes of association, make language an instrument which scarcely anything short of genius can wield with definiteness and certainty." Yet to divest language of its "fitful shimmer of many-hued significance," "its music and its passion . . . its vital qualities as an expression of individual character, . . . its subtle capabilities of wit" would be to deprive it of "everything that gives it power over the imagination," to make it "deodorized and non-resonant," "algebraic."[3] The realist author articulates multiple obligations: a duty to faithful representation, a duty to the truthful treatment of material, a duty to the everyday and the ordinary, and so on. But that author speaks these obligations into a discursive field felt as both enriched and disorderly, a place where ideal containers – words as well as concepts – have begun to burgeon with fitful, multiplicative, and contradictory particulars.

And so the realist's duty, that which the author enacts artistically in the work of writing, will come up against Art as well, or, more particularly, up against all formalized and aestheticized images of things that, when actually seen in their particularities, will prove themselves to be neither formally nor aesthetically consistent. "It is much handier to get at books than to get at men," says Howells.[4] Realism has it in mind to see beyond forms traditionally recognized as aesthetically permissible, and in particular it would scrap the pastoral as that which has costumed a vast body of work and otherwise under-dressed people in preposterous clothes. "Idyllic ploughmen are jocund when they drive their teams afield; idyllic shepherds make bashful love under hawthorn-bushes; idyllic villagers dance in the chequered shade and refresh themselves," says Eliot, whereas the real thing is not jocund nor merry nor beautiful nor light nor effervescent. "The selfish instincts are not subdued by the sight of buttercups," she says. "To make men moral something more is requisite than to turn them out to grass."[5] But realism wants more than merely this un-costuming, which is easy enough to achieve with a microscope or a photograph or a scalpel. (Sade sardonically prefigures the realist's suspicion of the ornamental in his eroticizing of the ugly and the old, as well as the beautiful and the young body. In his surgical fantasies of treating skin as merely one more layer to be penetrated or removed, or to be stitched, reshaped, and otherwise refurbished for more utilitarian purposes, he writes another version of Carlyle's story.) Realism would at once divest artistic vision of its habit of prettiness and give to art the right to paint and to write about that which is not pretty, *and* it would implicate one so thoroughly in this realness as to bring one to more genuine and immediate feeling (again, an affiliation with Sade): "We want to be taught to feel, not for the heroic artisan or the sentimental peasant, but for the peasant in all his coarse apathy, and the artisan in all his suspicious selfishness," says Eliot.[6]

The realist aspires to do what Barthes says that the realistic artist most particularly fails to do: to exit the loop whereby not only art but also language and desire feed off of art, and in so doing to bring art to the service of the immediately real, the contingent, and the unformalized, which is to say that the realist embraces the possibility of translating un-mediated sensations into words, an attempt as problematically complex when it is believed to have been effected as when, more often, one feels that it has failed. The English painter, says Eliot, paints his idylls while "under the influence of idyllic literature," and by extension one may as-sume that the writer recapitulates the painter's landscape as well; realism's premise is that one must learn to speak an art that is not itself filtered through art.[7] This may, of course, be impossible. Barthes says in *S/Z* that "the 'realistic' artist never places 'reality' at the origin of his discourse, but only and always, as far back as can be traced, an already written real, a prospective code, along which we discern, as far as the eye can see, only a succession of copies."[8] But, fishing up that metaphysical red herring "re-ality," this formulation begs the question whether or not one *can* exit the already written real.

My point is not to assert that realism succeeds where Barthes says that it must fail, but rather to argue that realism is not so complacent nor so decorous nor so ingenuous as its recent reputation would suggest; it is not so much estranged from desire as attuned to it, so much so that, to use Eliot's suggestive words in *Adam Bede*, "desire is chastened into submis-sion."[9] It buys its pragmatism at the standard price, which is to purchase one's ability to deal with things at the level of their human effect by giving these same things up as "reality" in any self-contained sense. "Consider what effects, which might conceivably have practical bearings, we conceive the object of our conception to have," says Peirce's pragmatic maxim, for "then our conception of these effects is the whole of our conception of

the object." This is realism's intuition of how to proceed – and thus metonymy necessarily prevails – but it is also a form of abnegation, a claiming
of performative efficiency within a system in which other forms of verifi-
ability have already begun to fail.

I do not mean by this to suggest that realist authors are philosophical
pragmatists, that is, that they yield up all metaphysical illusions in order to
formulate a philosophy of practical effects. I do mean that at one level they
choose to write in order to teach the lessons of what it means to function
humanly within a world increasingly oriented toward orderly, large-scale
productivities and that their hope is to communicate generally to others;
they have not willingly entered in any extended way into any of the secret
or limited discourses whose codes systematically alter the terms for their
initiates, and they are not primarily in the business of that obfuscation
meant to betoken a tortured soul beset by inner demons.[10] They cannot
(and they know that they cannot) afford to yield to the seductions of
existentialist reverie, although it is clear that they apprehend the instability
of their psychic position relative to the world; nor can they succumb completely to a formalism that would accommodate, contain, but not arrest,
"the perpetual exfoliations of personality" one suffers while progressing
toward death.[11] This open declaration of my choice to focus on realism's
often-noted pragmatic engagement with how the material world and character interact is an attempt to facilitate communication on this matter of
how I perceive realism, at one level, to work; the choice reproduces both
the impulse behind realism and the methodology of realism, as I see it.
The reader may, equally in realism's spirit, choose to enter temporarily the
terms of this particular contract.

At the heart of the realist's conscious agenda is a desire and an expectation to communicate effectively using the shared markers of materiality.
Realism cannot begin if it has its back up; rather, it must assume a willing
and competent audience that will know at the opening gambit the rules
of this most everyday of language games (this is not the premise of, say,
high modernist poetry or fiction or experimental film or avant-garde art).
Realism, like life, depends on the kindness of strangers, or, to appropriate
Donald Davidson's term, it embraces the "principle of charity" by which
a reasonable understanding is achieved and translation is more or less successfully effected.[12] A quotient of suspended disbelief, amnesia, and illogic

is built into the equation and accommodated accordingly. Realism's faith in materiality is problematized by a post-Kantian suspicion that these markers are compromised, delusory artifacts of one's own blind insight and the *Weltanschauung* that tinctures the productions of the ego; it is not so compromised, however, as to have become immured in irony and obfuscation. Like those road markers buried in snowdrifts in *Wuthering Heights*, materialities might still be of some value if one could only imagine seeing them clearly again. (Unlike the similar markers in *Women in Love* that would have led Gerald Crich away from death in the snow, these are not rejected before the fact as useless for finding one's way out of the labyrinth of inchoate loss.[13]) One is meant simultaneously to *trust* the material tautology of a given realism, its artifacts, its events, its influences, even as one recognizes the insufficiency and distortions of the data provided. Realism brings language (as we do even now) before what Davidson calls "the tribunal of experience," despite intuiting the quixotic nature of the enterprise.[14] When asked why, the realist might anticipate Austin's attitude about sufficient evidence: "Enough is enough, enough isn't everything."[15] Logically, conceding to a temporary reality is like being a little bit dead (or undead), but experientially we all, most of the time, accommodate competing assumptions about the world's place relative to self – even if we reject, on philosophical, logical, psychoanalytic, and political grounds that there *is* a self, and even if we have, philosophically, given up "the world" and "reality" as workable terms. Realism was and continues to be the literary embodiment of this opportunism.

Realism's willingness to appeal on a need-to-know basis to the tribunal of experience is then to be held separate from the notion of absolute or ideal "Truth," which it typically keeps in mind, but more or less bracketed; in using this double vision it shares the premises of a nineteenth-century historiography that mandated, as Humboldt said, "the exact, impartial, critical investigation of events" coupled with an intuitive reading of the "inner causal nexus" and the "inner truth" of these facts in time.[16] This combination requires delicate balance, for the novelist knows that language will want to have its fancy say. As George Eliot says in *Adam Bede*, "falsehood is . . . easy, truth . . . difficult," "even when you have no motive to be false, it is a very hard thing to say the exact truth, even about your own immediate feelings – much harder than to say something fine about them which is *not* the exact truth."[17] When one dons the hair shirt of an artistry that will draw "faithful pictures of a monotonous homely existence," when one forthrightly chooses to "turn, without shrinking, from cloud-borne angels" to ordinary old women eating plain food in a plain room, one tacitly suggests that a small but exact "truth" will take the place of Truth, just as history will take the place of History.[18] Eliot articulates – and does so from *within* her novel – realism's intuition of a double-sided truth, and in so doing she predicts the critical coin toss that will follow. On one side lies that which is historically verifiable because materially evident and artifactual, an external matter based in trade – of goods, of words, of ideas, of affections. And on the other lies that which is also true, often antithetically so: the hyperbolic, ontological truths that taunt externalities as meager and insufficient. The critical discourse calls heads or tails and proceeds accordingly, but the realistic texts themselves perform a less unilateral message.

Realism, often charged with blind-siding social, political, and epistemological complexities, with throwing its considerable materialistic weight against all that would challenge or suborn the status quo, manages nonetheless to communicate its sense of itself as a bifurcated and inadequate accommodation of any holistic reality. Depending on their predispositions, the critics may see this either as information freely if somewhat covertly given or as an unconscious truth extorted from an ingenuous text or a repressed text. Critics and marketing strategists who subscribe to the latter may thus promote realism as both fictional and true all at once: like the madman, incompetent as regards the really real, whatever the hermeneutic integrity of its visions, while, again like the madman, unimpeachable in its communication of a historical reality. Thus we see a paperback edition of *Adam Bede* using a fragment from the critical preface by Stephen Gill as promotion copy: " 'Reading the novel,' " says the cover, " 'is a process of learning simultaneously about the world of Adam Bede and the world of *Adam Bede.*' "[19] In this marketing strategy, fictional realism shares a space with texts produced within the asylum – Daniel Paul Schreber's *Memoirs of My Nervous Illness* (1903), for example. Realism is said to tell a (historical) truth despite itself even as it does not tell the truth, just as Schreber is said by the psychoanalysts to speak with absolute accuracy and precision about paranoia through a language he himself perceives as telling another kind of true story, that of his visions and visitations. Barthes makes the justification for analytic intervention explicit in his charge against the historians, a group that unambiguously asserts what the realists have been accused of claiming more obliquely: "a privileged ontological status" in which "we recount what has been, not what has not been, or what has been uncertain." "To sum up, historical discourse is not acquainted with negation . . . ," says Barthes. "Strangely enough, but significantly, this fact can be compared with the tendency which we find in a type of utterer who is very different from the historian: that is the psychotic, who is incapable of submitting an utterance to a negative transformation. We can conclude that, in a certain sense, 'objective' discourse . . . shares the situation of schizophrenic discourse."[20] For those who, for any number of reasons, ranging from the Althusserean to the ornamental, see realism itself as "a radical censorship of the act of uttering," this critical intervention may be used as a recuperative strategy.[21]

Yet however its intentions in the matter are read, realism does supply two histories for the price of one, one of them fictional, the other "real," but united inextricably in the detailing and circumstantialities to which modern historiography would also commit itself. Implicitly resistant to the grand narrative of Truth, while nonetheless in the service of a truth that is "historical" in proportion to its evidential materialities, the realistic novel eschews metaphysics at the level of practice. Gill's observations about *Adam Bede* are also more generally applicable, for the realist novelist reveals a world that is "simultaneously a real world, historically placed, specifically realized, accurate in verifiable detail, and a fictional one, artistically ordered by a *knowable* author."[22] This is not, of course, to argue that an articulated or fully realized skepticism about metaphysical absolutes necessarily motivates this diminution of terms in the nineteenth century; as Hegel's *Lectures on the Philosophy of World History* makes clear, both exegetically and through its own practice, one's acceptance of the necessary existence of Truth may in fact authorize a homely and dedicated empiricism, a preoccupation with craft over Art. Paradoxically, this metaphysical conviction may free one to assert that "history itself must be taken as it is; we have to proceed historically, empirically."[23] A sense of contingency, that which overrides, for Hegel, the "professional" historian's "*a priori* historical fiction" with its idiosyncrasies, may flourish within a system whose overarching formal integrity remains intact.

Unlike the productions of historiography, however, fictional realism's oxymoronic status ensures that both the realist's faith and the reader's faith in the judicial body – that which moderates the acceptable and the unacceptable, the sane and the insane, the real and the unreal – will be overtly contractual, contingent on the reality under scrutiny. One who reads very closely will see that the circle of fictional truth enacts its laws precisely by co-opting materialities into its representational bias through a system of synonymous elaborations, into the grammar of its given system of representatives,[24] whereas the "ordinary" reader – which is to say the reader whom realism so famously leads by the nose[25] – will respond to any number of less subtle warnings that realism throws out about its partiality. The ordinary reader – which is also to say the reader who engages these novels responsively, for pleasure (not so simple or domesticated an emotion as it often has been said to be) – is likely to feel realism's textual topography as rough, uneven. The *experience* of reading, which the critical discourse smooths out, translates at least as much anxiety as complacency in regard to the real: In realism, one is given to understand, in understanding the contractual and consensual nature of a given reality, that there is always a possibility that the terms will shift, that the bank in which one has deposited one's life savings will fail, that the currency may change. (As if to bring this point home quite literally, Gaskell shakes Cranford to its core with the bank failure that ruins Miss Mattie Jenkyns; *Cranford*, so devoted to the ordinary, the daily, and the non-hyperbolic as to become emblematic of realism's modest purview, must turn to the devices of romance – the long-lost and exoticized brother – for rescue.) Realism suffers from – is, in fact, in some ways activated by – the fear that *Frankenstein* makes literal: that one's own (horrifying, eye-opening) tribunal of experience may be obviated as madness in another court, that both the imperative to produce a given reality and the reality itself will, when presented before another judiciary body, be seen as phantasmatic. The imminently tangible monster, oversized as it is, potentially may be held not to exist in an alternative assize.

The realistic novel's preoccupation with lawyers, court cases, and trials reflects this apprehension of a reality that must be pled into existence. Godwin's *Caleb Williams* (1794), very early on, predicted realism's intuition of a world in which appearances might pose the most fundamental contradiction to the realities of the case at hand, and in which one's status would define whether or not, and how, one could be heard in court. The differend communicates itself variously in realism, which refines the degrees and kinds of victimization with an interest virtually Sadeian.[26] The eighteenth-century game of baiting lawyers, whose only competition as objects of derision were tailors and doctors, gives way in novels of realism to a generally more sober view of the judiciary: One thinks not so much of buffoons, but rather of coldly sinister barristers, of life-and-death matters, of trials of the falsely accused (Justine, in *Frankenstein*, for example, or James Wilson, in *Mary Barton*) and the equally horrific trials of the "guilty" ones (Hetty Sorrel, of *Adam Bede*, for example, who cannot, by definition of the childishness that propelled her into disaster, account for herself; only her seducer, the young squire entered into his inheritance, may plead her case successfully, the irony of which should not go unnoticed).[27] Realism both intuits and performs its own contingency, and it forces the question of what it is that constitutes the whole truth, and nothing but the truth. For Truth, systemically perceived within a given set of materialities, becomes something else, something, in fact, that contributes its mite to the ultimate subversion of the grand narrative, Truth: Like the word "realism" itself, such a word used within the necessary contextualities of a physical environment announces itself as already problematized.

Actuated under a pragmatic willingness to forget competing versions and extraneous details, whatever it might imply about its own metaphysical accuracies, realism is not then overly distracted with Truth or the absence thereof (its authors may or may not themselves be distracted, but such difficulties are not allowed to override the syntagmatic momentum within the text); it cannot afford to go either to the extreme of idealism – Truth in the Platonic sense – or to that of positivism – Truth as a finite condition to be reached through accumulation of all relevant detail. In her guise as Aletheia, truth makes a lovely seduction toward allegory and thus to exile in the "country of the blue," where one wakes to a good conscience but to a very small coterie of like-minded idealists.[28] An alternative anatomizing will lead one to the paradox of observation: The act of gathering details will produce enhanced methods of evaluation, which then, in revealing component parts, will require their further deconstruction. This inevitable conversion from macro- to micro-organization, of course, is accompanied by a necessity for name-giving that further compromises one's hope that words and things will have natural and necessary connections (when physicists named the "quark" by consulting *Finnegan's Wake*, the circle became complete). Realism, by virtue of its forensic attention to the tangible components of the environment at hand, *appears* to and often does consciously subsidize a positivist economy; it appears to contribute to the gathering of evidence that, when all the facts are in, will allow language to consummate its relationship to reality. Yet the literary process itself destabilizes the positivist program of fact-gathering, for things that appear to be facts can elide and metamorphose within the intricacy of the language game in which they reside.

Realism recognizes both the need for factual detail and the delusion of completeness that facts can come to represent, for the material world is exactly that place that is both too imperatively real in its effect on character and not "real" enough. Realism clearly senses that to speak without a degree of skepticism about "facts" is to be guilty of Gradgrindism, a strange mixture of the ingenuous and the hardheaded. At one level, such faith implies a Platonic "out there" that transcends individuated sensory experience, and at another level it perpetuates the notion of the possibility of full disclosure – that hopeful sense that when *all* the facts are in, truth will stand revealed, and that language will be equal to saying it. Yet the friction between the need for empirical rigor and the desire for holistic truth clearly generates anxiety in realism's texts. All those cabinets filled with specimens in *Hard Times* make a mute appeal to this acquisitive empiricism as a means to truth, even as they reveal by virtue of their fractured contents the inevitable partialities of the enterprise. And perhaps the sadist's compulsive avarice is another side to this fantasy of collecting enough evidence to make a fully presenced truth with precisely the correct and proper name:[29] Heathcliff, with his hunger for real estate, is another collector, as if acquiring enough land will finally bring into full resolution the oxymoron of his own terrestrial name, complete the half-truth represented in its ambiguous, univocal status as neither Christian name nor surname, and return him to the chthonic/maternal source from which he has been severed.

The very act of gathering things for a definitive totality calls up the futility of the gesture, and beyond that futility lies the exponential slippage between things and the words that speak them. The evidence of the things out there may *produce* the need for language, but the nineteenth-century novelist has begun to apprehend that language can be neither verified as "true" nor discredited on the basis of this other, entirely separate stuff that is, even as one speaks, proving itself to be so mutable and so willfully indifferent to standard terms and explanations.[30] Materialities in an industrial environment take their value less from what they are than from what they can be transformed into; they are both more than the sum of their parts and less, as they are amplified and reduced, assimilated and pried apart into components. There is the Rumpelstiltskin factor: One spins straw into wealth. There is the Midas paradox: One touches a thing, and it turns to gold. And there is the peculiar inversion of the Midas myth whereby those who make a given thing become contiguous with and inseparable from the machineries of production.[31] Sibylline, one deals in "futures" whose oxymoronic names prove a weighty ephemerality, things (hogs, rubber, copper) both there and not there at once. Time vacates its spatial correlatives to hide in the clockworks in this world. As Anthony Giddens points out in *The Consequences of Modernity*, an "emptying of time" begins when "it comes to reside in clocks, is standardized and available in timepieces to everyone," and when it is marshaled into the peremptory fiction of the industrial workday it opens the window through which it flies from itself in its more natural embodiments.[32] The Mad Hatter's tea party speaks to this estrangement, as does the impulse to doctor the watch with the very best butter, but Eliot's image most powerfully captures the watchbeetle hollowness of time and language on a White Rabbit schedule: In an attempt to escape the poetic for the scientific, the ambiguous for the factual, historians will reduce language to "a talking watch, which will achieve the utmost facility and despatch in the communication of ideas by a graduated adjustment of ticks, to be represented in writing by a corresponding arrangement of dots."[33]

Time flies, and "placedness" – one of realism's most intense preoccupations – loses its integrity as technologization reaches out to ensure that locales become "thoroughly penetrated by and shaped in terms of social influences quite distant from them"[34] (and thus the nostalgia of *Cranford*, a place out of time, or the isolative location in which *Silas Marner* enacts itself, or the purgatorial space that engulfs the Heights and the Grange and the Penistone Crags in *Wuthering Heights* – "the Heights is a bastion where, in De Quincey's words, ordinary clock-time becomes 'suddenly arrested, laid asleep, tranced, racked into a dread armistice,' " says Knoepflmacher;[35] thus realism's paradoxical affiliations, tonally and otherwise, with fairy tale). One must pause here to think how the chronotope functions when both time and space begin to be felt as arbitrary.[36] If language is, in Wittgenstein's account, an ancient city, with archeological density, realism sees Coketowns springing up like mushrooms, with no pasts and new vocabularies. Realism typically sets for itself a pedagogical juggling act within this all too tangibly real phantasmagoria, for if, as Mr. Sleary of *Hard Times* says, people must somehow be amused, they must also be taught – persuaded to a version of the real and to a humane amelioration of its errors. Realism takes seriously its obligation to mediate for humanness, even as it recognizes that, on the one hand, people impressed into technology's service risk reduction to dreary sameness, and that, on the other hand, these same dead souls risk an alienation from each other commensurate with the environment they have all come to metonymize. Deeply concerned with character, realism talks its people into a viability that functions both as example and as antidote.

The realistic text reciprocates this productively egalitarian intent with a paraphrastic energy that elaborates the terms as they are set until an understanding may reasonably be expected to have been reached.[37] One must notice, for example, that, for this very reason, realism never indulges more than momentarily in unstable irony; it is not premised on a reception by initiates or sophisticates; it does not look to separate, by a strategy of doubled meanings, the men from the boys; and it cannot afford to undermine its syntagmatic energy completely. In this milieu, aporia most appropriately functions not to distract or to disable, but to facilitate, as it makes gaps only where additional detail might constitute grounds for a competing reality or a distracting density or opacity. Shandian tomfooleries involving time, space, and character are necessarily to be kept to a minimum. Realism shows that the conversational possibilities for making oneself understood and for understanding what is being said may be kept more or less intact literarily, for the text may mimic those devices of repetition and connection that generate a mutual understanding. In fact, realism's evidential spirit licenses an analogy between oral sociableness and textual sociableness, enacting, as it does, a literary version of communicative competence. Davidson points out, in "Locating Literary Language," that the primordial triangle of speaker, hearer, and shared conceptual field repeats itself textually in writer, audience, and common background, although the distances that separate these elements are lengthened, and the connections among them can become "attenuated and obscure."[38] "Almost all connected writing that involves more than a few words and sentences depends on deictic references to its own text. . . . A vast network of anaphoric references connects parts of a text to each other through the use of pronouns, demonstrative adjectives, tense, and parataxis.[39] Realism is, by virtue of what it wants to be (i.e., real), a dream of connectedness, a resistance to the obscurities and attenuations to which the written word is prone.

Realism reduces the distances that separate author, reader, and shared world, basing its rhetorical tactics on the same instincts for repetition, incrementally articulated clarifications, and the other modes of connectedness one brings to conversation (publication by parts further enhances this recuperative project). Realism seems to intuit the value of the incremental repetitions inherent in conversational etiquette; one sees, for example, James and Wharton preoccupy themselves with the performative force of highly subtilized social interchange, sensing perhaps that it is in such verbal performances, interspersed with equally performative silence, that "truth" is forged and dissolved. James reduces the distance between narrator and character to an intimacy positively conversational, as if to bring everyone into his essentially circular discussions; through incremental repetition, endless reorientation, and nuanced variation the subjects (human, aesthetic, epistemological) make their realness apparent. In Wharton's *The Custom of the Country* (p. 335) there is a moment when a conversation is enough to change a character "as if a deadly solvent had suddenly decomposed [the] familiar lines" of his face. This is realism's apprehension of Davidson's famous assertion in "A Nice Derangement of Epitaphs" that "*there is no such thing as a language*," if language is defined, as philosophers and linguists have always said, as systematic, with rules to be learned. Davidson's "passing theory" is very much anticipated in the minute calibrations, the repetitions, the backtracking one finds in both the dialogue and the narrative structures of such quintessential realists as James and Wharton.

Realism chooses to speak of the ordinary world and the people in it. It subordinates its passions and its hobbyhorses to a representationalism both literal and metaphorical, and it uses common objects for illustrative purposes, as if aware of their pedagogical value. It is, as it has been accused of being, given to inclusiveness. Opponents of realism have seen these equable gestures as the soothing murmurs of the already brainwashed, middle-of-the-roaders who would lull others into seeing and speaking ordinariness and therefore into a perpetual re-creation of the status quo. Unapologetically anti-realism and pro-avant-garde, Lyotard says that "the *Salons* and the *Académies*, at the time when the bourgeoisie was establishing itself in history, were able to function as purgation and to grant awards for good plastic and literary conduct under the cover of realism." "When power assumes the name of a party, realism and its neoclassical complement triumph over the experimental avant-garde by slandering and banning it – that is, provided the 'correct' images, the 'correct' narratives, the 'correct' forms which the party requests, selects, and propagates can find a public to desire them as the appropriate remedy for the anxiety and depression that public experiences."[40] Yet this seductive and now-familiar opposition between realism and the avant-garde may only be the difference between the devil and the deep blue sea; while it accurately differentiates the "work" of understanding that each mode generates, it begs the question whether or not one can distinguish between the end products of those efforts of understanding. As in Lyotard's own brilliantly logical critical divagations (which are, paradoxically and necessarily, pushed to define "the corpus of the 'avant-gardes'" so as to counterpoint the work of, for example, the even more remarkable Barnett Baruch Newman), one finds that the text's original communicative intent – plain or fancy, straight or crooked, transparent or opaque – does not necessarily guarantee a transfiguration from a language made up of "the 'correct' images, the 'correct' narratives, the 'correct' forms" to a language natal and trailing clouds of glory.[41] "Charity is forced on us," says Davidson, and "whether we like it or not, if we want to understand others, we must count them right in most matters."[42]

Of course, the distinction of communicative intent is close to arbitrary, for it is evident that the act of speaking/writing proves our desire to be heard. There is no such thing as intending to be misunderstood, but only such a thing as wishing, sometimes perversely and with an infantile neediness, to have one's meaning pursued through the worst kinds of self-erected difficulties.[43] There are times when one cannot help but share with others who are similarly predisposed one's feeling of existential isolation, because silence – the only logical choice – would prove and enforce the existential dilemma all at once. Elias Canetti enacts this paradox in *The Conscience of Words* in his reading of Karl Kraus. "Thanks to him," Canetti says, "I started realizing that each individual has a linguistic shape distinguishing him from all others. I understood that people talk but fail to comprehend one another; that their words are thrusts ricocheting off the words of others; that there is no greater illusion than thinking that language is a means of communication between people. . . . Seldom does anything penetrate the other person, and if it does, it is usually twisted awry."[44] One must ask the philosopher's question, the question Davidson would ask as regards all such assertions of radical incommensurability, and the question that Tallis poses more tartly in *In Defense of Realism*: "if what he says is true, then how does he know it?" Or, as Passmore has said, "the speaker's action is the best possible counter-example to what he asserts to be the case."[45] One always assumes a fit audience somewhere, though it may be few. And in any event, it cannot be demonstrated that translations into "meaning" (in the critical discourse or within the more intimate space of a reader's participatory involvement in the text), even those from the most "difficult" of texts, are more than, or less than, translations into the common tongue of evaluative reorganization.

Where verification is unavailable, one might just as well posit commensurability as incommensurability, but while this choice may have pragmatic advantages, it does not necessarily follow that one who makes it will shed the anxiety, uncertainty, and even despair that attempts at communication, artistic or otherwise, so often provoke; it is, in fact, a position as much in keeping with nihilism as with faith, with Nietzsche as with Dale Carnegie; it may be heroic gaiety just as easily as stupid or slavish optimism. Realism proceeds as if there are common terms; it attaches human significance to materialities in such a way as to suggest that social and political and economic reforms are inextricably tied to spiritual well-being. It holds true to its reformative agenda even under the duress of its sense that language slips inevitably toward less upright pleasures. Conversational, well-mannered enough to consider its audience, practical enough, mostly, to give up ranting, and too humble to aggrandize its own anxieties in the matter of communication, realism works quite dutifully. But it also, in this process and because of this process, desublimates a more anarchic, personalized energy.

Realism becomes increasingly preoccupied with conversation, because the more it attempts to articulate itself, the more complex the communicative procedure reveals itself to be; if authorial interventions begin to take on an archaic character as the century progresses, this relocation of language into a fluid pattern of narrative, indirect discourse, and dialogue may be less than unilaterally determined by a conscious aesthetic program. Realism performs its apprehension of failure at multiple levels, beginning with *Frankenstein*'s extended reverie on the chasms that open between what is said and how it may be heard (or not), and reaching its quintessence in the delicate necessities one finds in the work of James, where the very subtilized linguistic environment bespeaks the potential and potentially irremediable insufficiency of words; the Dickensian comedies – people with lisps and verbal tics, malapropists and punsters – merely reveal the obverse side to that dark, legalistic world where language is incomprehensible and prosecutorial on the one hand and dangerously incriminating on the other. Realism clearly senses that conversation between two people involves what Beckett calls "two separate and immanent dynamisms related by no system of synchronization."[46] This flux, factored into the constantly shifting equilibrium of human interaction, further destabilizes an already uneasy truce. Moreover, and more bleakly, realism senses that it is only seldom that two people share equally in the desire to communicate with each other, and that even when the desire is present, the expectation of success is frequently absent. This conversational slippage is necessarily built into realism's contract with the reader, and it is also quite clearly a component of the internalized discourse within the novel. Realism makes the best of a shaky situation, and it does not do this blithely, for not only does it undertake itself at a time fraught with competing literary, philosophical, social, biological, and political imperatives, but also it places itself rather willfully under the duress of that inexplicable overage beyond the reach of the representational. The result is a series of enriched and internally dynamic novels whose best intentions to chasten desire into submission fail to contain the energies loosed by looking hard at the real; proprietous on the one hand, tropologically riotous on the other, realism does its work at multiple levels.

Tying the Knot

At this point in my narrative regarding realism, William Dean Howells, who in his critical persona knew precisely and unequivocally how realism was to be defined, would already have heard just about enough regarding realism's doubled capacity for straightforward, honest productivity and tropological delirium, and he might very well have announced that a critic who can talk about *Frankenstein* (Levine notwithstanding), *The Blithedale Romance* (James notwithstanding[47]), and *Wuthering Heights* (Charlotte Brontë and C. P. Sanger notwithstanding[48]) as if they live even close to realism's neighborhood is only "a realist according to [her] own conception of realism."[49] Austen, yes, Gaskell, yes, Eliot, yes, and himself as well; Chopin maybe, and Dickens in some of his less playful moments, but not the thoroughly anomalous vision of Emily Brontë, not the Gothic fantasy of *Frankenstein*, not *The Blithedale Romance*, whose very title announces its antipathy to realism. The inclusion of these texts, he is likely to have added, merely reflects the dubious taste of one who "likes to be melted, and horrified, and astonished, and blood-curdled, and goose-fleshed," and those who might be persuaded to include them among realism's efforts "have not taste enough; or, rather, their taste has been perverted by their false criticism, which is based upon personal preference and not upon principle; which instructs a man to think that what he likes is good, instead of teaching him first to distinguish what is good before he likes it."[50] And perhaps all that is so. As I have admitted early on, one sets up a circle and then moves within it, and Howells's more pristine and exclusionary tautology has a certain taxonomic and moral authority about it.

None of the books that I shall speak about at length would, for example, pass Howells's Austen test: "the simple verity, the refined perfection," "the exquisite touch," the honesty, the artistry, and the sheer truth of her novels bring Howells to proclaim "the divine Jane" as realism's paragon, her works unimpeachable. "She was great and they were beautiful, because she and they were honest, and dealt with nature nearly a hundred years ago as realism deals with it today. Realism is nothing more than the truthful treatment of material, and Jane Austen was the first and the last of the English novelists to treat material with entire truthfulness."[51] But it should be said as well (and Howells would expect this response from one who has already proved herself to be so perverse) that the work of Austen read through eyes other than Howells's is likely to be a very different kettle of fish; were I to include, for example, *Mansfield Park* among the novels I discuss at length, I would be provoked to do so not from a sense of Austen's "simple verity" but from a sense of her perversity, her ambivalence, her aggressive undermining, at levels other than exegetical, of the proprietous "real" she promotes by bringing Fanny Price to mature beauty and romantic and social triumph. Because *Mansfield Park* seems to me utterly riddled with a subtextual ambivalence – indeed, it seems positively ill-tempered, nearly querulous – and a nascent rebellion that finds voice only occasionally in Mary Crawford's wicked irreverences, I would question the "verity" of Austen's promotion of incestuous synthesis in the long-withheld consummation of Fanny Price's love of her cousin. I would not, in other words, at all question Austen's position as a realist, and I would see her infiltration of propriety with resistance as very good evidence of her commitment to the realist enterprise, but Howells and I would none-theless be speaking of very different novels as we talked of *Mansfield Park*. Yet at least Howells and I would agree in our admiration for the divine Jane, and though we would necessarily quarrel on the issue of her "entire truthfulness," neither of us would go so far as David Musselwhite, who sees *Mansfield Park* as a quintessentially venal "search for a market."[52] For him, Austen is indeed representative of realism as it emerges through the century, for he sees her as having sacrificed in *Mansfield Park* all of her "natural ideological affiliations" in order to appeal to (and, indeed, actively to constitute through suggestion) a "middle sector." This broad spectrum with all its idiosyncracies homogenized into a " 'Victorianism' " that would come to "constitute the very core of bourgeois ideology for the rest of the century" is for Musselwhite the reality she promotes: She is the original huckster, by his terms, who simultaneously creates a product and its consumers.[53] The point in this divagation on *Mansfield Park*, of course, is that realism defined as "the truthful treatment of material" begs a world of questions.

Howells's definitional circle is to the postmodern reader unavoidably apparent, and yet he lays out precisely the question of taste on which the critical discourse on realism feels itself to rest: How can one legitimate one's judgment relative to the term *realism*? Are one's extrapolations into theory motivated by the pleasures of the text or by "judgment"? Again, he says that "false criticism . . . is based on personal preference, and not upon principle"; it "instructs a man to think that what he likes is good, instead of teaching him first to distinguish what is good before he likes it." Hearing this indictment and responding from within the discourse it presupposes, we ask Kant's question: Is the pleasure (or pain) one feels in the aesthetic process antecedent to the judgment of taste, or is the pleasure (or pain) dependent on one's judgment, which has pronounced already the subjective universality of the thing perceived? In his section entitled "Investigation of the question of the relative priority in a judgment of taste of the feeling of pleasure and the estimating of the object" in *The Critique of Judgment*, Kant begins as follows: "The solution of this problem is the key to the Critique of taste, and so is worthy of all attention."[54] Kant, of course, comes down more or less on Howells's side of the question (with allowances for Kant's careful distinction between cognitive judgment and aesthetic judgment):

As the subjective universal communicability of the mode of representation in a judgment of taste is to subsist apart from the presupposition of any definite concept, it can be nothing else than the mental state present in the free play of imagination and understanding . . . : for we are conscious that this subjective relation suitable for a cognition in general must be just as valid for every one, and consequently as universally communicable. . . . Now this purely subjective (aesthetic) estimating of the object, or of the representation through which it is given, is antecedent to the pleasure in it, and is the basis of this pleasure in the harmony of the cognitive faculties.[55]

But even while wrestling with the personal issue of how judgment arises, the critic knows that post-metaphysical thinking does not allow for an answer to this question of which comes first, pleasure or judgment; because

Howells's "good" and Kant's "subjective universality" no longer apply, there is no possibility of grounding the question. The critic is only able to acknowledge yet once again that the circle is inviolably there and that *as* a circle it ensures the endless running together of the two modes. The critic cannot, other than arbitrarily, separate pleasure and judgment, but can only be disturbed by the sense that judgment *is* pleasure, that judgmental rigor, a kind of pain in the giving and the receiving, is pleasure: that Kant's rigorous and representative effort to assign priority to judgment is exactly the evidence one would need to conclude that pleasure, pain, and judgment have *never* been separate in Western metaphysics (one must think of the full and ironic implications of undertaking a critique of judgment, for example). It is a necessary thing to legitimize through judgment one's private pleasures, so as to disguise the probability that they are inextricable from judgment, which is meant to be rational and clear-sighted and altruistic [the sublime, which is not an aesthetic *judgment* by virtue of its powerful effect, is the (safely cordoned) philosophical and aesthetic version of an intuition of simultaneity, as sadomasochism is the sexual]. One comes to fear that it is impossible to escape implication in a system so juridically inclined as to have been predicated on that particular question and that answer.

Thus, what the critic of realism comes down to is exactly what realism itself comes down to: an economy of pain. How much knowledge, how many details, how specific a view of reality can one take and articulate without being either paralyzed or enraged by the complexities one sees and is brought to feel in taking off the blinders? How much suffering – and realism opens its eyes to this – is enough to bring one to responsible action relative to others, but not so much as to divest one of the capacity for action or drive one to ferocities of judgment? George Eliot speaks directly to the paradox of judgment, in its fullest sense, as that which derives from experience and from the experience of suffering. *Adam Bede* is an extended reverie on how one may balance judgment against understanding, how "Adam" will learn to function in the world of Duty after his egotism is tempered with pain:

Not that this transformation of pain into sympathy had completely taken place in Adam yet: there was still a great remnant of pain, which he felt would subsist as long as *her* pain was not a memory, but an existing thing, which he must think of as renewed with the light of every new morning. But we get accustomed to mental as well as bodily pain, without, for all that, losing our sensibility to it: it becomes a habit of our lives, and we cease to imagine a condition of perfect ease as possible for us. Desire is chastened into submission; and we are contented with our day when we have been able to bear our grief in silence, and act as if we were not suffering. For it is at such periods that the sense of our lives having visible and invisible relations beyond any of which either our present or prospective self is the centre, grows like a muscle that we are obliged to lean on and exert.[56]

Adam Bede has been called the "first major exercise in programmatic literary realism in English literature." Certainly, as if to sum up the lessons that realism has learned already, it precisely emblematizes realism's dilemma of preserving a delicate ecological system between soul and society in a post-Edenic world.[57] "Duty" – "how peremptory and absolute," says Eliot. And of the novel, J. A. Froude said that it "gave no pleasure. It gave a palpitation of the heart. That was not pleasure; but it was a passionate interest."[58]

Both the critic of realism and the realist author are forced at some level to face the possibility that what they wish to have pass for "judgment" in its valorized sense as rigorous, systematic, and externally and internally legitimated, is just another way of equilibrating their own disturbances and desires. As *Wuthering Heights* makes very clear, realism sees that judgment is not bound to forward motion but is always also recuperative, and this is an insight whose adumbrations fill the critical discourse as well. Judgment is retroactive and retrospective more than forward-looking (the precedent is its icon), and it all too frequently recovers characters as guilty or innocent, unworthy and therefore to be sacrificed or worthy and therefore to be saved, based on what it has allowed to happen to them. Those who have been so injured or damaged as to have failed in the performative recuperations that win pity will be seen as deserving of whatever punishment has befallen them. The critic who writes of realism shares realism's apprehension of how claims of legitimation are made by a constant process of assimilation, a ravenous appropriation along a line that extends backward into the past and forward into the future. Metonymy begins to seem an almost sinister trope, as it recognizes the essential barrierlessness and the consumptive energies of one's linguistic progress through the world. (And this brings us back to the infantile and needy monster, who can stand as a figural prediction of metonymy's multidirectional as-

similative force and as a warning about how a "sensible" economy of pain –
Sewell's model in *The Rise of Silas Lapham* – can very easily elide into violent
excess. The monster, having been formed from pieces of humanness, is so
hungry to make the justice of his claims to inclusion felt that he becomes
something of an avatar.)

The critic who speaks today of realism is more than ordinarily aware of
the necessary insufficiencies of a theoretical ordering of the field, but this
is at least in part due to realism's own ambivalent relationships to the
competing imperatives of duty and pleasure, of judgment and mercy, and
of inward and outward compulsions. Yet, as with realism itself, one makes
the obligatory teleological gesture of tying the whole thing off. And as with
realism, one hopes to have fashioned a slipknot, for, as realism knows, it
is only in the act of claiming a reality that one has "a reality." The gesture,
in order that it be complete, must be carried out again and again.

Chapter One

Real Realism

I mean to ask whether a bed really becomes different when it is seen from different points of view, obliquely or directly or from any other point of view? Or does it simply appear different, without being really so? And the same of all things.

—Plato, *The Republic* (bk. X)

Once noticed, it continued to occupy one's mind. It even persisted, as it were, in going about its own business. . . . The striking thing was that it was neither simple nor really complex, initially or intentionally complex, or constructed according to a complicated plan. Instead, it had been desimplified in the course of its carpentering. . . . As it stood, it was a table of additions, much like certain schizophrenics' drawings, described as "overstuffed," and if finished it was only in so far as there was no way of adding anything more to it, the table having become more and more an accumulation, less and less a table. . . . It was not intended for any specific purpose, for anything one expects of a table. . . . Its top surface, the useful part of the table, having been gradually reduced, was disappearing, with so little relation to the clumsy frame-work that the thing did not strike one as a table, but as some freak piece of furniture, an unfamiliar instrument . . . for which there was no purpose. . . . A table which lent itself to no function, denying to itself service and communication alike.

—Gilles Deleuze and Félix Guattari, *Anti-Oedipus*

"I'm telling you stories. Trust me."

—Jeanette Winterson, *The Passion*

The Critical Question

Real realism might be,[1] one begins to take it after a great deal of reading on the subject, the dull-as-dirt, earnest stuff said to have been produced by the only plain realist on the two continents: William Dean Howells. That definition, based more on what Howells said in *Criticism and Fiction* about what realism should be than on what he made of it while in the throes of novelistic text production, works precisely so long as one does not actually *read* Howells's novels (if they are so many advertisements on rocks, they are nonetheless painted with deep Persis-brand colors).[2] In fact, Howells does very clearly articulate and to a great degree perform a baseline truth – perhaps *the* baseline truth – of realism: that literary realism has the question of human decency in mind and that it sees threats to the ecology in which this decency may be enacted.[3] That the historical specifics of British and U.S. technologization produce localized and distinguishable responses to this anxiety has been clearly documented; that realism takes variable shapes as it reacts to historical circumstances is also clear. That it can be periodized, with some useful organizational results (standardly, for England, 1870–1914; for the United States, 1865–1900), is undeniable. That it can be significantly distinguished, in product and in motivation, from nineteenth-century European realism has been carefully premised;[4] indeed, that there are important divergences between the British and U.S. varieties has also been implied and demonstrated in the critical habit of taking them on individually.[5] That for every generalization about the mode there is a disclaimer to be made and a contradiction to assert is the obligatory preface to any recent discussion of the field, no matter how rigorously it limits itself otherwise; that every such critical generalization does, in fact, obscure crucial distinctions is true. And yet to say that realism cannot be defined is nonsense, for it has been defined in multiply fruitful ways. To say that it can be defined finally, or that it should be defined only through the positivisms of formalist cataloging, taxonomies, and correlations, or alternatively through a meticulous genealogy of historical, political, and cultural circumstance, is also nonsense.

In fact, critical discussions of realism always to some large extent reify the texts they choose to include, and in these reifications they produce correlative meta-realisms enriched by the double resistance and capitulation inevitable to their authors' own critical/artistic preoccupations; more particularly, the enterprise of literary realism enforces a critical mirroring of realism's essential duplicity as a term that begins historically in idealism and reverses itself into an affiliation with empiricism and positivism.[6] This mirroring is caused by and is reproductive of the dilemma of representationalism that is at the heart of realism itself. A token whose double face puts idealism at the back of particularity, realism generates an equivalent tautology within the critical discourse.[7] This assertion will seem offensively reductive or, at the least, counterproductive unless one takes it as it is meant, in realism's own spirit of flexible accommodation: as a celebration of the irreducible productivity of the realistic mode and of the field of inquiry such a protean energy as realism generates. Critical involvement in any given text or texts guarantees a specific, documentable, and largely unconscious reproduction within the critical analysis of many of the semantic and tropological terms of those texts; and the enhanced parallelism between the necessary interdependence of a given material "reality" and its mediating language game becomes another part of this equation in critical evaluations of realism.

As Michael Riffaterre points out in "The Discourse of Criticism," the relationship between critical text and primary text is always intimate and on multiple levels:

From the mimetic level to the hermeneutic, from representation to interpretation, the similarities between the object text and the critical text are many. Criticism, for instance, like literature, integrates the representation of its object with that of the subject's viewpoint. Criticism, again like literature, dictates a tendentious reading, reflecting the distortion of planes and lines, the anamorphosis that disappears only when the subject's vantage point is found, regardless of whether he or she is the writer, the narrator, or the character who enables the reader's cathexis of that subject. Finally, criticism, like literature, controls readers' attention so as to insure a relative unanimity in their reactions, or at least in their identification of the salient features of a text.[8]

One who writes criticism, and particularly one who attempts to write about realism, begins to discover experientially the truth of Riffaterre's assertion and to recognize the influence of text on the respondent as ongoing and as a crucial, indissoluble part of the analytic and semantic process. Rather than dissipating as the critic progresses through understandings of the texts, this influence intensifies, as language becomes less reducible and more seductive in its effects the more closely it is examined. Realism packs a hidden punch in this regard, for its interest in a salutary representationalism and its putative commitment to "simple, clear, direct prose" often obscure, at first reading, a concomitantly enriched tropological energy whose affiliation with the surreal gradually makes itself felt.[9] Realism promotes linearity, a certain easy movement down a path whose most interesting landmarks are clearly tagged, and whose materialistic landfill (the rustic's endless babble, the over-lengthy physical descriptions, etc.) may be passed over, mostly unnoticed; but like those nineteenth-century pictures of children blithely crossing a rotten catwalk over a precipice, an unseen angel hovering just over their heads, realism communicates its reassurances while also noting the chasm at its feet. For in fact, the topography of realism is wonderfully treacherous, as riddled with shafts and tunnels as Coketown's meadows, and if one stays *within* the text rather than above it one may fall down any number of rabbit holes.

The reader/writer's relationship to the teleological field of the text(s) under consideration is gravitational, and the weighty materialism necessary to the realistic vision of things enhances this textual pull: this is true for the critic reading the literary text, and it is true for the critic reading the critic's text. As Riffaterre says, anamorphosis can be fully corrected in either case only through complete consciousness of the subjects' vantage points. This anamorphosis is, of course, irremediable, for one cannot, after all, verify a subject's full vantage point – even the Riffaterrean model is asymptotic. But it is the critic's sore point as regards realism in particular, because of realism's putative capacity to lull one into a sense of its representational sufficiency: In the thrall of that sufficiency, says the Althusserian line, the reader will lose clear, full sightedness and see only through the distorted, co-optive lenses of a mode whose materialistic biases predispose it toward the ideological status quo. Thus critics, with the authority of Althusser's "Ideology and Ideological State Apparatuses" behind them, may reject the realistic mode as itself conceived through a skewed vision that thinks of itself as straight and as producing in the reader and ordinary critic an equivalent anamorphosis.[10]

This line, in its intuition of the formative power of the text as regards reader response and critical response, is, it seems to me, reasonable; in its assumption that one might see the text for "what it is," it ignores or forgets the systemic life of that text, whose words are the *material* – in every sense of that word – from which one will reconstitute and redescribe and re-envision. One can, of course, enact what Pierre Macherey calls a "symptomatic reading," psychoanalytically astute in its uncovering of what his translator describes as "those gaps and silences, contradictions and absences, which deform the text and reveal the repressed presence of those ideological materials which are transformed in the labour of literary production";[11] one cannot, nonetheless, exit the textual web and still speak of it; one can never, as Dickinson would say, see to see. One may make slogans – "To deprive the bourgeoisie not of its art but of its concept of art, this is the precondition of a revolutionary argument"[12] – but it does not necessarily follow that such reeducation of the readership through critical intervention amounts to having the scales fall from one's eyes. As long as one answers to a literary text, that text will enforce reciprocity, and it has the advantage of being an already stable artifact, as unarguably closed as words carved on tombstones. In the case of the literary critic's work, this covert influence is further obscured by the critic's conscious appropriations of the text under consideration: a critical borrowing that seems fully controlled – the evaluation of tropes, the redirecting of quotations, the cryptogramic rescues of "hidden" meanings and subtextual energies – can disguise the full range of the object text's own powers, which are considerable. And if the relationship between the critic and the object text is always intimate, the critic's engagement with realism may be said to prefigure a marriage made in heaven – similarly predisposed partners in a single, thoroughly recalcitrant epistemological and ontological quest for the "real" realism.

This position relative to the defining of literary realism is not incompatible with the playful (or melancholy) nihilism of deconstruction, for it, like deconstruction, does not imagine the likelihood of an escape to taxonomic perfection through the achievement of a view from nowhere: "objectivity" is in both cases an illusionist's game. If methodological precision may reveal a certain stability inherent in texts and the responses they provoke, this is only to premise a powerful "fictional truth." There is, then, no covert Platonism in the offer, but there is, I would argue, a certain comforting reinforcement of a sense of contiguity between language and materialities. It is the nature of critical commentary to engage itself with its texts *as if* it were possible to find the real, untransmuted treasure hidden therein; it is also commentary's nature to be double-minded, on the one hand creating a new discourse that takes the original text and uses it as an "open possibility for discussion," and on the other seeing as its role "to say *finally*, what has silently been articulated *deep down.*"[13] "The infinite rippling of commentary is agitated from within by the dream of masked repetition: in the distance there is, perhaps, nothing other than what was there at the point of departure: simple recitation."[14] If, as Riffaterre says, "the discourse of criticism is fundamentally paraphrastic," if "in describing and interpreting its object, and in evaluating its art, criticism appropriates and develops the form it glosses," then a critical discourse on literary realism will share an intimacy with the materialities that the realism it is evaluating has set out to represent.

There is no trickery in this claim of intimacy between word and thing, no unacknowledged metaphysic that would suggest that literary realism has a privileged semantic relationship to the things its verisimilitudes attempt to mirror (if realism's preoccupations are at one level material, its definitions of material things cannot be verified as any more valid or accurate or transparent than in other modes). Its purpose is, instead, to assert a demonstrable connectedness between the interventionist tactics of the object text and those of the critical text in consideration of a commonly articulated material environment: The reader-critic and the author share and together enact a primary concern with the possibilities for "true" representation and an interest in and commitment to the represented world (of the novel, of realism) and the people in it. The resulting critical meta-realisms will, by virtue of their protean subject matter (the "real"), reformulate a world of perspectives, but the crucial enactment of an anxiety about ("ordinary") character in the ordinary, extraordinary world will recapitulate itself – both in the critical text's necessary evaluation of realism's preoccupation with the character/environment equation and in its enactment at the level of process of exactly the dilemma of human character it describes. Disclaimers such as George Levine makes early in his exposition of terms are and are felt as precise extensions of the novels under consideration: "The critical narrative I imagine here is . . . presented as a fiction whose closure emphasizes the distance between it and the truth it seeks, metonymically, to shadow forth."[15] How *does* one produce a defensibly coherent (critical or novelistic) reality out of such multiplicity? How much (critical or novelistic) control should one, and can one, wrest from the infinite permutations of the real to make one's point? How much of any given (critical or novelistic) narrative remains hostage to the very determinisms of time and place that the narrative seeks to examine and clarify?

Defining the real through fictional truth entails doubled hearing and doubled sightedness, and these imperatives communicate themselves to the engaged critic. The ear must attend both to inner voices and to other voices; the eye must see form both as stable and as metamorphically, tropologically, and entropically fraught. The realistic author must orchestrate tangibilities in a way that neither mimics the formlessness of random, inexhaustible detail nor succumbs to the crassly opportunistic propagandizing that neglects any artifacts in competition with its message;[16] defining realism through these texts, the critic necessarily enters an assimilative relationship with this epistemological double-mindedness. The work that these various critical approaches to the subject of realism do is thus to some large extent performative and inevitably feels itself to be so. The authoritative and persuasive critical voice, in defining the "real" temporarily, produces therein a solid sense of its presence. But if it is performative, the critic feels, it also must recognize both the Austinian and the dramatic implications of the performative: If it is Austinian performativity of the simple type, then its power is authoritarian, and it makes its point through a device (authoritarianism) that realism posits as a primary danger to the formation of character; if it is dramatic, then its power resides within the persuasive persona one adopts (derives, in other words, from merely *acting* as if it were real); and if, as is more usually apprehended, the two modes are inextricable parts of the text's performative impact, then the critical invocation of a real realism becomes exactly that tour de force of seductive persuasion that realism has meant to eschew for a more responsible fiction.

The critical discourse on literary realism is thus, as I have said, a reification of realism's own worthwhile, earnest, and conflictual agenda, an attempt to produce under significant duress a meta-narrative that is at once representative and productive. There is, in the case of realism and critical evaluations of realism, a matching of impulse before the fact, a similar willingness to resign sheer tropological pleasure for duty, a similar desire to make workable order out of chaos. It is, of course, no accident that those critics whose theoretical affiliations have disallowed the possibility of resigning tropological pleasure for duty have also been said to have dismissed realism as "at best a historically inevitable mistake";[17] a charming promiscuity and a requisite contempt for what must necessarily be felt as realism's stolid reductionism make a virtue of deconstructionist necessity, but participation in realism's protocol takes a more stoic, domestic valor. The difference is, perhaps, not so much in the degree of skepticism with which one approaches the task of articulating the "real" but in the standard, good Greek recognition that one must *act* as if responsibility were possible, whatever the seduction of the nihilism, desire, or doubt underneath (again, it is no accident that critical discussions of realism have increased exponentially of late as the (a)political implications of deconstruction have been articulated but not resolved).[18] One might, then, posit that it is the very intimacy of this marriage of essentially domestic textual predispositions that guarantees an inevitable similarity between realism and the critical evaluations of the mode; like the husband and wife who have long been together, they begin to look alike. More overtly "aesthetic," less candidly propagandistic forms than realism might enforce, through obvious disparity, a greater distance between object text and critical text or, alternatively, as Bersani points out, awaken a playfulness within the critical text itself, but the meat-and-potatoes industry of realism parallels and produces the solid and well-balanced offerings of the critic's labor.[19] One could even premise that the critical resistance to realism as a form that is not *good* for readers, because it brings them to illusion rather than to a recognition of the real (metaphysically physical) condition of the world is realism's most inevitable, truest reification of itself within the critical discourse (and one could make a further move in this mirror game and suggest that this last critical wave brings realism back into intimacy with its original source: idealism). The text – realistic, lyric, epic, romantic, etc. – in every case may be said to infiltrate the language in which it is anatomized, but it can be premised that realism's very affiliation with evaluative and definatory procedures more thoroughly tinctures the correlative mode of critical assessment with the specific terms within which these procedures display themselves.[20]

The nineteenth-century critical discourse on realism reinforces and to a large extent predicts this claim of artistic/critical compatibility and inter-

dependence, for many of the most cogent definitions of the realistic mode
are found in authors' prefaces or are embedded in the very novels whose
goal it is to create a given reality (James, in his New York edition prefaces,
offers a quintessential case of the generative relationship between the production of realism and the production of theoretical justifications for one's
view of realism; it is a dialogically energetic project that *performs* reality's
own double status as a fiction and a fact).[21] One can hardly fail to notice
the effect of critical prefaces that bracket the "realness" of the novels that
follow or the paradox of critical interpolations within the realistic novel
itself; by claiming methodological, sociological, moral, or political justification, the novelist interrupts the illusion of reality that the novel claims is
its business to create (the critical reifications of this tactic can be seen in
Levine's candor in announcing his narrative to be a fiction, and, more than
that, a fiction "whose closure emphasizes the distance between it and the
truth it seeks to shadow forth," or in the standard confession that literary
realism is in fact in excess of the critical definition at hand).[22] For instance,
Eliot does not simply suspend the story of *Adam Bede* to defend its procedures; she carefully enumerates the biases that will obviate other realisms:
She will produce "a faithful account of men and things as they have
mirrored themselves in [her] mind," though the "mirror is doubtless defective"; she will assume the necessity to embody an aesthetically compromised subject so that her audience will say " 'do improve the facts a little.
. . . The world is not just what we like; do touch it up with a tasteful
pencil, and make believe that it is not quite such a mixed, entangled affair' "; she will proceed from a candidly moral position that dictates that
"these fellow mortals, every one, must be accepted as they are . . . and it
is these people . . . that it is needful you should tolerate, pity, and love."[23]
She lays her terms out on the table in a chapter whose heading is "In
Which the Story Pauses a Little," and in an apparent qualification of fictional illusion she performs a fundamental, if thoroughly paradoxical, realist's duty: to keep readers from a sense of having been hypnotized into
fictional truth by reminding them of real reality outside the text. This meta-
textual gesture, which interpolates a form of critical commentary and displays the ordering devices by which the fiction will perform its magic,
enacts precisely the balance among circumstantial detail, theorizing, and
methodological justification common to the critic of realism.

The final turn of the screw is, of course, that such candor at the same time increases rather than diminishes one's faith in the text's realist intent: *this* is not reality, the text seems to say, but you are in it, out there.[24] In reading such statements as Eliot's, one senses that invoking, analyzing, valorizing, and castigating the "real" produces for the novelist an inescapable, if often subliminal, anxiety, that every reality premised within the teleological space of the novel generates the apprehension of something forgotten or left out; the correlative realization must be that to create an unbroken illusion of fictional truth for the reader is to obscure the partiality of the attempt (being by definition dutiful, realist authors and critics of realism are vulnerable to this guilt before the fact). It is not, then, sufficient to respond that these interpolations of realist theory are merely conventional, another form of authorial meddling in a venerable history of such devices.[25] James and Howells and others call for all the obvious machineries to be expunged from the novel proper in favor of a seamless narrative – as James says in "The Art of Fiction," "certain accomplished novelists have a habit of giving themselves away which must often bring tears to the eyes of people who take their fiction seriously"[26] – but often this particular form of commentary merely shifts its position relative to the text it protects and justifies (and those authors themselves cannot always practice what they preach). When such theorizing disappears from the narrative structure, it often surfaces in contiguous, auto-referential prefaces – which thus become metonymies for the fictional products they hand off to the reader – and in reciprocally developed critical essays by the realist novelists themselves.[27]

The novelist's very task of creating a productive representationalism, a burden the critic then necessarily shoulders in writing about realism, seems to goad both novelist and critic into what is at once a brag and a lament: The irresistible confession of the particular and therefore limited "real" that one makes it one's duty to substantiate is also a most effective performance of one's watchful, responsible engagement with reality. The artist knows that she can beguile her readers into the perilous territories of her imagination and make chimeras seem real; it does not take factories and ditches and dustbins to convince a reader, for the good novelist can bring monstrosities and angels to life and make them seem irrefutable for the space of the experience. Cervantes and Jane Austen tell us what the realists know as a body when they set out to create a less fantastical, more ethically oriented fiction:[28] that otherwise ordinary citizens can be seduced into taking the elegant hyperboles of art – romance, the Gothic – for "real" life, that the hermeneutic circle is as snug when populated by heroes and insatiably wicked monks as it is when filled with the fallen and instantly recognizable masses of the ordinary. Howells sees this "fiction habit" as a kind of opium-eating, the brain "drugged, and left weaker and crazier for the debauch."[29] And so Eliot gives the lesson: One must go about the task of realistic writing "dreading nothing . . . but falsity, which in spite of one's best efforts there is reason to dread. Falsehood is so easy, truth so difficult."[30]

Eliot knows, the realistic writer knows, that regardless of the text's putative interest in reform and its commitment to "the faithful representing of commonplace things," the artist is pulled always toward the seductions inherent to writing: "The pencil is conscious of a delightful facility in drawing a griffin – the longer the claws, and the larger the wings, the better; but that marvelous facility which we mistook for genius is apt to forsake us when we want to draw a real unexaggerated lion."[31] In some crucial ways, in fact, *Adam Bede*, the novel in which these observations about one's artistic commitment to the everyday, the ordinary, and the unlovely are made, is a most precise enacting of Eliot's own ambivalent relationship with the realist duties she sets forth in this core chapter, for it is very much a reverie on the innately seductive quality of sheer beauty. Hetty Sorrel, not very smart, not very wise, not very deep, is nonetheless very, very beautiful, and not only with the kind of beauty that men can see and women impugn as tartish (I speak a stereotypical shorthand here, for a certain ironized version of beauty). Eliot makes it clear in description after description that Hetty is genuinely, ravishingly beautiful, the kind of perfection that overbalances common sense, even that of so canny a man as Adam Bede, even that of so canny a woman as Eliot herself, with its pure, pleasurable loveliness. It is not sufficient to say of *Adam Bede* that it repudiates Hetty for Dinah Morris's more contained and subdued beauty, that it makes, as usual, a cautionary example of her, for her story works within the novel in a much more complex way; as Eliot well knows, Hetty is fraught with an entire history whereby female figures allegorize textual and spiritual conditions, and she embodies not simply Eliot's resistance to the seductions of the beautiful, but her homage as well. Realistic novelists and their critics enjoy the essential paradox of confession, which allows them in all genuine piety to repudiate griffins for real, unexaggerated lions, while invoking both. Like Dinah Morris blushing, this combination of rectitude and desire can create a most wonderfully charged eroticism.

When Eliot proselytizes for the "commonplace" over sublimity, rarity, and romantic oddity, she does not deem the latter to be nonexistent, but only non-typical, among the deserving and slightly dumpy set she has chosen to champion; yet though the realist and the critic of realism may attempt ordinariness, they sense and often admit textually through tropological and subtextual enrichments that if they choose to promote a given typicality, it can be done only at the expense of such demonstrably existent residues as sublimity, rarity, and oddity. "I turn, without shrinking, from cloud-borne angels, from prophets, sibyls, and heroic warriors," Eliot claims, "to an old woman bending over her flowerpot, or eating her solitary dinner . . . ." (p. 223). No griffins for this novelist. First, one thinks of F. W. H. Meyers's description of Eliot herself: Eliot speaks – of God, Immortality, and Duty – and Myers watches: "I listened, and night fell; her grave majestic countenance turned toward me like a sibyl's in the gloom."[32] Then one thinks of *Silas Marner*, filled with the realest of real people talking the way people talk in the places, domestic and social, where they talk, and dominated by a man who, demonstrating one of realism's most basic tenets, has become a metonymous extension of his work and his religion. Silas has been, as stereotype would have it, a psalm-singing weaver, representative right down to his Methodism.[33] And yet in the very pit of the novel lies a mystery that infiltrates the tale from almost the beginning to the end: The transmutation of Dunstan Cass from pedestrian boor to memento mori, a skeleton whose ballast is a full measure of miser's gold, effects a virtual alchemy of plot and symbolic value. Eliot's enactment, at a most explicit level, of a vivid materialism and her insistence on Silas's metonymous identification with his work and mode of production (his "face and figure shrank and bent themselves into a constant mechanical relation to the objects of his life, so that he produced the same sort of impression as a handle or a crooked tube, which has no meaning standing apart")[34] are realism's duties performed at the very mouth of this pit; her reclamation of Silas through the reverse metonymy of dead gold turned to living golden hair balances on the grim irony of Cass's most fitting regression to a cold materiality. If the realist, giving up angels, prophets, sibyls, and warriors, at one level often makes the "implicit Benthamite assumption that the life lived by the greatest number is somehow the most real," that realist also knows this assumption to be more useful than it is true;[35] if the critic performs a similar Benthamite disregard of the exceptional and the idiosyncratic in the service of order, that critic will enact it under an anxiety arising from and reifying the object texts' discomfort with the notion of a unilaterally defined "real."

The realist's often-noted tactic of claiming to repudiate extremisms – of character, of tone, of style – for a more recognizable if less exciting vision is both political and pragmatic, and it is a gesture that the critical discourse has in many cases dutifully reified, if not without apparent skepticism, then at least with similar (lip) service to the pedagogical efficacy of clear, functional definition. Eliot commands that "these fellow-mortals, every one, must be accepted as they are: you can neither straighten their noses, nor brighten their wit, nor rectify their disposition";[36] the standard handbook definition of realism not only reproduces this dubious claim for realism's consistent interest in a worthy mediocrity but also, in making it, reifies realism's "do as I say, not as I do" complexity. Realism, says the handbook, is "the ultimate of middle-class art," focusing through "simple, clear, direct prose" on "the surface details, the common actions, and the minor catastrophes of a middle-class society," and in so saying it reproduces exactly the quotient of muted condescension and dutiful brotherhood one hears in Eliot's protests. But the novels belie both the novelist's claim and the critic's claim of mundane propriety, as soon as they speak individually for themselves. This is perhaps what brings Raymond Tallis to say in *In Defense of Realism* that "there is a certain amount of hypocrisy in the relationship between many critics' theoretical beliefs and their evaluation of individual novels";[37] once drawn into the gravitational field of a specific text, a responsive reader tends to be distracted from generalities. (There are times when "hypocrisy" may be a legitimate charge, but I would argue, and I have structured my own book to reflect this belief, that the theoretical enterprise and the more intimate pleasures of close reading may inform each other, not least in revealing precisely the discrepancies – necessary and inevitable – between the two modes of sightedness. And *this* is, after all, the larger point to be made. "Hypocrisy" is an insufficient concept for this interplay.) And in fact, both the realistic novelist and the critic of realism know better; they know very well that the exceptions to this egalitarian agenda will in every instance outweigh the democratic majority who fill the taverns to talk of life and the weather and the town's business. If realism looks, for methodological purposes, toward a Benthamite reductionism that it invariably exceeds, many of the standard definitions of realism have reproduced precisely, and for the same purposes of order and methodological precision, this leveling of realism to a mythical common denominator of the mundane, the workmanlike, and the thoroughly domesticated. Do as I say, not as I do – a good, socialist intent, this preemptive strike against the anomalous and the excessive, but subverted at the level of the specific by less proprietous, more disorderly preoccupations.

It would be a much simpler matter for novelist and critic if realism could keep intact its social commitment to plain, compassionate observation of the "more or less ugly, stupid, inconsistent people" who seem on first cursory glance, to make up the bulk of one's daily encounters.[38] As Edmond Duranty says in the opening of *Realisme*, "simple uncomplicated creatures" are more synthesizable for the purposes of reform and representation than are "overly civilized beings whose sharp originality consists entirely of nuances, halftones, and all those impalpable nothings. . . . "[39] Obviously, Byronic figures do not lend themselves to an argument for the public good or to the enactment of the deterministic dilemma or to the exploration of a representational ethics or to an ethical aesthetics (the most beautifully subtilized James character is representative in this sense). Edith Wharton explains in her "Author's Introduction" her choice of a narrative structure for *Ethan Frome*:

It appears to me, indeed, that, while an air of artificiality is lent to a tale of complex and sophisticated people which the novelist causes to be guessed at and interpreted by any mere looker-on, there need to be no such drawback if the looker-on is sophisticated, and the people he interprets are simple. If he is capable of seeing all around them, no violence is done to probability in allowing him to exercise this faculty; it is natural enough that he should act as the sympathizing intermediary between his rudimentary characters and the more complicated minds to whom he is trying to present them.[40]

But, of course, realism is precisely the proof that the real begins to slip the bounds of ordinariness as soon as it is subjected to genuinely watchful and receptive observation. Seeing "all around" her "rudimentary" characters, Wharton clearly feels their atavistic, Stonehenge power even as she claims to have them under control: they are *"granite outcroppings;* but half-emerged from the soil, and scarcely more articulate," and this image professing for simplicity invokes at the same time an archeological complexity of character (p. xx). If it is clearly a hallmark of the realistic mode to claim an interest in and an affiliation to commonness, this affiliation proves that a close look at people, even those with crooked noses and less than rapier wit, will reveal an uncommonness most profound. Ordinary humanness is, as Howells points out, the most complicated thing in the world, and the harder one looks, the harder one falls: "If you had asked that character in fiction be superhuman, or subterhuman, or preterhuman, or intrahuman, and had bidden the novelist go, not to humanity, but the humanities, for the proof of his excellence, it would have been all very easy. The books are full of those 'creations' . . . and it is so much handier to get at books that to get at men."[41] Ethan Frome, a man so bent and broken as to fulfill the realist's most severe requirements for a salutary unloveliness, proves the rule that if one examines a human closely enough, one will find the extraordinary.

However censored or displaced, these intuitions of a nonreducible excess of spirit, as well as other competing material realities, insist on themselves either explicitly or more obliquely in the form of anxiety. Engaging the realm of the physically real in the name of the "real" manufactures a sense of infinite complexity, and further, maddeningly, one's anti-materialist resistance suggests that real realness is precisely *not* to be found within the meticulous enumeration of things, but within the vagaries of the soul (with all of its pathological, exasperating, and uplifting affiliations).[42] Positivism, no matter how enthusiastically embraced as a philosophy, seems always to translate artistically into the sense that it protests too much its optimisms. Among novelists and critics whose province is a language that pulls one toward griffins and away from real lions, but whose business is representative representationalism, one finds consistent evidence of what Freud called negation – the expression of unconscious desires through a complex mathematics of disclaimers.[43] The realist who announces a stalwart, no-nonsense evocation of the real world also, at the same time, signals an equal and opposite energy that tends to exude itself tropologically (Howells, for example, in a character like Silas Lapham, produces an almost palpable sense of the explicitly repudiated, bestial side of things; one has only to look at the metonymy of Lapham's hands to find a window into Howells's intuition of a darker place). The critical discourse on realism is frequently marked by an equivalent awareness of the necessary amnesia within the ordering process and an equivalent resistance to the anarchic energies emanating from the unconscious; it is marked by an equivalent apprehension that a preoccupation with materialities obscures rather than constitutes the real real of the human soul (and the postmodernist critic, having modernism's introspections as a formalizing of this reactionary spiritualism, is immersed in the realist's original dilemma without the half-illusion that it is an answerable issue). Realism is an anti-fanciful impulse toward taxonomy balanced against the competing seductions of a reciprocal impulse toward the indeterminacies of the spirit; the critical engagements with realism cannot exit this tautology, but must reify it. A matter of predisposition, perhaps, the critic's placement on the slippery slope between an ordered materialism and subjectivist chaos is reflected in the books the critic chooses to examine, and it both produces and is produced by the compromise with "realism" that is worked out in the end.

A scrupulous accountability to competing definitions of the real translates itself from novel to critical text: It is not simply academic prudence that generates the critic's defensive/apologetic negotiations for realism's territories, but an anxiety mobilized by the very texts themselves and often articulated in their terms. For example, Eric Sundquist's introductory essay in *American Realism: New Essays* recapitulates in form and content his claim that there is "a remarkable intrusion of romance into the work of nearly every writer of the period" (1865–1900), and this assumption (which I share) is a means by which the critical dilemma of definition and ordering is mitigated.[44] It can be said to recapitulate a more generalizable duplicity within realism as well, the infiltration of realism with romance being another manifestation of realism's historical polarity between idealism and particularity. Sundquist very beautifully has his critical cake and eats it too (much as does realism, often enough): The perennial distinction between realism and romance is "useful" in exactly the sense that it can be shown to be both ideally true and artificially exclusive when applied to American fiction.[45] In making this elision, Sundquist reproduces Hawthorne's own wily game of playing in the territory be-tween real romanticism and romantic realism. Hawthorne's explicit performance of the author's realism/romance dilemma in "The Custom-House" section of *The Scarlet Letter* enacts the very cross-pollination it seems to be repudiating in its definitional segregation of the terms, and it carries this out both within the complex romantic/realistic "The Custom-House" and, by intertextual force, within *The Scarlet Letter* proper. Sundquist's introduc-tion, standing in a similarly detached and yet intimate relationship to the col-lection of essays with which it resonates, takes on a similar formative power for the text that follows as a synthetic statement of the book's revisionist po-sition relative to American realism (as editor, he must see these essays both as his, by virtue of editorial intervention and choice, and as not his; the one, the introduction, is a business matter, a commentary designed to catch the spill-age from the other essays, whose autonomy gives them an anarchic potential analogous to that of romance itself). And it, too, at one level, segregates re-alism from romance – the title of the book is, after all, *American Realism* – even as it performs a subversion of that elemental distinction.

The set piece by which diversity is united, objections forestalled, and ec-centricities contextualized, an introduction such as Sundquist's must elide the "real" circumstantial details of the critical essays and their primary texts with unifying invention; it must come up with authority (the packet of doc-uments left by Surveyor Pue) through the claiming of a fictional truth, and if it recognizes, as Sundquist clearly does, the irresistible power of romance, it must also create the productive authority of realism. Hawthorne professes, at once ironically and genuinely, to wish to be a real man doing realism, but he confesses that his unalterable predilections seem to lie in the airy world of ro-mance. At the same time, he enacts a formidable authority, through his wit, his use of detail, and his irony, and he effects a substantial revenge on real people and a real political situation. Sundquist articulates a similar impotence in the face of an insurmountable opposition: "No genre – if it can be called a genre – is more difficult to define than realism . . . ."; realism "virtually has no school" and is represented by "a group of writers who virtually had no program." "If it had a definable life at all in America, realism has surely had a life that stretches beyond the boundaries proposed by this collection."[46] And he performs, as surely as does Hawthorne and all of the realists who find themselves seduced into temporary romanticisms, a textual contradiction to his claim of bafflement. The texts of realism, perhaps more than any others, infect the criticism with their epistemological ambivalence at the same time that they also guarantee an infusion of their vigorous stoicism. Following realism's lead, the critic makes the best of a hopelessly muddled situation using the means at hand.[47]

Sundquist's essay, the dominant motif of which is realism's inevitable infiltration by a romantic value system that valorizes the " 'aesthetic possibilities of radical forms of alienation, contradiction, and disorder,' " performs a version of the fruitful dilemma it describes, and it reproduces as well, if very obliquely, the Hawthornian confession that realism is manly, whereas romanticism is not.[48] Using a combination of quotations from primary and secondary sources, Sundquist re-creates the dynamic relationship between realism's attempt at unilateral productivity and the resonance and density of romance. He appropriates James's metaphor in "The Next Time" of the "country of the blue" (the place Ray Limbert wakes into with a "good conscience and a great idea") as a figure for the realist's romantic dilemma, but he claims it most forcefully for his purposes by using another critic's words, Blackmur's, to make the image emblematic for realism. James's story, says Blackmur, and the story of realist authors, says Sundquist, is a fable of the writer " 'who struggles desperately to make society his prey, but fails because he cannot help remaining the harmless, the isolated monarch of his extreme imaginative ardent self.' " It is also, clearly, the critic's fable as well, a story so concentrically inclined that the unilateral involvement between the critic, Blackmur, and the story, "The Next Time," becomes a stone dropped in still water: my citation of such a quotation begins to suggest the complexities of its resonance, which increase rather than diminish as the marks multiply.[49] Quoted but also transmuted from Blackmur's intervention in James's fiction, the critic's statement, doubly invested, is made to communicate the shared condition of the artist/critic/person who struggles to manipulate terms that are both insufficient and in excess of any possibility of definition: To allow romance into realism, novelistically or critically, is to risk becoming "harmless," "isolated," impotent; to forgo it is to give up "a good conscience and a great idea."

This oxymoronic condition of awaking in the country of the blue is not then merely Sundquist's metaphor for the realistic author's double affiliation to a morally driven productivity and to a more isolative and introspective energy; it is, as well, the covert announcement of his own parallel inability to cut, merely for the sake of critical simplicity, the threads that weave realism and romance together in an intricate and unreproducible form, and it is the confession of his own resultant anxiety about the production of a valid and forceful critical position relative to the real.[50] Sundquist signals from the outset of his essay the danger for character, artist, and critic of giving in to the seductions of this blue country. At the end of his opening paragraph he quotes James, who says of "his admitted fictional double," Ray Limbert, that " 'he had merely waked up one morning again in the country of the blue and had stayed there with a good conscience and a great idea.' " Sundquist adds a brief coda of his own to close the paragraph: "He dies shortly after." If Hawthorne preoccupies himself with the bones of Inspector Pue and otherwise fills "The Custom-House" with memento mori, living and dead, of the effects of nonproductivity, Sundquist communicates a similar sense that, good conscience notwithstanding, one who yields to the country of the blue becomes history.

(Un)admitted fictional doubles for the critic himself, Ray Limbert and James become contiguously involved in Sundquist's enterprise of settling up with reality while under the spell of romance. One who fails to settle, whether character, critic, or realist, will die shortly after, at least to the world outside the country of the blue. Critics of other genres less punctiliously ambivalent than realism may reproduce the elegant certitudes contained therein or, considered more skeptically, may reproduce, in a rather ironic textual determinism, the illusion of epistemological certitude or formalist authority. However the critic of realism may struggle "to make society . . . prey" by enforcing a version of realism that will, finally, stick so wonderfully as to be universally definitive, that critic will inevitably recapitulate the realist's obligation at some level, overt or covert, to demur. That same critic, reifying the authorial ambivalence of the artist caught between productivity and self-expression, will feel with every fiber of an "extreme imaginative ardent self" that reality is a highly personal, remarkably idiosyncratic matter.

By investing Blackmur's assessment of James with an emblematic authority that then, circling back, further authorizes James's metaphor of "the country of the blue" as emblematic for realism, Sundquist participates in and extends the contiguities of the critical/artistic field. Blackmur's statement mediates between fiction and criticism as seamlessly as does Inspector Pue's fortuitous bundle of evidence; it is both a simple, "real" thing, an apt borrowing from another critic whose main business is fact and not fancy, and a token for passage into the country of the blue. Sundquist's production of a controlling metaphor for his definition of American realism through an appropriation of Blackmur's words conveys the dilemma of realism and of the critic of realism: its need for simple commonality and its correlative instinct toward the allegorizing of romance. For the critic on the horns of the realism/romance dilemma he perceives to lie at the heart of American realism, Sundquist's finding of the quotation from Blackmur is like finding that beautifully embroidered piece of work in Pue's packet, the artifact into which is knotted the unrecoverable "answer" to realism.

George Levine's introductory remarks on realism in *The Realistic Imagination* give evidence as well of how the realist critic (the critic of realism) reifies the balance between uncertainty and authority, anxiety and stoic productivity, that he sees as manifested within his chosen texts. Levine candidly professes to reenact the terms of the realism he chooses to evaluate, and more subliminally and perhaps less consciously his text reproduces, in its statement of methodology and epistemological affiliation, exactly the value system he ascribes to realism: "Realism posits 'mixed' conditions. So do I," he says, and this is a fruitful rather than an ineffectual environment.[51] Realism "belongs, almost provincially, to a 'middling' condition and defines itself against the excesses, both stylistic and narrative, of various kinds of romantic, exotic, or sensational literatures" (p. 5). He himself reacts similarly to the exotic or sensational tendencies, both stylistic and narrative, in recent critical theory: He will recognize, and to some extent respect, "the antireferential bias of our criticism" and the methods of deconstruction, with its "dazzling regressions," but he will proceed, nonetheless, "at the risk of ideological and metaphysical complicity with things as they are," "as though something is out there after all" (p. 4). He will, like the realism he promotes, mediate among extremes. Levine acknowledges the seductions of uncertainty and the dangers of an unreflexive corroboration of the ideological status quo, but he premises a critical alternative to deconstructionist play or Marxist disapproval in terms that reiterate precisely his definition of nineteenth-century realism: "The ideology lurking in the details

43

of experience and of texts can emerge through the habit of attention and of encouraging the very liberal-humanist tradition of skepticism toward the big idea that may, indeed, lead to 'submission.' It can also encourage a dialectic between systems and particulars essential to human and responsible thought."[52]

He will himself announce a middling position between deconstructive nihilism and an impossible but productive positivism, between a dismissal of realism's texts on the grounds of ideological contamination and an ingenuous disregard for the political effects of those texts; the realism that he defines produces its critical double, a combination of nearly irascible forthrightness and conciliation. If one is to enact criticism's responsibility to create "communities of meaning (if only to agree on unmeaning)," one must proceed as if there is something out there, regardless of anxieties to the contrary.[53] He announces before the fact an assumption that will shape the rest of his book: that nineteenth-century English writers of realism were already self-conscious about the "real," that they were "aware of the possibilities of indeterminate meaning and of solipsism, but they wrote *against* the very indeterminacy they tended to reveal. Their narratives do not acquiesce in the conventions of order they inherit but struggle to reconstruct a world out of a world deconstructing, like modernist texts, all around them."[54] This is exactly the position that he will adopt, using realism's habitual device of metonymy to locate himself in a contiguously intimate relationship to the conflictual field he will analyze: "there is a direct historical continuum between the realists who struggled to make narrative meaningful and modern critics who define themselves by virtue of their separation from realism and even from narrativity itself," and there is also clearly a direct historical continuum between the realist who struggled to make narrative meaningful and modern critics who despite anxiety and inescapable skepticism, seek to do the same.[55] Levine projects a correlative alliance to that layer of the continuum that, in realism and in criticism, will continue to articulate communities of meaning, despite anxiety, uncertainty, or despair; he will, to reiterate his words once again, present his critical narrative as a "fiction whose closure emphasizes the distance between it and the truth it seeks, metonymically, to shadow forth."[56]

Realism's dominant trope is metonymy, and thus it is no surprise that the critical analyses of realism discussed earlier seem to become metonymous extensions of the texts they consider: if Levine sees his critical effort as a shadowing forth, through metonymy, of truth, this is realism's gambit as well. The fictions and the meta-fiction can be superimposed. Pared down to fighting weight, the critical text becomes the contiguous part that represents the whole, and having taken its shape and methodology very specifically from the terms of the primary texts under consideration, it both stands for (in its representational capacity) and refutes (in its formative, revisionary capacity) the "reality" responsible for its presence.[57] Through the appropriation of images that, though taken from the object texts, come to speak emblematically for the critic's organizational procedures, through such doublings as the James/Blackmur collaboration in Sundquist's argument, the relationship of critical text to novelistic texts takes on the reciprocal energy of a trope that refuses to extend its meanings or energies unidirectionally. The realistic novelist's tendency toward self-referential commentary on the defining of reality as it is premised within the text licenses this contiguity, as it establishes through the very authority of the fiction-making process itself that literary realism is a fluid and unstable interdependence among competing concerns: aesthetic and anti-fanciful, playful and pragmatic, objective and propagandistic, idealistic and circumstantial.

This dynamic is preserved as the critic lifts quotations from primary texts and invests them with dual novelistic and critical significance; offered as covert testimonials to the analytic dilemma of defining realism, within both the primary text and the critical text, these fragments of fictional truth prove the metonymous energy that at once generates and thwarts versions of the real. Macherey, in *A Theory of Literary Production*, formulates a sternly dichotomizing statement: "either literary criticism is an art, completely determined by the pre-existence of a domain, the literary works, and finally reunited with them in the discovery of their truths, and as such it has no autonomous existence; or, it is a certain form of knowledge, and has an object, which is not a given but a product of literary criticism."[58] Macherey takes the latter position, necessary, of course, to his assumption that one can exit the terms of the text so as fully to expose them: "Literary criticism is," he writes, "neither the imitation nor the facsimile of the objects; it maintains a certain separation or distance between knowledge and its objects. . . . What can be said *of* the work can never be confused with what the work itself is saying, because two distinct kinds of discourse which differ in both form and content are being superimposed. Thus, between the writer and the critic, an irreducible difference must be posited right from the beginning: not the difference between two points of view on the same object, but the exclusion separating two forms of discourse that have nothing in common."[59] Macherey's either/or proposition is neither necessary nor sufficient; indeed, it seems to be the product of exactly those repressions – those erasures and amnesias he would have the critic lay bare – for the critical discourse is neither a clone of the object texts that it takes as its subject nor a purely autonomous product. The interdependence between critical text and realist novel is far more complex, a necessary and inviolable pact premised in a shared desire for communicational competence, a shared resistance to and ambivalence toward the pleasures of fancy, and a shared sense of how materialities, including language itself (for words are things, after all), present themselves phenomenologically within a universe felt as contiguous.

Realism discovers in metonymy a compromise in the conflict between real consumable stuff and real spirit, and so, I think, does the criticism it generates. Metonymy both exhibits the powers of and suborns the materialist environment felt to be in competition for the souls within its province. Metonymy premises a troubling contiguity between materialities and character, so that one sees human contours adjusting themselves to the geometries of industrial production (Gradgrind's warehouse-shaped head, Marner's spider-to-web/man-to-loom identity, which is so potent as to bring him to tie Eppie to the loom as if to draw her into this fabric, etc.); but realism's metonymy also turns that contiguity back on itself. The very gesture of tropological appropriation refutes the determinism it invokes and asserts creative individuality even as it argues for the dehumanizing consequences of alternative productivities. This is the essential paradox of realism, this combination of pride in and loathing for an environment exponentially changeable, and it infects every level of the discourse: Author, hero, and critic successively prove that to produce and consume a thing (the novel, mineral paint, literary criticism) is both to shape it and to be shaped by it.

If goods commodify their consumers, and in realism you always *are*, to some extent, what you eat, buy, drink, wear, paint your house with, and live in, consumers also produce, reformulate, expunge, and invent goods. Sundquist obliquely addresses this paradox:

> For in the anatomy of American realism, the possible distortions of character that might lead the hero out of a society whose debased values and hypocritical entanglements of virtue he appears to reject are countered by those distortions of character that can make the hero the exemplary figure of power within that society. Such a hero does not reject society but masters it. . . . The hero is democratized not by being swallowed up by the fierce oblivion of materiality . . . or by being leveled to insignificance . . . but rather by being permitted to incorporate the age's own dream of success, its own special romance.[60]

If, in other words, people become thingified by a technologically coercive or spiritually damaging environment, they also are shown frequently to use this mutation in a reciprocity that alters the terms of the environment that has produced them. There is a certain Darwinian irony in Sundquist's description of the American realist hero that extends to realism generally and to the critical discourse on realism: One who successfully engages the dilemma of the "real" – one who neither capitulates to a putative determinism nor succumbs to the country of the blue – turns reality back on itself. Through one's poetically inclined language, spiritual resistance, or ontological willfulness, and equally through adaptation and appropriation, material reality is made, in literary realism and in critical discussions of the mode, to seem as mutable as it is formative.[61] The novelist's primary source is the material world (this is not to discount the effects of other texts on the novel at hand); the critic's primary sources are the novels that speak of these materialities, and in each case the variables are wrested or cajoled into order. The basic question of literary realism remains intact: how to preserve the possibility for human decency within a material environment that threatens the delicate ecological balance between spirit and flesh. But both realism and the critical discourse on realism *perform* an answer to this question as they enact the responsibility of speaking responsibly about the real.

Realism, Historiography, and Allegory

My working premise is, then, that real realism, literary or critical, is not a place one can get to from here; in other words, the critic can no more give the true history of realism than the novelist can give the true history of the people and events that the novel describes. Yet one can equate the metaphysician's fantasy of objective Truth with the alchemist's determination to turn lead into gold and still proceed as if there is truth of a sort – if not to be found, then to be created over and over. As far as the novelist's or the critic's methodological procedure goes, this hopeful empiricism may be only an apparent contradiction, but one typically labeled (from within the system that it has itself, at least for practical purposes, exited) as "relativism." The hopeful empiricist can run her shop under all kinds of landlords: metaphysicians and skeptics, positivists and pragmatists, new critics and deconstructionists. As Humboldt and Hegel make very clear in regard to historiographic procedure, one can enact a particularized quest for specific evidence, carry out such a search with the intention of producing a history whose teleology will not be predetermined, and undertake this project believing, nonetheless, that "history is . . . 'the autobiography of God.' "[62] This approach, a candid effrontery to simple logic, allows for a play of ingenuity, a subtlety of argumentation, and a brashness of tone. One can also work from a thoroughgoing pragmatism, operating on the Rortian logic that there can be no relativism when, all things being equal as far as final and definitive verification is concerned, there is no stable, objective thing to be relative *to*. Either way, the gathering of detail, the close attention to particulars, the (temporary, partial) removal of a priori blinders, may be felt as valuable and potentially revelatory procedures.

There is, however, a position in between metaphysics and pragmatism (or skepticism, or deconstruction) that does indeed sense itself as working under the duress of contradictory and therefore potentially debilitating obligations regarding the "real"; the critic of realism and the historian, both preoccupied with the really real (as opposed to the novelist, who chooses the mediative form of the fictional real), may feel themselves impossibly torn between recognizing endless permutations of specificity and the organizing imperatives of "truth." This is the place held by covert metaphysicians who lament the rise of subjectivism and relativism while at the same time having come to the conclusion that one's only options as regards evidential procedure are subjectivism and relativism. At best, this confusion emerges as a sort of Episcopalian largesse, the sense that one can believe in God and not believe, more or less at the same time, since faith is a series of plateaus receding infinitely into the distance. Nietzsche and Derrida see history as "disguised theology," and therefore as the field in which this hypocrisy becomes inevitable;[63] putatively committed to a non-teleological assessment of evidence in pursuit of the historical truth, while nonetheless proceeding under the old ontotheological rules, such historiography, say its critics, wants to have its cake and eat it too. Yet what Dominick LaCapra says of historians can be applied to some critics of realism as well: "Historians have traditionally accepted the Aristotelian stabilization of the universal and the particular, between intemporal 'synchrony' and changing 'diachrony.' In this decisive gesture, repetition is idealized and fixated on an ahistorical level while 'history' is identified with change."[64] Thus the book jacket, with an acute sense of marketing strategy, may offer realism both to the ambivalent and to the hearty, the aesthete and the historian, for "reading the novel is a process of learning simultaneously about the world of Adam Bede and the world of *Adam Bede*."

Yet historians and critics who maintain their metaphysical superstitions, but reject the specific Hegelian dispensation for this Aristotelian balance (and the Hegelian philosophy of history, indeed most philosophy of history, is unpopular among working historians), must suffer the duress of genuine contradiction, a problem felt at the level of the text, as the analyst must articulate both the endless diversity of change and a stability of meaning: "It seems to me," says Nietzsche, "that such historians cease to be instructive as soon as they begin to generalize; their weakness is shown by their obscurity. In other sciences the generalizations are the most important things, as they contain the laws. But if such generalizations as these are to stand as laws, the historian's labor is lost; for the residue of truth, after the obscure and insoluble part is removed, is nothing but the commonest knowledge."[65] This conflictual system does relatively little damage within the densely populated site of the realistic novel, for while the author may interpolate various messages (theoretical, political, methodological, etc.), the fiction has immense absorptive power. The novel, taking itself as a novel, proclaims itself holistically as fictional truth, and it pulls the author into its gravitational field; one reading the novel feels the candid interventions of the author in the narrative flow as a difference not so much of kind as of tone. But the critical discourse *about* realism is threatened, at the same levels and in the same ways, as this version of historiography. The critical discourse, faced with literary realism's multiplicity, its internal and contextual contradictions, and its necessary metamorphoses over changing time and space, must balance between an isolative specificity that would obviate the concept of literary realism entirely and a generalizing and assimilative movement toward the generic. Nietzsche's warning is well taken: Realism, concerned with ordinary people as they are engaged in that most complex endeavor of surviving from day to day, more or less intact, more or less unruined, can easily be reduced to a banal humanism that translates itself into the critical discourse at the inextricable level of form and content. As Nietzsche says, "but if such generalizations as these are to stand as laws, the [realist's, the critic's] labor is lost; for the residue of truth, after the obscure and insoluble part is removed, is nothing but the commonest knowledge."

The relationships between a certain kind of conventional historiography and nineteenth-century literary realism are too complex to be given sufficient space or attention here, except as they inform the methodological procedures regarding the assessment of realism to be found in this book; and at the heart of my assumptions about the two endeavors, and the correlative work of critical analysis, lies the conviction that historiographic narrative has a deep affiliation with realist narrative. As Hayden White says, "it was no accident that the Realistic novel and Rankean historicism entered their respective crises at roughly the same time."[66] Both the realist writer and the historian face the paradox that evidence becomes meaningful – and thus can begin to lay some claim to truth – only when it is removed from listings and chronologies, from the randomness of its artifactual content, and is reoriented, placed within a narrative structure and given flesh. As White says in "Narrativity in the Representation of Reality," real events, that is, "events . . . offered as the proper content of historical discourse [and of realistic discourse as well]," are real

not because they occurred but because, first, they were remembered and, second, they are capable of finding a place in a chronologically ordered sequence. It is the fact that they can be recorded otherwise, in an order of narrative, that makes them, at one and the same time, questionable as to their authenticity and susceptible to being considered as tokens of reality.[67]

Realism and the critic of realism are well acquainted with this paradox. Critic or novelist, one must guard against reproducing exactly the effects of reality, with its welter of detail, its bewildering subversions of expectation, and its capricious tendency toward a coincidentally perfect order that would embarrass any artist worth her salt. On the other hand, one must avoid a translation so aestheticized as to arrest reality's disorderly conduct.

Ranke's famous dictum, and Humboldt's before him, says that "the historian's task is to present what actually happened," a formulation that echoes as well throughout the nineteenth-century discourse on the writing of novels.[68] Yet, as Stephen Bann points out in "The Historian as Taxidermist," one who wishes to reconstruct the real must act from the initiating premise that it is somehow lost: the utopian fantasy of lifelike reproduction is a reaction to the fact of death, a "strenuous attempt to recover" a state recognized as past.[69] Bann's analogy to naturalist Charles Waterton's pioneering work in taxidermy is as informative regarding realism as it is for historiography (and provides an image that resonates perfectly with the image of Frankenstein's monster that permeates this book). Waterton revolutionized taxidermy by discovering that to reanimate a corpse, one had to take considerable artistic liberties with it. The beak of a dead toucan soon loses its bright blue color, but if the beak is altered and then painted blue on the inside, it is as if the bird were still alive. Before Waterton, preserved animals could not appear to see, but after his ministrations they peered out at one through precisely replicated glass eyes. As Bann points out, this realism can be wonderfully abused as well, as when Waterton produced a stuffed monkey aping precisely the expression of a learned judge. Catachresis, as the historian, the artist, and the critic know, is always just around the corner when one begins to reformulate the chaos of the real. The realist's imperative to present what actually happens – ordinarily, every day, humanly – is very close to the historian's mandate to present what actually happened, and both enterprises are thoroughly, irremediably complex.

These observations do not lead to the facile and reductive conclusion that everything is fiction, including historiographic narrative; they do begin to suggest the scope of one's dilemma in speaking with anything like comprehensiveness about realism and, more specifically, about particular novels within the realistic mode. Realism is pragmatic, refusing to throw up its hands when confronted with the endless qualifications that the real so perversely insists upon, and the approach I shall take as regards historical context is pragmatic as well. I find certain conventional and typically interlocking historiographic practices troubling: the unselfconscious, complacent, or defiant assumption that one can reach an evidential sufficiency that will make narrative "true" rather than something more tentative;[70] the correlative assumption that certain truths are valuable, whereas others (domestic, feminine, etc.) are not; and the resultant narratives, in which contingency, partiality, and predisposition are not acknowledged or, given lip-service confession, are countermanded by a text that projects its own sufficiency at the expense of counternarratives that might enrich or actively deny the premises at hand. These reservations, funded both by my own theoretical biases, including my sense of how narrative works, and by historians' repeated observations about their craft, do not by any means suggest that I devalue historical contextualization.[71] They are meant instead to announce both my temerity and my timidity in this area.

For my investigations have, in revealing what I believe to be certain problematic habits within conventional historiography, only increased my respect for a classic question: "What is the use of history?"[72] Its uses are so immense, its field of inquiry so rich, that one is left aghast at the possibilities. The nature of this book is to be somewhat perversely extremist: to speak in the first half in ways more generalizing and theoretical than intensively oriented to single texts, and to speak in the second half, for the most part, as if each novel, unique in time and space, is a hermeneutic miracle. Neither half is a complete truth of realism, and the two halves added together would make yet another version of Frankenstein's monster; their juxtaposition is meant to be felt as performative, a recapitulation of realism's own uneasy complexity. A full-fledged historicizing of any of these novels would provide another way of seeing; a book like Baldick's *In Frankenstein's Shadow: Myth, Monstrosity, and Nineteenth-Century Writing*, for example, places *Frankenstein* within a context that both explains the novel and makes it richly explanatory of later nineteenth-century texts.[73]

Reading Dickens or Gaskell in the context of Henry Mayhew's remarkable *Morning Chronicle* series (eighty-two letters on London working conditions, written between October 19, 1849, and December 12, 1850) would enforce a revision of both historiographic and novelistic terms, as these articles, poignant, novelistic, and impassioned, prove the hyperboles of the real at the same time that they prove historiography's affiliation with the narrative devices of fiction.[74] I am not by any means indifferent to the value or even to the necessity of an awareness of historical context; for the space of the discussions of individual novels, however, my focus is rather willfully more internal than contextual.

This admission leads to one final explanation of my own critical practice, having to do with what can be called my tendency toward allegorical perception. This vision will seem justifiable only if one agrees with or becomes convinced by my apprehension of realism as fundamentally metonymic, in complex ways that the book seeks to clarify over the entire space of its endeavors. By my reading, realism's textual field is suffused with meaning *because* it takes as its task an accountability to understand how humanness is shaped by and how it shapes the material world. The more nineteenth-century novels I read, the more powerful becomes my sense of realism's intuition of the reciprocity between things and people. Such contiguities are hardly a new preoccupation: Carlyle ruminates on where the material ends and humanness begins, and Sade articulates another version, whereby flesh can be peeled away like yet another suit of clothes. But realist writers, implicated in the real of which they speak, are provoked into the task of merging humanness with its increasingly technologized surroundings. Writing about realism, it is as if one's very fingertips begin to appreciate the infinite complexities of that interaction. Thus my tendency to invest textual fragments with full-bodied significance, and thus my predisposition in the latter half of this book to treat the body of each text as a speaking thing.

The realist writer and the critic of realism will, by definition of having taken up the task, feel inadequate to it (a more blithe and less beleaguered sort would not bother in the first place). There is a world of details to be gathered, and neither world enough nor time in which to gather them. So one takes instead the rather immodest tack of performing for all the world as if the Real were a county someplace just down the road. One person calls a horse a herbivorous quadruped and uses it for plowing or circuit preaching, whereas another takes to bareback riding in flamboyant circles. But there is, as we know from *The Wizard of Oz*, always a horse of a different color to be found. Realism and critical evaluations of realism are willful and necessary fictions, and if they do not definitively quantify or expose a real reality, they do at least usually perform one whose intentions are good. If, as Riffaterre asserts, "a metalanguage functions as if it presupposed the reality of the topics it glosses, when it actually presupposes the reality of the language in which these topics are broached," then the critical discourse on realism enters a looking-glass world where the fiction and the criticism form one inextricable meditation on the really real fiction.[75] "Till the world is an unpeopled void there will be an image in the mirror," says James in "The Future of the Novel," and realism and the critic of realism must share in the mirror's dispensations of a solipsism actualized as a phantasmatic projection of self onto the planes and surfaces of its material surroundings.[76]

My observations on realism make their own meta-realism, which arises directly from the texts most nearly considered. I can project in these opening chapters only a purely theoretical, ground-zero realism, the terms of which are a mixture of extrapolations from the specifics of texts arbitrarily chosen from years of reading and teaching novels and generalizations that favor some details and forget or fail to see others. My immediate corrective, undertaken in realism's spirit, is to follow up my theorizing with close readings of texts, each of which I see as both anomalous and representative: to *enact*, in other words, the same conflictual relationship between theory (the Real) and practice (the real) that literary realism itself embraces. I see myself, in other words, under the same duress that literary realism suffers and enjoys. So, like Levine, I must acknowledge that my own criticism is yet another fiction, carried out with the sense that it is as truthful as I can make it (which is not the same as being true). With Oz and the Emerald City in mind, one thinks of *The Vicar of Wakefield*: Moses trades the horse for a gross of green glasses, and though the silver rims turn out to be copper, "we will keep them by us," says the vicar, "as copper spectacles, you know, are better than nothing."[77] Realism's point, exactly, and the critic's point as well.

Chapter Two

Talking about Things

━━━━━━━━━━━━

Two men were traveling by train from London to Edinburgh. In
the luggage rack overhead was a wrapped parcel.
"What have you there?" asked one of the men.
"Oh, that's a MacGuffin," replied the other.
"What's a MacGuffin?"
"It's a device for trapping lions in the Scottish Highlands."
"But there aren't any lions in the Scottish Highlands!"
"Well, then, that's no MacGuffin."'

The Ineffable

Realists are nudged by the immemorial even as they are compelled by ma-
terialities:² stunned by some weighty piece of fact falling on them, they look
first to outer causes for a pain that continues after the fact is lifted off and the
bones are mended. Like Mrs. Gradgrind, they find (and we find) that the
source of this particular, other suffering is unlocatable, the thing itself a phantom: " 'Are you in pain, dear mother?' 'I think there's a pain somewhere in
the room . . . but I couldn't possibly say that I have got it.' " Mrs. Gradgrind,
worn out, says simply what the philosophers say in other, less poignant
terms.³ The realist senses that there is some felt thing just out of sight that will
not stay to be examined, the memory that cannot be recalled. It is about the
room, somewhere, but unlike the furniture that may be pushed and pulled
into place for a given tableau, its presence is not negotiable. Hawthorne's
name for it is Romance, and he gives it form in Zenobia, drowns it, and
hoists it, hook-poled through the breast, up to the surface in the hope of ex-

orcising himself of its most anarchic powers. At last he can look his fill at this conflictual body that he has with an avid reluctance brought to life, but he finds that what is left is a contortion of the thing he had hoped to discover and then recuse.[4] Brontë also gives the Thing a name and a form – Cathy – and it comes, only when it isn't called, and to one who doesn't wish to see it and has no understanding of what it is, to tap at the windowpane. When Heathcliff calls its name it disappears, this phantom of an unnameable desire, incestuous, brutal, and exquisite. It is this thing that incarnates itself for Heathcliff in the insufficient and maddening metonymies of every flagstone and every face; its objectification is "Cathy," but its true name is Heathcliff – "I *am* Heathcliff" (p. 74) – that part of himself felt to be both unrecoverable and imminent. And if this incarnative force is a hyperbole in Heathcliff, with his endless metonymizing, it is also Brontë's way of showing how one inevitably uses the world as a sop for that excess and how, more particularly, one often gives that demonically willful essence a woman's name. Realism, a pragmatic and essentially unpretentious mode, accommodates this non-negotiable energy without being subverted by it, and in the process is able to accomplish good works; if, in disciplining this pleasurably painful manifold, it also comes to know and to reveal that familiar affiliation with sadomasochism produced by any domesticated will to power, it works as well to keep that energy contained.

Within the post-revolutionary, pre-modernist moment of the nineteenth century and early twentieth century one finds a condition of imminence, a novel neither innocent of nor yet entirely self-conscious about how any interest in that oxymoronic thing, "human nature," inevitably problematizes the "real." It is perhaps not entirely ingenuous to suggest that the relative newness of the novel as a genre in the nineteenth century provided for a resilient and capacious space in which one's engagement with the unnameable energy that exceeds and thwarts representationalism could be more safely contained, that the world and the novel, growing older together, have suffered constrictions even as the possibilities for experience and perversity may have grown. One may look at the playgrounds of the late eighteenth-century Gothic for an exuberant, infantile (and veritably polymorphously perverse) psychosexual fantasy that strips bare neoclassical pretensions to moderation and rational self-control: teenagers and imaginative women in the drawing room, alas, who leave no doubts as to one's own imperatively undirectable and non-socializable energies. Alternatively, one can read in all those trails of tears in the late eighteenth-century novels of sensibility the melancholia and mute hysteria of such Gothic/Sadeian impulses deferred or denied, or see in the resurgence of such quixotic heroes as Smollett's Sir Launcelot Greaves a piquant mixture of this double-sided coin of the innocently high-minded and the sadistic. Take these two complementary strains and impose upon them the exigencies of the realist's sophisticated and earnest agenda and you have a warm, conflictual body familiar to us all. (Gross generalizations, of course, storytelling, but it is a narrative whose crayon strokes echo realism's intuition that one *must* forget virtually everything to tell any story.[5]) The responsible, the social, the productive working to hold themselves in an Aristotelian equilibrium of virile moderation, the "middling position" defining itself against literary extremisms[6] – against this rectitude plays another irremediable energy that representationalist language does not obviate, but in fact enables. Even the anxiety of a flamboyant influence like the late eighteenth-century Gothic or the self-indulgence of the novel of sentiment cannot produce complete propriety; if realism is on the surface of it like the dowdy offspring of a wild and wooly parentage, it is beleaguered nonetheless by its own self-generated engagement with the ineffable.

The Asymptote

This unnameable thing, neither seen nor spoken as itself, may well thrive best in the sidelong glances of realism; most certainly it retreats under scrutiny, with the atavistic urgency and unimpeachable guile of a dog diving underneath a couch. Yet if, as Lyotard asserts, "writing is this 'work' that is nourished by the thing excluded in the interior soaked with its representational misery, but which sets out to represent it (this thing) in words, in colors," then realism, with its faith in and reliance on the representational, would seem to be one of the last places within writing to look for the thing hidden.[7] It is, of course, a much-maligned orientation. For Baudelaire and Beckett, realistic art is " 'the miserable statement of line and surface,' and the penny-a-line vulgarity of a literature of notations"; its practitioners are those "worshipping the offal of experience, prostrate before the epidermis and the swift epilepsy, and content to transcribe the surface, the façade."[8] Frank Norris, for whom naturalism is the real romanticism and realism is a tidy fraud, advises that we "let Realism do the entertaining with its meticulous presentation of teacups, rag carpets, wall paper and haircloth sofas, stopping with these, going no deeper than it sees, choosing the ordinary, the untroubled, the commonplace."[9] But it is not exactly so. Realism is the purloined letter all over again, the secret (or, more precisely, the apprehension of the secret) disguised by its very mundanity, black mail under false cover – smudged, tattered, brazenly addressed to the wrong party, it nonetheless envelops an alternative set of possibilities. It is not surprising that realism subsidizes the new genre of the detective novel, nor that the nineteenth-century detective novel is so invariably linked with the supernatural, the inexplicably mysterious, and the pathological; realism sets up its own "crime" as it harbors this troublesome Moriarty – this shady and obtrusive "past" – without setting up the hue and cry. Yet as tensile a form as can be imagined, realism is thus able to make the best of an irremediable impulse to thwart its own responsible agendas.[10]

Realism is a tacit obeisance to a "real" reality that, as Clement Rosset says in *Joyful Cruelty*, "situates its sentence at the very level of execution from the start" (it *is* and it *happens* at once) – mute, its inexpressibility is absolute. To speak of "realism" is both necessary and impossible, and it reminds one of that unutterable cognizance that Rosset sees as most notable and crucial in the human condition: "to be equipped with a knowledge . . . but simultaneously to be stripped of sufficient psychological resources to confront one's own wisdom, to be furnished with a surplus of knowledge or with 'one too many eyes,' . . . which indiscriminately is our privilege and our ruin, in short, to know but to be completely incapable."[11] Searching for a representational language, realism exceeds the language that would describe it; it is, ironically, compelled by its own name and on its own recognizance to wrestle with that importunate waif, the ineffable. That thing makes its own energy, refutes predictabilities of character and behavior, imbues representationalism with a conviction of insufficiency, and thus ensures that language will be felt to fall short: the real Thing that makes of real things a waxworks.

Realism is, then, in an asymptotic relationship to a baseline of communicational efficiency – regardless of its good intentions, always veering away from its self-imposed obligation to produce pragmatic, pedagogically effective discourse (teaching responsibility by what it says *and* what it is) – and it is further complicated by its engagement with its own literary progenitors. Nineteenth-century realism is, in fact, no less literarily informed than psychologically and philosophically acute, and it is in part the novel itself, with its lush but recent history, that energizes the impulse toward realism and marks its boundaries. If one may postulate for the text a triangle of author, reader, and shared world that reproduces the "primordial triangle" of conversation, one must also see that engagement as in competition with the triangle of author, past authors, and shared world.[12] Reacting against the putatively low status of the novel itself (a form favored by women), realism invested the genre with seriousness and social and political purpose. Nineteenth-century authors witnessed the novel's power over the public, over themselves. They saw what it could do. And in this sense realism becomes a code for an acceptance of the genre's potential and imminent legitimacy: to think in terms of realism is to take the game, and oneself as writer, seriously at last. This is, for some critics, of course, the very root of the problem of realism; what is seen as realism's eager compliance with normative values is also seen as marking the novel's transition into a form more concerned with marketing strategies than with play or with desire.[13] This is a neat, convincing, and now-familiar formulation that often begs any number of questions about what language can and cannot do, how language actually performs, and what the novel did with itself before realism whipped it into mercantile shape. One might do well, then, to set aside, temporarily, this version of righteousness and to reconsider the question of realism's complex productivity (noting, of course, the immense, oxymoronic weight of this word, both in a Marxist sense and in an anti-Oedipal sense). For what comes to be called realism by earnest men like Howells, whose political affiliations have been forgotten in the hue and cry against realism as a cog in the bourgeois machine, is at once both self-reflexive and socially aware, with the beliefs (religious, political, social, philosophical) that generate teleological inevitabilities resting on and endangered by more anarchic impulses.

Realism's ideological energy is at once both a necessary condition and a partial one; it compels order, teleological and otherwise, even as it puts into play a series of erotic distractions, pleasures of the text, that awaken one's apprehension of a general systems failure. One who subscribes to the standard line regarding realism's Germanic orderliness will see a form not only given to closure but also predicated on it; with only a slight shift of focus, another might see that same gridwork – which often enough is quite remarkably florid or haphazard itself – as mere tracery over a burgeoning and fitful subtext.[14] Bersani says that "even when novelists seem to become more skeptical about their ability to find a saving form for the disconnected, fragmented lives they represent, they make a last-ditch stand for the re-demptive pattern rather than simply abandon the whole pattern-making enterprise."[15] For Bersani, this "pattern-making enterprise" is anti-erotic, producing, as his image would suggest, the templates for a psyche more ordered and controlled than anarchic and desirous: a veritable sewing-circle repression. Musselwhite makes a specific argument along these lines in his chapter "Dickens: The Commodification of the Novelist," as he differ-entiates between a Boz-language whose chaotic urgency actually does the *work* of destabilizing the reader relative to the status quo and a "Dickens"-language that performs through a glib persona only the simulacra of anger, comedy, and dark despair.[16] Whether or not Musselwhite's textual exam-ples from the "Autobiographical Fragment," *Dombey and Son*, *The Pickwick Papers*, and *Sketches by Boz* would speak these two languages without his help as translator remains unclear, for his formulations are themselves so elegantly convincing and rhetorically polished that one cannot help but accede to his assertions that said passages can be differentiated into the "nomadic buz of Boz" and "the labelled identity of Dickens."[17] To some extent these critics are correct: Realism assumes a *telos*; it knows, still, more or less where it means to get and what it means to accomplish. Yet it also dodges the circle at every opportunity, subverting its own program of or-derly productivity.

Realism, essentially pragmatic in enacting its social responsibilities, thus inevitably balances itself between the willfulness – the heroism, even – of pragmatism's dismissal of anything to do with unusable, unnameable surplus and an alternative nostalgia for that magisterial loss that intrudes itself as unrecoverable and unspeakable. Lyotard describes this loss in terms of memory: it is "a past located this side of the forgotten, much closer to the present moment than any past, at the same time that it is incapable of being solicited by voluntary and conscious memory – a past . . . that is not past but always there."[18] Realism senses that one may too easily be mesmerized or distracted from action by this forceful absence, this "past" that exceeds historicizing, because, unlike the past it metaphorizes, it does not yield to the quiescent forgetfulness of narrative. This is not a place one can ever get to, not even through the wardrobe door of involuntary memory, and thus it remains impossible fully to anticipate its effects in the present. Yet it is, paradoxically, the most present of things; one's efforts to suppress, or to repress, its interference in one's daily business virtually guarantee its sidelong intrusion into conscious memory and desire. It thwarts language, producing metaphor and a maddening repetition of insufficient terms, and it cannot be fully accessed in terms of use. Willful dismissal amounts to an admission of its powers. The pragmatist's injunction to consider the conception of the practical effects of an object as all that can, or needs to be, known is restful and resolute in its promise to obviate the inaccessible. Realism at its most starched would find the pragmatist's maxim both congenial and efficacious, for it ditches the issue of the unnameable, its implicit antagonist, at the same time that it is in accord with realism's concern for the effects of one's material circumstances. But when one's guard is down, the intimations of a hidden life – a forgotten past – make one restless, and perhaps in any case it does not do to repudiate the unnameable altogether. Realism hedges its bets, and, subscribing fully to neither, makes room for both.

Realism enacts a pragmatic appropriation of this unnameable disruption, recognizing the energy, to some extent respecting it, but at the same time rebuffing its seductive allure with its own performative energies: it has a world to bring forth, a reality to sustain, and a social agenda to fulfill, and it must, on the face of things at least, make itself authoritative. Its resistance to being derailed by its engagement with this anarchic energy makes realism seem to many a hopeless stuffed shirt, the most unregenerate propagandist of the status quo. Those who suspect the written word, and the novel in particular, of subsidizing by definition whatever rotten conditions are in place find in realism's resilience a covert slavishness: like Dickens's Mrs. Sparsit on the watch, they spy out the wet noodle disguised as manliness. In an environment sensitized to and suspicious of any such ideologically driven fiction, realism has been labeled as a collaborator, the Vichy of the literary world.[19] And this common assertion makes a certain experiential sense, as it detects most easily in realism's accommodative and apparently egalitarian impulses exactly that stabilizing capacity to include, assimilate, and detoxify resistance. Even Howells, whose leftist political sympathies became the informing energy within such novels as *Annie Kilburn* (1888), felt his beloved realism inadequate to the task of producing change in a world capable of the Haymarket affair: "the longer I live the more I am persuaded that the problems of life are to be solved elsewhere, or never."[20] It is felt that, as Bersani says, there is a "secret complicity between the novelist and his society's illusions about its own order."[21] The insistent mundanity of realism's surface preoccupations, its dependence on the thing-iness of things, further aligns it with a fundamental and unchanging ordinariness. But this (apparent) equilibrating effect is only more patent in realism than elsewhere. There is, after all, no verifiable escape from such complicity, and it is arguable that extremist positions only beguile one into a false sense of radicality. Derrida, in "The Ends of Man," argues that when "a declaration of opposition to some official policy is authorized, and authorized by the authorities, [this] also means, precisely to that extent, that the declaration does not upset the given order, is not *bothersome*."[22] This assimilation of all that is bothersome happens within *"the form of democracy"* and in fact defines, to a certain extent, democracy: the very freedom to speak, however radical one makes these utterances, ensures that all seismic activity will be absorbed. I would agree that to some extent the imprimatur, however reluctantly it is granted, is always also a stamp of commodification, but I would add that realism's preoccupation with stuff only makes this contract more palpable than elsewhere.[23]

In fact, perhaps precisely because the diurnalizing is more patent, realism often includes a rueful awareness of its own potentials for complicity in the status quo, and this intuition, while it does not suffice for anarchy, does at least ensure a deconstructive, destabilizing movement at a level more sub-liminal than overt.[24] Dicken's ambivalent placement relative to the Preston strike both within *Hard Times* and within his *Household Words* pieces is paradigmatic. His refusal in his commentary and in the novel to privilege unequivocally either the unions or the bosses seems on the surface to epit-omize this betrayal of the workers' cause to the existent power structure. In "On Strike" he makes his dual allegiance clear: Mr. Snapper tells him that "a man *must* be a friend to the Masters or a friend to the Hands," and

Dickens answers that "he may be a friend to both."[25] The novel carries out this program most overtly in its corrective lambasting of both Bounderby and the corrupt union official, Slackbridge, and the conflict remains irresolvable. The standard reading of such ambivalence is that the tied game always goes to the dealer, but *Hard Times* refutes this premise,[26] for Dickens carries his undecidability into the text and makes a virtue of it; the residue, immanent from his tropological manuevers in this odd territory, exceeds and destabilizes the ideological field. As Howells suspected, this may be the best that can be hoped for in the way of political effect, from realism or any other fiction; certainly it follows pedagogical wisdom to suggest that instruction takes place at many levels other than that of straight exegesis. The novel becomes a location for a fluidity of purpose; far from instantiating the bottom line, it makes its negotiations on a tightwire. It encodes its sense of this precariousness throughout, but most literarily in the circus scenes, with their inevitable descriptions of balancing acts – horseback riders, gymnasts in teetering pyramids, plates spinning on sticks, wire-walkers. Sissy Jupe's concern over her father's poor legs and indeed the virtually obsessive leg imagery throughout the novel keep one subliminally off balance, riding side saddle at hard gallop without the full use of one's limbs. Realism is apparently businesslike, apparently devoted to a confused materialism that, while interested in and often appalled by how things and people interact, is nonetheless out to make sure that everyone gets enough stuff; it also holds its own alternative entertainments, sideshows just off the main road (and perhaps all those holes and pits and ponds that people fall into communicate a textual danger as well as a geographic one).[27]

Thus it is not surprising that nineteenth-century novels otherwise committed to material precision and evidential truth may also, and sometimes in the same figure, unembarrassedly hypostatize mystery, romance, and the unspeakable. From the paradigmatic forms of Frankenstein's monster and Dracula (historically, scientifically "real" and hyperbolic all at once) to the momentary supernaturalisms that permeate the work of, among many, Dickens and the Brontës and James and Hawthorne, one sees this intuition displayed. The woman in white moves like a specter through text after text; the veiled lady shows up for exhibition. The fallen governess and the sinister valet in *The Turn of the Screw* are the quintessence of this undecidability, as James makes the conflict between inner and outer realities quite palpable. But the ineffable may pitch like King Billy bomb-balls, as it does in *Wuthering Heights* and *Dracula*, and the town never lies beaten flat, because there is too much else going on. This energy is never aggrandized into full (non)presence at the expense of the rest of a very complicated and rich picture. Realism's depth of field is like Brueghel's, with whatever Icarus is presently on the wing plummeting, small, through myriad other details.[28] This quality alienates those who see the novel as a vessel that should be capacious enough to accommodate in its characters the great soul of its author: Lawrence says the "trouble with realism" is that, among the best writers, it becomes a case of "a truly exceptional man . . . [who] tries to read his own sense of tragedy into people much smaller than himself."[29] But in refusing to reify a grandiose fantasy of heroic individualism and existential anxiety in its "small" characters, realism remains open to multiple encodings, among which are the invariably oblique manifestations of this indirectable, unnameable energy.

Realism implies always that our (and its) preoccupation with the persistent (non)appearance of this energy may in fact be mostly hypochondria, a possibility it subsidizes by resisting the solemnities of an unequivocal subscription. It is not immune to despair, but entertains the thought that this conviction of loss may be in part a communicable melancholia – one person describing a set of symptoms to which everyone else lays claim in some local manifestation of the disease.[30] Edna Pontellier's ennui and despondency, Coverdale's impotent watchfulness, Louisa Gradgrind's vacancy, Cathy Linton's lapse into enervation, Lily Bart's slide toward narcosis – each of these characters is burdened by a sense of lack that the text both acknowledges and, in offering reserved sympathy without aggrandizement, withstands. Henry James, intuitive and ironic, sympathetic and unsentimental, takes this complex to its conclusion in a series of characters infiltrated with angst so enriched as to have become erotic: these Jamesean creations are the figures for realism's body, the allegories of reading. "It is nothing," says Nelly Dean of Cathy Linton's self-willed dissolution, and she comprises Brontë's sense of both the (nihilistic) long and the (pragmatic) short of it without for a moment knowing. Sometimes, impatiently populist, realism implies that serious notice of the ineffable's disruptive inevitability signals the will to alter, all at once, one's epistemological, spiritual, and social status, like giving up the Baptists for the Episcopalians or the New Critics for the deconstructionists: Dickens raises this possibility when he makes Harthouse, the only resident aristocrat, a half-hearted nihilist; Hawthorne, compulsively admitting through a series of effete characters his own introspective obsessions, throws the privileged Coverdale into a "vortex of . . . meditations" that essentially unman him (p. 65). In the world, economic, political, and physical duress distracts one from attempting through language a direct engagement with the ineffable, although it is arguable that ignoring the energy empowers rather than disarms it; artistic realism, predicated on a willful pragmatism in resistance to the distractions of a surplus energy, keeps itself together by refusing to engage in producing a taxonomy of its conflictual condition.

The necessary exclusivity of a given realism's social program will force the issue of this conflict, as it pits the tropological displacements by which one signals and concedes the unnameable against the necessity of creating an illusion of facticity. Dickens builds *Hard Times* on the paradox of this dual productivity; he speaks of two factories, one manifest and the other secret. The plant to enforce regularity and order and to create people so "equally like one another" as to be representative of their material conditions is manifest; the secret plant is run by Time, the keeper of memory, and "his factory is a secret place, his work is noiseless, and his Hands are mutes" (pp. 20, 87). One begins to feel that realism's characters, cut to order for a specific social purpose, have come through this secret place behind the scenes of its more candid productivities: Lily Bart, to name only one, looks to be, to herself and others, the most perfectly constructed artifact of her social condition, and she is as bewildered as her social fellows by the secret internal mechanism that holds her from complete conformity (even Wharton herself seems to find this recalcitrance somewhat mysterious). Blake's wily and ironic *Songs of Innocence* playing themselves off against the *Songs of Experience* predict early on realism's doubleness, for Lily suffers from (is redeemed by) a faint, antiphonal unworldliness that experience can overman but not obliterate. She embodies the condition that Rosset ascribes to one who, seeing the real, is always one step behind its simultaneity: Lily is "equipped with a knowledge . . . but . . . stripped of sufficient psychological resources to confront [her] own wisdom," she is "furnished with a surplus of knowledge or with 'one too many eyes,' " and she is shown "to know but to be completely incapable" of acting on her knowledge.[31] The secret factory is noiseless, its Hands are mutes, but one feels its effects nonetheless.

Realism overtly concerns itself with talking about real things – real factories, real towns, real rocks and furbelows and chairs and sideboards – but it remains resistant to the coercions of objectification even as it makes these coercions one of its themes. A solid, willfully unromantic citizen, it nonetheless has the wisdom to see that its own objectifying mode is always potentially a kind of madness – one looks to Stoker's Renfield, with his meticulous account book, as the figure for the "faultless armature" of a discourse both eminently logical and utterly mad – and that one's divagations from the delusion or pretense of objectivity represent the accommodative gestures of sanity.[32] ("Romance" is an alternative gambit within this same game for exploring the parameters of the real.[33]) Realism remains cognizant of, and it concerns itself with, social, economic, and political conditions and their effects, but the candor with which it engages materialities *produces* rather than allays ambivalence about realness. Yet the term "realism" is, after all, a most essentially optimistic one whose very utterance, regardless of the epistemological or ontological skepticism with which one compromises its name, suggests a willingness to recognize and to wrestle with the definition of some place outside one's own insistent ego. Realism, literary as well as philosophical, has always known at some level that it begs the question of itself; what Kaplan says of American realism is more generally true as well: "Realism simultaneously becomes an imperative and a problem. . . . "[34] Thus, as Levine says, "there [is] no such thing as naive realism – simple faith in the correspondence between word and thing"; "positing the reality of an external world, it self-consciously examines its own fictionality."[35] The conundrum of the flowered carpet that opens *Hard Times* is the paradigm for how realism calls up for itself two modes of thought, and the parodic nature of the confrontation signals realism's rueful humor about its own conflictual agendas. "You cannot be allowed to walk upon flowers in carpets," carps the third gentleman, the government officer, in a *reductio ad absurdum* of realism's anti-fanciful duties; the author, however, knows full well the seductions of the imaginary gardens that realism works to populate with real toads (or, to use Howells's version, with a "simple, honest, and natural grasshopper").[36] Realism thus brings itself with every material detail to confront the enigma of how the physical conditions of one's environment compete with an inexplicable, preexistent core of human recalcitrance for priority. This ambivalence, far from vitiating realism's force, is generative of it: the unnameable is free to flourish in this environment of undecidability in a way that it cannot under the perspicuous, inquiring modernist gaze or the sardonically wistful postmodern glare.

Assuming that what one can see and taste and smell and touch is more or less independent of and influential upon the perceiver, realism cannot, nonetheless, divest itself of the compulsion that skews into unpredictability or even obviates the effects of externalities; realism consciously addresses this paradox, and it also reifies it in a way that the less resistant mode of romance does not, and this reification generates and sustains a productive complexity. As the "romantic" Hawthorne most energetically proves, the world is real enough for government work: Hawthorne's name stenciled on "pepper bags, and baskets of anatto, and cigar-boxes, and bales of all kinds of dutiable merchandise" is an ironic version of Johnson's refutation of Berkeley, for it implies both the robust tangibility of objects and their power to transmute humans into versions of themselves.[37] But although these bags, baskets, and boxes named "Hawthorne" are meant to stand as metonyms for the author's psychic commodification, they are also meant to stand as evidence of how the perceiver marks solid realities with his individual impress. Hawthorne claims this stuff through remarking it in his text: Communicating the painful irony of a ubiquitous commercial imprimatur purchased at the cost of creativity, he revenges and restores the artistic power that the stencil itself has denied. In fact, the masterful, enriched realism of "The Custom-House," with Hawthorne's "confession" of his inadequacy as regards the production of realism, is the next concentricity in this game of tropes and toads. Then comes the stunning *coup de grace* of *The Scarlet Letter*, a text that both deconstructs and enacts the "reality" of its archival evidence.[38] Hawthorne, intuiting exactly the ways in which the "real" is most clearly posited and confirmed by its indissociable relationship with romance (and vice versa), reveals realism's presencing as absolutely dependent on the inevitability of its being subverted by the tropological energies of the language that manifests it.

Accepting of its putative contract with the prosaic, realism does not hold itself in abeyance from habit, keyed up to a Proustian susceptibility that courts the exquisite pain of surprise – hears with virtually unbearable acuteness "the explosions of the clock," feels as if assaulted by "the hostility of the violet curtains."[39] It is rather, at one level, an acceptance of (in fact, a veritable insistence on) habit, a vision that allows things their dullness as tacit recognition of the reciprocities between perceiver and object. Realism involves both a willing forgetfulness and a sense of the unrecallable that does not include in its equation the perfect recollection that involuntary memory may afford. Resistant to such joyful cruelties as those afforded, acutely, by involuntary memory, it is at home in that everyday memory that for Proust, and with him one major strain of the "modernist sensibility," was a bowdlerized account of the past, "as far removed from the real as the myth of our imagination or the caricature furnished by direct perception."[40] Nelly Dean, Lockwood, Coverdale, Edna Pontellier, and Victor Frankenstein, self-absorbed and assimilative, are all tacit admissions of the necessity for a productive but almost brutal indifference or incomprehension regarding the past; Undine Spragg, of Wharton's *The Custom of the Country*, is the quintessence of this motif, with her willed metamorphoses based on incremental amnesias. Lockwood returns accidentally to the locus of *Wuthering Heights* less than a year after his tenure there and says, unselfconsciously, "my residence in that locality had already grown dim and dreamy" (p. 241); this thick-skinned forgetfulness is realism's necessary mode because it allows it to remain socially and politically involved, rather than introspective and bound to the past. This refusal to engage the historical and psychoanalytic pasts except as they may be used to inform the present is perhaps more stoic than stolid; this resistance is, at any rate, what pushed modernists like Lawrence and Woolf to complain that realism, at least of the Edwardian variety, fails to provide characters with "souls."[41] That modernist investment in seeking for things that one knows beforehand cannot be found is not yet fully present in realism, as if some Lord Jim, in Conrad's litanic phrase, "one of us," must first sacrifice himself to the fool's errand of being chased and hounded eternally by the very ineffable thing from the past that he so hotly pursues.

Realism's recognition of habit is both a methodological choice and an epistemological choice, for realism concerns itself precisely with how a given set of materialities eventually may cause some people to behave predictably within it (and it is equally fascinated by the sense that there are some who will never come to fit the mold) – how some are lulled by its logic until alternative systems are, quite simply, forgotten even as possibilities. Realism senses that this is both the good news and the bad news, of course, because it perceives that the very forgetfulness that turns people into automatons also allows people and texts to address themselves sufficiently to productivity. To remember too much of the past is to lose the present advantage; if Silas Lapham rises spiritually as he seeks to recuperate his ousted partner's fortunes, he sacrifices, in looking backward, his financial future. As long as he remains the metonymous extension of his product, tough and impenetrable, he can whitewash past dealings, but when he views the past stripped of its surface elaborations, he sees and reacts to alternative imperatives. Lily Bart holds history – "a long history" – in her hands,[42] but the packet of love letters that could restore her to full social (and therefore economic) power is tied to and reinforces a personal honor, a remembrance of herself and her connectedness to others. It must be kept as "history" and withheld from reinscription in the present. Nelly Dean, on the other hand, is a monster of self-sufficiency and a certain kind of efficiency as well, having discovered through "hard discipline" her precise terms of engagement with the story at hand; she is able to order her account to Lockwood only because she is not beleaguered by the memory of what she must leave out nor plagued by any recognition of her own potential incomprehension. Nelly illustrates, page by page, that the willfulness that represents rationality as sufficient and complete is founded on multiple amnesias, and she reveals just how absentminded one must be to be any kind of realist, or to speak any kind of language as if it were enough.[43] Dicken's Bounderby, verbose and materialistic in the extreme, is the caricature of the realist who must stick to the story he has invented for his purposes. Born in a ditch, bedded in an egg-box, he must alter the terms of his past to legitimize his present argument.[44]

As if to embody its sense of producing a willed truth, realism is populated with orphans and amnesiacs who have lost or repudiated their pasts, just as it is filled with stories built on locations and worlds said no longer to exist: Frankenstein's monster, of course, is the original figure for an old brain wiped clean to carry out a new agenda; Dickens's Bounderby and Wharton's Undine Spragg prove realism's premise of a material present dependent on annihilation of one's past. But there is also Hawthorne's Priscilla, the veiled lady, as well as Dickens's Louisa, who professes to no memory of past dreams or feelings, and Stoker's Lucy Westenra and Mina Harker and Jonathan Harker, none of whom can summon even the memorable past fully to conscious memory. These authors reify in amnesiac characters their sense of a text always partial, necessarily forgetful; that they so often invest this intuition in lovely women signals both the desire and the ambivalence with which they approach the generation of their texts. (Collins's wandering, distracted woman in white, the mirror image of another character who is brought, finally, to a similar state of bewilderment, is another figure in this equation.) They communicate this forgetfulness in spatial terms, as if amnesia is metonymously reciprocal to physical places that become altered, or disappear, or take on new identities. Realism apprehends continuity as broken. As memory is translated in realism into spatial terms, one finds a whole world of markers for these disjunctions, of which the mythic landscape of *Wuthering Heights* and the clockwork sameness of *Hard Times*'s Coketown are only among the most remarkable. The writer who proceeds resolutely onward nonetheless, and the reader who is, regardless of her own alternative realisms, politely pragmatic enough to be forgetful for the space of the novel, can understand that there is in realism a contractual obligation to proceed syntagmatically.

One is struck, in fact, by realism's equanimity, which is neither ingenuous nor uncomprehending, but perhaps merely pragmatic; it creates all those characters besieged and ultimately conquered by their own too-acute sensibilities, all those suicides, all those drownings, and observes them with a reserved compassion. The females who are invariably sacrificed are killed off not only as women but also as virtual allegories for the pleasures of the text, the erotic tropological energies that threaten the syntagma by creating vivid spots in time; that they so often drown communicates this intuition of a depth that thwarts syntagmatic and diachronic forward movement toward efficiency. The trope, turning, becomes a vortex – Eustacia Vye, the very embodiment of Hardy's pleasure in sensual, tropological language, casting herself into a maelstrom, man-made, productive, and unforgiving. Maggie Tulliver, most painfully " 'cute," but "half an idiot i'some things," stands as emblematic of a text in danger of forgetting its business for a mad lyricism: sent to fetch a thing, "she forgets what she's gone for, an' perhaps 'ull sit down on the floor i' the sunshine an' plait her hair an' sing to herself like a Bedlam creatur'."[45] Floating *down* the river produces an erotic plot;

sinking beneath it becomes an almost ritualistic purification of both text and character of the tendency toward a regressive poetic density. Edna Pontellier, the most absentminded and dreamy of suicides, is another such sacrifice of introspection to a more practical agenda, and the fluid indirect discourse and the poetic litany through which she sinks at the end are the seductive antitheses to an alternative, more linear textual productivity. Zenobia, fool for romance, suffers the ballast of double repudiations, from within the text by the reformist/fanatic Hollingsworth and from outside it by an author threatened by his own capacity for such erotic distractions as she represents; her British sister, Eustacia, Queen of Night, is so disruptive of Yeobright's reformist/evangelical agenda that she must be launched into a whirlpool. [Lily Bart wants, right before her death by chloral, "a brief bath of oblivion," as if to acknowledge her affiliation with all these submerged fictional sisters (*The House of Mirth*, p.322).] Read within this intertextual space, the fact that Hetty Sorrel of *Adam Bede cannot* drown herself, that she seeks out and stands by the still, dark pond but cannot submerge herself, becomes an enriched gesture, for she is all beauty and no substance, Eliot's refutation of Keats and Plato. She, unlike the powerful others who may stand for the body of a text torn between desire and rectitude, is only distraction. These drowned figures, potent and, like Edna, impossible to kill off definitively, are the proof that beyond realism's agreement with mundanity there is something else, which it circles, signals, and encodes without the illusion of an access proportionate to one's neurasthenic sensitivities. Yet, too, these reveries on drowning instantiate one's desire for consummation at all costs; it is a fantasy whose equivalence, when brought to the surface, is death: "One ought to sink to the bottom of the sea, probably, and live alone with one's words," says Virginia Woolf, who knows herself what it means to be not waving but drowning.[46]

Realism's Accommodative Gestures

Realism's doubts, produced by an underlying awareness of both conflicting materialities and some unreachable, inarticulable interior space, serve to keep the form open in ways that other, less accommodative forms are not. This fiction often preaches a closed message, and seriously so, but only at the most overt level, and even then it often, and with self-referential irony, mocks preachers at the same time: grandstanders like Zenobia, Hollingsworth, Bounderby, and Brontë's "vinegar-faced Joseph" (p. 18) are among its cautionary figures. Realism works, and it does its work at a complex level beyond these demagogues and bullies of humility; its pedagogy is subtle, often despite itself. Howells, in *Annie Kilburn*, a novel springing from his outrage over social and political conditions and an attempt to address "the social as well as the individual conscience," makes his spokesman for the working class a minister; Mr. Peck, however, like the author, works quietly to persuade, his methods virtually Socratic. ("You beg the question," he says, and sustains the conversation by replying "I will answer your question by asking another."[47]) Realism is a mediation, effecting a balance between two virtually essential human impulses – one pragmatic, the other disruptive, one optimistic, the other seductively shadowed.[48] It is often said of realism that, bound to the terms of verisimilitude, it is hard-pressed to discover endings; progenitive forms like the picaresque exposed the difficulty of providing any ending that would not by definition signal a hyberbolic fictionality, and indeed realism clearly faces a more complex version of this practical dilemma. Yet if the picaresque could not, by virtue of its being predicated on unregenerate rogues, turn convincingly to transformations of character for its endings (for one could hardly say, under picaresque circumstances, "and so, Lazarillo, having plumbed the depths of his soul, married, fathered children, and became a productive member of society"), it could at least depend on this class and genre-based assumption of character stasis to define its dilemma. But realism's intuition of character as both assimilative and intrinsic produces a more enriched and ambivalent response to the demands of closure. Offering a hermeneutic space within which conflicts play against each other, realism's *telos*, revealing itself by virtue of elaborate plots and conclusive endings as both inevitable and arbitrary, proves at the same time the willfulness of its own ordering.

One begins to discover beneath the apparent certitudes of realism's closures a virtual nihilism at work, an opening up that leaves room for multiple productivities; there is a pattern throughout realism's stories of +/minus pairings that nullify each other and further destabilize the textual status quo. Leo Bersani argues that "the *dénouements* in realistic fiction make havoc of the verisimilitudes which the novelist has appeared to be so scrupulously observing," as the tying up of structural elements betrays the particularity and randomness that realism makes it its business to reveal.[49] Catherine Belsey says that "the movement of classic realist narrative toward closure ensures the reinstatement of order, sometimes a new order, sometimes the old restored, but always intelligible because familiar."[50] I would argue that the very self-consciousness of these gestures in realism produces the opposite effect. Dickens, for example, announces his sense of fiction as willful arbitration between order and the ineffable, even as he is calisthenically teleological.[51] *Great Expectations*, with its two endings, quite simply pulls the flowered rug out from under the whole realist project of sustaining the illusion of being in a reality, and *Hard Times* enacts a more subtle subversion in the remarkable double knot of Louisa's end: "Herself again a wife – a mother – lovingly watchful of her children, ever careful that they should have a childhood of the mind no less than a childhood of the body, as knowing it to be even a more beautiful thing, and a possession, any hoarded scrap of which is a blessing and happiness to the wisest? . . . Such a thing was never to be" (p. 274). Bounderby's story, pricked by his mother's rebuttal, deflates to nothing. Dickens well knows the realist's trick of claiming merely to report a historically "true" event or story (there are documents and evidence, and one can dig up the bones of the man who constructed the file), and thus the layers of self-referential irony amass themselves as Bounderby's "real" history, based on a disappeared text (his mother), shows up to impugn his fictional one.

This willful undoing is common, as if realism's teleological responsibilities generate subliminal resistance. Hawthorne pulls something like Dickens's trick in *The Blithedale Romance*. Having handed the story over to Coverdale, he causes him retroactively to suborn his entire account in his final, startling confession ("I – I myself – was in love – with – Priscilla"), for if that declaration is true, then the story he has told changes utterly, and if it is false, then he is a liar and thus not to be believed in this or anything else (a version of the "all Cretans are liars" paradox). Brontë allows Heathcliff to tell a story of Isabella's "innate admiration" for his brutalities, particularly the hanging of her spaniel (p. 127), and to speak with such authority that he subverts but does not discredit Isabella's own more reliable testimony, leaving the "truth" in some empty and unclaimed space. Chopin tells the world that Edna has become capable of speaking for herself, even as Chopin increasingly speaks for

Edna, almost without our noticing, through indirect discourse; this double claim for Edna's authority and her incapacity creates the enigma of how the ending is to be read. Hardy, pressed by his editors to sacrifice his five-act tragedy for a happier ending to *The Return of the Native*, offers a recalcitrant footnote elaborating the enforced and artificial nature of what is to follow, and he further enacts his resistance through the virtual caricature of closure he then supplies. And Howells performs, in *The Rise of Silas Lapham*, the mirror trick of using an imaginary novel, "Tears, Idle Tears," to produce a treacherously unstable irony within his own text: the sentimentality that Sewell scorns as genre and that Penelope rejects as plot reproduces itself within Howells's novel to become both valorized and repudiated at once (and regarding nihilism, Howells once wrote this: "for the greater part of the time I believe in nothing, though I am afraid of everything").[52] Realism, only superficially conclusive, proceeds by double negatives, seeing the world and character from a place just before unstable irony. Its subliminal nihilism offers a procedural compromise, a placement relative to the world and others just sufficient to hobble one's aggressions without also inducing the paralysis of deep introspection.

Operating its shop with an underlying apprehension of a place beyond words, realism signals its double connectedness to inside and outside through its dominating trope, metonymy.[53] If a postmodern sensibility articulates its apprehension of the duplicity of language through puns and oxymorons, realism's dependence on metonymy is equally revealing: Metonymy establishes the baffling contiguities between the soul and its material concentricities as if both to predict and to defend against a coming fragmentation. It is as if, without pretension, realism does its bit to hold the Cartesian split together, but like one knitting socks for the war effort instead of making bombs or speeches, it is not grandiose in its resistance. The motif of an excitation spilling over its articulable components, a preoccupation with the supplementarity of a language always both in excess of and insufficient to representation, has come to fruition only after long and persistent literary and philosophical meditations on the essential unavailability of the thing in itself. And it is possible to see in this most quixotic of quests for the very thing a manifestation of the tropological inevitability that renders the search futile. For what have those discussions been but creations of metonymies for (contiguous outward projections of) one's somatic memory of a free-based, eternally illusive intrapsychic thing, or if not extensions of a somatic memory, then the mutated leavings of some first, ancient metaphor, "the detritus of other metaphors – language speaking itself, then – and the line between first and last tropes is very thin"?[54] This shared fantasy of making successful, unmediated contact with externalities is, finally, not a dream of objectivity, but, as Heidegger suggests, the opposite, a dream of de-objectification.[55] Realism, its eye on things, intuits in them both possibilities: the utopia of full presence and the dystopia of the commodified soul.[56] This intuition inevitably disturbs realism's social program of displaying a contamination of character by outside forces, and those novelists who wish to effect a "complete transparence of person to environment or mind to matter" both discover and create opacities, attuned and implicated as they necessarily are in this circularity.[57] Metonymy is simultaneously a measure of both hope and resignation, for if it argues a connectedness between inner and outer worlds, it also implies inevitably that we are contaminated by the deadness of all the things that perceptually we cannot let alone. What we objectify turns on us; as with Gradgrind, our heads become warehouses; as with Zenobia, our heads become hothouses. And, too, metonymy is a *trope*; it is itself the evidence of inevitable displacement.

Paradoxically, realism's use of metonymy exposes its apprehension of the seamlessness of real and surreal, as it infects materialities with the caprice of the very humans who are shown by metonymy to suffer materialization. Realism acknowledges that a dead-on stare at such enriched materialities often makes them go queer. Realism thus inevitably manifests itself as a set of conditional assumptions always in flux, caught in the play of fancy and romance and the surreal. That paragon of surreal realism, *Hard Times*, is wonderful proof that traditional genre distinctions are Procrustean acts of will and habit; and its counterpart, Hawthorne's grimly realistic, politically cynical *The Blithedale Romance*, is the other side of the coin. One thinks one has sighted a realist, and suddenly there is nothing left but his grin; romanticists turn from flamingos into croquet mallets at the drop of a hat. Artistic realism, that fruitful oxymoron, is nowhere better effected than in the "high realism" of Henry James; yet nowhere is there a more potent confluence with what has been designated Hawthornian romance.[58] Realism proves that "magical realism" is only a virtual oxymoron invented by ingenuous rationalists; according to lived, perceptual experiences, realism reminds us, the balance between magic and real is as mercuric as a carpenter's level held in one's own two hands. One could go further and say that realism invents and necessitates a full-blown magical realism as it provokes language into speaking metonymously, articulating the contiguities that come, over time, to erode the boundaries between people and things and between the (humanly) possible and impossible. As if to reconfigure some primal split – the one that Freud summons forth in "The Antithetical Meaning of Primal Words" – realism restores to words their double truths, and "nature," both human and otherwise, becomes (un)natural. Brought by realism's very practice to a state of doubt about what constitutes the "real," even the ideologues seem, at some level, to sense that the microscopic lens and the anatomized soul only enrich each other. It is not insignificant that the century opened with Frankenstein's meticulously piecemeal monster and closed with Dracula's desirous and infectious bite, reported with forensic accuracy, verified by rational and minute scrutiny, and recorded faithfully with the most up-to-date equipment as a matter for both the scientific record and the spiritual record.

Conventionally, realism is seen as antithetical to this enrichment of the real – just as romance must, by these terms, play Ariel's game as proof of itself – but it is realism's deadpan agenda as regards materialities that inevitably brings with it the vision of the transformative nature of things. Anyone who reads Dickens or the Brontës rides effortlessly on this continuum of real–surreal. The likes of Dickens's Mrs. Sparsit may put character on the Giants' Staircase headed down, only to find a certain Escheresque complexity in the matter of descent (this is another of Dickens's self-referential jokes about plot and character).[59] Even a female, typically the most gravity-bound of creatures, does not hit bottom in this anxiety dream: Louisa, whose only cathexis is to the double father, Gradgrind/Dickens, is this free radical embodied, her suspended animation at the end ("Such a thing was never to be") an admission that reality is a Cheshire cat, here and then gone, all but its smile. Dickens's tropological inventiveness throughout *Hard Times* may, in fact, be seen as a model for this dynamic interplay. He is forced by his reformative agenda to stare hard and long at a singularly ugly set of endlessly repeated forms and to drill them into the reader. He must teach of a hard world, hard times with no respite: "all

very like . . . still more like . . . equally like," "same hours . . . same sound
. . . same pavements . . . same work," "every day . . . the same as yesterday," "every year the counterpart of the last" (p. 20). And his tropological
resistance is directly proportionate to his reformative obligation to communicate this deadly reiteration.

With realism's pedagogical obligations in mind, realists often show
themselves to be painfully aware of the consequences of a unilateral and
humorless approach in matters of instruction. Gradgrind and Hollingsworth, whose metonymous identifications with grim institutions suggest
their inadequacies as teachers, stand as emblematic of a pedagogy unrecep-
tive to its audience and unaware of its own prejudicial perspective (Stoker's
Van Helsing, with his utterly meticulous, cautiously gradual "teaching" of
the terms of the reality constituted in Dracula and Dracula's transformation
of Lucy into vampire/harlot, is the model pedagogue, his patience in instruction virtually psychoanalytic). Hollingsworth is the type of the philan-
thropist-reformer-realist who fails pathetically to effect his agenda even as
he is destructive of the lives he touches; in *Annie Kilburn*, Howells uses
him thus: " 'Oh, that's the way with these philanthropists,' said Annie,
thinking of Hollingsworth, in *The Blithedale Romance*, the only philanthropist whom she had really ever known. 'They are always ready to sacrifice
the happiness and comfort of any one to the general good.' "[60] Mr. Gradgrind, "with a rule and a pair of scales, and the multiplication table always
in his pocket, . . . ready to weigh and measure any parcel of human nature,
and tell you exactly what it comes to," is the cautionary representative of
the Henry Cole, Department of Practical Art school of realism.[61] Gradgrind
and Hollingsworth, lodged at the fulcrum of the century, and both predictive of future and evidential of past abuses, prove the failure of a pedagogy that alienates itself from fancy – a realism that has no persuasive force
– even as Gradgrind becomes, under Dickens's enriched vision, a testamentary figure for the power of realism's double attachment to the ineffable
and the material. One is given to see, too, the serious consequences of
failed teaching in the students who bungle their lives as a result of it, and
not only in the tragedies that accrue under Gradgrind's and Hollingsworth's
tutelage. Frankenstein attributes his own abortive production to his father's
inadequate pedagogy: "My father was not scientific and I was left to struggle with a child's blindness." "If, instead of this remark, my father had

taken the pains to explain to me that the principles of Agrippa had been entirely exploded. . . . " (pp. 25, 24). (Shelley also implies that Waldman and Krempe do not sufficiently contextualize their own dangerous teachings.) Realism knows that in order to be effective, it must not yield completely to the fanciful – Mr. Sleary, whose lisp slurs into near incomprehensibility his speaking up for imagination and artistry, signals Dickens's oppositional but equal sense of the dangers of yielding to tropological acrobatics – but neither can it be overly earnest and humorless. Its vision must displace all other realisms for the space of the novel, but it cannot be experienced as browbeating and still remain effective.

Realism's claiming of real space is clearly felt as an imperialistic gesture and is always under threat of reapportionment, either by another reality or by one's own irresistible and elusive unrest (it is the candor of this claiming that makes it bearable), and this intuition generates what might be called a realists' melancholy, as if the duty to organize the furniture for a particular kind of conversation wears them out. One is given to feel this melancholia quite explicitly in *Hard Times*, which is filled with madhouse images of a populace/town/text/author under threat of terrible depression, and in *The Blithedale Romance* to sense in Coverdale's distracted fidelity to detail the half-depression of a man who cannot escape his own watchful, realist's habit of mind. Lockwood is another such; at once enervated and (dis)possessed by his own spectatorial gaze, he cannot bear eyes that are raised to meet his. Hawthorne's mysterious Priscilla, one moment running about, leaping and laughing, the next moment slack and out of focus with the world around her; Edna Pontellier's rebounding between a virtually manic energy and a commensurate ebb; Eustacia Vye's oxymoronic condition of potently restless enervation – these figures embody realism's recognition that it must be stoic in its resistance to the inner voice. And perhaps *Dracula* as well is at some level a quintessential reverie on the realist's necessary ambivalence; pulled between a daylight world of proprietous obligation and a delirious midnight that threatens to leave it exhausted, vitiated, and irrevocably changed, realism both knows and signals its endangered commitment to rectitude.

Like all of us, the realist both entertains and resists the fantasy of waking up from the nested series of impediments to a full and unmediated contiguity with the past and the "real" present. Chopin's novel is only the distilled reverie on this subject, its ambivalence about its protagonist and her angst evidence of the realist's necessary resistance to dwelling on the subject. A complete awakening (an oxymoron that signals in advance its own condition of hopeful futility) would not only recover the present but also restore what time has relegated to memory; without it, the past is always bowdlerized and the present blurred. Like Edna Pontellier dazed by the heat and trying to recover the waist-deep meadow of her childhood, one feels both the past and the "past" only as what Edna names as a "retrace": narrativizing may partially redeem the memorable past for the present – "Oh, I see the connection now!" she says, as she struggles to discover her thoughts – but this same narrativizing is itself the reminder of its insufficiency as regards the immemorial. A place to which the child Edna went in order to run from prayers, the oceanic bluegrass represents an antitheological fantasy of immediacy, irrevocably lost to the displacements of the necessity "to think about thinking" (p. 17). To apprehend things as contiguous, and not merely as seen, distorted, across a chasm of time and space, not metaphors for the thing, but the thing itself, to swim in the gulf – that is, ironically, the ultimate metonymy for a full sighting of the forgotten. But her nostalgia for full consciousness notwithstanding, Chopin remains equivocal in her flirtation with the unknowable. Schopenhauerean idealism (and that whole epistemological wanderground) makes a nice metaphor, spices up the dream imagery, suffices to swell a progress, start a scene or two, but it competes with furniture polish and dress patterns and irony and naturalism.

Maligned as pedestrian and inelegant, realism has an industrial strength, and thus its uneasy accommodation of the immemorial seems, in retrospect, to predict how less robust or more self-indulgent forms will cave in to introspective paralysis or lyric despair. As Lawrence says in "Surgery for the Novel – or a Bomb," in the manner of having his teacake and eating it too, Joyce and Proust and Richardson are "absorbedly, childishly interested" in themselves. " 'Did I feel a twinge in my little toe, or didn't I?' . . . Is my aura a blend of frankincense and orange pekoe and boot-blacking, or is it myrrh and bacon-fat and Shetland tweed?"[62] Looking to define exactly the enigma of the "soul," one may trade what Beckett calls realism's epidermal preoccupations for an endless reading of entrails.[63] When Norris asked for a fiction that would see into "the unplumbed depths of the human heart, and the mystery of sex, and the problems of life, and the black, unsearched penetralia of the soul of man," he could not have known how completely his wish would be fulfilled.[64] At best, one comes to the paradoxical impasse of a lyricism so acute in its reading of this irretrievable knowledge that it is itself an epiphanic, sublime, but hopelessly ephemeral cure: Lily Briscoe's sense, in *To the Lighthouse*, that "words fluttered side-ways and struck the object inches too low," her reverie on how "the urgency of the moment always missed its mark," and her question, "how could one express in words these emotions of the body?" are the terms under which realism tacitly operates. But her cry "to want and not to have. . . . And then to want and not to have – to want and want – how that wrung the heart, and wrung it again and again!" brings the text to a full awareness that being true enough to wring the heart also irrevocably alters the terms of the game.[65]

If one collected all the expressions, lyrical and psychoanalytic and philosophical and economic, that are the rich and infinitely subtle varia-tions on this modernist theme of the immemorial, one might conclude, for the sake of argument, at any rate, that such a trenchant, goading for-getfulness is a common denominator, virtually an essentialism located so-matically within humanness: call the fantasy of its hypostasis *Dasein* if you will, or "the sublime," or one of many less inclusive terms; once ac-knowledged, it drives one to search for it, to speak of it, and to give it names. Realism apprehends this restless displacement and accommodates it without attempting direct engagement. Embodied in *Wuthering Heights* as desire, it is a lovely, dark-haired specter at the window luring one out into the weather; and as desire, it is also Dracula, at once undead and freed of formalisms and also coffin-bound, the irresistible catachresis for realism's apprehension both of how the ineffable seduces one from home and of how it may dispossess one into an unquiet grave. Its meta-morphoses are infinite and opportunistic, and its energy can be neither destroyed nor conserved; like Dracula, it may come in the guise of a wolf or great dog or in "a thin streak of white mist" (p. 258). "Like smoke – or with the white energy of boiling water," it is at once both palpable and immaterial (p. 259). Potent, it chases after the one who chases after it – Dracula's hypnotic and corruptive link to Mina Harker's psyche is a figure for the unimpeachable circularity of the hunt – driving one, in both poetic and Heideggerean terms (the same thing, after all), to homelessness.[66]

Realism, its feet on the ground, nonetheless feels and responds to the diasporan consequences of the restlessness that language itself awakens and projects them into its texts in bodily form: the wandering and utterly bereft monster in *Frankenstein*; in *Wuthering Heights*, Heathcliff, starved and sleepless, night-walking, driven by the ghost from all domestic comfort, whose death, staring wide-eyed at the mockery of an open window, is exactly the proof that one cannot get outside to find the lost thing. Or, as a figure for us all, there is Coverdale/Hawthorne hounding himself out of Arcadia in *The Blithedale Romance*. (It is this restlessness, in fact, that obviates forever any possibility of utopia, as Plato well understood when he denied poetic language a place in the Republic.) Or, as another figure for us all, there is Lily Bart hounding herself out of, if not Arcadia, at least a materialist paradise. In *Hard Times*, Louisa, sitting among the fallen trees and the fallen leaves in a dark opening in the woods, stands within the text as the very emblem of homelessness, and she is the figure of the artist's desire and the father's desire. In the hope of seeing clearly this immemorial thing, modernist fiction looks beyond materialities; it says eternally, with Heathcliff, "Last night, I was on the threshold of hell. To-day, I am within sight of my heaven. I have my eyes on it – hardly three feet to sever me!" (p. 259). Realism, not looking so hard, manages close encounters; knowing the difference between its obligation to communicate the real thing and its obligation to accommodate the Thing holding itself incommunicado, it manages a bit of both. But, as events have proved, the straight-on search for this forgotten thing is pulling a short thread through a needle's eye, an endless, futile twirl to catch sight of that thing at the back of one's mind, an apotheosis endlessly deferred.

Therapeutic Containment

Realism keeps this immemorial force contained, a remarkable and therapeutic event, as it allows for a text that is pervaded by forces pathological in dimension and yet is not co-opted by those forces.[67] Heathcliff is perhaps the most potent example of how realism genuinely problematizes and ultimately curbs the impulse to aggrandize such anarchic power as transcendent, as Brontë tarnishes his sadistic appeal with the toad-like ugliness of acquisitiveness and petulance, while also holding him within the bounds of sympathy (Brontë achieves with Heathcliff what Milton was unable to do with Satan). Separated from the cluttered and homely milieu of realism and given incarnative priority, the unnameable may be either aggrandized to Byronic proportions or invested in misogynist and racist name-calling. Freed from realism's insistence on material and spiritual reciprocities, this excitation at the heart of Western anxieties and desires has taken its names and claimed its places prejudicially; postmodernism reminds us of this result and signals its resistance through its embrace of the eclectic and the ordinary (and outside of literature, Heidegger stands as the warning for how such a focus might swell into fascist proportions). When it has been located cerebrally and called something ineffable, something sublime, something grand and illusive – Lyotard's "anamnesis of the Thing," for example – it has been gendered male: it is the Beast in the Jungle, that very grandiose Thing for which men have waited at the expense of women. But when, frustrated and ill-tempered, one tires of calling it out with Heideggerean subtlety, one names it something else, this prick-teaser that produces an excitation but no relief, and locates it in women or other conveniently othered species. Zenobia is this fantasy embodied, but, notably, with chains;[68] Hawthorne, resistant, puts his mythically proportioned heroine between Pulpit Rock and Hollingsworth – a rock and a hard place, indeed – and, turning the screws, proceeds to press the real woman from the romance. Sometimes the seams are apparent, the gendering slightly botched: "Down from the waist they are Centaurs, though women all above" – as Aretha Franklin would say, Who's zoomin' who, here? Freud's urbane question, "What do women want?" and his Alice in Wonderland assertion that "you are yourselves the problem" involve precisely this displacement of the enigma onto the Other.[69] Tired of courting the ineffable within one's own purview, one reduces it to "irrationality," "nature," "the female," the whole gamut of stale euphemisms for unsatiated and inexplicable restlessness, dead metaphors for the Thing itself (if compromised women routinely get killed off in fiction, it is because consummation, as it proves such women attainable, also proves them to have been merely fraudulent advertisements for the ineffable; it is an excision of the already dead, a vision brought to full life in Eliot's extended references in *Adam Bede* to Hetty Sorrel, after her murder of her child, as a living corpse, on trial but already nullified).

Or if not women, then other scapegoats are postulated in an environment in which the ineffable is privileged, and they are partially disguised, as women always are, as enigmas. And in a way, this enriched, aestheticized racism is almost more egregious than its less elegant nineteenth-century counterparts, as it metaphorizes race (in the same way "woman" has long been assimilated) as a locus for its preoccupation with the otherwise inarticulable foreignness of that unnameable energy. Realism's dubious courtesies of defensive hostility or crude caricature seem preferable because less disguised. Sim Rosedale performs, in *The House of Mirth*, Wharton's egregiously unselfconscious anti-Semitism, but he is also accorded a place, a character, a part in the metonymous landscape of a materialized existence. Conrad's more "modernist" *The Nigger of the Narcissus* might stand as the symbol for all the less candid racisms used to articulate, aggrandize, and humiliate the mystery of self; it reifies in James Wait this preoccupation with a potent black nothingness that will not let one alone for a moment and that goads one into a veritable madness of introspection. "Wait" is exactly the watchword for one's sense of the eternal enforcement of a large-voiced and resonant inaccessibility that may be the Darkness or just as well some charlatan in blackface; that he floats on the *Narcissus* puts us all in the same boat. We have all been trained to speak thus metaphorically of this enigma of our own forgetfulness, and our language makes such misogyny and racism easy. But realism, an oxymoronic condition of perspicuous amnesia in which both the world and the forgotten can be accommodated, does not privilege the mystery, and this accommodation, to some small extent, desublimates that provocative phantom that finds itself, by virtue of the inevitability of its aliases, being more or less criminalized when given female or other-racial form.

Held by ambivalence from any sustained illusion of transcendence and tethered to the very material artifacts that represent one's commodified condition, realism by its nature reminds one rather of the comedic aspects of humanness: realism's use of metonymy to signal the soul's associative relationship to materialities virtually guarantees that character will always verge on catachresis, monstrous or motley. Lyotard has scraped his knuckles against the question of the "inhuman" in an attempt to discover the precise human residue that can be neither translated nor dismissed, and he finds it in suffering. If, indeed, it is this bereavement, this suffering toward the nearly present memory of what has been lost, that marks "man" as human, then realism maintains, by virtue of its preoccupation with mundanities, that this amputation, with its phantom presence, is also at the same time to be perceived as more or less comedic. In a world of half-realized representations, the loss of one more thing, even such a precious one as full consciousness, provokes a certain strange mirth, like the boy in Frost's "Out, Out – " whose "first outcry was a rueful laugh" as he saw his hand devoured by the chainsaw. "The Beast in the Jungle" springs to mind as a paradigm for the ambivalent character of a realism that is simultaneously very serious and irremediably skeptical; whatever James's sympathies with Marcher, he also consciously reveals the comical pretentiousness of a fantasy that predicts before the leap that what will descend will be kingly – a lion or some such creature – and not a bunny or a hyena or a gadfly, that it will, in fact, reveal itself as a "beast," with all that the term connotes of size, desire, and ferocity (James's novels are permeated with his genuine appreciation of the comedic view one might, in moments of rare freedom, take of one's gorgeously introspective self). A pessimistic modernism may put the carcass of the snow leopard at the summit of Kilimanjaro and leave the hyenas prowling the camp perimeters in the lowland, but this exchange of the grandiose vision for the venal is a solemnized abasement, emblem of a gangrenous suffering that cannot be remediated. Trading beasts is not the point; realism's doubled sense of the sublime and the ridiculous emerges in the catachreses of Frankenstein's monster and Dracula, as if to bracket the century with a veritable menagerie of names for that "beast" within.

Realism allows us to intuit the humor in our mournful solemnities, reminding us in what it does rather than in what it says that the safe, deliciously melancholic conviction that the lost thing must have been quite grand makes the human condition as potentially funny as it is tragic. If Frankenstein creates a gargantuan specimen of a man, it is in part because Shelley is constructing a physical and tropological figure to represent the whole human, both flesh and Promethean soul. The problem is, of course, that providing physical space for that chimera that lurks in the jungle of one's psyche means ending up with a monstrosity of pathos and violence: the inelegance of the comic or the grotesque is the price we must pay for our oversized estimation of the unknowable thing. That curious mixture of comic and serious tones one finds in Brontë, Hawthorne, Dickens, and James, among others, a mixture suggesting a rueful awareness of one's own complicity in the self-aggrandizing gestures of tragedy, signals this double sensitivity. And if one chooses to call this excitation Desire, which is one of its commonest names, then realism inevitably reminds us of desire's unlovely and earthy side: the beast with two backs, the original catachresis, which, in the missionary position at any rate (the most appropriate position for a propagandistically inclined form like realism), precludes anything but alternating views of the two sides of the question. Realism has the capacity to signal a double message of travail and mundanity, for it is, by its nature, incapable of being grand (and when it is grandiose it simply reinforces the double code). It manages to communicate the possibility that what is lurking just beyond the reach of memory, imagined as an immemorial gray eminence, might be everything or nothing: it could be the key to the soul, or it could as well be the eternal MacGuffin. Either way, realism acknowledges that this memory remains an irresistible lure, coming from a place beyond the rational and pulling one away from logic and precision and reformative effectiveness and toward a stuttering, seriocomic eagerness to spill one's compulsion.

Chapter Three

Domestic Violence

=========================

"Miss Temple, Miss Temple, what – *what* is that girl with curled hair?
Red hair, ma'am, curled – curled all over? . . . Why, in defiance of
every precept and principle of this house, does she conform to the
world so openly . . . as to wear her hair one mass of curls?"
"Julia's hair curls naturally," returned Miss Temple, still more quietly.
. . . . .
"Madame . . . I have a Master to serve whose kingdom is not of this
world: my mission is to mortify in these girls the lusts of the flesh; to
teach them to clothe themselves with shame-facedness and sobriety,
not with braided hair and costly apparel; and each of the young persons before us has a string of hair twisted in plaits which vanity itself
might have woven: these, I repeat, must be cut off. . . . "

        —Charlotte Brontë, *Jane Eyre*

Rapunzel, Rapunzel, let down your hair.

Realism and Character

The nineteenth-century novel is in a privileged position to hypostatize the
mutually corrective serious and comedic impulses typical of a realist's habit
of mind, for it stands at the congruence of two competing assumptions
about character: that character is a spiritual matter, predetermined and in-
alterable, and that it is malleable and environmentally susceptible.[1] Realism
premises that observable realities can be and should be articulated novelistically through verisimilitude and that these realities are contingent on
character, which is, in its turn, contingent on the realities within which it

---

86

is formed and exists. The ratio between inside (psyche, character, personality, soul, morality, etc.) and outside (reality) is not, of course, stable, for no one of these writers is able to sustain absolutely a fixed position regarding the soul's processing of those societal bytes that compose *Bildung*: good and evil are both inside and outside; sometimes they coincide appropriately, so that reality reflects character and vice versa, and sometimes not.[2] (The *Bildungsroman*, with its double agenda of personal growth and societal integration, comes alive in nineteenth-century England under exactly this exhilarating ambivalence.) One way of handling this equation is quite clear, and it is reflected in the critical assessments that see realism as attempting to create a transparently univocal relationship between environment and character: The novelist (or perhaps it would be better to say the critic) subdues, to some large extent, her awareness of those who remain immune even to the most coercive physical and economic environments and, with moral purpose firmly in mind, enacts a ruthless metonymizing of character to the things it touches. This is a position very difficult for fiction to sustain; one sees humans in the real world both conforming to and refuting the premise at every turn (often the *same* human, malleable in some things and resistant in others), and the very trope itself generates a resistant energy that subverts the propaganda at hand. More often, the relationships between things and people prove reciprocal, and character emerges from within the generous parameters of this ambivalence. But though by its nature mediative (if full determinism, then not plot, not fiction, not character), realism signals a darker intuition as well, for it sees past the possibility that one is coerced and altered by one's environment to a recognition that one so abused may come to use the metonymous force of one's own materialization.

Realism senses that the masochism one often learns at the hands of a voracious technological or capitalistic environment may produce a reciprocal sadism in the mechanically charged victim. This intuition of instability enforces a full range of insights into the matter of the human soul and helps give to realism its peculiarly metamorphic character as a genre; it also further destabilizes realism's already considerable tonal complexities into a virtually manic–depressive vacillation between hilarity and gloomy sobriety, both among novels within the mode and within a given novel. In its calm and equable moments, realism is able to feel that metonymy is merely its chosen trope, used in its service, called to witness against materialism's formative and dehumanizing impact on those souls involved in a world of assembly and production; and it is in this mode that realism's capacity to produce a productive equilibrium is realized. It enacts a sensible balance between objectification and resistance: an "economy of pain," to use once again Sewell's words in *The Rise of Silas Lapham*. Walter Benn Michaels points out, in his examination of Sewell's position in *Silas Lapham*, that

the goal of realism, literary and moral, is . . . to minimize excess; in literature, to replace the monstrously disproportionate role played in the sentimental novel by love with a more balanced vision of "human feelings in their true proportion and relation" and in ethics, to teach people that their duty lies in following the natural economy of pain, in refusing unhappiness that is the product not of a real cause but of a "false ideal."[3]

Yet if realism frequently makes the covert recognition that an economy of pain may segue imperceptibly into a sadomasochistic economy, it maintains, nonetheless, its overriding obligation to "minimize excess." Critics are not often so explicit as Bersani in making connections between sadomasochism and an anarchic and thoroughly undomesticated eroticism; yet at the heart of the party line on realism's desireless condition may lie, in fact, this sense that its economy of pain is a modest one, small change compared with the Sadeian excess to which untrammeled desire must inevitably lead. However one wishes to read realism's bookkeeping (and one might premise that whatever the delights of sadomasochism, it does not necessarily follow that its absence constitutes desirelessness), it is indisputably *not* excessive relative to what it might be. Flexible, realism assimilates a world of potential pain and gives out a more balanced character than it gets.

This equilibrating is realism's hallmark, but it should not be presumed to derive necessarily from self-satisfaction or certainty; its apparent balance is, in fact, rather the product of its uncertainty and ambivalence, and thus akin to the gymnasts and bareback riders in *Hard Times*, or to all those tipsy stacks of secondhand things in *Dombey and Son*, always felt as on the verge of toppling. Once this precarious equilibrium between character and external reality shifts, realism itself modulates into something else that, while seeming more fully enriched with an anxious sensibility, is in some ways far less (dis)equilibrating. One looks at Lawrence's *Sons and Lovers*, for example, and finds that the most rigorous verisimilitudes, the most linear of chronologies, are impeached by an obsessional process of self-revelation; there is no thought of a social program, no generalized notions of human character until after the fact, but only a virtually infantile exploration of a single need (how else could Lawrence, as if it were a here/gone game, put Walter Morel down a coal mine every day of his life and bring him to the surface, blackened, as symbolic evidence of the intrinsic deficiencies of Morel's character – it is as if the coal mine, not seen by Paul/Lawrence, could not exist as a formative materiality).[4] Realism is not innocent of the existential problematics that make the logics of cause and effect less than fully explanatory of the human condition, but neither is it mesmerized by this apprehension. Still, it is not only the modernists who cannot resist looking inward toward the soul.

This ambivalence leaves room for character to exist as unfinished and at one level destabilizes conventional gender distinctions: If one gets the whole humanist thing finally reticulated, *Frankenstein* seems to predict, one inevitably ends up with a clumsy approximation of a man, no matter what one originally set out to make. (One sees this happening again and again; a most notable recent attempt is in Le Guin's *The Left Hand of Darkness*, which removes all the barriers of human genetic determinism and leaves Earth altogether, only to find its utopia populated by a race that manifests itself masculinely, despite Le Guin's resolute attempt to make it otherwise. It is as if language, functioning with entropic inevitability, falls back into inescapable paradigms.) Raymond Tallis begins *In Defense of Realism* with the pugnacious assertion that he will use the masculine pronoun throughout, according to convention, but he registers his feminist intuitions by saying that "if those who defend realistic fiction have natural allies, they are to be found among the ranks of the feminists." Sensitive to realism's tendency to refute, through its own process, formalized versions of itself, he also senses that characterization – as idiosyncratic and non-stereotypical – may thrive in this environment. It is common to find this condition literalized in characters whose pasts are deficiently represented or completely contradictory to their present characters. Heathcliff is only the most compelling of the halflings, with half a name and half a history, and no recuperative childhood past to link his Liverpool self with his current condition; there is Priscilla, as tenuously present as the veil under which she floats; there is Bounderby, as solid as mud, and with a past that contradicts completely his present personality. Or there is Dracula, inexplicably undead, *sui generis*; it is precisely this void that rebuffs any effort to explain him, and his metamorphic physicalities merely reify the indeterminate nature of his character.

The myth of the transcendently rational man and the oppositional stereotypes it projects onto others cannot prevail unscathed in realism's environment, precisely *because* of realism's inability to decide on how character is produced; if humans are inextricably bound to their material conditions in realism, they cannot also be unaffected by them, but they are also the products of their pasts, historical and spiritual, memorial and immemorial. As Tallis says, "reality is the *asymptote* of narration; and a just expression of reality – one that is equal to its greatness and its misery, to its distances and its depths – is one of the central regulative ideas (in the Kantian sense of this phrase) of literature and the supreme regulative idea of fiction. Realistic fiction is capable of being the highest expression of the fundamental task of consciousness – that of imagining what is actually *there*."[5] To find what is *there*, ontology's dream, may be impossible (as some post-structuralist visions would have it, there is no "there" there to find), but to mobilize a genuine scrutiny can only work to the advantage of those who otherwise would be seen through the anamorphoses of racism and sexism. In realism, neither the present, with its tangible artifacts always deploying themselves unpredictably, nor the past can be allowed to prevail; the struggle is irresolvable. We see Wharton literalizing this struggle (which earlier had been played out more covertly in Lily Bart's subliminal resistance to her own venal and materialistic self in *The House of Mirth*) in the very landscape of *Summer.* The mountain-born, town-raised girl, Summer, is pulled with near-physical force between competing versions of material reality; her love affair is played out on the middle ground between the high mountain and the valley town, but the oppositional topographies of her socialized history and her sexual history make unbearably oppositional demands. The frequent fits, the inevitable faints, and the brain fevers these otherwise strong men and women endure stand as emblematic of this virtually unendurable double responsibility.[6] Count them as they fall: Frankenstein, Cathy, Coverdale, Harker. And Edna Pontellier's inescapable sense that she is in a fever dream stands as evidence as well, as does Lily Bart's frantically hallucinatory wakefulness.

But more than just rational control is compromised in this milieu of forthright ambivalence: character stereotypes are willful necessities produced under the duress of this ambivalence, and thus they are also revealed, at the same time, as constructions. In this universe of reciprocal forces, where neither intrinsic "character" nor socially constructed character is sufficient alone to explain a given fictional personality, stereotypes achieve a certain stolid precariousness. Authors cannot make a fully charged, "heroic" character in this environment of undecidability, any more than Frankenstein can make an elegant man from Petrarchan bits and pieces (white teeth, fair skin, glossy hair, etc.), for both the past and the present are imperative forces. Critics past and present have cited this middling condition as one of realism's unattractive features, but such deflationary necessities as realism imposes make room for multiple characters to coexist within a text and enforce a sense of humanness as interactive and unstable as well as autonomous and deterministically set. Thus, realism is acutely tuned to the Frankensteinian problems faced by the self-made man. Bounderby, with his preposterously hyperbolic stories of a degraded childhood, concocted to aggrandize his present success and to explain his pomposities and his foolishness, finds himself confronted with his "dead" "slattern" mother, who reveals his past with an innocently prideful and utterly devastating candor. Undine Spragg, in *The Custom of the Country*, ends where she begins, with Elmer Moffatt, after a series of metamorphoses to match herself to a playbill of other, incrementally differentiated men.

Realism's characters are perpetually deconstructing under the forced labor of their socializations; sometimes, like Mrs. Sparsit turned mad detective, they cross the line, but realism's stereotypes are always just before such breakdowns. Louisa Gradgrind Bounderby, taut as a bow pulled too tight, is only the most unmistakably disintegrative of these constructs, and her cathexis with nothingness is the emblem as well of other, more superficially therapeutic models. It takes the likes of a D. H. Lawrence to theoretize an obsession with his own sexual ambivalence into a stereotypical femality that masquerades so convincingly as complexity as to be persuasive: as if to take up Frankenstein's failed task, he makes a woman of virtually megalomaniacal proportions and then deploys it, like some seductive and dangerous cyborg, within a series of texts.[7] Realism is not certain enough of its footing relative to inside or outside matters to postulate such secret sharers.

Realism is quite a humble mode, and, socially inclined, it rejects such masturbatory pleasures as these grand embodiments provide. One must, in fact, be genuinely monstrous in ego to enforce this will to power that obliterates the past: Ursula, of *Women in Love*, "wanted to have no past . . . wanted to have come down from the slopes of heaven to this place . . . not to have toiled out of the murk of her childhood and her upbringing, slowly, all soiled. She felt that memory was a dirty trick played upon her. . . . Why not a bath of pure oblivion, a new birth, without any recollections or blemish of a past life. . . . What had she to do with parents and antecedents? She knew herself new and unbegotten, she had no father, no mother, no anterior connections, she was herself, pure and silvery" (p. 502). Whatever his ambivalence relative to Ursula herself, Lawrence fantasizes through her a complete repudiation of realism's anxieties, about character, about text production, and he scorns realism's relative humility, but he purchases whatever relief he gets with characters driven by a complex but inflexible ideology of gender; for all their appearance of a magnificent effrontery, Lawrence's characters are more truly one-trick ponies than is any simple soul in realism's stable.[8] Ursula might just as well be proclaiming herself as the new text, empowered by its own willed separation from everything that has gone before, but reduced to sheerest ego; comically, she might also be seen as speaking with the same bombast as Dickens's Bounderby, who is, alternatively, proud to claim "the murk of . . . childhood," since he pretends to have been born in a muddy ditch.[9] Realism accepts the double yoke (or in Bounderby's case, yolk, since he was raised in an egg-box) of the past, historical and immemorial, and the material present. In doing this, it keeps character "real" by revealing it as a tenuous, artificial construct balanced between socialized habit and capricious changefulness, and between personality, intrinsic and immutable, and persona.

This is not to say that stereotypes do not exist – and most certainly not to suggest that female and other-racial characters are not portrayed stereotypically – but to say instead that realism by its very nature destabilizes the conviction behind those stereotypes. There is an advantage to being seen as indeterminate, neither fish nor fowl, when the alternative is a deeply entrenched conviction of one's spiritual and intellectual inadequacy; realism's ambivalence as regards character formation can only benefit those already otherwise discredited by virtue of their "innate" predispositions. Zenobia is the hyperbolic embodiment for this ambivalence, at one level a virtually allegorical figure of torture realized literally in the contorted rigor of her corpse. Hawthorne does his best to discredit and stereotype his character through the evidence of her political affiliation with feminism and through the evidence of her unregenerately "romantic," "womanly" passion: not one stereotype, but two, and the complementarity throws both of them slightly, almost subliminally, off kilter. Her political and social engagements and her sexualized demeanor are meant both to represent her flawed condition and to exacerbate it. But she emanates another energy so powerful that her head flowers with it, and thus she becomes as potent a refutation of stereotyping as she does a stereotype. Louisa, of *Hard Times*, is another such enigma, as are the maddening Edna Pontellier and Eustacia Vye, and as Cynthia Kirkpatrick proves, in Gaskell's *Wives and Daughters*, this complexity does not necessarily depend on the security of being able to kill off such a seductively complex character in the end. All of these women stand as virtual embodiments of realism's ambivalence about its position as regards character (that it is so often female characters who are thus enriched should not be ignored, coming as these figures do from within a discourse that sees all embellishment, textual or cosmetic, as feminine).

Predicting the necessary catachresis that will emerge from a vision of character so conflictual in its loyalties, Frankenstein's monster stands huge at the beginning of things, and if it is grotesque and pathetic and violent, it is also the figure, paradoxically enough, for realism's recognition of a humanness that exceeds the sum of its parts. Enforcing a reassessment and an attempted redefinition of all the canonical terms (goodness, nature, justice, evil, etc.), the monster predicts a semantic disturbance that will work in realism to undercut rote misogyny with uncertainty. Torn between crediting the world with the production and formation of character and recognizing some irresistible predisposition that remains immune to the depredations or enhancements of history and material circumstance, realism undermines its own stereotypical impulses. Thus the standard, old-fashioned misogynists speak their set pieces about women into a precarious reality that renders both themselves and their pronouncements anachronistic and slightly quaint, not because their auditors are enlightened, or even, necessarily, because their authors are speaking ironically, but because they speak a language of spiritual determinism that has already begun to erode within a textual environment whose very form acknowledges the fact. This does not make the smug stupidities uttered by such characters as Mr. Gibson in *Wives and Daughters* less annoying: "Don't teach Molly too much," he says, "she must sew, and read, and write, and do her sums . . . and if I find more learning desirable for her, I'll see about giving it to her myself. After all, I am not sure that reading or writing is necessary. Many a good woman gets married with only a cross instead of her name; it's rather a diluting of mother-wit, to my fancy; but, however, we must yield to the prejudices of society, Miss Eyre, and so you may teach the child to read."[10] But such pronouncements, even without the intertextual disturbance Gaskell introduces by calling her governess "Miss Eyre," and without Gibson's own implicit acknowledgment of his old-fashioned ideas relative to societal expectations for women, are spoken within a larger context of deepening uncertainty about how people are formed. The more rabid misogynists, like Bartle Massey of *Adam Bede*, speak a language meant to be felt as at once deeply familiar and insufficient: "You don't value your peas for their roots," he says, "or your carrots for their flowers. Now, that's the way you should choose women: their cleverness 'll never come to much . . . but they make excellent simpletons, ripe and strong-flavoured" (p. 569). Even without Mrs. Poyser to answer Massey's knee-jerk calumnizing, his auditors cannot any longer credit his wit, because it is uttered into an enriched environment that must locate him as archaically unilateral in his assessments of character.

Women writers have clearly found the realistic mode congenial, and one may speculate that realism's accommodation of competing energies and its intrinsic resistance to reductionisms of character provide an opportunity for expression that less flexible forms deny. This openness to female writers is not a negligible fact, for nineteenth-century women created novels that continue to do an immense amount of work today by virtue of their irresolvable contradictions and complexities; it is clear that realism's accommodative venue has allowed people to speak at multiple, even contradictory levels, which has subverted *telos* with open-endedness. Kate Chopin can, perhaps ironically, perhaps seriously, repudiate the troublesome hero of *The Awakening* (and it is realism's strength that it enforces the undecidability of her position): "I never dreamed of Mrs. Pontellier making such a mess of things and working out her own damnation as she did. If I had had the slightest intimation of such a thing I would have excluded her from the company. But when I found out what she was up to, the play was half over and it was then too late."[11] She cannot, however, after the fact, reduce Edna to feminist or anti-feminist parameters, not having got her up that way to begin with (and neither can anyone else). There is room in realism for characters to be up to things, up, in fact, to the same conflictual things as their authors, but without the burden of the paradoxically revelatory censorship born of introspection. "Having a group of people at my disposal, I thought it might be entertaining (to myself) to throw them together and see what would happen," says Chopin, perhaps innocently, perhaps ironically. Not yet bound by the modernist paradox that makes character at once highly enriched and ultimately a coherent picture of the fragmented, amnesiac self lost to its own Being, she can still throw a party (and indeed does within her text) that exceeds the conscious expectations of its host.[12] Like Gouvernail at Edna's party proceeding superficially within the bounds of decorum, realism mutters Swinburne under its breath: " 'There was a graven image of Desire / Painted with red blood on a ground of gold' " (p. 89). There is space left within which to breathe, and to breathe such secrets.[13]

Necessarily bringing their own ambivalence about gender and character to the already overdetermined conflict between intrinsic and extrinsic forces, women writers could appropriate a space for themselves that remained unclaimed by the imperialistic gestures of strict Aristotelian definition. Realism's amorphous nature made it too capacious to be turned into an exclusive club for men; the pact of a friendship prior to rule-making, a friendship that did not by original charter include women, could not, as with other forms, come up with a paradigmatic structure.[14] Shelley would thus embody in her monster the conflictual, Promethean fantasy of power, rage, and pathos that might emerge when character was unchained from stereotypical inevitabilities. Chopin, defanging Schopenhauer's misogyny with the universality of Edna's dilemma regarding wakefulness, would fall into a reverie about how one learns, or doesn't learn, to *see* the world as if wide awake; if she drops Edna into the gulf in the end, this fictional cliché comes almost to seem a sardonic reference to the meta-text that sentences female character according to type (the necessarily disguised equivalent to Dickens's two endings for *Great Expectations*). It is not, in any event, a gesture sufficient to discredit Edna, and in fact it sets up a resonance between stereotype and unpredictability that lingers yet. And it was not only the women who were relieved, but also many men, who could, for example, look lovingly and long for the first time at their mothers, memorializing their own regret for a thing – happiness, love, desire, wholeness – felt to have been once apprehended but irrevocably lost: Thackeray's *Pendennis*, unselfconscious, and Lawrence's obsessively and unembarrassedly Oedipal *Sons and Lovers* bracket the period as if to mark the beginning of realism's quest for the lost thing and its end in modernism's unrelenting inward gaze. At one level preoccupied with the socially constructed, the mundane, and the stereotypical, realism at another level, and for the very reason of its distraction by daily matters, allows a virtual ungendering. Realism delivers character from its humors even when seemingly most intent on caricature – Gradgrind is the type of this complexity – for despite its other agendas it cannot bring itself either to conscript or to deny the ineffable entirely.[15]

Obliquities

Realism knows that the very act of speaking necessitates amnesia or else risks a heteroglossia too monstrous to be comprehended, and it couples this intuition with the further psychoanalytic insight that there are, quite simply, stories that cannot be told as they "happened" and still be (safely) heard (this apprehension is more or less endemic to artists, but it is an inescapable fact of female existence that to speak without subterfuge is dangerous folly: women artists are doubly cursed). Realism's superabundance of materialities is a paradoxical reminder of alternative catalogs of the things not present: all the stuff forgotten, in the attic, in another country, of another class, and all the stuff it would not do to mention. Dickens's famous dustpiles, heaped with visceral ambivalence and archeologically layered with the detritus of a vision of embattled bodies and things, are only among the most complex of the metonyms for this state of willful forgetfulness. Those things it explicitly repudiates as unimportant or unmentionable intrude themselves through the looking glass of negation (where "*x* is not important" always, also, means "*x* is very important").[16] Frankenstein's fear that he will be taken as mad if he tells the monstrous truth of the situation regarding the murders, and Harker's assumption that either he will discover himself as mad or will be taken as mad if the contents of his journal are revealed – these are openly premised engagements with the artists's similar sense that there are things she simply cannot say and expect to have heard. *Wuthering Heights*, with the distancing convolutions of its narrative and its translation of events through the mouths and eyes of the egocentric Lockwood and the self-contained Nelly, is a model of authorial protectionism, for the novel tells a splendid, violent, and quite unladylike story whose shocking effects would otherwise either disqualify its being heard or raise an unholy ruckus. And *Wuthering Heights*, though extraordinary, is nonetheless representative in this matter of displacement. One sees an inventive series of narrative gestures designed to accommodate the unsayable in forms that ingratiate themselves with the promise of an unhysterical, even inartistic, rationality. *Frankenstein*'s similar concentricities defuse the monstrosity at the heart of the book; Coverdale's phlegmatic and somewhat enervated urbanity disperses the erotic vision that produces *The Blithedale Romance*; *Dracula* protects itself with a virtually juridical methodology. *The Awakening* appropriates and tempers the increasingly inflammatory opinions of its heroine by claiming them through indirect discourse. *Ethan Frome* reclaims the 24-year-old story of a tragic eroticism through an engineer's distancing curiosity (it is as if he stands, with his assignment "on a job connected with the big power-house," as emblem for the necessary authorial task of careful construction of which Wharton speaks in her "Author's Introduction").[17] When the normalization, mature productivity, and social integration of a central character are by definition built into the *telos*, as is often the case for the *Bildungsroman* of the early and middle nineteenth century, one may risk a simple first-person narrative; when there are competing distractions that threaten this integrative end, this disarming of all that is bothersome, narrative displacements act as spin control. Realism has work to do and cannot afford to alienate its audience with its apprehension of alternative energies and desires; pragmatically speaking, it enforces the rhetorical strategies necessary to ensure its reformative efficacy. This accommodative normalcy is neither callow nor Heepish, but is instead productive of texts that refuse to be rendered down to their ideological messages or to be inflated to tropological play.

Realism also safely channels its fascination with the immemorial into a middle ground, outside the "real" but within real experience, by filling itself with dreams. Nelly Dean, for example, can listen, albeit unwillingly, to Cathy's raw fantasies as long as they are couched in terms of dreams (and so, too, may we). The exposition of dreams can no more get at the Thing than can Freudian analysis, where primary repression is inaccessible, but one may achieve the illusion of having tapped the source, productively and without harm. Lockwood, for example, can *dream* all he likes about sawing the dream-child's hand from her wrist or being flagellated by men with long staves; dream stories within fiction are relatively safe for both author and character, for one is assured before the fact that they are symbolic for the purposes of the narrative and are not "real." Lockwood's character is not impugnable merely on the evidence of his dream, and, of parallel and equal importance, neither is the author's character damaged: the dream provides license to slip the confines of propriety and rectitude without meaning it. The dream, when brought into any language, but most undeniably so when created within realist fiction, becomes all metaphor, all displacement, all allegory, all analogy, but its often obvious connections with experience and its responsiveness to what would come eventually to be called day-residue make it a respectable way to work symbolically within the larger agendas of realism.

Dreaming is, after all, itself a standard nineteenth-century metaphor (the predominant metaphor of Schopenhauerean idealism, which uses it to problematize the notion of an outside reality); correlatively, it is also a metaphor for the artist's mode of perception. Dreaming is a safe haven between madness and rationality and between desire and control, and these are the Scylla and Charybdis of text production as surely as of character; *Dracula* conflates these terms in a more than ordinarily undeniable way, so that madness/desire and rationality/control are compartmentalized in dreaming and wakefulness. Stoker also links dreaming inextricably with hypnosis, as does Hawthorne in *The Blithedale Romance* in the story of the veiled lady, as if simultaneously to signal and to repudiate the text's powers to mesmerize and seduce.[18] Harker's "dream" of the three beautiful vampires saves him temporarily from both full horror and guilt, and this is the dichotomy within which the novel resonates: *Dracula* writes large how realism's use of the dream both encodes desire and denies its tangibility, its force in the real world. One can kill a vampire in the daytime. Dreaming stands as a code for the epistemological and moral ambivalence of both author and character, without compromising the social or political agenda at hand. Thus when Louisa says in *Hard Times* that she does not dream and has never dreamed, she articulates an artist's nightmare, for without dreams she must stand within this realistic context either as inexplicable or as thoroughly and satisfactorily evidential within her waking life. When Dickens deprives her of dreams and of reverie, as he does when she looks into the fire and sees nothing in it, he creates a phantasm for an acute authorial anxiety. She prefigures the hysteric in her painful quietude, a malady whose workings Dickens intuits for himself by virtue of his own malaise, well before Freud and Breuer would lay out the terms.

If, in postmodern aesthetics, realism is often estimated dismissively as standing "somewhere between academicism and kitsch," nineteenth-century fiction intuits that it is precisely between these poles that the body does its business, without the easing reconciliations of sublation, but forever deferring, disguising, denying the excitations that lure one, hapless, to academicize the heart and sentimentalize the head.[19] Taut, brief, and urgent, *Hard Times* is shorthand for this conflict: a persistent and inescapable imagery of headlessness balances against the circus's great heart and productive loins, and because they cannot be merged, the novel is littered with body parts – legs and heads populate the imagery, the language, the tropes, and the story as figures for this disjunction.[20] Realism claims this conflictual space for itself, and the tropological consequences follow, with Shelley's stitched-together giant as a prediction of how incongruities can be galvanized into power. Paradoxically, it facilitates, through its instincts for catachresis, the humbling apprehension that there is always an irretrievable other forgotten that sublation cannot raise up into a new, coherent shape and name; this residue remains covertly displayed in hyperbolic forms, personified in deconstructively inclined figures like Cathy's ghost or the monster or Dracula, or metonymized in Zenobia's tropic flower in order to disguise it through partial desublimation.[21] If, as Ricoeur says, the very term "figure of speech" conveys the fact that tropes give to discourse "a quasi-bodily externalization," then a body torn between a dialectic of desire and control and an alternative energy that refutes sublation will project itself as catachresis.[22] But there is value in the instinct for teratology, for it subverts the text as reification of the well-made man. By positing its monsters, modest and immodest, within the context of surrounding materialities, realism enacts tropologically a refutation of the very stereotypes it so frequently posits.

Realism is the last place one would look for a failure of synthesis and sublation (the purloined letter, again), for its domestic orientation and its investment in the marital contract make it the veritable model by which sublation (at least in its popularized form) was conceived; yet, as in other ways, realism performs in its very domesticity an apprehension of an oppositional, less manageable form of desire. Robert Frost, poetry's modernist version of the realist, and himself given to playing in the wild place, mocks the standard version of Hegelian synthesis as at heart only a fancy version of a reciprocal sexual reality (although, tautologically, he may himself have tied the lead horse's head to the back of the cart); his analysis clarifies how realism's domestic venue might beguile one by procreative analogy into the assumption of a movement always toward resolution:

Hegel saw two people marry and produce a third person. That was enough for Hegel – and Marx too it seems. They jumped at the conclusion that so all truth was born. Out of two truths in collision today sprang the one truth to live by tomorrow. A time succession was the fallacy. Marriage, reproduction and the family with a big F have much to answer for in misleading the analogists.[23]

Tying the knot is a perfect teleological gesture, but realism does not allow one to forget how that knot may slip or be sliced. By filling its pages with cautionary tales, realism undercuts any delusion of marital bliss. For a putatively domesticated mode, it is often fiercely ironic about domestication; for a mode putatively given to thinking, during coitus, about whether the clock has been wound, it has some powerfully erotic couples and threesomes; and for a mode said to be procreatively earnest and family-centered, it features an awful lot of women who share Mrs. Gradgrind's perpetual headache.[24] Austen has the young Henry Bertram speak ironically to this matter in *Mansfield Park*: "I am of a cautious temper, and unwilling to risk my happiness in a hurry. Nobody can think more highly of the matrimonial state than myself. I consider the blessing of a wife as most justly described in those discreet lines of the poet, 'Heaven's *last* best gift.' "[25] There are many ways in which the strangely insistent motif of enacting Kotzebue's *Lovers' Vows* may be read in this same novel, not the least of which is in its function as erotic play – as a play, as play in which the characters may both reveal and disguise their desires, as the play of a text that means to signal its resistance to the marital and domestic proprieties it must at another level uphold, even if by main force.[26] Edna Pontellier, at the other end of the century, is not so ironically coy as Henry Bertram: "She says," reports Léonce, "a wedding is one of the most lamentable spectacles on earth."[27]

If, as Ricoeur says, metaphor predicates itself on the model of the body, and if, as Frost says, marriage and the family produce from family-minded men the idea of sublation, it is not surprising to find that in realism, marriage is only putatively sanctified and is successful in spiritual and emotional terms only once in a very great while. In fact, it becomes the country seat of an immense social, political, and spiritual anxiety. Austen signals this ambivalence very early on, for while her novels use marriage for its teleological neatness, its affiliation with comedy, and its insistent and lamentably necessary "normalizing" of character, she also displays a thoroughly wicked irony regarding matrimonial bliss. And if the marital reality produces, as Frost so reductively asserts, the analogous notion of a sublation whose directional impulse is upward, then Undine Spragg's social climb up the matrimonial ladder from commoner to nobility is a precise parody of the Hegelian ascent.[28] Only a peculiar form of repression can have allowed critics to gloss over realism's deeply conflictual apprehension of human relationships in order to assert its desireless stability; it is as if Oedipal necessity (or the habits of Oedipalized thinking) has dictated its own simultaneous exaltation and abasement of mothers, wives, and daughters, producing within criticism a discursive environment whose systemic equilibrations are projected outward as a binding characteristic of the realistic text.

It is noticeably the case that nineteenth-century fiction tends to dispatch mothers with fairly ruthless economy (it is even more common to kill off a mother than to drown a daughter), thus lending itself quite naturally to the Oedipal predispositions of its critics. But if the fiction is itself "Oedipal" (and we shall bracket the question whether or not the Oedipus complex is a viable or true reading of human development, saving only the assertions that it is a teleologically influential concept whose premises have been applied retroactively to texts that seem to court the attention[29]), it lacks the overriding imperative of exegetical authority common to critical discourse. One could almost say, as a corollary to this thought, that the critical commonplace of realism's bad habit of closure may also arise from a specular gaze that cannot, as Irigaray would say, see beyond the rings and reversals of reflective distortion. Pragmatically speaking, absent or ineffectual mothers facilitate action, of course, and allow characters to compromise and to resurrect themselves, to sink or swim (the case of Lily Bart makes this equation very explicit, and Edna Pontellier, taught to swim by a lover, has no mother to keep her afloat), but realism's marital troubles are more than merely pragmatic, as reflective of textual and linguistic intuitions as of Oedipal ones. The assertion that realism's relationship to language is still an innocent one is only relatively correct, at best, and even so the fiction is filled with performative contradictions to its surface complacencies.[30] One sees the specifically marital implications of the dead-parent syndrome, worked out in permutations of disaster from *Great Expectations* to *Wives and Daughters*. These nineteenth-century marital anxieties are not simple markers, for if they reflect an undeniable reality of human relationships, they are also articulated in a milieu devoted to protecting the sanctity of the domestic institution and thus reflect a needful subversion of the very proprieties realism is said to have pledged itself to uphold. One must feel, then, that Frost's reduction of the philosophical to the sexual is not so simplistic as it seems, for it reinforces the felt contiguity between personal and public, between the perceived world and how one comes to say it: A language that has begun to intuit itself as both impotent and excessive as regards the "real" is hard-pressed to reify itself in domestic bliss and progenitive virility, whatever its best intentions (Fourier's ideas of free sex as a means of effecting solidarity seem to subsidize Frost's intuition).[31]

One discovers, in fact, that in realism the marital relationship becomes the locus for chaos, for discord, for the refutation of conciliation: all those drowned women sing a mermaid's song of repudiation by two-legged men, and Old Stephen's tumble down the "black ragged chasm hidden by . . .

thick grass" is merely the inevitable correlative of his having fallen into a wanton, heartless wife (*Hard Times*, p. 244). It is habitual to see these domestic failures as the sordid inevitabilities of realism's close look into people's houses, and, surprisingly enough, it is also habitual to gloss over these failures in favor of the Howellsian assumption that realism should (or at least that it does, to its detriment) sanctify marriage, that it is most essentially "domestic." But what emerges from the rack focus of a more cynical gaze is something quite different, a set of people maddened by their own energies into incivility, rebellion, betrayal, and abandonment: Frankenstein distracted from his procreative duties by his more irresistible attraction to himself, Zenobia estranged from Westervelt, Edna estranged from Léonce, Lucy Westenra estranged from Arthur Godalming, and on and on – the Eustacia Vye/Damon Wildeve/Clym Yeobright/Thomasin Yeobright muddle; Undine Spragg and her four husbands. *Sister Carrie*, "arguably the greatest American realist novel," according to Michaels, has Carrie leave an entire string of men in her wake.[32] Or consider Heathcliff abducting Catherine Linton and forcing her into marriage with the dying and virulent Linton Heathcliff, or, for that matter, Catherine Earnshaw's double (in)fidelities with Edgar and Heathcliff. Again, Dickens's *Hard Times* makes a most emblematic statement, as marriage becomes, in both Stephen Blackpool's case and Louisa's case, the antithesis of true artistic productivity and genuine desire; the right to divorce, tied explicitly to class, would free the "Hands" to do a very different kind of work. There is in all of this marital mayhem something more than mere social realism, for such a fundamental disruption as this necessarily impugns the social productivity of the realistic text. It speaks at an allowably oblique level to something else: to an unmanageable surplus of energy that both enriches and threatens the socialized elements within the text. It concedes a "dark, inscrutable power, 'that which *shuns the light*'": Hegel's third stage of reality, "Absolute Necessity," in which the individual is so inevitably overmastered by some inner excitation as to seem implicated in "blind fatality."[33] Put another way, it is what takes Ethan Frome and his lover down a dark slope at breakneck speed into a tree. That unnameable thing is ungendered, and because it cannot be given a proper name that is sufficient to it, it exceeds its aliases.

One feels, thus, in realism a frustrated energy that sometimes plays itself out in (mostly covert) fantasies of a sadomasochism contradictory of realism's goal of minimizing excess; having expressed through metonymy its sense of a humanness replaced, piece by piece, with the prosthetics of its technologized function, realism affords glimpses of the Edward Scissorhands who waits in the wings. Given razor-sharp scissors for hands, Edward can create more wondrous topiaries than any ever seen before, but he can also wound and scarify himself and anyone else he touches with the prosthetics of his craft. Pushed to extremes, he might learn to enjoy his disability. He is the artist, the Frankensteinian hyperbole of a soul whose desires goad him into using his "Hands," for livelihood, for art, and, *in extremis*, for weapons. This is realism's vision of empowerment and self-laceration: The metonymy that transforms people into the extensions of their work and their automatized lives also gives them frighteningly enhanced capacities for harm.[34] Realism's "economy of pain" sees very well that people left with (self-)crippling weaponry will sometimes use it. The only surprise in Heathcliff's desire to use his hands to rip off the fingernails of his bride-to-be, Isabella, to paint her face with bruises, and to blacken her blue eyes is in its precocity (p. 93). In realism's world of things, *hands* seem to signal with mute eloquence metonymy's doubled intuition of power and powerlessness. Only in part is this an intuition of a Marxist recognition of an industrial economy that, in debasing workers, may bring them to perilous life. Realism senses that the psyche, forced to accommodate an economy of pain, may forget how to separate desire from pain; and because the mode is domestically oriented, this knowledge tends to play itself out in the sexual arena. Fitful, and either trained to sadomasochism or born to it, the human parties involved in realism's transactions with the mundane cannot, thus, always stick to a vision of what is best or most productive or healthiest or wisest or most ethical.

What happens, realism is forced at some level to wonder, when "Hands" become so hardened that a blow from them can be killing (Bounderby's nightmare)? What happens when such a chimerical man-machine, which realism sees being turned out daily and by the thousands, responds to pain? In madness, one finds the unimpeachable logic of this circularity realized; having invented in his paranoia the electrical machines that he cannot now escape, Robert Gie turns them to advantage: " 'Since he was unable to free himself of these currents that were tormenting him, he gives every appearance of having finally joined forces with them, taking passionate pride in portraying them in their total victory, in their triumph.' "[35] But realism sees (and Dickens is a most candid witness of this) that the real disposes itself increasingly in such a way as to push humans toward madness and a paradoxical empowerment; realism sees that as reciprocities between machines and people multiply, the borderline between madness and despair breaks down. Lyotard says that "thinking and suffering overlap," and this is not an imposition from outside, but the very mark of true thought, and its impetus. To make machines human, you would have to make them "suffer from the burden of their memory."[36] The fact that realism sees that humans may be made into machines suggests a possibility that Lyotard does not here mention, for it is precisely the oxymoronic truth of the human machine that it does suffer from the burden of its memory – a burden that is complex, made up of what one remembers, what one forgets, and what one cannot forget that she cannot recall, and made, too, of a distracting concurrency. For if it remembers the past, it also remembers dualistically in the present moment every time it thinks itself. Levine says, in "By Knowledge Possessed," that empiricism makes it clear that "to be human . . . is to make oneself into two – the observer and the observed. To know is both to register experience on one's senses and to reject the validity of the senses";[37] realism, sharing in the empirical endeavor, enforces an equivalent doubleness, the "power to think [and] the power to be aware of one's own thinking."[38] This is memory potently enforced and maddening, as it holds in the present moment both the grounds for future action and the history on which that decision for the future will be based.

Although realism may choose an amnesiac position as regards the non-relevant circumstances and details of its surroundings and effect an agreement with the reader to do the same, it remains under the duress of these other memories, this sense of something to be brought forth and this pain of unremitting failure, each time it inscribes the insufficiency of its attempt. One learns to expect this pain and, in the curious economy of necessity, to take some pleasure in it. There is in it at least an incandescent moment. As futile as one's effort to turn on the light fast in order to see the blackness clearly, it bursts as blindness upon that vacant space we try so hard to see, but it has the value of affording for a moment full presence.

Sadomasochism and the Sublime

Realism cannot but see itself as implicated in the paradox it reveals in its potently impotent characters, as at once a very powerful and a very compromised mode. Realism, epistemological and literary, created itself partially in response to having been impugned by the increasing precedence of the material things it was meant to represent; the very technologization that provided a means of environmental control also proved itself uncontrollable as part of the original bargain; the very positivism and empiricism that made investigation of phenomena possible and necessary began at once to prove language insufficient to the precisions of the pursuit. Samuel Butler's *Erewhon* (1871) registers this anxiety through a satire whose visions of a mechanistic reality have proved themselves accurately predictive; its tone suggests Butler's doubled intuition of technology as both the good and the bad news, even as he more overtly suggests that England is, in general, either unnecessarily fearful of or foolishly utopian regarding machinery's power. "The Book of the Machines," written by a learned gentleman of the Erewhonian Colleges of Unreason, embodies the literal field of dispute from which realism's metonymies gain their force. Among its claims are the following: that machines may develop consciousness and thus challenge humanness for precedence, that "machinery [is] linked with animal life in an infinite variety of ways," that "man's very soul is due to the machines; it is a machine-made thing: he thinks as he thinks, and feels as he feels, through the work that machines have wrought upon him, and their existence is quite as much a *sine quâ non* for his, as his for theirs."[39] He goes on as if to define realism's affiliation with metonymy:

A machine is merely a supplementary limb; this is the be all and end all of machinery. We do not use our own limbs other than as machines; and a leg is only a much better wooden leg than any one can manufacture.

Observe a man digging with a spade; his right fore-arm has become artificially lengthened, and his hand has become a joint. The handle of the spade is like the knob at the end of the humerus; the shaft is the additional bone, and the oblong iron plate is the new form of the hand which enables its possessor to disturb the earth in a way to which his original hand was unequal.[40]

Butler's is a very provocative "satire," as it mocks those doomsayers who would rid the world of machinery entirely even as it displays an insightful measurement of that same machinery's very real powers to mold and shape its users. "The Book of the Machines," with its uncannily correct and yet "satiric" predictions, embodies realism's doubled sense of impotence and empowerment, both as a measurement of a material environment and as a language game.[41]

Along with this accelerated recognition of insufficiency and ambivalence relative to a burgeoning environment, realism's authors also typically participated themselves in a significantly accelerated textual productivity, a partializing of work to fit the fast-paced demands of parts publication. If human character was seen as under the duress of compartmentalizing forces that made it monstrously productive in one area and arid in others, so too was text production often felt as a disjunctive enterprise simultaneously successful and compromised (and one's sense of urgency might be doubled, as with Hawthorne, by the sense that there are plenty of scribbling women turning out an addictive fiction to be consumed eagerly by the masses). This apprehension of fragmentation, of disproportion, of power and powerlessness alternating in a perpetual cycle, is a condition the text shares and reproduces.

Speaking, juridical creatures, caught between the imperatives of a real reality whose sentencing and execution are simultaneous and the expression through language of this precipitous eventfulness, declare a realism through language that is as persuasive as the virile performativity of the speaker who makes it, while *at the same time* they recognize the belittlement of a world of things too precise in its executions to be susceptible to appeal. Dickens's fascinated outrage over industrial accidents, his graphic accounts of "split brain, puddles of blood, crushed bones, and torn flesh," is a figure for this sense of a reality that does not announce itself in advance and makes itself definitively felt when it descends.[42] It is as well an alternative figure for what metonymy becomes in such a violent materialism, whose dangerous machinery has been harnessed for the production of goods rather than for the waging of wars: spilt brain, puddled blood, crushed bones, torn flesh, the contiguous parts for a whole commodified soul who has become, in this environment, the sum of its Sadeian pieces. The sentence becomes doubly fraught: it contains a recognition both of its power to compel and of its own relative failure of immediacy, and this oxymoronic condition sets up a circuitry of humiliation and self-aggrandizement.

A speaking creature will find that this environment refutes all best guesses about "character" and where it is made, for the more real that things get, scientifically and empirically speaking, and the more complete the taxonomy of things and the parts of things becomes, the more they reveal themselves as inadequate, alone, to explain character; yet they cannot be dismissed. So character, too, is caught in this tautology of control and servility. One seeks necessarily to impose one's will on a world of things that in its turn manipulates one and enforces itself with a degree of ruthless inevitability. Heathcliff stands as only the most hyperbolic representative of this combination of avaricious, acquisitive, and sadistic control, coupled with an impotence made delightful by the phantasm that mocks him. The imagery of cannibalism that accompanies this dynamic in *Wuthering Heights* is only a most literal instating of the inescapable circle: those starved hatchlings (who could not have died all together in peaceful resignation) on a plentiful moor, and Heathcliff self-consumed and starving before a table covered with food, are the figures for the consumptive teethings of sadomasochism. Sade is no accident, but rather the inevitable caricature of this environment, and if, as has been claimed, he creates in sadism a thing that, before his name, did not exist as such, it is because he is the parodic front man for this circuitry of abased domination and indomitable surrender, this accelerating reciprocity between a technologizing world and the human "desiring-machine."[43] Realism, putatively prosaic, billed as stolid, as far from sublime as stump water is from champagne, called by the Handbook "the ultimate of middle-class art," finds its capacity for sadomasochism in the very prosaic environment whose artifacts it seeks to master through verisimilitude,[44] for it discovers that it cannot cede character entirely to circumstance, despite circumstantial imperatives: it sees that it is driven, and that character is driven, equally by some irrepressible other energy.

Thus, as restless as it is rectified, realism inevitably deviates from the straight and narrow pragmatism of its socially oriented mission; sublimating this excitation, it creates characters and situations that reify the double energies of a language that must answer both to the maddening demands of productivity and to the importunings of its own tropological nature. Driven by despair and desire, caught by the imperatives of duty, the realist may feel himself a veritable Ethan Frome: one fast, exhilarating sled ride into one real, immovable tree, and a lifetime of restitution. One is accustomed to accepting realism's insistence that it is a thoroughly domesticated form, upright, rather prudish, rather too much the sissy.[45] One takes at face value Levine's assertion that "it is striking how difficult it is to locate in realistic fiction any positive and active evil," but it is exactly this resistance to Satanic seductions that facilitates a more covert and ambivalent violence.[46] The century is littered with Sadeian images, but because they fall, by virtue of their locus within realism, into the broad category of "domestic violence," they are seldom recognized for what they are. A montage, very partial, would include Frankenstein's female monster strewn in pieces on the floor, multiple fragments of *Wuthering Heights* (dead rabbits, hanged puppies, a half-strangled bitch, starved baby birds in a sardonic cage, a wrist raked hard against broken glass, a brutalized Isabella, a violated, half-murdered Linton Heathcliff, a consummately violent and desirable Heathcliff), the drowned and disfigured Zenobia, her breast naked and torn, a terrified Priscilla, Louisa held by Dickens suspended inside a desire felt only as the painful numbness of bonds tied too tight for too long, Lucy Westenra alive, dead, and undead, her sexualized staking and beheading only the most egregious of many such images. These figures speak obliquely about realism's will to discipline its pleasurable relationship with a reality to which it feels itself insufficient. Sade stands emblematic, across the Channel, gargantuan in his lust for physical detail. He waits leering outside, as predictive for realism as is the revolution in which his work is entangled, as the ultimate caricature of the realist brought to recognize that verisimilitude, even in fugal repetition and jumbo size, is insufficient to account for this energy.

Realism, working to accommodate its tropological restlessness to a vision of industrial efficiencies and a reformative response, suffers under the duress of its own pedagogical impulses. It is no accident that the sites of sadomasochism and schooling so often overlap in both fantasy and fact; as Deleuze points out in *Masochism: Coldness and Cruelty*, sadism's pedagogy is embodied by an authoritarian "instructor," while masochism enacts a fantasy of the patient "educator."[47] Nor, of course, is it surprising that nineteenth-century realism has more cruelly punitive schoolmasters and dominatrix relatives and housekeepers than one can shake a stick at. Dick-

ens's Murdstones might stand as perfect representatives of this strong un-
dercurrent of sadism, for they together embody a virtual textbook case:
brother and sister, incestuously linked in the pleasurable, debasing instruction of the wife and the vicious tutelage of the boy, their names suggestive
of sadism's delight in coprophilia, and all got up in the gear. Jane Murdstone, embellished in "numerous little steel fetters and rivets," "arranging
the little fetters on her wrists," and called after one of Sade's favorite
scourges, "the Cat," is a most thinly disguised version of the dominatrix.[48]
The siblings Murdstone are, after all, not unique, and in fact they are quite
immediately recognizable as familiar types, for realism's obligation to teach
how character and environment constantly interpolate each other's stories
inevitably arouses its Brocklehurstian side: if realism may not sanction a
mass of natural curls, unregenerately tropic, it must learn at some level to
enjoy the "disciplinary" instruction of cutting these tangled coils off before
the entire school. It is a measure of realism's essential responsibility that it
encodes this impulse and at the same time so frequently and resolutely
repudiates it.

Not yet having been hypostatized psychoanalytically or philosophically –
as primary repression, *différence*, the trace, *Dasein*, the anamnesis of the Thing
– this disruptive energy disperses itself among a series of metaphors, a whole
corps of embodiments, but the nineteenth-century umbrella euphemism for
this inexplicable residue of excitation is the "sublime." As Lyotard suggests,
notions of sublimity mirror and contain sadomasochism's double capacity for
self-humiliation and self-aggrandizement, for one both sees and identifies
with an element of immense and fearful grandeur and knows at the same
time one's smallness and insignificance relative to it.[49] Kant's discussion of
sublimity in *The Critique of Judgment* weaves a motif of pleasure and pain:
"The feeling of the sublime is, therefore, at once a feeling of displeasure, arising from the inadequacy of the imagination in the aesthetic estimation of
magnitude to attain to its estimation of reason, and a simultaneously awakened pleasure. . . . "[50] Burke begins his discussion of the sublime by saying
that "whatever is fitted in any sort to excite the ideas of pain, and danger, that
is to say, whatever is in any sort terrible, or is conversant about terrible objects, or operates in a manner analogous to terror, is a source of the sublime;
that is, it is productive of the strongest emotion which the mind is capable of
feeling."[51] He goes on as if compelled associatively to speak of the torture re-

cently inflicted on the regicide Robert Damiens; one who remembers Foucault's grim and extended description of that event in the opening of *Discipline and Punish: The Birth of the Prison* will see the multivalent possibilities of Burke's gesture.

"Sublime" is a term that, by locating itself at the borderline between philosophy and aesthetics, reinforces the connectedness of inner and outer states and predicts realism's similar modalities;[52] it is, however, because of its association with the extra-ordinary, a notion that realism approaches with significant ambivalence and that is conceived by critics as antithetical to realism's mundanities. Holistically perceived, sublimity may manifest itself within realism as an enrichment, a dis-ease, a figure for this borderland territory between ecstasy and rectitude, but it cannot reach "heroic" proportions; it may be embodied in Mademoiselle Reisz's Chopin sonatas or in such a one as Cathy's ghost, lovely, here and then gone, but it is exactly its ephemerality relative to the grosser stuff of existence that asserts itself. It has the status of revenant, a return that can be neither summoned at will nor declined, a visitant whose loving bite comes within a space outside of time, as it is apprehended both as instantaneous and as interminable, within the space of a heartbeat and as the only sensation that matters in the world [Edna Pontellier is a casualty of the sublime, its propaganda and its addictive effect; Dracula is its (non)corporeal representative, suffused with blood and transubstantiative all at once].

Yet the two concepts of realism and sublimity are, finally, dependent on each other for the generation of mutual terms; one might argue that they are conceptualized out of the same, shared source of anxiety. As with realism itself, theories of the sublime work to articulate the conundrum of where volition is charged; as with realism, these theories postulate an inextricable complex of inner and outer necessities, and they reify the linguistic difficulties such an enigma imposes. The Alps may produce the sensation of the sublime, but the question of what preexistent source within humanness it awakens and depends on remains unresolved. Shelley instantiates this enigma in *Frankenstein* and locates the question of the sublime as precisely and literally entangled with the issue of character formation (a term that takes on a new meaning in the context of the monster). The monster is not cowed by snowy peaks and crags that make his "human" double seem even more than ordinarily puny; the source of the monster's affiliation with a landscape that Shelley repeatedly designates as sublime is unclear, however, for it may be an index of his relative receptivity of soul or, as well, of his enhanced capacity for evil. Is the monster sadistic or masochistic? As Stephen Knapp points out in *Personification and the Sublime*, "the most notorious obstacle confronting historians of the sublime is the difficulty of deciding who or what, in any given case, the critic means to call 'sublime.' " Is it the object itself, the agent producing it (God or artist), or the agent who encounters it?[53] The sublime is the very figure for this circuitry of internal excitation and external stimulus, and it predicts that when the terms are teased apart, they will reveal in the human subject both a will to power and a concomitant will to abasement intertwined like a bed of nesting snakes: the composite monster, a literal everyman, is both sadist and masochist.

Thus, even the most resistant of realists may be brought to court sublimity's double punch and, like Edna Pontellier, to feel the burdensome ennui of its absence. To imagine it gone or inaccessible – really forgotten – is to presage death; like Edna Pontellier, who walks into the gulf, one who fears that this energy has forsaken her no longer intuits the sublime abyss – Heidegger's *Ab* – and the *Abgrund* opens to become instead a grave: one hits bottomground, which, in the mythology of dreams, is to die.[54] To focus on it to the exclusion of materialities is also death: Heathcliff's painfully ecstatic preoccupation with the specter is a figure of this distraction that makes one look just beyond what is at hand – beyond solace, beyond sustenance, beyond sleep – for what cannot be reached by any available means. Hawthorne is, of course, the one who knows best the dangers of an overweening desire to see inside, to waken the bosom serpent, to find the unpardonable sin, and his obsessional treatment of the subject holds him, mostly, from the realist's end of the continuum; he feels the degrading attraction of the sublime to be resident in his very choice of romance over realism, a mode he impugns but cannot abandon because he finds it, and speaks of it as, a pleasurable debasement. Coverdale articulates the seductions of such an examination, which produces in the analyst a "diseased action of the heart," and which promotes the Sadeian capacity "to put a friend under [the] microscope, . . . insulate him from . . . his true relations, magnify his peculiarities, [and] inevitably tear him into parts," and, of course, to enjoy the guilty pleasure of doing so (*The Blithedale Romance*,

p. 64). Sublimity and sadomasochism are resident in realism's preoccupation with character, and if they are forces that are obscured by the propagandas regarding realism's stolidity, they are nonetheless very much at home within the mode.

Their presence is disguised by the same definitional circularity that characterizes virtually all domestic excitations, for such tautologies were from the beginning imposed on realism, the most domesticated of that highly domestic form, the novel.[55] These are a few of the domestic tautologies: if marriage, then not rape; if marriage, then not murder; if marriage, then not assault and battery; if marriage, then not child abuse; if realism, then not sublimity; if realism, then not sadomasochism. It is a truism to speak of the nineteenth-century romantic poets in terms of sublimity and thus by the usual either/or procedures to see in realism a failure of the sublime; this dichotomy does not generate realism's prosaic reputation, but serves rather as an extremism by which realism's less grandiose engagement with the sublime is rendered more or less invisible. Romanticism becomes poetry's "Byronic" mandate and creates the tautologies by which poetry and prose are defined and alienated from each other. Even so demure a figure as Emily Dickinson knows an extensive Sadeian vocabulary of pleasure and pain by which she defines poetry: "If I feel physically as if the top of my head were taken off, I know *that* is poetry," she says; "Perhaps the Balm, seemed better, because you bled me, first," "I had rather wince than die." This tautology – if pleasurable pain, then poetry; if poetry, then pleasurable pain – claims sublimity for itself. Prosaic, unheroic, stolid, overly righteous, in short, domestic, realism was at once an announcement before the fact of sublimity's absence.

Thus if Frankenstein wants to galvanize a monster (and never mind what he says about a glorious new race emerging from this preoccupation with large body parts), it is hardly surprising: Shelley has perhaps more than ordinary reason to embody a monstrously desirous violence that moves from the pre-linguistic to the eloquent with no loss of power, for being neither a man nor a poet, not being Percy Shelley and not being Lord Byron, she is driven to the "platitudes of prose" and must make up the difference with size and violence. "The illustrious poets . . . annoyed . . . speedily relinquished their uncongenial task" of story production, presumably for the much-vaunted sublimities of a less overtly embodied fantasy,

but Shelley must make her prosaic way through a more mundane productivity (*Frankenstein*, p. xxiii). Shelley, pressed by her husband to abandon
her idea of a short tale and "to develop the idea at greater length," enacts
in her monster a parodic version of the sublime: he is a gross sublimity
made to last a long, long time – a couple of hundred pages worth. Like
the Burkean sublime, he is also a force both humiliating and self-
aggrandizing for the perceiver/creator (this is why the monster becomes an
inextricable part of its natural surroundings when it is in the Alps or the
vast frozen wastes of the North).

And Victor is an original sadomasochist for whom masochism is dom-
inative, and his ambivalence regarding the monster he constructs suggests
that he finds its sheer, hideous grace irresistible, its unbounded capacity for
lawlessness attractive. Frankenstein does not *want* it domesticated (nor does
Shelley), and he performs his own Sadeian ritual in the dismemberment of
the female he begins to create. Left to itself, the monster might, after all,
decide to tear him apart, and it is testament to Shelley's own insight into
sadism that she quite explicitly withholds this painful pleasure from Frankenstein, who leaks away his substance in an interminable confession – yet
another quintessence of masochism – and invests it in a marriage-night
consummation with Elizabeth worthy of Sade. It is not at all surprising that
realism shades, at the century's end, into naturalism's grimy assumptions
about a human nature more bestial than divine; this is only the logical, if
simplistic, conclusion to realism's increasing recognition that the residue
beyond representationalism – virtually deterministic in its authority – is its
most compelling subversion. Fiction invents (as do we all, perhaps) all kinds
of evasions, in fact, to deny or disperse this apprehension that one may be
goaded by the ineffable into the extremities of sadomasochism.

Realism's doubled intuitions for the social and the ineffable ensure both
that the sublime will make itself attractive and that its attractions will be
appropriately chastised; one ends up with authorial gestures that simultaneously acknowledge and repudiate the seductions of the sublime. Such an
impulse is what makes Dickens, in *Hard Times*, throw his most righteous
character down a hellhole (not that we miss him) and then pull him back
up, nearly dead, to say a few words, and it is what makes both Heathcliff
and Dracula equally repellent and irresistible. It threatens to compromise
realism's social agenda and makes the earnest reformer grumpy, with his

sense that, "objectively speaking," human desire in all its sadomasochistic complexity is both inevitable and problematic. A realist who wished to speak forensically or scientifically about such matters could turn to *Psychopathia Sexualis*, with its multiple case studies of blood-drinking, flesh-eating sadists, penny-ante Draculas without the panache, but that would be to localize a pathological state in extremisms, when in fact these writers feel it to infiltrate our desires. This leftover, galvanizing stuff – one wonders if it is the secret force by which the monster quakes into violent and loving life – insists upon itself, and it pushes one toward catachresis and toward the oxymoronic conditions of sadomasochism and sublimity as the only means by which it can be, for a moment, trapped. The space between sadism and masochism, the space, wherever it is, in which sublimity resides – these are the oppositional places that generate the proof of an unnameable thing and reify both its potency and its unmanageableness. Real reality, whose activism diminishes the space between sentence and execution to the interminable instant when the guillotine blade falls, holds the secret, but it is unavailable to language. And realism cannot violate the terms of its social contract by chasing directly after this energy, although, having conceded it as nonrepresentational, the mode is obliquely hospitable to it. "I think there's a pain somewhere in the room . . . but I couldn't possibly say that I have got it" – this is realism's fortitude and its haplessness, all at once.

Chapter Four

The Inhuman

The well-shaped *Changeling* is a Man, has a rational Soul, though it appear not; this is past doubt, say you. Make the Ears a little longer, and more pointed, and the Nose a little flatter than ordinary, and then you begin to boggle: Make the Face yet narrower, flatter, and longer, and then you are at a stand: Add still more and more of the likeness of a Brute to it, and let the Head be perfectly that of some other Animal, then presently 'tis a *Monster*, and 'tis demonstration with you, that it hath no rational Soul, and must be destroy'd. Where now (I ask) shall be the just measure; which the utmost Bounds of that Shape, that carries with it a rational Soul? . . . I would gladly know what are those precise Lineaments, which according to this Hypothesis, are, or are not capable of a rational Soul to be joined to them. What sort of outside is the certain sign that there is, or is not such an Inhabitant within?

—John Locke, *An Essay Concerning Human Understanding* (bk. IV, ch.4)[1]

Assimilations

Realism, consensually oriented, is most particularly a mode whose success is actuated by the assumption of a basic congeniality among addressor and addressees; it courts the kindness of strangers, but the seduction is based on a preexistent pact of friendship that assures beforehand that they will privilege as initiates the tautology they choose willingly to enter. (The *illusion* of being included, a familiar and necessary paradox among non-initiates, also works; one must think here within the context of Daisy Miller's simultaneous understanding and repression of her knowledge of exclusion: "There isn't any society, or, if there is, I don't know where it keeps itself." "Well we *are* exclusive, mother and I. We don't speak to everyone – or they don't speak to us. I suppose it's about the same thing.") Sustaining a conviction regarding the "real" depends, as I have said, on a certain willfully habitual vision of things; it depends as well on the paradox of an apprehension of the real sensed at one level as a virtual anamnesis and at another as circumstantial and arbitrary selectivity. The game of anamnesis is also a game of amnesia, a choice to forget the twists and turns in order to move unimpeded down a path one recognizes, perhaps opportunistically, as having been lived already in some previous version of the brotherhood. This is less precarious a game than it seems as long as it is conducted among people, fraternal or otherwise, who know and will concede to the rules. It gets out of hand only when certain recalcitrant players suddenly remember all those left-out details, including the details of their own real exclusion from the terms of the game. Like the grandmother in O'Connor's "A Good Man Is Hard to Find," they suddenly realize themselves as operating in the wrong state, negotiating a path through Georgia that exists only in Tennessee. Startled, chagrined, they let the cat out of the bag, the car rolls over, and the Misfit appears to blow them away.[2] And once you let the Misfit have his psychopathic/prophetic say, the terms dependent on a more congenial circularity go hopelessly askew. Or, less extreme, once you give up the assumptions of a humanism whose commonalities were modeled in the Forum and its Peripatetic discussion groups, once you no longer agree to amnesiac simplicities of form and content, "reality" may well (but not necessarily) become something else.

What counts as acceptably real may be – and often has been – opportunistic, or corruptly political, or sexist, or racist; this is a fact, as Blatchford would say, that no man lately attempts to deny. In realism's network of common sense (using that term in its full, ironic implications) one can easily spot the "ordinary," but it becomes more difficult to tell the seers from the madmen, except when they are dressed up for work. The seer wears a robe, the madman a straightjacket; the poet wears something hyperbolic, the madman wears a straightjacket; and their clothes, free-flowing on the one hand and circumscribed on the other, offer one more metonymous signal not just of the relative positions of freedom and confinement but of souls as well, the one expansive, the other locked inside its tight madness. Incorporative, reality reveals itself as having an immense appetite: the poet drinks absinthe and eats opium, and the madman drinks potassium bromide and eats saltpeter, proving metonymy's premise that you are what you eat, and you eat what you are (thus the monster's vegetarianism has been much commented upon; thus when Heathcliff abandons reality for a phantasm, he can no longer perform realism's transubstantiative gesture of eating). There is an immense risk of losing all sorts of diversity – not just hyperbolic, the eccentric and the prophetic, but the alternatively sensible and workable as well – to this hungry system. For those who like a crazy salad with their meat, there is little hope. Yet there is, still, the small, pesky matter of the Misfit, who does after all see to it that a family is dispatched quite economically, the small matter that not all monsters are vegetarians (the literal and recent proof of which needs no elaboration). There is the inescapable intuition that "monstrosity" is not always the invention of a culpable status quo, that often it is both real and, except in limiting-condition cases, comprehensible, which is to say that one *understands* through potential complicity the arbitrary and shifting nature of boundaries between good and evil.

That realism's assimilative power is the bad news, that it threatens everything that does not mirror the status quo, is well known; that this assimilative power is also, at the same time, the good news has been less well documented recently. Backed up by nineteenth-century historiography's articulated preference for "facts" – small, integrative, structural units as precise as bricks and made of material evidence – realism does, as it has been accused of doing, first externalize the "real" and then incorporate it; contiguous, an endless reticulation of people and things, things and things, people and people, realism creates (or reflects) an intimate sphere of apparently inescapable influences. Metonymy in the prison-house of language: in a Marshalsea cell, the "man spat suddenly on the pavement, and gurgled in his throat. Some lock below gurgled in *its* throat immediately afterwards.[3] My point is not only the obvious: that the same realism that enforces and indeed creates a powerful catalog of what counts as real also, *by its nature*, therefore creates an exclusionary system whose abuses are to be deplored. Rather, it is more pragmatic: that the system of realism, which has more than proved that it can generate critical opposition, perpetuate discussion, and otherwise goad people into observations of the sort I am about to make on *Frankenstein*, serves not only a useful purpose but also an inevitable purpose. Focusing on realism's potentially co-optive formulations does not provide, as well, a viable alternative, as long as one is speaking of discourses whose functions are to be explicitly or implicitly political. As the critical discourse on realism suggests, even conscious resistance cannot subvert the material power of a text whose legitimating premise – that there is a real to speak of in some responsible way – is shared.[4] Language does various kinds of work at various levels, and lyric poetry, for example, may have a moral, ethical, erotic, or political effect that is felt as radically different from the way realism's effect is felt. But to stay within narrative, broadly defined, and within a presupposition, on which political activism must rest, of the realness of everyday things, is to join an inevitable process of regression to certain basic assumptions and the formulations that bespeak these assumptions. To imagine otherwise has, perhaps, a utopian value, but it is a fantasy that necessarily must repress certain systemic givens. *And yet*, there is still the exclusionary side of the system to be considered, and it is that context in which I shall think here of *Frankenstein*.

One cannot responsibly think of realism without first addressing this most basic of prohibitions: How does one excluded from the canonical discourse by virtue of being a woman, a monster, a child, a lunatic (and all the other synonyms of exclusion), summon her audience? It took Wittgenstein to say, with profoundly revelatory simplicity, "If a lion could talk, we could not understand him."[5] Which is, in part, to say that as long as you define "lion" and "talk" and "understand" and the rest of the words in this sentence one way and in one set of relationships to each other, you cannot define them simultaneously another way. (Yet one cannot help but think of how it would be if the sentence read, "If a lion could talk, we could not understand her.") If a monster could talk, we could not understand it. If a woman could talk, we could not understand her. If these creatures "talk," as Shelley's monster talks and talks and talks, it is a language perceived as garbled by definition of its having come from the misshapen lips of an alien species. Only a member of the club could be truly stunned by the tautological elegance of this declaration regarding language, which has nothing to do with lions at all, although it has everything to do with taxonomy. Wittgenstein's friends heard him, and the halls echoed with the mournful sounds of "radical incommensurability," and, again, in response, with Quine's no-nonsense "radical translation" and with Davidson's "radical interpretation."[6] Such philosophical theorizing, seductive, pristine, intelligent, is *possible* as such only within the brotherhood to whom they speak, and those unhearable Others who have been saying something like the same thing all along may feel an ironic exasperation that the club members have, after a ritual purification of it, taken up the theme as their own (for their having taken it up only means they have assimilated it to their own program). Those who had been excluded all along from full enfranchisement did not need this dopaminic awakening to the treachery of language to sense themselves as having long been unhearable, unseeable, and unsayable. These Others could have spilt the beans long before Davidson: It is a matter of *choice*, has always been a matter of choice, to facilitate communicational competence, or at least the mutual illusion of it: all it takes is a genuine assumption of commensurability from both parties. But as long as lions, women, monsters, and other misfits are held outside the magic circle, strewn round the perimeter with holy wafers, such communication and the realities it authorizes for the purposes of the moment will be subverted.

Entertaining from within the dominant discourse the (impossible) question of how a monster, or a woman, or a lion, might *see* the world does nothing to obviate the problem of communication and instead reifies the dichotomy at hand: being taken by the compatriots as, by definition, inexplicable, ensures that these creatures will still be used primarily to establish the snug parameters of the brotherhood. Such speculation about alternative visions may alter one's complacencies regarding the real, although the epiphany it affords has something of the same sublime goofiness of a revelation one might receive while stoned (and about the same durability and practicality). These Others may well see a set of verisimilitudes different from the conventionalized versions, or they may see the same artifacts through alternative lenses, but this is not particularly the point, since all "realism" is a matter of negotiation among different perspectives, and such speculations are in no way verifiable in any case. This uncertainty

merely reinforces, paradoxically enough, the need to declare or, if necessary, to negotiate a reality: Quixotic, one declares for a windmill or, alternatively, for a giant; one declares for Dulcinea or, alternatively, for the
whore. One finds oneself on a rotten canvas covering over a pit, with a
language that threatens to unravel at every moment to nothing. Such self-
reflexiveness subverts one's confidence in language's capacity to translate
anything without the willing consensus of a "reasonable" group who will
say, with Putnam and Austin, "Enough is enough, enough isn't everything."[7] But, of course, until "reasonable" opens to include what has traditionally been felt as the monstrosity of the inhuman – or, in other words,
what is felt as an essential *femaleness*, wherever it is seen to reside (in
women, in Jews, in men who don't fit the mold, etc.) – that which is
perceived by initiates as "enough" will be, to one outside the terms of
friendship, always the same radical insufficiency.

The Friendship

"Oh my friends, there is no friend" – Aristotle, Kant, Montaigne, Heidegger, Derrida – this oxymoronic lament and the echoes of this lament filter
themselves through the philosophical discourse and permeate the literary.
Isolated and distilled in Derrida's "The Politics of Friendship," this paradoxical cry is felt to reverberate between a performative, an apostrophic call – a
prayer, if you will, predicated on faith in immanent friendship, a listening
christ – and a concession to the impossibility of the reification of this summons in "friend." An installment, he says, in "one of the great canonical discourses of philosophy on friendship," Derrida's ruminations weave [the
(im)possibilities of] justice, expressibility, and visibility together inextricably
with the notion of the friend; one can only make this double claim, "Oh my
friends, there is no friend," within a prescribed place that allows the calling
forth of friendship/language/justice because it has kept a space open that is
immanent with that trinity.[8] The least epiphanic of Derrida's insights – and
yet, perhaps, the most inescapably essential of them – are his final recognition
that the canonical discourses on friendship are predicated on the "sublime
figure of virile homosexuality" and his implication that friendship, and, by
necessary extension, justice, expressibility, and full visibility, cannot be ac-

corded to such Others as are too completely Other.[9] Plato's myth of the Whole Man from which men come accords each man his half of the tessera, a perfect match for the lost other half (perhaps the artistic preoccupation with the image of intercrural postures in Greek homoerotic coupling, a figural manifestation of the "beautiful" form that such relationships both mirrored and produced, is relevant here[10]).

Women, and monsters, very much the same thing after all, exceed or distort the template and thus need not apply: their "realities" perceived from within the brotherhood are the realities of dreams, hallucinations, fevers, the hyperboles of fear and desire. Allegories, emblems, receptacles, and properties, these Others have no place in the terms of friendship: a *"double exclusion . . .* can be seen at work in all the great ethico-politico-philosophical discourses on friendship, namely, on the one hand, the exclusion of friendship between women, and, on the other hand, the exclusion of friendship between a man and a woman."[11] This is, of course, at heart a truism, hardly news, but Derrida, in exposing the connections between friendship and law, between friendship and the possibility of discourse, and, more obliquely, between friendship and visibility, awakens a vision of the full implications for any notions of realism, philosophical or literary, of a debarment from friendship. It is, indeed, a *politics* of friendship, and the disfranchised may be seen to have been declared, in political effect, null and void: chimerical, not "real" enough even for government work.[12] "Reality" is a term whose only existence lies in its actualization through law; its parameters are established through the discourse arising from that law; its verisimilitudes – its coming into visibility – are predicated on how one reads the law (madness and its certification come under this heading). Realism is a negotiation that will fail the moment a competency hearing is called; it may see both sides of the idealism/particularity coin, but it must cast its lot with the material status quo. *Frankenstein* reveals the necessary teratogenesis of language spilling from mouths perceived as monstrous; it suggests what will become realism's intuition of an enterprise imperiled before the fact by a language that is essentially uncontainable, a material environment that is radically metamorphic, and a human condition, both within the artist and within her characters, that resonates in a field somewhere between hyperbole and understatement.

Frankenstein is an enriched space in which to examine realism's necessary complicity with and resistance to a language game whose rules have been laid down at the club. For what is Mary Shelley's *Frankenstein* but a woman's cry, a monster's cry, this time all too true: "Oh my friends, there is no friend"[13] – the baffled and aggrieved cry of one who, having been steeped already in Godwin's theories of justice and Wollstonecraft's theories of gender equality, and having also heard the assumption of universal human rights implicit in the "Declaration of the Rights of Man and Citizen," finds nonetheless that women remain excluded from full "human" rights.[14] The apostrophe is addressed to a masculine literary establishment whose very ears will be dulled to alternative voices because attuned so fraternally to homoaesthetic expectations for reading pleasure ("At this time he desired that I should write, not so much with the idea that I could produce anything worthy of notice, but that he might himself judge how far I possessed the promise of better things hereafter," writes Shelley[15]). But more than these, there is the sheer, inescapable truth of what it means to have no (right of) appeal, to have been constructed by an other who, deluding himself that he is making something beautiful, has instead merely put together a monster composed of male effluvia. Shelley's novel is, among other things, a reverie on friendship and friendlessness, on how it feels to be imbued with what many have argued is a cognitive predisposition for a knowledge of "the right" – the basis on which Enlightenment humanism is founded – while remaining excluded from justice, without protection and without redress (Justine is the sacrifice, the literal instating of this awareness in the text, while the monster plays out an alternative fantasy of power and impotence).[16] The theme of friendship in the novel is primary, overt: "I have no friend. . . . I bitterly feel the want of a friend. . . . I greatly need a friend. . . . I shall certainly find no friend," these in the space of one paragraph and the opening sentence of the next (pp. 4–5). "I desire the company of a man," moans Walton: the homoerotic element is clear, as if in the transvestitism of her authorial voice Shelley knows the game from which she is excluded (p. 5). Walton may rhapsodize over Victor – "I never saw a more interesting creature" (p. 11) – may detail his human features lovingly: his eyes, his countenance, his physiognomy, his form. And Victor may love Clerval. But the monster, unnamed, reifies both the powerful linguistic, erotic, political, and social aberration and the paradoxical impotence of the female. His tragedy is doubled, as if the mathematical neutrality of Aristotle's +/− phrase is skewed; his dilemma involves playing out the full implications of the second half of the Aristotelian lament, "there is no friend," when the initiating call to friendship cannot be heard. Without friends, he cannot *be* a friend; perceived only as a monster, so does he necessarily become a monster in the end. He becomes, quite literally, a murderer of brotherhood, for if he leaves the father(s) to stand in judgement, he slaughters the beloved brother William and the beloved "brother" Clerval. Given the capacity for friendship, lawfulness, and eloquence in a (post-revolutionary) society whose call to arms was "Fraternity, Equality, and Liberty" (that revolution to create "a vast lodge in which all good Frenchmen will truly be brothers"[17]), he is deprived of access to the prerequisite by which one makes oneself seen and heard: he has, and can have, no friend, for (the) fraternity cannot include monsters. And it cannot include women.

Thus it is not surprising to see a fantasy of gigantism emerge from a woman's pen, a vision of sheer size, strength, agility, and intelligence coupled with a righteous insistence on being heard and seen and felt by the father. And it is not only the literal monster that is huge, but also the form in which Shelley invests her energy: At the same time that she will remain rigorously within the confines of the "real" − real science, theoretically productive of real monsters − she will also produce something Gothic, a story that will "speak to the mysterious fears of our nature and awaken thrilling horror − one to make the reader dread to look round, to curdle the blood, and quicken the beatings of the heart" (pp. xxiii–xxiv). She will write her verisimilitudes large: "As the minuteness of the parts formed a great hindrance to my speed, I resolved, contrary to my first intention, to make the being of a gigantic stature. . . . " (p.38). She will locate the monster's voice at the very physical center of the book, nestled there like a bomb in a narrative labyrinth that rivals Brontë's structure in *Wuthering Heights* for complexity.[18] She will turn him out into a nature that epitomizes the Burkean sublime, with all of the sublime's implications for man's sadomasochistic nostalgia for some unrecallable potency, and she will make him, unlike the puny Frankenstein, an equal to the Alps and to the snowbound wastes. *Frankenstein* reveals Shelley's awareness of an exclusion from the fully human, which her gendered experience proves and literature reifies in its lifelong flirtation with the model of virile homosexuality; she translates into the form, the story, and the tropology of her text the full, inchoate clarity of living as a woman (artist), of being that which may only watch life from the pigsty, through the cracks, of being that which must disguise or bury or repudiate its fullest sense of "the real" in order to fit the parameters set by the brotherhood. The monster knows that the difference between an ass and a lapdog is that the lapdog may make itself pleasing in a way that the ass, even gentle and with affectionate intentions, may not (100); a woman speaking to make her version of reality *heard* knows her place on the lapdog–ass continuum.

One who is outside the brotherhood remains inevitably within the realm of the objectified, and, as Habermas points out in *Moral Consciousness and Communicative Action*, those who are objectified – children, drunks, madmen – exist outside the boundaries of moral discourse, their competence as participants in communicative action obviated:[19] They are not to be judged culpable, but neither are they to be acquitted. Habermas quotes Strawson on objectivity: "If your attitude towards someone is wholly objective, then though you might fight him, you cannot quarrel with him, and though you may talk to him, even negotiate with him, you cannot reason with him. You can at most *pretend* to quarrel, or to reason with him."[20] It does not matter that a "wholly objective" attitude is a fiction, for fantasies of objectification are based on the necessary enforcement of not simply a radical incommensurability, but an incommensurability of human worth; the assumption that the other does not sufficiently *share* one's humanness reproduces exactly that chasm between the (hu)man and his subjects, and the subsequent failure of discourse then confirms his assessment and perpetuates the circle. For such an objectified Other, then, to try to force a recognition of her existence is only laughable or histrionic, if it is noticed at all. For women this is an experiential commonplace. Thus Shelley makes her monster the very paradigm for the objectified matter that is called "woman." His pieces chosen objectively from dead figures, he is a Petrarchan conceit gone mad, all parts and no whole, with his "hair . . . of a lustrous black," his "teeth of a pearly whiteness" (p. 42), but his skin yellow and shriveled, his eyes dull and watery, his lips straight and black. Hair and teeth, which for a corpse are almost the last things to go, remain intact, but the bright eyes, the rosy lips, and the alabaster complexion are effaced to reveal the inhuman beneath such artifices. One thinks of Hawthorne's similar fantasy in *The Blithedale Romance*, where beneath the veil of the lovely woman in white may lie "the lips of a dead girl, or the jaws of a skeleton, or the grinning cavity of a monster's mouth."[21] Hawthorne has Zenobia (herself in the throes of storytelling) speak this vision for him, as if he imagines it to be a virtual anamnesis; the reverie that is *Frankenstein* suggests instead that it is the propaganda as regards a woman's inherent monstrosity that is polluting and, ultimately, corruptive. So consistently "objectified" by others, one may come to objectify oneself. Infantilized, animalized, pathologized, one may not merely be excluded from, but may actually exit, the bounds of moral discourse.

One does not have to be politicized to feel the weight of this shared and typical vision of a monstrousness, immanent and disguised only by the thinnest veneer of female charm; Shelley would not have needed her mother's feminist program to intuit the consequences of such a burden.[22] Anatomized so insistently, their features and form scrutinized, compartmentalized, and judged, women are trained to conceive of themselves as figural. One learns to feel oneself as tropic, on a precarious slope toward catachresis.[23] One might ask why Shelley did not make her monster a woman, and my response would have to be, without substantial irony (or, at least, I mean what I say, despite the inescapable irony of the assertion itself), that to do that would be to commit a redundancy. A doubled monstrosity of woman and monster would cancel itself out as too egregious, so far-fetched as to obviate the symbolic potential of the story altogether; as Frankenstein says, "she might become ten thousand times more malignant than her mate and delight, for its own sake, in murder and wretchedness" (p. 150). ("Woman is indescribably more evil than man," says Nietzsche.) The she-monster is inconceivable as a character, for by that impossible paradox of womanhood, she would have to be simultaneously more malignant and less effectual than her male counterpart. Such restless mobility, coupled with such fixity of purpose as the man-monster demonstrates, is unthinkable in a female, of whatever type. One must consider the film *The Bride of Frankenstein* (1935) in this context – and it was a remarkably insightful gesture to have had Elsa Lanchester play both Mary Shelley and the monstrous bride –; even the well-stitched woman falls apart under pressure (the bride's first response is a coy glance at Frankenstein; her second is to scream at the sight of the monster who is to be her mate; her last, before the walls come tumbling down, is to hiss spitefully, catlike, at the love-struck monster – already fickle and fainthearted, erotically powerful by the monster's needful estimate, and the more vile in Frankenstein's eyes for her attraction to him).[24] Yet Shelley does encode within the text her sense of the literal impossibility of translating this vision into character, and if the monster embodies a walking catachresis, one can only shudder at the energy that in addition produces the phantasm of a woman, half made and then torn to pieces, called forth to be violently repudiated. "The remains of the half-finished creature, whom I had destroyed, lay scattered on the floor, and I almost felt as if I had mangled the living flesh of a human being" (p. 155). It is as if realism's enriched ambivalence about how character is produced cannot bear, here, the additional burden of an engagement with the female; it is as if Frankenstein's gesture merely accelerates the deconstructive violence implicit in a figure so conflictually constructed. All rhetorical flourish, a woman's dissolution is always imminent; she will either fall apart of her own accord or be deconstructed by the masculine gaze. She cannot therefore speak, except to be heard through the fancy figures that overlie her voice.[25]

This is thus a novel whose first fantasy is polar, a search for a place beyond turmoil, "a country of eternal light," a "region of beauty and delight," the still point, the "calm sea" around which all the turning goes on, from which the tropes emanate: the still point where "reality" exists, unmetamorphic and unadorned, in a whiteness that transcends the white mythology of Occidental metaphysics. This fantasy may be a reaction, in part, to Shelley's ambivalence about a revolution whose aftermath suggests that mere anarchy has been loosed under the banner of equality, fraternity, and liberty. By this reading, it is not insignificant that Felix instructs Safie in English by reading Volney's *Ruins of Empires*, a text that, while celebrating "the stupendous genius and mental activity of the Grecians" and denigrating the "slothful Asiatics," also details the rise and then the "subsequent degenerating" of the Romans (p. 104). It may be as well a hyperborean vision of creative (and procreative) stability, for the hyperborean is a place behind the north wind and also, at the same time, the north wind itself – a whiteness that is everything and nothing. But even more basically, the novel's figural message challenges the Occident, whose vision is predicated on a centrality that valorizes structural integrity and beautiful form over the arabesqueries and the orientalisms of the "slothful Asiatics."[26] Walton imagines that he will find the center, "that very thing within a structure which while governing the structure, escapes structurality," true, quintessential north, the secret of the magnet (pp. 1–2).[27] What he finds is a land of dangerous flux, where even in the stillness of being icebound one risks being ground to bits; into this world, too, the monster comes. Shelley's novel, askew and thus itself a radical decentering, knows by instinct that for a woman writing the putative center always lies elsewhere, for woman is a paragon of mutability: soft, transformative, hysterical, given to involuntary gyrations emanating from the treacherous womb.[28] All creators are, after all, hard. By the logic of the canonical discourse on friendship, Shelley must concede that any hope of polar quietude – a "real" as seen through a view from nowhere, her own vision of the Grecian urn, the still unravished bride of quietness – is traversed by a monster, whose self-immolation is the poignant final sacrifice. And thus a woman, and not just any woman, but one surrounded at the very conception and gestation of her story by men playing out the game of friendship with each other, gives necessary birth to realism's sense of its inevitable slippage. She cannot enter the discourse on friendship at the level of discourse ("Many and long were the conversations between Lord Byron and Shelley, to which I was a devout but nearly silent listener," she says, p. xxiv); it is arguable that she cannot even "know" the terms of the game. But Shelley clearly does know at some most essential level how one risks being mutilated, deconstructed, and parodically reconstructed into the figure of a "man" when one has not, and cannot have by the terms as they are given, a friend. It is not the least of the ironies associated with this dilemma that Shelley saw the very body of her text, a reverie begun in dream work, grafted by her husband's hand. She does not even summon her own text forth in the Preface, for, she says, "as far as I can recollect, it was entirely written by him" (p. xxvi).[29]

The monster, friendless, is thus divested of all linguistically based performative power, and this divestment condemns him to the brutish alternatives of one without kinship and without power to authorize a version of the real or even to locate himself within any reality. "Listen to me," "make me happy," love me, see me as I am, destroy me (pp. 84–5) – the monster cannot enforce any of these commands, nor can he, by performative authority, bring a proclamation of friendship to pass that would validate his claim to command these things. As J. L. Austin claims, early in his discussion of performatives, in *How to Do Things with Words*, one must be invested with certain powers in order to utter a performative – which is so called only *because* it causes something to happen. One cannot command, create, or conjure friends merely by saying "Oh my friends" unless one has a preexistent, anteriorly validated position relative to the brotherhood; strength alone – of will, of anatomy, of sexuality – is insufficient. Such an apostrophe assumes inclusion within "a kind of asymmetrical and heteronomical curvature of the social space," assumes "the relation to the Other prior to any organized *socius*, to any determined 'government,' to any 'law' ";[30] man is located in a law that precedes and thus actualizes "the Law." To be excluded, by definition, from this space is to be rendered invisible, impotent, and voiceless; it is to be placed such that, once the formalized and articulated Law emerges from this prior law, one can only remain extraneous to it, ruled by but never fully within it.[31] And, more dangerously, it isolates one from connectedness within a "lifeworld" in which intrinsic moral feelings, ineluctable, manifest themselves in performative attitudes.[32] This is Prometheus unbound, indeed, for a creature excluded from "the web of moral feelings" within which one's humanness is enforced may swell to the proportions of the monster himself, huge, lithe, strong, canny, farsighted, and uncontrollable. Lawless.

Shelley sees that without law, language, too, may exceed safe bounds, and at the same time she acknowledges in the gender of her monster her conviction that in order to remain within language at all, even in polysemic discord, she must create a male and leave the females *in flagrante delicto*, tossed aside and broken. *Frankenstein* reifies the failure of a necessary linguistic reciprocity, a model of communication based in "homological, immanentist, finitist, and politicist concord," in its monster, who as a "male" character may remain symbolic and therefore at least serially unified, but who, as a figure, becomes language unshored by law.[33] This creature without a name, a proper name from which he can speak, and thus " 'answer for [himself]; 'answer to [others],' 'answer before [the law],' " embodies the tripartite failures of justice, expressibility, and visibility.[34] He is, in other words, outside all of the conditions of being that are necessary to one negotiating a realism. He is made to be lawless, in all three senses of that term "made" (caused to be, made by Frankenstein, made by Shelley), and his lawlessness, his monstrosity, exists at the tropological level as well as the political level. If he is sheer power run amok, he is also a language game gone awry: "my form is a filthy type of yours," cries the monster (p. 115).[35] Made piecemeal, and divested before the fact of that pre-text of concord intrinsic to a man's relationships to other men, he is not just metaphor, not just a prosopopoeia for a revolution gone crazy or a father/son relationship turned ugly or a mother/daughter dyad predicated on either maternal death or abortion. He is also a nightmare of language: metaphor and metonymy bungled, a catachresis, parts put together so that metonymies are at once both ensured and severed, multiplied and amputated simultaneously. "Something monstrous lurks in the most innocent of catachreses: when one speaks of the legs of the table or the face of the mountain, catachresis is already turning to prosopopoeia, and one begins to perceive a world of potential ghosts and monsters," says Paul de Man, and the monster, though he is "innocent" where innocence may not be made visible, is to the eyes a catastrophic tangle of disharmony.[36]

The monster is polysemy; he is a figure at once real – physically irrefutable, scientifically thinkable – and hopelessly outside the realism into which he is born; he stands emblematic of realism's doubled and antipathetic obligations to the solitary soul (always monstrous, always unthinkable, always unparalleled) and the well-made, socially inclined figure, both physical and linguistic. This is why one cannot pin him down to any univocal meaning, why he can be, in defiance of everything Platonic, both hideous in countenance and good at heart, bleary about the eyes and acute of mind, graceful and strong yet ungainly in form, unnatural and yet most at home within nature. His metonymic status is hopelessly problematized, for no single part can stand forth to epitomize the whole man, as, for instance, Gradgrind's warehouse-head epitomizes him in *Hard Times*; neither can these discrete and ill-sewn parts reflect anything consistent about the environment, as the "Hands" of *Hard Times* speak of dehumanizing industrialization. To be thus polysemic, all remainder and no whole, is to be, by philosophy's reckoning, monstrous: "Each time that polysemia is irreducible, when no unity of meaning is even promised to it, one is outside language. And consequently, outside humanity."[37]

If metonymy is subverted in the figure of the monster, so too is metaphor, for the nameless creature resembles nothing that those in the brotherhood are equipped to recognize as existent within their realisms. Metaphor, "the trope of resemblance," the trope associated with vision and visibility, with light and enlightenment, cannot function without law; it is, in fact, arguably within its power to predicate and to readjust, to enact a form of law in itself.[38] Thus the word "chimera," which figures so prominently in Shelley's opening pages, is not simply a foreshadowing of literal monstrosity, but of linguistic deformity as well (pp. 24, 32, 33). As Locke says (poetically) of catachresis, "he that hath *ideas* of substances disagreeing with the real existence of things, so far wants the materials of true knowledge in his understanding, and hath instead thereof *chimeras*"; one must ask how a woman's vision, by fraternal definition alien to "the real existence of things," and outside the bounds of "true knowledge," could be anything but chimerical.[39] The monster is a vision of inchoate desire, of what might be born from the head and hands of one who is not granted the right to speak or to be heard within the terms of the brotherhood that defines true knowledge and the real existence of things; it is what one must envision when the mirror finally proves that homology cannot be shaped out of one's monstrous mouth. The monster speaks for everyone who is at last persuaded by the propaganda regarding her soullessness, her essential formlessness, and her fundamental irrationality: "I started back, unable to believe that it was indeed I who was reflected in the mirror; . . . [and] I became fully convinced that I was in reality the monster that I am" (p. 98). What must a "trope of resemblance" become within this specular trap?

One cannot answer the question of what the monster *is*, for by detailing its appalling parts one discovers only a parodic homonymy; the naming of parts reveals that the flesh called by the names from human physiology is something else, not "man." Frankenstein can only say what he is not: "A mummy again endued with animation could not be so hideous as that wretch" (p. 43).[40] This is the paradigm by which woman – "at their best . . . but mummy possessed" – are perceived, with their "heads" that are not really heads (too much irrationality, not enough brains), their torsos deformed, their crotches unsewn, incomplete, and irreparable. It is no accident that the newly awakened monster brings Frankenstein to a dream of his lover Elizabeth liquefying into his mother's worm-eaten corpse: they are all one within Shelley's vision of excludedness. This odd homonymy threatens all lawful tropological comparisons, for the turn cannot be com-

pleted within that "curvature of the social space" that contains the cen-
trifugal energy of its movement.[41] Metaphor must fail under these
conditions, for comparisons are predicated on a filial confidence in baseline
similarities that necessarily erode under the pressure of such parodic simulacra. As Ricoeur says, "the very expression 'figure of speech' implies that
in metaphor, as in the other tropes or turns, discourse assumes the nature
of a body by displaying forms and traits which usually characterize the
human face, man's 'figure'; it is as though the tropes gave to discourse a
quasi-bodily externalization. By providing a kind of figurability to the message, the tropes make discourse appear."[42] Metaphor's best capacity is "to
set before the eyes" whatever comparison it seeks to display, and its further
capacity, by Ricoeur's definition, is to enforce a brotherly bond of shared
understanding and mutual feeling. Metaphor has an illocutionary force; by
displacing literal meaning, it *creates* by predication a meaning that is "the
solution of the enigma" it poses; it is productive of that poetic feeling that
joins men in brotherhood ("On the basis of this analysis of . . . poetic feeling, it is possible to do justice to . . . a claim of Heidegger's analytic of the
Dasein that feelings have *ontological* bearing, that they are ways of 'being-
there,' of 'finding' ourselves within the world. . . .").[43] But the monster's
grotesque, watery yellow eyes suggest Shelley's doubled sightedness, and if
they are monstrous, seeing the world through a grotesque filter of monstrosity, they are also far more acute and farseeing than men's eyes. Metaphor is predicated on a certain accord, a shared vision, which the monster's
eyes can only fail to see. In the homonymy by which female otherness is
seen to be composed of parts that only *look* (hu)man, "eye" and "eye" –
"if eyes they may be called" (p. 43) – are homonyms, the one a radical
distortion of, a despiritualized version of, the truth of the (male) other.

It seems inevitable, then, that Shelley feels these sharp eyes to be monstrous for precisely this reason: that they see *beyond* the curve, make straight
for the pole. Like Emily Brontë, like many writers, she must necessarily
feel the threat of making her vision manifest within an environment whose
accepted "realism" is based on alternative insights.[44] Lyotard has said, in
The Inhuman, that it is for the artist to transgress the bounds of the merely
human and to threaten the quietist assumptions of humanism; according to
Adorno, "art remains loyal to humankind uniquely through its inhumanity
to it."[45] But this cannot be realism's position (as Lyotard implies when he

locates realism somewhere between academicism and kitsch and focuses his energies on the avant-garde), and one who assumes the responsibility of realism must be felt to see with eyes neither too sharp nor too dim. This is a game that may be played close to the net for those within the brotherhood, for one covered by the law, who exceeds from *within* the law the terms of the standard humanist subject, retains a modicum of safety: For a man among brothers, to be "inhuman" – to be an artist – is only one more language game from which there is a retreat.[46] One who successfully performs a realism, even if he is a member of the anti-metaphysical club, must sustain the fiction that there is some order, some meta-metaphor by which metaphor may be described, whose lodge-secret may be shared. As Irigaray sees it in "Plato's Hystera," "a whole conception of language here halts – or runs up against – the illusion of a system of metaphor, a meta-metaphor, postulated by the preexistence of the truth that *decides* in advance how conversation, interventions, will develop. These 'inters' are dictated by a specular genealogy, by a process of images, reflections, reduplications which are rated in terms of their conformity, equivalence and appropriateness to the true that is meant to be uncovered."[47] The eyes have it, and within this specular genealogy, metaphor must become a form of productivity that perpetually remediates the human; but built on the model of the (male) body, designed to produce a reality emanant from the body of the brotherhood, metaphor may remediate for the chosen few by perpetuating their versions of the real.

For one felt to be outside the boundaries of the fully human, the transgressions necessitated by art (and particularly art as conceived romantically) threaten to push one from realism into the realm of monstrosity. This seeing beyond must always threaten to produce lawlessness, as it removes one from the structures by which order is made and kept. Although, outside of realism, there may be something Zarathustrian about such a penetrating gaze (if, at any rate, it proceeds from a man's head), within realism one so sighted is likely to be named as mad. Shelley instantiates this knowledge in Frankenstein's conviction that his story (Shelley's story), if told to the magistrates, would prove him insane before the law, so that he could not be heard as telling the truth and thus could not call forth justice on his own behalf; and unlike Frankenstein, who enjoys the protectionisms afforded by race, class, and gender, a woman who communicates the monstrous may most certainly become punishable under the law, but not protected by it. Inspiration, which for Percy Shelley, in "Ode to the West Wind," is felt as a maenadic assault, will, by extrapolation from this logic, amount instead to maenadic possession for a woman, a lawless rampage that is the very antithesis to domestic, social, and political order: the maenad brooks no "friends." Shelley *shuts* her eyes, and "imagination, unbidden, possessed and guided me" straight to a "hideous phantasm" (p. xxiv). Thus the monster, his demand for justice unanswered, feels his resentment as an incipient madness, one "so great, that not only you and your family, but thousands of others, shall be swallowed up in the whirlwinds of its rage" (p. 84). One might translate this threat as follows: I, the monster, will destroy these three people within the text – lover, brother, and friend – who represent the domestic and politico-fraternal law; but I, the author, will disseminate such rage through the "thousands of others" who read my book.

Thus, though Derrida's sense of "a kind of asymmetrical and heteronomical curvature of the social space" in which friendship is always immanent may also be perceived as a form of myopia, it is nonetheless a necessary boundary within which the enactments of paternal justice are played out and in which desire may be named and controlled. Within this space, men may see each other as reflections of self, as, indeed, completions of self. Together, they form the parameters within which justice may occur. Walton fantasizes a man, "gentle yet courageous . . . whose tastes are like my own." "How would such a friend repair the faults of your poor brother!" (p. 5). The man he finds for a friend, he sees as "lighted up . . . with a beam of benevolence and sweetness" (p. 11), as "so conciliating and gentle, that the sailors are all interested in him." He begins "to love him as a brother" (p. 12). Victor Frankenstein has had a similar love in Clerval, and he merely preaches the Platonic party line to Walton when he says that " 'we are unfashioned creatures, but half made up, if one wiser, better, dearer than ourselves – such a friend ought to be – do not lend his aid to perfectionate our weak and faulty natures' " (p. 14). This is a vision that calls itself straight – both in the sense of its philosophical rectitude and in the sense of its putative heterosexuality – but it fits the curve that preexists it. And it is this vision, this agenda at the heart of the great philosophical discussions of friendship and at the heart of philosophy itself, this "brotherly" love, that supersedes all other claims to justice, this filial authority whose imperatives are as irresistible as one's own will. (" 'If your will should command you to kill your daughter, would you do it?' And I should answer that I would. For that bears no witness of any consent to do so because I have no doubt at all of my own will, and just as little of that of such a friend," asserts Montaigne.[48]) Montaigne has loved his friend so well that his death provokes a fantasy of justice denied and, implicitly, a fantasy of suicide as necessary recompense: "We went halves in everything; it seems to me that I am robbing him of my part."[49] Brothers look to each other for themselves, imagining that they see "truth." (Is it any wonder that George Sand demanded to be called *mon frère?*) Yet as Irigaray says, "if man once thought that straight vision could allow him to escape the opaque barrier that every body presents to the light, now, in his impetuous desire, he is plunged into the darkness that a supposedly enlightened gaze had projected in its very rings and reversals."[50] What passes for enlightened humanism is more properly described as a play of lights dependent on darkness, a veritable aurora borealis of ego projected against the curvature of that social space. What *seems* real is in fact legislated, and while this is a fact very difficult to see from the inside of the curve, it is not so theoretical a notion to those on the other side.

One who sees through can only disrupt the discourse, altering the terms of the real and threatening to turn metaphor to catachresis by imagining, even without intending to, monstrous linkages, unthought-of comparisons. If metaphor has the power to predicate, as Ricoeur suggests, or even if, as Davidson argues, metaphor "belongs exclusively to the domain of use," where it has an *effect* rather than a "meaning," then such a linking, pro-duced by such a vision, may be perceived as terribly irresponsible.[51] One who senses that her sightedness is "flawed" or perverse by all the usual criteria, but who gives in to the temptation to create because the urge to do so is "a resistless and almost frantic impulse," a "slow fever" (pp. 39, 41), will necessarily feel that she gives forth with monstrosity. "The dis-secting room and the slaughter-house furnished many of my materials," says Frankenstein (p. 39), as if to declare Shelley's instinct that the language from which she constructs her own "hideous progeny" (p. xxvi) must necessarily be chosen from out of the charnel house. (Men may, instead, feel themselves locked within language's prison, but at the least such a place supplies, notoriously, an excess of homoerotic energy.[52]) The monster is then virtually inevitable – for masculine discourse, when appropriated by a woman, is, by definition of her own spiritual vacuities, divested of its soul, its filial place in "the very movement and time of friendship," and its location within the law.[53] There could be no better figure for this dilemma than the carefully crafted disaster that is Frankenstein's monster, for it is begun under the artist's delusion that she will escape the trap by creating a new genre and, at the same time, a language in which she can be named as friend: "A new species would bless me as its creator and source; many happy and excellent natures would owe their being to me," says Frankenstein (p. 39). But one soon discovers that the careful juxtaposition of all the best parts of a figure – the strongest limbs, the whitest teeth, the most lustrous hair – will stay dead under such fingers, despite having been galvanized into action; one cannot animate language so that its function is pleasing and therapeutic when, by virtue of speaking and writing it, one perverts the discourse into a teratology. Thus, Frankenstein cries, "How can I describe my emotions at this catastrophe, or how delineate the wretch whom with such infinite pains and care I had endeavoured to form?" Frankenstein does not describe these emotions, because Shelley cannot describe them unambivalently; Frankenstein does not kill the monster, because Shelley cannot bring herself to kill him. Shelley must remain ambivalent about her own progeny, for, ugly as it is, it is the only literary birth that can fully represent her sense of power and her otherwise unacknowledged burden of friendlessness.

In the 1931 film version of *Frankenstein*, the monster cannot speak, but only articulates himself in grunts and snuffles and howls, and this may be felt to be a typical Hollywood oversimplification of a complex text. But it is, actually, an insightful gesture, a translation of a truth about language hidden at the heart of Shelley's text. There is no more articulate, no more thoughtful, no better-read monster anywhere than in *Frankenstein*; he knows Milton, Goethe, and Plutarch. He is reasonable in his argumentative strategies, which are based on an enlightened notion of rationality and justice as being in necessary accordance with one another. He believes that if he can bring Frankenstein to see the error and injustice implicit in his repudiation of one to whom he has a responsibility, then Frankenstein will, seeing the light, mend his behavior. Justice is blind to externalities, the enlightened gaze sufficient, and so the monster, in order to make himself heard, places his hands across his creator's eyes: "thus I take from thee a sight which you abhor," he says. "Still thou canst listen to me and grant me thy compassion. . . . Hear my tale" (p. 85). But the monster, known by all others to be at heart a monster, simply cannot make himself heard except *as a monster*. Not here and not to the De Lacey family, toward whom he takes a watchful maternal role designed to conciliate in advance, to prove his humanness through acts of domestic responsibility (and when have such gestures ever accomplished this?). He can no more convince his accusers than can Justine, before the law, convince hers (her own domestic services also go for naught): they cannot hear him. Justice may be putatively blind − all ears − but, as in the case of the elder De Lacey, when it finds itself dealing with monstrosity, its hearing fails. One cannot get a hearing, really, under such a prohibition, but only a pretense of one ("You can at most *pretend* to quarrel, or to reason, with" the inhuman/rationally incompetent subject[54]).

To know that one will be, by definition, substantially unheard necessitates a rigorous double-mindedness, both epistemologically and literarily: One listens, often with interest, with appreciation, even with sympathy, to the "best" productions of a brotherhood whose exclusivity as regards women, based as it is in opportunistic prejudice, does not then prohibit an outsider from reading, writing, thinking, and feeling, but (only?) from participating in the dialogue (like the monster reading Goethe in the pigsty). The anxieties of influence that produce the mode of realism out of reactions to and readjustments of past texts undergo subtle shifts in this schizophrenic landscape. Within this context, the monster's dualities − his anti-Platonic, oxymoronic condition of lithe awkwardness, bleary acuteness, soulful soullessness − only reify the willed amnesias of a woman reading canonical texts that require her to occupy both ends of the spectrum simultaneously. Shelley instantiates this necessary double vision within her text in her monster's reading list. But by providing bipolar visions of manhood, she covers the canonical bases even as her texts, either implicitly or explicitly, prove the female extraneous to the extremes of either soulfulness or sociability: Plutarch's *Lives*, with its moral-political examination of famous men, designed to elevate one above the "wretched sphere" of one's own reflections, versus Goethe's *Sorrows of Werter*, sourcebook of romanticism, with its "divine being," its "lofty sentiments and feelings," its "disquisitions upon death and suicide," its loving fascination with that "wretched sphere" of one's own reflections; Milton's *Paradise Lost* versus its nineteenth-century revision, Frankenstein's journal, both of which give the monster (woman) "the minutest description of my odious and loathsome person" (pp. 112–15). "I sickened as I read," says the monster (p. 115). Within the discourse of friendship that binds oppositions within a tight intercrural fit, these visions may be felt as compatible. But a monster reading, a woman reading any one of these canonical versions of the real must read both masochistically and in a state of dispossession.[55]

Nonetheless, the monster can read, he can be moved, he can love across the boundary line, and the bottom line here is that he learns that such capacities are not necessarily reciprocal. The monster is a woman's nightmare and realism's nightmare, for his metonymous existence as the sum of random pieces of a contiguous environment remains unilateral. He can read and speak and act, but he cannot begin to transmute his metonymized self by turning what he has learned back upon the world that produced it in a way that would *make his mark*. Certainly, he can alter his world, but not through realism's pedagogical finesse; his only option is to produce physical contortions – dead bodies – that will only decay (one understands here his need for a mate, to produce an offspring both assimilative and assimilating). The realist who gives in to this vision finds herself in an absurdist universe whose most emblematic text is (to leave Wittgenstein out of it) Gary Larson's *Far Side* cartoon captioned "What we say to dogs. What they hear." The text is in a double frame: First, a human pointing his finger at a dog: "Okay, Ginger! I've had it! You stay out of the garbage! Understand, Ginger? Stay out of the garbage, or else!" Then, from the dog's point of view, as it sits, head cocked: "blah blah GINGER blah blah blah blah blah blah blah GINGER blah blah blah blah blah."[56] (One thinks of those recent theories of language for which justice – its immanence and its actualization – is an inseparable component: Habermas's theory of communicative competence, Lyotard's postulation of a pragmatics of language particles used to facilitate a non-zero-sum game by which justice prevails over totalitarianism,[57] Davidson's argument for a "passing theory" by which humans learn to understand each other, thus obviating even the notion of those scheme –content dualisms that might prohibit translatability – each of these presumes a hearing within compatible species.) For one to be heard, one must be accounted a rational subject, and one must be accorded a soul. Otherwise all transactions become null and void; the world may dispose of the mad, the subhuman, the monstrous as it will. And those changelings who fall somewhere in between the rational subject and the monster will be consigned to limbo, a place for the dead souls suspended in a metonymy that will yield access neither to the soul nor to external surroundings.[58]

"Languages we will not think of as separable from souls; speaking a language is not a trait a man can lose while retaining the power of thought," says Davidson.[59] Even when the conversants are, as with Davidson, Plutonians, Saturnians, and Earthmen, the intrinsic expectation is that they will listen, charitably, as if to another soul.[60] But what of the soulless? "I know these charming maenads," says Nietzsche, "Ah, what a dangerous, creeping, subterranean little beast of prey she is."[61] The bitch can't be expected to understand, for, like a dog walking on its hind legs, she can neither philosophize nor reason for more than a few moments at a time. Davidson, in "A Nice Derangement of Epitaphs," makes an elegant argument for the passing theories by which people come to understand each other, and he ends, famously, with "I conclude that there is no such thing as a language, not if a language is anything like what many philosophers and linguists have supposed. There is therefore no such thing to be learned, mastered, or born with."[62] Making yourself heard and listening to others is the only game, and it is not dependent on "assumptions about shared meanings, concepts, or beliefs."[63] In other words, the "prior theory," which "expresses how [one] is prepared in advance to interpret an utterance of the speaker" and includes "all the features special to the idiolect of the speaker that the interpreter is in a position to take into account before the utterance begins," is insufficient; it is, in fact, unnecessary, "for the passing theory is the one the interpreter actually uses to interpret an utterance, and it is the theory the speaker intends the interpreter to use."[64] Now this is a wonderfully convincing argument read within the humanist mind-set, for here even Mrs. Malaprop has a good chance of being interpreted, if only as a pompous "creature" not quite human. But Davidson is operating in good faith, with the rational assumption that one who wishes to understand another human will suspend his prior theory in order to conduct the business of communication by "entering hypotheses about new names, altering the interpretation of familiar predicates, and revising past interpretations of particular utterances in the light of new evidence."[65] In abandoning the search for a theory of meaning within the non-natural languages constructed by analytic philosophers, he claims to address the baseline functions of natural communication, where what counts is one's "knowledge of the character, dress, role, sex, of the speaker, and whatever else has been gained by observing the speaker's behaviour, linguistic or otherwise."[66] He neglects the distortive potential of the residue of the prior theory, however; assuming the brotherhood, he fails to take the monster into account. It becomes an amusing game to apply Davidson's ideas on communication to *Frankenstein*, for there, the prior theory is everything, and it keeps the passing theory from functioning at all. The monster speaks like an enlightened man, but he *looks* like a monster; the woman may speak like an enlightened man, but she *looks* like a woman.[67]

The predisposition that allows Aristotle to say, knowing that he will be heard, "Oh my friends, there is no friend" is at the heart of philosophy itself and it is, thus, also at the heart of a realism whose epistemological orientation is toward determining what *is*; the "question of essence or truth, has unfolded itself, as the question of philosophy, on the basis of a certain experience of *philein* and *philia*."[68] The very central question "What is?" is bound up in filial heteronymy, a rule of brotherhood that is intrinsic; "a friendship prior to friendships, an ineffaceable, fundamental, and bottomless friendship, the one that draws its breath in the sharing of a language . . . and in the being-together that any allocution supposes, including a declaration of war" (p. 636). To enter the philosophical discourse whose opening gambit must always be the question "What is?" one must begin in good filial faith, knowing already at some level what brotherhood is. "Vico would remind us that men know how to speak like heroes because they already know how to speak like men," says Eco in his argument for the underlying semiotic network by which metaphor is produced.[69] I would further say that men know how to speak like philosophers because they already know how to speak like men, and they know how to speak like enemies because they already know how to speak like brothers. A man knows these things, in part, by knowing what brotherhood is not and cannot be: the not-masculine. The basis for knowing the one is knowing the other, and it is a discrepancy one forgets at the peril of losing philosophy altogether. Thus the monster does not stand a chance. Only a blind man can imagine it to be his "countryman" and can say "do not despair. To be friendless is indeed to be unfortunate; but the hearts of men, when unprejudiced by any obvious self-interest, are full of brotherly love and charity" (p. 118). But both the monster and the woman writing know their odds: "I have good dispositions; my life has been hitherto harmless and in some degree beneficial; but a fatal prejudice clouds their eyes, and where they ought to see a feeling and kind friend, they behold only a detestable monster" (p. 118).

Shelley's novel remains irreducible, and it remains deeply compelling, as it reifies at every level what it means to write, to think, to exist as a monster; and it accomplishes this density by locating its production within the gestures of a new realism whose most basic assumptions would come, increasingly, to force the issue. In fact, among the multiple allegories of reading it inspires, the novel's birthing of a monster could stand as predictive of realism's cumbersome and conflictual obligations. *Frankenstein* has been seen traditionally as a "flawed" novel, one that fails the tests of naturalness of language and of beautiful form.[70] Yet it stands, by itself, intact, as the thing Shelley herself called it: her "hideous progeny." Its very disjointedness, its very lack of a language that seems able to fit exactly what needs to be said, its seams and fissures and disproportions, all testify to Shelley's racked vision of how she might create a story real enough to be persuasive, even while being named as inadequate to do so. She represents in *Frankenstein* the possibility that the female voice will somehow make itself heard, or at least felt; yet she shudders at what this might mean. She is both visionary and repelled, for as one who witnesses uneasily for revolution, she is "faced by the as yet unnamable which is proclaiming itself and which can do so, as is necessary whenever a birth is in the offing, only under the species of the non-species, in the formless, mute, infant, and terrifying form of monstrosity."[71] But unlike other realists who "turn their eyes" from this borderland between the real and the ineffable so that the engagement will be oblique, she meets the monster more or less straight on, for she knows herself to be outside of friendship, and thus outside such expressivity as might be deemed therapeutic among the brotherhood.

This displacement of women from the politics of friendship has been achieved and sustained by a irresistibly transformative propaganda that both valorizes and discredits the inhuman. The immemorial – that thing which refutes all attempts at being bespoken, that thing for which the trope of visibility is always insufficient – becomes phantasmatic, made of monsters, women, beasts, and Others. This excitation is, depending on one's mood, felt variously as (painfully) pleasurable or exasperating, but in either case it is given form in embodiments from outside the circle of friends, embodiments that, by definition of their failing to meet the lodge requirements, will always be catachreses. This tautology enforces and legitimizes a conscious masculine exclusivity that has used Others, and women in particular, to aggrandize itself and to keep political and social power to itself. The discourse of friendship is not an adjunct to philosophical or literary discourse; it has been and continues to be at the very heart of the matter, the given on which effective discourse rests (this is, in part, why the academic discipline of philosophy continues to be dominated by men; literature has a space for aberration, for the "inhuman," that philosophy lacks), the space in which reality, and realism, is negotiated. Fraternity is the safe investment without which philosophers like Davidson and Putnam and Habermas could not afford to be such spendthrifts, so generous, so magnanimous, and so optimistic. They are able to say of communication, with Putnam, "enough is enough, enough isn't everything," because, in their brotherhood, they have unrestricted access to the "enough" that makes wasted words less precious. In this economy, a man may easily exercise a Principle of Charity; yet, under the circumstances, such largesse must seem to Others yet another invitation to join the Hatter's tea party (" 'Take some more tea,' the March Hare said to Alice, very earnestly. 'I've had nothing yet,' Alice replied in an offended tone: 'so I can't take more.' 'You mean you can't take *less*,' said the Hatter: 'it's very easy to take *more* than nothing' "[72]). Even the iconoclasts reside, at some level, within the white mythology that first took language for itself to create a metaphysics of presence synonymous with God/Plato/Man/Humanism and that even now continues to make something of nothing, to make elegant and kindly meant apologias for the fraternal status quo, to soothe and comfort and seduce even the non-initiates (the monsters, the women, the Others) with their visions of sufficiency – at least until one stops to think or starts to talk or falls asleep to dream. Shelley's vision includes the apocalyptic side of a desire to seize "justice" by the throat, but it ends in immolation (or so we are told – is this ending, like Chopin's in *The Awakening*, another moment in which the law says the monster must die, but the author cannot in good conscience fully kill it off?). But beneath her resignation something clamors: Enough isn't enough, because there isn't yet enough. One must resist with constant vigilance the fantasy of inclusion, that lapdog gratitude for what is offered as "enough." The first step in this program is to out the fantasy of virile homosexuality that informs the humanistic trinity of justice-visibility-expressivity and to proclaim the covert misogyny disguised within the concept of the humanist subject. And the second is to repudiate the externally imposed assignment of monster altogether, while, at the same time, accepting the responsibility to become one.

Chapter Five

Brontë's Variations on a Theme by Sade

___

"My dreams appal me."

—Catherine Earnshaw

Catherine Earnshaw speaks to Nelly Dean:

I've dreamt in my life dreams that have stayed with me ever after, and changed my ideas; they've gone through and through me, like wine through water, and altered the colour of my mind. And this is one – I'm going to tell it – but take care not to smile at any part of it.[1]

But Nelly Dean refuses to hear her, and she so resolutely refuses to listen that Catherine *never utters this dream aloud within the text*. Catherine recounts an alternative dream, slipping it into the conversation so deftly, with a laugh and a disclaimer – "This is nothing . . . I was only going to say" – that Nelly misses her cue to rush off to bed; she hears the dream despite herself, and she makes nothing of it. Catherine relates her dream in its most reduced terms, purged of its somatogenic enigmas, blurting out the barest outlines of plot before Nelly can stop her (p. 72), saying "that will do to explain my secret, as well as the other" (p. 72). The reader is not accustomed to being treated in this way. This breaches the contract of fictional realism, flagrantly. Catherine *must* tell the first dream, the "real" dream, as opposed to the substitute, having signaled its transubstantiative symbolic value. That she does not has profound implications within this text, for it suggests that

___

she *cannot* articulate what Nelly (the most resolute of realists) cannot re-count, that she cannot speak what Nelly cannot hear.[2] It suggests that Brontë has a conscious awareness of the interdictions laid on the (woman) writer under realism's manifestoes, the censorship of convention and ex-pectation, and it predicts her rebellion; it also encodes her intuition that there is an untranslatable energy so profound that it permeates both inter- and intra-subjective interchanges.

For Brontë, there is rational discourse and there is something else that cannot be rendered within a discursive mode, something felt as a heady transformation of water to wine, or, as Bataille says, "a divine intoxication which the rational world cannot bear."[3] Cathy articulates this intuition as a perceptual shift, as if her dreams move her away from seeing through that substance which, transparent, allows the world to impose its material "realities" and toward a sightedness filtered through the blood-wine color of the unexpurgated and uncensored dream state. Like Cathy's, Brontë's is in part a dream vision, and "the dream-work does not think, calculate or judge in any way at all; it restricts itself to giving things a new form."[4] The dream is the work of desire, with its daylight residue a synesthetic tincture "like wine through water" that alters the color of the mind.[5] Brontë lit-eralizes this link between dreaming and desire by having Cathy give a bowdlerized substitute for what was, implicitly, a dream of Heathcliff, who stands within the text for all that is unsanctified; and she codifies within Cathy's memory of being flung out of heaven the perceived transgressive-ness of the untold dream (p. 72). "Desire does not speak; it does violence to the order of utterance," says Lyotard, and Cathy's promise to lay bare her dream − "I'm going to tell it" − is an explicit threat to the linguistic order that Nelly, the consummate realist, holds so dear.[6] Brontë, too, in-tends to tell it, to subvert a more ordinary realism with an enriched reality perceived through the voracious receptivity of a consciousness that sees beyond the ideological predispositions of the apparent reality within which it functions.[7] *Wuthering Heights* is the irreducible "new form" born of this sightedness.

But as if it is an inevitable correlative of her desire to do violence to the order of realistic utterance, while yet remaining within it, she awakens a fantasy of sadomasochism, that nexus at which an erotic cruelty comes up against and is sustained by the very punitive social and political "reality" that is both its paradigm and its antithesis.[8] Her actors play out variations of an erotic game whose teleology is, finally, inherent in the bondage imposed by their words; the restrictiveness of a language that invests itself in material verisimilitudes compels Brontë's resistance as certainly as the Bastille and Sainte-Pélagie enhanced Sade's literary elaborations of exquisite torture.[9] Through *Wuthering Heights* wafts the air of Sade's Château of Silling, as Brontë locks out from her novelistic landscape all the pretenses of direct intervention that society may afford and then allows Heathcliff to burgeon irrepressibly within it.[10] Her environment is hermetically sealed, as if to give weight and shape to the incestuous enclosures of language; those sarcophagi (coffins, bed-closets, oak dresser, locked rooms) that permeate the story are compact metonyms for this state, written large in Brontë's isolative heath-land. Her perversion of the Trinity in Heathcliff's sarcophagous fantasy of sideless coffins and the erotic consummation of inextricable decay is the desacralized reduction of the three into one: Father, Son, and Holy Ghost made synonymous through a degradation that may be found to be no more than a physical extension of the realist Lockwood's habitual linguistic reductionisms. That undiminished corpse that must not be exposed to air, that grotesque parody of the sleeping beauty who, at one kiss from the prince, would melt into a coprophiliac's delight, is the emblem for a linguistic system whose hermetic seal is the necessary insurance that it will not be discovered in its moribundity. And the wandering female spirit, that holy ghost, is its refutation, for as Brontë says elsewhere, "The Dweller in the land of Death / Is changed and careless," immune to upland realities.[11]

Brontë speaks in *Wuthering Heights* about language and desire, about the raw need to reveal an unexpurgated dream and the trace of the immemorial versus the need to say what can and what will be heard in an environment that demands good, productive realism. Her book is filled with stories of texts, because she clearly feels her textual body as an extension of herself, as a physical manifestation as connected and tactile as one's "hand" (another layer of contiguity within a text filled with palpable connections). Van Ghent's sense of the technical patterning of *Wuthering Heights* translates this energy into a taut, hourglass figure on the page: "the design of the book is drawn in the spirit of intense compositional rigor, of *limitation*," she says, "the characters act in the spirit of passionate immoderacy, of excess."[12] A fantasy of sadomasochism *must* accompany this potent vulnerability, and thus the terrifying dream vision of the severing of that hand. When Brontë has Cathy fill the margins of her books with alternative realities (p. 15), she implies the essential effort of insinuation that her own art entails: when she sees the same book on the windowsill stanching the flow of the dream-wraith's blood, when she imagines Catherine's books as used to dam the bloody hole (p. 30), she suggests both the power of the text and its mortal price. Joseph, his "large Bible on the table, and overlaid . . . with dirty banknotes" (p. 267), produces a more nearly rectified text than Brontë, and he parodies Cathy's interpolations by crossing one ideological text with an apparently oppositional but really quite compatible second ideology. His is the parodic realism of Mammon and hypocrisy, of preachments whose only effect lies in the punitive measures with which they are accompanied. Her realism is a more dangerously subtle and pedagogically sophisticated one; as Van Ghent says, the book "works as a level of experience that is unsympathetic to, or rather simply irrelevant to the social and moral reason."[13] Thus the textual body as a communicable arousal is, for Brontë, mortal; she looks with wide-open eyes straight at the dissolutions of the corpus, and while Cathy's corpse remains unaltered, her books decay. They have bodies that age and corrupt, skins that may be flayed and burned. She tells how they look and smell in their degenerations – "mildewed books," "a Testament, in lean type, smelling dreadfully musty," "antique volumes" (p. 15). Filled with blood, like the books on the sill, they might pulsate with violent life; testamental, they are "lean." They burn with the smell of burning, sacrificial flesh – "an odour of roasted calf-skin" – and are hurt as living things – I "spread open the injured tome on my knee," says Lockwood (p. 15). Cathy can fling *The Helmet of Salvation* across the room and knock its cover off, and she can write between the lines and thus cosmetize the library to match her contempt; but when she loses her cathexis with the text, she is, in essence, already dead. Even Nelly sees her dissolution, as Cathy's expression during her illness "stamped her as one doomed to decay" (p. 131). Brontë confirms Cathy's deathwatch metonymically: "A book lay spread on the sill before her, and the scarcely perceptible wind fluttered its leaves at intervals. I believe Linton had laid it there, for she never endeavoured to divert herself with reading. . . . " (p. 131). Once a girl who co-opted Branderham's patristic sadisms, she is now metonymously identified with an unread, and therefore dead, text.

Brontë's is a world in which two kinds of pleasure can be dreamed, but only one articulated directly, in the terms as they are set by realism's overt program of productivity: a dream-desire, violent by its nature, but not punitive or hostile, becomes co-opted by the hard, coercive thrust of a necessarily politicized language. Desire must struggle to hold its value in the economy of realism, for in order to fulfill its social promise, it recognizes the need to flay all erotic mystery into elements of flesh.[14] The tutelage that permeates the final pages of *Wuthering Heights* brings Hareton to beauty even in Heathcliff's eyes; Hareton looks like Cathy Earnshaw when he is fully awakened to language – like, Heathcliff cries, "the ghost of my immortal love, of my wild endeavours to hold my right, my degradation, my pride, my happiness, and my anguish" (p. 275). And, remarkably, one finds in these moments Heathcliff's only approach to a non-sadistic erotic response, as Hareton becomes the text from which Heathcliff reads "the thousand forms of past associations, and ideas he awakens, or embodies" (p. 274). *He* moves me differently," Heathcliff says (p. 274), as if the fully illuminated masculine text performs a seductive brothering irresistible even to a man immune to all other non-sadistic eroticisms. Yet it is not *this* text that is the permissible one, and it is not this kind of tutelage that is offered during most of *Wuthering Heights*. Instead, one sees the sadomasochist's educative process, that which disciplines a "reality" that exceeds the sum of its parts by enacting punishment on its corpus. The palimpsestic, amorphous, and fertile heath abutted and abruptly abridged by the stony cliff – Heathcliff is its animus, the place where natural force and a voluble and therefore corrupt human "nature" coincide in a speaking subject. He is the quintessence of realism's treacherous, double-invested metonymies. Brontë's is thus a world where sublime "nature" is the predominant metaphor, but *only* a metaphor, as it must be brought to social service, as language is brought to the service of a paternal justice.[15] The skeleton babies in their nest on the heath epitomize this vision of a natural world trapped in a latticework of sadistic masculine artifice – the nestlings, their view of the surrounding heath virtually unimpeded, starved nonetheless on the very bosom of plenty.[16] This is thus a book in which mothers die and fathers prevail, and in which the symbolic set piece is Lockwood's first ecstatically painful dream of clashing staves.

Yet in her reverie on the subject, Brontë transcends the bipolar equivocations of sadomasochism by showing a deep insight into its nature, while finally repudiating its power. Swinburne, who knew Sade's work, speaks to the charge against Brontë that she struck a "savage note" or showed "the sickly symptom of a morbid ferocity"; he feels in the novel a "wild and bitter pathos," a "passionate and ardent chastity." "As was the author's life, so is her book in all things: troubled and taintless, with little of rest in it, and nothing of reproach."[17] She proposes sadomasochism as a caricatured or hyperbolic version of an intrinsically cruel ordinary life – everyday expectations turned up a notch or two for effect – and thus reveals in realism's reformist energies its necessary affiliation with judgment, punishment, and pain. (The French Revolution has been a most vivid proof of how reform may career into violent retribution; its images of headlessness mirror a grotesquely comic metonymic dispensation in a country whose Heads are being replaced by its Hands.) She intuits the extremist possibilities inherent in a form whose ethical responsibilities might push it at any moment into obsession and fanaticism, whose pedagogy might veer from instruction to sharp discipline. She thwarts, somehow, all convenient reductions; she intercedes in that will to power that ensures that a figure such as Heathcliff will continually shed his most impeachable weaknesses through the self-purification of a sublation whose movement is toward refinement. She neither valorizes nor castigates the sickness of sadomasochism; understanding it, she does not see it univocally, and so, unscathed, she may keep spiritual company with Sade without sharing in his opportunistic reductionisms. Her refutation of the paternalism that Sade carries to its logical extreme lies not in repudiation but in non-aggrandizing acceptance, in a patient *withholding* of judgmental authority (and in this she enacts realism's equilibration of extremes even as she articulates them). *Wuthering Heights* thus explodes, from within, the standard fictional dichotomy, which earlier had reached a predictive excess in Sade, between an uncomprehending, helpless innocence and a fallen knowledge that, knowing its power, uses it to enforce control.[18] The novel itself proceeds by an acute sightedness that apprehends a painful reality without then necessarily enacting an aggressive judgment and an "equivalent" punishment based on a conviction of guilt.

Because she thinks beyond dichotomy, she recognizes but does not succumb to the Sadeian caricature of realism's double-mindedness as regards
character. The Sadeian world is all Bounderbys or Priscillas: humans either
are pragmatically rapacious (because rapacity produces both physical pleasure and economic profit) or are lamb-like innocents, with women necessarily at the most extreme end of either extreme (a Justine/Juliette pattern
repeated in muted tones throughout realism's texts – Zenobia/Priscilla,
Catherine/Isabella, Eustacia Vye/Thomasin Wildeve, etc.). Brontë, in fact,
seems relatively resistant to the female stereotypes produced by a paternalistic assessment of "reality," the one sublated from the virgin and the other
from the whore, and epitomized in Sade's Justine and Juliette (Sade takes
his models from, among others, those paragons of masochism, Pamela and
Clarissa[19]). The purely inviolable, utterly impenetrable but constantly violated Justine, Sade's sardonic rendering of the woman of unthinking, non-
philosophical, and inflexible "virtue," is one side of this paternal "reality,"
and Juliette, cruel, rapacious in her sexual and economic appetites, is the
other side. Brontë constructs *Wuthering Heights* as an unfathomable refutation of this self-reproducing system of dichotomous yet complementary
femality and reifies her alternative vision of female sexual/intellectual complexity in the two Cathys, even as she offers up enriched Sadeian stereotypes against which the irreducible females may be held: the sadist
Heathcliff, the duenna Nelly, the bruisable, blonde Isabella, Justine-like in
her incapacity to assimilate and process what Cathy tells her in plain English
of Heathcliff's monstrosity, are the social markers – the politicized extremities – to which the Catherines respond unpredictably.[20] While Brontë
clearly senses that the realist's passion for punishment and reward and his
penchant for order may, and very likely will, produce Sadeian extremes as
the powerful and the powerless reveal themselves within this system, she
confounds sadism's powers by ensuring that one will apprehend *Wuthering
Heights* always at two levels simultaneously: that "reality" beneath which
sadomasochism lurks, and its undoing in some ineffable, non-punitive acceptance of things as they are, a form of perception that accords a genuine
respect to reality, as it sees beyond its own egoistic need for control and
beyond those ideologies that order one's vision by predisposition. By Iris
Murdoch's terms in *The Sovereignty of Good*, Brontë may be said to approach

an acceptance of the real, exterior world – the "unself" – by qualifying any univocal "realism" as her operative perception.[21]

Apparently attuned to the necessary and piquant affinity between sadomasochism and (linguistic) domination – "You are welcome to torture me to death [with your words] for your amusement, only allow me to amuse myself a little [with someone more defenseless] in the same style," says Heathcliff (p. 97) – Brontë is, however, infinitely more resilient than Sade as she shows a commensurate faith in the regenerative, language-based eroticism she realizes so explicitly in Catherine Heathcliff's tutelage of Hareton Earnshaw. Even as she creates a landscape in which pleasure may be derived from giving pain, and in which, in the Cathy/Heathcliff and Cathy/Edgar pairings (and, too, in Hareton's anguished obsession; perhaps even in Nelly's fidelity to Hindley), pleasure and pain are inextricable, she can imagine an erotic alternative in which two people, profoundly *uninnocent* by virtue of their enforced degradations, may resurrect themselves together through language. Unlike Sade, who may have been so ingenuous as to believe his own unequivocal "reality," Brontë refutes, in *Wuthering Heights*, the unilateral assumptions of her given reality of a humanity degraded by circumstance, even as she examines its consequences. Her lack of ideological single-mindedness is both what distinguishes her insights into the pleasures of cruelty from those of Sade and what, in a paradoxical way, makes critics invoke his name (only elliptically) when speaking of *Wuthering Heights*, for they sense in her novel a *freedom* of perception that seems monstrous ("A free woman in an unfree society will be a monster," says Carter, in *The Sadeian Woman*[22]). Yet Brontë's freedom is all the more incomprehensible as it lies outside the mode of thesis/antithesis, which generates its extremisms predictably.

Brontë formalizes the reciprocal nature of desire (both that which is interdicted and that which is unspeakable) and of repression (that which functions to bring language to order and usefulness) structurally and at the level of her story and image patterns, even as she exceeds the sum of these parts. One such manifestation is in the Cathy-Heathcliff pairing that cannot be reduced to language or satisfactorily explained, as placed against the normative and comforting Cathy-Edgar union. In the one house, where desire is sanctified in marriage and thus dispersed and vitiated, language is also sanctified; the library, set apart, but within the heart of the structure, signifies the Horatian civility and social rectitude of the Grange. In the other house, whose very portal-arch of "shameless little boys" metonymously signifies it as an appetitive construct, and where marriage is either parodic or intensely anti-social,[23] books are the most abused and subverted of objects, and instead of a library, the kitchen-dining-living area, with its huge oak dresser hung with sides of meat, dominates the scene. At a structural level, this conflict between desire and repression is objectified within the language game that ensues between Brontë's narrative permutations, which embody the voices of impenetrable rationality, and her subtextual subversions of the narrators' authority and candor. But the novel does not yield its sum completely from such articulations; it is as if Brontë herself whispers, knowing that we also may fail to hear, "I've dreamt in my life dreams that have stayed with me ever after. . . . And this is one – I'm going to tell it."

Nelly's enforced and panicked censorship – "I won't hear it, I won't hear it! . . . I won't harken to your dreams" (p. 72) – conveys Brontë's fear that even the ear of the Other may be so scarified, so suborned by terror, so co-opted by the putative reality of the existent power structure, that its receptivity will be dulled to nothing. "I have undergone sharp discipline which has taught me wisdom," says Nelly, and it is precisely the wisdom of a cultivated amnesia she has learned;[24] Brontë writes within a world trained by the pilgrim's cudgel to hear only in limited ways and forget the rest. This scene also suggests a truth the novel itself reifies: that (her) language, being power, is subject to (self-)disciplinary strictures, that for a woman to speak or to hear too oracularly is to risk (a desire for) punishment. Only to be "merry," to dream "nothing dreary," to sleep "sweetly" like the child is permissible (p. 72). As Foucault says in "The Discourse on Language," "in every society the production of discourse is at once controlled, selected, organized and redistributed according to a certain number of procedures, whose role is to avert its powers and its dangers, to cope with chance events, to evade its ponderous, awesome materiality."[25] The novelistic mode, moving in 1847 inexorably toward a self-consciously articulated and programmatic realism, imposes its own set of restrictive procedures; it sets its agenda and fulfills its mission. In order to do its work, realism predicates its overt agenda on a priori assumptions of truth and propriety, and it measures those things that deviate from and thus threaten to corrupt these truths; it assumes a community of ideologically compatible listeners – whose parodic equivalents would be the Branderham congregation – who will nod their agreement to both what it approves and what it repudiates.[26] But Brontë, like her spirit(ed) Cathy, appropriates the realist's most pristine library "not altogether for a legitimate purpose" (p. 26).

Brontë's vision, acutely observing, exceeds a narrowly defined realistic mode, spills out of it and thus enriches it. Realism's social, reasonable, and responsible impetus can seem so upright as to generate such arguments as Jon Stratten's, in *The Virgin Text*, that "realism developed as the expression of a society founded on repression";[27] it is, in any event, in realism's best interest to discipline and subdue the erotic potential of the word by linking it to pragmatically deployed materialities (not the least of Brontë's subversive gestures is to use texts aphrodisiacally, so that the virginal, "handsome book . . . in white paper" Cathy places on Hareton's thigh is an initiatory step in arousal). It is, thus, that metonymy reads all contiguous physicalities as reciprocal evidence of realism's accuracy of observation, and materiality may be divested of its nonfunctional status as pleasurable in and of itself.[28] Based overtly on a plea for reason and reasonableness, realism must, at the level of official protocol, preclude "gratuitous" violence, including the violence intrinsic to intense pleasure – it is officially against those extremisms of emotion, instinct, and artistry that erode the avenue to a safe, profitable forward progress – and like other taboos, it may generate its own extremist reactions to its repressiveness (Sade may be said to epitomize, linguistically and sexually, the connections between an intense repression and a correlative extremism; *Wuthering Heights* is also notably "extreme").[29] Realism requires a tacit contract – a gentleman's agreement – with the status quo, and it may thus feel obliged to fill itself with object lessons about those who cannot or do not subscribe. In her poetry, Brontë speaks of the stern rebuke of Reason "to judgment come," prepared to punish the speaker for leaving the "common paths that others run" for a journey down a "strange road"; she invokes her "God of visions," even as she calls him (her slave, comrade, and king) "My darling pain that wounds and sears / And wrings a blessing out from tears."[30] The novel, imbued with this spirit, is so topographic as to trip up those who are syntagmatically inclined, pursuing forward motion down the common path to an (ideological) end:

the Penistone Crags, looming as sheer erotic provocation to exit the loop between Grange and Heights, is a reminder of this density, this visceral attraction to a sublimity that brings one to eschew propriety for its dangerous delights.[31]

Stolidly anti-sublime, Nelly Dean and Lockwood are the interdictory figures who filter Brontë's intensities while simultaneously revealing both the cruelties and the inadequacies of the system for which they speak and from which they perceive: they are thoroughgoing, virtually parodic realists whose ontological convictions preclude alternative apprehensions (they are similarly rigidified, but brought to that state by different roads). As Van Ghent points out, these two "belong firmly to the world of practical reality."[32] They do not merely disallow alternatives but, in the profoundest innocence, fail to see that there may *be* alternatives to their astute realism; they are the purest forms of interdiction, because their ideologies are absolute. And reality may be forced more or less to behave itself within an absolute ideology; every empirical detail, every spiritual vagary, every flight of fancy falls into place, so that Nelly can say "I was superstitious about dreams then, and am still" (p. 72). In this she confirms the realist's social contract, which cheerfully acknowledges the ineffable, and in calling the feeling "superstition" accommodates it benignly within the system. These two even perceive their mistakes as a kind of rectitude, as their errors occur when events deviate from the way they ought to behave. They work from the most logical scenario, eliminating possibilities as they go: Lockwood's puzzling out the question to whom Cathy Linton Heathcliff belongs represents this method, which takes its precedent from the logical game.[33] They thus continually confirm their own mistakes, which they "see" retrospectively when all the particulars are in, and they do so with the unabashed self-congratulation of those whose forgiveness of seventy times seven sins first includes their own defensible – nay, commendable – fallibilities: one can't be expected to see *everything*, since the logical system is susceptible to diachronous caprice.

Lockwood represents the first order of obtuse perspicacity, and as he bumbles around he represents every reader of *Wuthering Heights*. We, as much as he, begin as tenants within this strange book. We *are*, in these first moments, Lockwood, if for no other reason than because there is no one else to be (and, as Bersani says, "a fact about all fictions by an essentially manipulated, passive narrator: they are told from the reader's point of view"[34]). This being the case, Brontë commits another abuse of the fictional contract of realism as she meddles with a proleptic marker: she has Lockwood say that "some people might suspect [Heathcliff] of a degree of underbred pride; I have a sympathetic chord within that tells me it is nothing of the sort: I know, by instinct, his reserve springs from an aversion to showy displays of feeling – to manifestations of mutual kindliness" (p. 15). Now, Lockwood is a gentleman, and when he makes this assessment, one reads it as a prolepsis; by all the rules of the old-boy club and of fiction it *ought* to be revealed as true, because a gentleman is supposed to be able to spot a bounder at first sight. His epistemology equips him for such things, if for nothing else, and when Lockwood says, "I have a sympathetic chord within that tells me. . . . I know, by instinct," one is not to be faulted for taking this as an anamnesis of breeding (p. 15). When Lockwood admits, then, with a kind of ephebic candor, "No, I'm running on too fast: I bestow my own attributes over liberally on him" (p. 15), the realistically inclined reader is not prepared to assume him mistaken. "I knew, through experience, that I was tolerably attractive," Lockwood confirms (p. 21), and he never exits this self-admiration based on the presuppositions of his class and education. His "experience" is so tautological as to confirm and congratulate itself, endlessly. Yet the reader who persists in operating within Lockwood's epistemological mode must maintain faith in his methods, even though Brontë repeatedly makes him (and the reader who trusts him) look like a fool. A socially inclined realism, with its renewable faith in evidential metonymy (truth manifests itself materially within its correct system), seems at once both too cynical and too ingenuous a method for seeing Brontë's world, and that Heathcliff, "in dress and manners a gentleman," utterly confounding his sartorial persona (p. 15) signals from the beginning this potential for discrepancy. The reader who fails to heed Lockwood's mistakes goes like a lamb to the slaughter, a pup to the rope: the innocent, socially integrated realist taken by his own predilections into a Sadeian territory of excess where dead rabbits lie strewn on the cushion where, by all standard conventions, kittens should be curled.

Indeed, Lockwood suffers the exigency of a realist whose prime necessity is to make things fit within his system: that which cannot be accommodated must be excised – the hand that would lead one into an alternative reality must be severed at its wrist. That Lockwood thinks categorically and comfortably within the narrow bounds of habit is made quite clear in his assessment of Nelly's relationship to her class: "Excepting a few provincialisms of slight consequence, you have no marks of the manners which I am habituated to consider peculiar to your class" (p. 58). He is incapable of more than realignments within preexistent categories; his mode is compartmental, a fact that makes his residence in the fatal cupboard-bed a neat spatial irony. He soon discovers that Heathcliff, instead of being "in dress and manners a gentleman," has "a genuine bad nature" (pp. 3, 9); the dialectic is, for him, as simple as good/not good. It is quite comically malicious of Brontë to put such a man into another's bed, to force him to accommodate a strange bedfellow, and it is inevitable that Lockwood suffers nightmares during his confinement.[35] His first dream is a parodic logical game, its permutations multiplying uncontrollably in a way that reveals the weakness of his daylight methodology: the 490 possibilities are all covered, but the 491st will always be a big surprise. If not that one, then the 492nd. And in contrast to his own capacity always to forgive himself his reasonable mistakes, his dream adversaries want to pronounce judgment and enact punishment – "Drag him down, and crush him to atoms, that the place which knows him may know him no more!" (p. 29) – and they become so aroused that they fall to beating one another in a Sadeian ecstasy; having failed once too often within the paternalistic system of limited errors, Lockwood is divested of his "club," which is to say with a dreamer's candor that he is unmanned. What Brontë envisions for Lockwood's second dream is equally telling, as it follows the first with psychosexual inevitability: having been humiliated, both in dream and reality, he now vents his own frustration by mutilating the fragile girl-child (p. 30). Exposing almost at once Lockwood's own sadomasochistic affiliations, Brontë also lays bare realism's potential for enacting a ruthless economy and a necessary protectionism when some alternative reality importunes, with "tenacious gripe," "Let me in – let me in!" (p. 30).

It is not sufficient to see Lockwood only as insufferable, for his density is so profound as to lock him into a parodic version of the realist's system of notation, whereby matter is disciplined to yield meaning in a set of one-to-one correspondences; realism predicates itself on translatability, and Lockwood reveals the logical extension of this assumption of commensurability into egoist incomprehension.[36] He wants all the details from Nelly, chronologically ordered, as if to construct a syntagma; he has a case-study mind for whom circumstantialities are everything in the toting up of values. He operates without apparent skepticism within a system of second and third-order translations, because it is not "meaning" he seeks, but that message "rich in information" that might be stored in bytes.[37] One set of common words is as good as another to represent what he knows can be seen, like bricks that are necessary but interchangeable, and he intuits that he and Nelly are compatible systems. What Nelly gives in a fairly generous periphrastic way, he reduces, forgetting everything "unimportant." He can, thus, paraphrase Nelly's story with no fear that something may be lost: "I'll continue it in her own words, only a little condensed," he says complacently (p. 130), and because he has summed up her previous narrative with "yes, I remember her hero had run off, and never been heard of for three years; and the heroine was married" (p. 80), one knows something of his methods of condensation. Brontë refutes Lockwood's crude synonymity in her own naming, for the Earnshaw and Linton houses are constructed of proper names laid across each other in mobile superimposition: this is the most potent proof that even within the *same* word – "Cathy," or "Earnshaw," or "Heathcliff" – meaning elides and even reverses itself. Yet Lockwood has an ear only for what the realist must consider the main point: an exegesis of place, character, and circumstance that confirms the (political, epistemological, artistic) assumptions of the given realism.

Lockwood's ego-based precision of detail, devoid of any insight into the transformative or hidden nature of matter and the word, is so tautological that it makes him at one level fallible even within realism's most undistracted system; precise in detail, he is weak in the metonymic instincts whereby the realist makes sense of place and personality by making them contiguously interdependent; he suffers the necessary amnesia of the realist, only so acutely as to become almost parodic.[38] It is as if his self-absorption is so profound as to be a virtual malady, a near-madness of narcissism that puts his observatorial powers in the same camp with a figure like Stoker's meticulously logical Renfield. He is so distracted by himself that he can barely extrapolate from toponymy to topography or from topography to toponymy, which is, in part, why he can't be trusted to find his way home in the snowstorm. His most ludicrous error, over and beyond his mistaken reading of Heathcliff, is, in fact, just of this sort, for he proclaims that "Mr. Heathcliff forms a singular contrast to his abode and style of living" (p. 15). If Lockwood doesn't get the palpable metonymic connection between the house and the man, this suggests the fundamental particularity within which he thinks; and the comfort is that when he describes one or the other, we know that it is description untainted by the attempted sophistication of conscious metonymy. Architectural and topographic contiguities, contexts outside the self, are not his strengths, which reside in the ego-tinted perception of particularities.[39] This perceptual weakness displays itself in spatial terms in a kind of cartographic amnesia. When he removes himself for a few months from the material site of Nelly's story, he can barely remember having ever lived there: "Gimmerton? . . . my residence in that locality had already grown dim and dreamy," he says, as if to confirm quite literally the infantile assumption that what is not seen does not exist (p. 258). There have been other explanations for Lockwood's arranging to have Catherine's portrait placed above his mantel, but one reading is that, "seeing" her, he can keep his place in the narrative surrounding her. Lockwood's epistemology is the purest accountability to circumstantial detail; his amnesiac sensibility assures that he will not think consequentially, so that contexts, with their diachronous complexities that hold one from judgment (and thus from punishment), remain for him essentially nonexistent.[40]

In Lockwood's world of particulars there can be no genuine mystery and no real passion; his own stigma is a fatal incapacity to love, his own madness an inability to exit the impenetrable armature of his narcissism, and these are both the causes and the effects of his narrow vision. Like the Sadeian hero, he never for an instant loses his (faulty/perverted) analytical eye to become a yielding body.[41] He reads every text through unblinkingly egoistic eyes that see only how things look to him; thus, only when his eyes are closed in sleep may Cathy attempt to invade his cubicle. It is inevitable that his trauma locate itself within the gaze, that he can "look" his own language to the beautiful young lady at the resort but is appalled when she returns the favor.[42] Within Lockwood's materialist linguistic economy – words for things – there are no secrets, and thus he feels that his gaze reveals the full tale of his passion to "the merest idiot" who cares to watch (p. 15). The world displays itself to the realist's analytical eye with anatomic (im)precision, and thus is it articulated: Lockwood, plumbing Heathcliff's psyche, says that "he turned . . . a peculiar look in her direction, a look of hatred unless he has a most perverse set of facial muscles that will not, like those of other people, interpret the language of his soul" (p. 21). It is fitting that metonymy is the hallmark of realism, as it reveals character piece by piece. (Lockwood's malady reminds one of Sade's syndecdochical logic reducing woman to anus/sewer. Replicating Lockwood's progress from delight to disgust, Sade concludes: "Is it really worthwhile going into raptures over a cloaca?"[43]) So locked within his materialist perceptions, Lockwood can see only material fragments; completely insensitive to the subtle nuances of language, his capacity for synonymity in the case of the female gaze is frightening.

As Sade the anatomist shows us, one cannot articulate beauty (or, indeed, any concomitant value, including "the real") holistically, and in its dissection, a certain recapitulation of terms (for the several orifices, only beginning with the eyes, for the cheeks, for the mounds of forehead, breast, and pubis) is inevitable. Barthes says that "being analytical, language can come to grips with the body only if it cuts it up; the total body is outside language, only pieces of the body succeed to writing; in order to *make* a body *seen*, it must either be displaced, refracted through the metonymy of clothing, or reduced to one of its parts."[44] This is another way of saying that language cannot get at the interstitial spaces where limb is joined to limb, or where beauty is joined to an excitation nameable only in caricature. Beauty succumbs to language that, with its limited sensual vocabulary, links body parts through the act of naming them. Even benignly Petrarchan language creates an erotic series implicitly linking head and body: forehead like snow, eyes like sapphires, lips like cherries, cheeks like roses; breasts like snow, (vulvar) lips like cherries, (nether) cheeks like roses (the paradigm for myths about Cyrano's nose). Sade turns this decorous Petrarchan reticence into explicit linkages between cerebral and erotic physiognomies: cheeks like a springtime rose, mouth like a rosebud, belly like satin; ass like a springtime rose, anus like a rosebud, and so on, in endless sardonic tautologies.[45] One knows through linguistic intuition, then, that Catherine Heathcliff's "unnatural" eyes imply the genital abyss, and her sharp-tongued speech, her red lips, the *vagina dentata*. The realist Lockwood, his faith in the reportorial function of language, like his faith in the metonymic conversions inherent to materialities, unskeptical and intact, is, at his best, no master of reticulation. For one who so perceives the world, to be seen in moments of looking his passion is to be caught *flagrante delicto*; thus the sexual implications of his shrinking icily into himself, "like a snail" (p. 15). Far from erotic, the loved other's gaze becomes particularized enough to frighten Lockwood away, as it is tied, by a metonymic process of downward contiguities linking one aperture with another, with a guilty sexuality that for Lockwood – or for any "virtuous" realist – makes the woman more punishable than desirable (one cannot help, here, thinking of Lockwood and Hawthorne's Coverdale as if, as their names suggest, they are virtual doubles – both ineffectual, enervated, beset by illness, both fearful of women who look them in the eye, both given to a perceptual and imagistic reduction/empowering of women as witches). Lockwood's mode of sightedness anatomizes beauty and thus endlessly defers spirituality by moving reciprocally back and forth between those evidential materialities that keep one tied to the flesh. Incapable of seeing beyond his own (socially valorized) misogyny, Lockwood the realist is, potentially, Lockwood the sadist, whose dreams of bloodletting exhibit what his decorous facade refutes.

Nelly, the good servant, is also absolutely dependable in her account of detail, and in her precision she, like Lockwood, always fails to see the forest for the trees; the crucial differences between them lie in her sex and class, both of which remediate and extenuate her behaviors to a large extent. This being said, however, her unequivocal advocacy of the status quo seems slightly unsavory, as it threatens to relegate her to the position of a (co-opted) duenna.[46] As a servant, she is subject always to the vicissitudes of her masters and mistresses; if she speaks disapproval, "forgets" her place, or remembers too much about family business, she risks being cast out or punished. "To hear you, people might think you were the mistress," Cathy rages. "You want setting down in your right place!" (p. 96). Having "undergone sharp discipline," Nelly has learned the wisdom of a forgetful propriety; that she has been trained by punishments, explicit and implied, to her current "reasonableness" may be inferred from her rigorously pragmatic methodologies. She seems devoid of the capacity to fantasize outside the system of paternalistic realism; instead, she says, she "gather[s] intelligence" (p. 110) for the paternal overlords. If the drama in which she is involved has a precedent, she can function with the autonomy of a decent lawyer; thus, having no doubt looked into, for example, *Clarissa* in the Grange library – though her lack of training allows her no Greek, Latin, or French, no alternative cultural narratives (p. 59) – she is able to predict the erotic consequences of Catherine Linton's secret letters and thus burn them. She knows her catechism and Bible, repositories of patristic authority, and thus she knows how to scold Isabella for her pleasure in Heathcliff's trouble: "Fie, Fie, Miss! . . . One might suppose you had never opened a Bible in your life" (p. 153). But if the narrative is a foreign one, she cannot complete it on her own, so that when Heathcliff overhears Cathy's decision about marrying Edgar, she has no memory for two such extremities as these lovers; not just a realist, she is the parody of an English realist who, unlike her European counterparts, remains sexually ingenuous and who, unlike her American counterparts, remains resistantly "unromantic."[47] Moreover, not feeling the lack, Nelly makes no attempt to alter Heathcliff's misapprehensions.

Nelly is thus given to making errors in judgment; like Lockwood, she can't see too far down the road, and her charges' unfailing capacity to step geographically beyond her boundaries is a reification of this shortsightedness. When Cathy takes to her room in a fury over Heathcliff's and Edgar's behaviors, she becomes (so Nelly discovers after three days of letting her sulk unseen) really quite ill. But this is not Nelly's fault, nor is it her affair, for she has read the signs correctly by her terms, which are also the terms of the pragmatically committed realist. She is the English counterpart of Howells's Reverend Sewell, who will not countenance romantic excess and who slices the knot of the Irene-Corey-Penelope disaster in one definitive pronouncement that it is better for one to suffer than for three; like Sewell, she sees such suffering as more literary than real and therefore without real consequence. All those good English books in the library that she has "looked into, and got something out of also" have reinforced her proprietous notions of reality (p. 59): one puts something in, one gets something out that is roughly equivalent, and the grossly disproportionate consequences of Cathy's tantrum make no sense. Realism's putative commitment to an "economy of pain" is so skewed by some unfathomable excess that Nelly is genuinely bemused.[48] By the realist's rules, a healthy, selfish girl may work herself up, may drop a few pounds, may go a little pale. She may not, by these rules, become so distraught as to endanger herself. The doctor even says so, and his authority in matters of reality can be measured in pounds of flesh: "A stout, hearty lass like Catherine does not fall ill for a trifle" (p. 111). That Catherine has not behaved within the proprieties of Nelly's realism is her own "wicked waywardness" (p. 109), and thus Nelly can say, even on discovering Catherine's anguish, "it is nothing" (p. 109).

One must decide Nelly Dean's fate at the moment of this assertion that Cathy, going mad, is fine: "she would admit none of us till this evening, and so we couldn't inform you of her state, . . . but it is nothing" (p. 109), she tells Linton. If this is a craven lie, designed to ward off Edgar's fury at her negligence, then Nelly is less subtly corrupted by the fear of paternal retribution than we had imagined. We had partially reconciled her unsentimental pragmatism as justified politically by her class (one *must* ask why Nelly should be expected to coddle or to sentimentalize Cathy Earnshaw or Heathcliff), had concurred, if somewhat resignedly, with Charlotte Brontë's assessment of her "true benevolence and homely fidelity" (p. xxvii). But we look for the woman who spits Hindley's knife from between her teeth, that bit being less to her taste than a more covertly sadistic paternalism, and we more or less get her. Only more or less, however, since Nelly herself at times reveals her own taste for sadomasochism: watching Catherine, corpse-like, blood on her lips, cheeks blanched and livid, Nelly tells Lockwood how she urged Edgar to remain resolute in his punishment. " 'There is nothing in the world the matter,' I whispered. I did not want him to yield, though I could not help being afraid in my heart" (p. 102). It is safe to assert that Nelly is less fearful of Edgar than willfully uncomprehending; she is convinced, at the point of Catherine's illness, that "the Grange had but one sensible soul in its walls, and that lodged in my body" (p. 103), and she is quite correct by her definition – the only one she can know – of "sense." Nelly can only believe that this thing she sees in Catherine is "nothing." The terms for the something that Catherine manifests do not exist for her; the language is not there because the conceptual recognition of Catherine's state is nonexistent, and vice versa. She can no more know Catherine's despair than she could hear her dream. Paradoxically, only in that ineffable contradiction produced by her double sense of fear and pleasure at Edgar's coldness, that sadomasochistic voyeurism, lies a tainted connectedness with Catherine's despair. She does not despise Catherine, but is fond of her in an impatient way; she can become, thus, terribly alarmed (p. 104) at Catherine's behavior in the same way that dreams make her "superstitious," without believing for a moment that these feelings may have credibility.

Brontë quite ruthlessly places her story in the mouths of the two people whose language is most insufficient to articulate its enigmas, and thus she reveals the cruel ingenuousness of the system in which they work at the same time that she implies its inadequacies. Nelly Dean and Lockwood are the least reticent of narrators, because they quite literally tell everything they remember. Every circumstantial detail is pellucid in its clarity because it is not fraught with significances beyond the most ordinary, materially bound realist's perceptions. Crucially, neither one is free to be desirous, and whatever their inevitable brushes with the immemorial might be, they each have a significant investment, for different reasons, in repressing these intimations of an unnameable excitation: Lockwood because he cannot bear the female gaze that awakens such terrible anxiety (either for what might be called forth or for what might be discovered lacking), and Nelly because she may well have invested passion in a source – her employer – that necessitates its dispersal. Their agendas, set, are perfectly straightforward, and all details perform their service within these agendas determined by class, gender, and character. For Brontë, sighted, knows that it is no good being Lazarus come back from the dead if no one else is equipped to receive the knowledge one gains there. There is, in this, both frustration and a modicum of safety, for prophets lead dangerous lives, and female prophets are burned as witches. She has an instinct for the terrors of the Inquisition, a sense that anarchic desire must be encoded, disguised in hieroglyphics. Because the "truths" one can tell and expect to have heard are only those for which one's audience is equipped, the profoundest wisdom about the real may be met with howls of derision or inquisitorial torture: one can be locked away as mad for affirming too soon that the earth revolves around the sun. One learns early on that, as Foucault says, "we are not free to say just anything, . . . we cannot simply speak of just anything, when we like or where we like; not just anyone, finally, may speak of just anything."[49] Brontë does not, thus, place her secret knowledge in the hands of those who might inadvertently reveal it. It is as if she has slipped some dangerous contraband into the luggage for Lockwood and

Nelly to carry to its destination all unknowing, and if they should be stopped and questioned, even if they should be tortured (and her fictional world is rife with that possibility of torture and with the sense that the torturer eagerly awaits his pleasures), they cannot reveal what they do not know, and thus they cannot implicate her. They are thus almost as unsentimental as child narrators; what James has Maisie know, Nelly and Lockwood know here, and that is how to describe scenes and events despite – or indeed because of – innocence of their significance beyond the realisms resident in mundane things. But like the child, they keep getting the analysis mucked up. One comes to recognize, if only subliminally, the serious limitations inherent in realism's necessary dependence on an amnesiac taxonomy, whereby one reality is circumstantially detailed only by forgetting all others; these are people who make error after error, and because they cannot step outside their own rigid ontologies, they are doomed to continue forever making the same kinds of errors. Yet, never learning, always availing themselves of the retroactive justifications their system affords, they will always exact punishment from those who function for them as alterities (Heathcliff, a Lascar, a Spaniard, a gypsy, is Brontë's embodiment of this truth).

Just as Lockwood's dream-state may be said to reveal the necessary cruelty of the realist's egoistic economy, so Nelly's response to Cathy's illness suggests the retributive, potentially sadistic capacity within realism. Nelly is another of those hardened "Hands" whose function as a metonymous extension of her service within a corrupt environment has given her an enhanced capacity for harm arising directly out of her diminished possibilities within a larger sphere. In a given realism, cause and effect become both equivalent and reciprocal, as do the uses of "meaning," which perpetually adjusts itself to maintain the status quo of that realism; thus actions, events, and characters do not merely develop through forward motion, but are redefined retroactively. In this kind of system, people are seen *to be* what happens to them, in a fierce tautology of retroactive justice.[50] Nelly cannot compassionate Cathy because Cathy is a transgressor who behaves and reacts according to some non-Nellian, "unrealistic" system. Within Nelly's realism, it is not sufficient that Cathy is desperately unhappy, desperately ill; her condition is itself a deserved "punishment" for her excesses, which are confirmed as excesses by the weight of the punishment inflicted.

(Again, Sade clarifies this reasoning: Justine is a fine example, as her virginal, blue-eyed gaze and fair skin are felt to beg, by virtue of their bruisability, to *be* bruised, much as Heathcliff envisions "painting" bruises on Isabella's irresistible palette, her "mawkish" face, p. 93.) Brontë knows, too, that it will not be only Nelly who feels this way, but most readers as well; trained to a paternalism that demands "justice," we all become judges, and judges require evidence, demand "proof," inflict punishment. In this dispensation of judgment after the fact, one feels metonymy's reciprocal energy, for if the punishment is made to fit the crime, one could also say with grim irony that the "crime" is often adjudged only after the fact of some otherwise inexplicable punishment – a metonymous vengeance, indeed. Cathy is dying of grief; operating within the realist's system of commensurability, we must suspect that, being so punished, she must deserve her punishment.

This recognition – that, realistically speaking, the world does not tolerate intense pain or ecstatic pleasure, but must explain and justify them, even retroactively, by making them culpable – is at the very heart of *Wuthering Heights*, and one has not so far to go from this insight to a fictional world that delights in punishment. *This* is the sin past all forgiveness, the 491st sin: this sheer suffering, this madness of (artistic) desire, that cannot be alleviated or assuaged or satisfactorily accounted for by any terms the realist knows. One can just glimpse its face by gazing obliquely at Cathy and Heathcliff. One resents that which cannot be saved – again, the Branderham congregation makes this message explicit – and Brontë's novel, permeated with sadomasochism, suggests that she understands the self-preservatory instinct to delight in punishing what has proved itself to be punishable and therefore is deserving of punishment. Brontë is a woman writing, and this alone, were there no other anomalies of place, circumstance, or personality, makes working within the realistic mode a form of mimicry or ventriloquism (thus the narrative structure); more explicitly, she is a woman writing from an enriched, multidimensional reality, one that subsequently has been devalued as Gothic or perverse, and thus the dynamics of punishment infiltrate a text that presumes to contest its own structural and epistemological imperatives. In "The Philosopher's Conclusion," she has her philosopher cry, "No promised Heaven, these wild Desires / Could all or half fulfill – / No threatened Hell, with quenchless fires, / Subdue this quenchless will," and yet the speaker prays for death as the turbulent streams of her desires tumble into "an inky sea": Brontë's pen will not resolve its flow into the Apollonian clarity of the page illuminated by reason.[51]

Brontë has an acute sense of the double text of which she is the author (this image is, of course, notably reified within her story), and if she is writing between the lines about spiritual, sexual, and artistic oppressions, she is also writing *on the line* as well. Obliquely addressing the consequences of her realist methodology that examines the world piece by material piece and then extrapolates spirit from physicalities, she lays bare the Sadeian impulses that may inform such accountabilities, such rigorous defining and delimiting of terms. If the word is made flesh in realism, it is flesh that may be anatomized, flayed to reveal its component parts. Brontë, no more than Cathy with her tight interlinear interpolations, does not then merely appropriate the masculine book, for she senses that it is *not enough* to have co-opted the paternal text. A pleasure, perhaps, it is also a kind of degradation. Brontë recognizes that, using the language of paternalism and of realism, she must not simply attack or simply subvert paternalistic systems (of literature or of society); using that language, she must feel herself complicit in its punitive force, even as she senses what she makes so clear within the novel: that women will bear the brunt of its habit of aggrandizing itself by degrading what it defines as alterities. For a woman with this knowledge, writing is itself a pleasurable pain as the revelatory and ecstatic repudiate language's insufficiency to reveal them and repudiate realism's virtuous propagandas. Realism, at the level of its social program, wields the knife – its duty to bring everything into its own systematic propagandas and to excise that which cannot be made to fit. The relationship between text and text, between the "legitimate" lines and the feminine interpositions, is dialogic; the female text answers back, and this is, as Sade's world makes most explicitly clear, the most punishable of sins for a woman.[52] Thus, within the book the bitch is hanged, almost to her last gasp, and so, too, are the whelps: the woman and her text may both be excised.[53]

Brontë's creation of the consumptive Linton Heathcliff is a stunning reification of the personal and dual implication she feels in this hardest of "realisms" that brings language always back to "justice" and punishment: he is a cautionary portrait of the artist as rendered in-valid by fear, an object lesson for those who would give in to hysteria, defeat, or terror in a world ruled by a paternalistic realism. Reduced to a parodic androgyny, neither man nor woman, neither child nor adult, he resides in a terrible limbo; yet if he manages to come of age, he will most certainly be eradicated by the father.[54] His hand is guided, quite literally, by the father's words and cruel threats; his letters of wooing are perverted by Heathcliff to effect Heathcliff's own erotic desire to inflict pain and to gain power and property. Divested of all stoicism, terrified by endless brutalities, motherless, Linton is made to be ignoble and undesirable – guilty – by his own pain, which must exist for him in profoundest isolation because no one else can fully understand or forgive him for suffering it. Sadistically, he passes on to others the pains he has received, others who cannot or will not hurt him, for he has been degraded by the father into a nightmare creation of physical and spiritual ruin; he is the text overwritten and dominated by the father, who "talks enough of . . . defects, and shows enough scorn" to make Linton think himself vile (p. 203). He is a test few can pass, either within the story or outside of it, and that Catherine Linton comes close is evidence of the regenerative power that will rescue two ancient houses: "I know he has a bad nature. . . . But I'm glad I've a better, to forgive it; and I know he loves me, and for that reason I love him," she tells Heathcliff (p. 228).

Linton Heathcliff is the pure embodiment of Brontë's insight into the complementary and endlessly regenerative relationship between sadism and masochism – "I heard him draw a pleasant picture to Zillah of what he would do [to Cathy], if he were as strong as I," says Heathcliff (p. 228) – as he stands within the text both for that weakness that should be most profoundly pitiable and that weakness that is most viscerally disgusting and most makes one want to see him punished. By the metonymic reasoning of realism, his character, flawed and puny, is merely manifested outwardly in his crippled and wasted body. As his body goes, so goes his character; as his character goes, so goes his body, inexorably consumed in a tautology predicated on culpability and punishment. Brontë addresses pain with an utter lack of sentimentality; she creates a world as treacherous and cruel as is imaginable, and then she looks for those who, bereft, brutalized, or abandoned, nonetheless refuse to be corrupted by their own sufferings even as they are educated by them. Brontë reifies both the (female) artist's dilemma and her triumph in her characters: Linton is a dark casualty to paternal sadism, while Cathy and Hareton prevail. That they have resisted the dual seductions of sadomasochism – loving neither to inflict pain nor to bear it – suggests that the artist, too, may find her way with some dignity in a phallocracy.

She sets herself the most rigorous of tests, however. Enacting a matricidal necessity that will give her the power, and the danger, of the pen,[55] she reifies this claim to artistic autonomy within the text as she removes the first order of protection from all of her characters with ruthless precision: She dispenses completely with mothers and maternal figures in *Wuthering Heights*, leaving within the text a paternally dominated structure that mimics a system of authorship predicated on a unilateral and unequivocal realism.[56] It may be argued more generally that mothers are no more compatible to the realistic mode than they are to the Sadeian, at least mothers who fulfill their maternal functions wisely and well. Feminist philosophers, in searching for a distinctively female epistemology, have defined a "maternal ethic" as one in which retributive actions are patiently deferred. Recognizing the contextual above the immediate, the spiritual potential above the determinisms of material surroundings, the maternal ethic finds its model in child-rearing, and its antithesis in the epistemological patterns Lockwood manifests.[57] The good mother does not enact, inflict, or impose her own reality on her child, but proceeds with watchful respect to keep the child safe during its progress toward selfhood. This necessitates a procedure alternative to the judgmental and retributive impulses inherent in rationalist thinking. One should be, Murdoch says, "watchful" of others, with eyes that are not predisposed by egoism;[58] by these terms, Lockwood's malady, located so specifically within the gaze, is a direct consequence of his penchant for his own egoistic reality. Yet this acceptance of things as they are, rather than things as they "should be," does not play well within the realist's social and political agendas, for it argues against action, reformist and otherwise, and for conservation – a suspension of judgmental and punitive reaction. Thus, nineteenth-century novels are filled with compromised and killed-off mothers. By the terms of the maternal ethic, Cathy Linton's despair would inspire in the maternal figure the deepest empathy; the point would be her pain, not its justifiability. Healing would prevail over chastisement. One need not dispute the rarity of this ethic *in the world* (Mrs. Earnshaw would "fling [the foundling] out of doors," p. 39) or argue against the impossibility of its full realization to see that the idea has experiential roots and a non-paternalistic agenda. This dichotomy generates dialectical energy, and in excising the mother, Brontë thus leaves the paternalistic mode to go unchecked.

Paternalism taken to one of its extremities, sadomasochism reduces and clarifies the relationship between highly systematized, self-enclosed order and punishment, and it locates women within this structure as the most debased of the debased; Sade distills the truths implicit to sadomasochism, and he articulates its relationship to women with a candor that strips away the pretenses of a less overtly misogynous vision. One finds in Sade that the enumeration of women's parts reveals both a tangible and a systemic perversion of the male body – that essential, undeniable realism of correct form.[59] (Freud institutionalizes this tautology: Women *must* regret the lack of a penis, for it is inconceivable to him, who presumably has such a lovely one, that they would not.[60]) Sadism is, by Krafft-Ebing's account, virtually confined to males, and his case studies corroborate Sade's pleasure in excision, in scoriation, in mutilation: women's bodies invite the sadist's knife, and if he takes pieces of femality away with him, whether out of covetousness or disgust, his surgeries address at once both the punishable difference and the exquisite sameness.[61] Among the sadist's pleasures is the enumeration of the anatomy by marking it as having been counted and scourged simultaneously: "I'd wrench [her nails] off her fingers," says Heathcliff, in a sadist's version of "This Little Piggy" that is also a reprise of Lockwood's dream (p. 93). As a type, the sadist is the realist taken to his furthest extreme, as he first physically accounts for and then slices off or rebukes all parts that from his perspective as a man appear to be systemic anomalies.[62] In a world that harbors that from which Sade takes his cues, Brontë senses the danger of *l'écriture féminine*, for to write the female body within a masculinist system is to enact a self-mutilation. Yet to be cowed by threats of violence or by pain is to become Linton Heathcliff, that nightmare of compromised sexuality and humanity.

Brontë, on the line, seems to have had a Tiresian vision that vouchsafed her some insight into the kind of paternal "reality" that could produce Sade, and she incorporates, as if by uncanny instinct, Sade's own sense of the metonymously endowed enclosures that reify the tautologies within which such realities confirm and justify themselves.[63] Both her imprisoning

spatial organizations and her incestuous kinship patterns confirm her suspicion of the circularity intrinsic to a realism that confirms itself through
its own observation. Sade, being what Barthes defines as a "logothete," is
the realist particularized, for his system of language creates and sustains an
inviolable, incestuous reality that does not brook linguistic interference; he
takes the tautological justification to a fine and curious art and reifies his
linguistic self-sufficiency in his mathematical elaborations on the theme of
incest (another version of the logical game). Sade makes women the most
deservedly punishable of all his victims, but it is wives, mothers, and sisters
who most necessitate correction through degradation, as their kinship enforces their inexcusable differences from their husbands, sons, and brothers.[64] Working within a realist's system of reciprocal metonymies, Brontë
senses this Sadeian truth and thus, like Sade, invents an incestuous system
of kinship that intensifies Heathcliff's loathing and his rage; all of the bodies
in this world of hers share those genetic markers that justify and provoke
Heathcliff's punishment of them. All metonymous reminders of Cathy
Earnshaw, either by opposition or by similarity (the eyes, the mouths, the
hair, the gaits, the very bodies), proclaim their need for punishment by
being, so provokingly and provocatively, both Cathy and not Cathy, which
is also a way of saying that they are all both Heathcliff and not Heathcliff,
that they infuriate him with their otherness, making explicit the fierce
solipsism implicit within the realist's vision.[65] Brontë apprehends the univocal nature of a given realism, with its metonymous appropriation of the
world to its needs, and she embodies it in Heathcliff's subsuming of all the
world into his own voracious reality. It is not simply every detail of his
world – every flagstone, cloud, tree, the very air (p. 255) – that feeds his
one realism, but every body as well: "The most ordinary faces of men and
women – my own features mock me with a resemblance. The entire world
is a dreadful collection of memoranda that she did exist, and that I have
lost her!" (p. 255): the serpent's tail down the serpent's throat.

Heathcliff embodies the self-mutilation one must suffer to work within
a system of (ideologically driven) realism. When Cathy speaks of her unity
with Heathcliff, she articulates a natural form: "My love for Heathcliff
resembles the eternal rocks beneath. . . . I *am* Heathcliff! He's always, always in my mind – not as a pleasure, any more than I am always a pleasure
to myself, but as my own being" (p. 74). Yet this union is from the be-

ginning harried out of doors, refused sanctuary or domicile. Cathy herself records their expulsion from Eden: Having made themselves snug in the arch of the oak dresser, Cathy fastens their pinafores together and hangs them for a curtain. The arch functions as both stage and house (and allows them to "play house," with its connotations of eroticism and of fantasy), and the two pinafores signal the innocence of their intimacy. Within the spatial symbolisms that pervade the novel, their placement beneath the organizational cupboard suggests that their fantasy is a quite literal enactment of Brontë's subtextual energies; that Joseph, crying "shame," rends the veil and drives them out is inevitable (p. 27). This dresser, which figures so significantly throughout, appears first in the text to Lockwood, and it is a figure of evisceration that predicts retroactively that it can remain no sanctuary: "its entire anatomy lay bare to an inquiring eye," and it is over-laid with "clusters of legs of beef, mutton, and ham" (p. 14).[66] Beneath it is the "huge, liver-coloured bitch," guardian of Heathcliff's possessions, and her "swarm of squealing puppies" (p. 15). Appropriated temporarily by Cathy/Heathcliff, the underside of the dresser is one integrated world in which love and play and the play of fantasy are inextricable, but appro-priated by paternalism it becomes a figure of anatomized functionality, the bitch underneath turned watchdog for the master. "Cathy-Heathcliff" can-not exist as one name within the realist's intuition of a dichotomizing system of world and self; there is no name to speak the form of a total humanity, *uncompromised*, sublime: Cathy's testament is not mere roman-ticism, but a most literal assertion of Brontë's sense that salvation lies in discovering the *whole* name, which is the name of the maternal father and the phallic mother[67] – not parts, not things represented metonymically, not crude synonymies, not the "truth" of that realistic mode whose agenda does not merely shape the forward movement of the text but works ret-roactively and archeologically to reduce its complexities to a definable *telos*. For a time, Cathy can retreat to her daughter-name or to her wife-name, but when Heathcliff returns, she loses those names. Pregnant, she is filled with another name that is yet the same name – Catherine – delivered of it, she ceases to exist, as if she is canceled out. But Heathcliff must exist within the truncation of his one name – the name of the dead son – after Cathy is excised from his life, made into half a being, with all that is Cathy/female cut away: "Oh God! it is unutterable!" he cries, as if to affirm the death of that ungendered name (p. 139). His obsession with conjoining coffins is thus utterly consequential to a fantasy of wholeness: "I'll have it made so, and then, by the time Linton gets to us, he'll not know which is which!" (pp. 228–9). And not knowing, one must love both together or love none.

With the acute instinct of one who extrapolates from the realist's tautological self-justifications the extremities to which the paternalist/realist system may give rise in its sublimation of the ineffable, Brontë vivifies a Sadeian hero. It is as if she objectifies her most potent fantasy of pure force – her own – in order to contain it, and by following paternalism's laws to their bleakest outposts, she ends up inevitably in Sade's territory. Harold Bloom (like Van Ghent) sees her as deriving her insights primarily from the flourishing "cult" of Byron: "Byron's passive – aggressive sexuality – at once sadomasochistic, homoerotic, incestuous, and ambivalently narcissistic – clearly sets the pattern for the ambiguously erotic universes of *Jane Eyre* and *Wuthering Heights*."[68] Yet one must also, as Swinburne did, apprehend an originality of insight that exceeds external influence. Just as Shakespeare and Aeschylus are originals, so, too, is Brontë, says Swinburne: "The book is what it is because the author was what she was; this is the main and central fact to be remembered."[69] Embodied, the paternal no longer functions as muse/destroyer (though she often called on the masculine muse to inform her poetry, she seems to have felt that she could not overmaster the alien and potentially brutal powers that muse would visit upon her).[70] Embedded, Heathcliff may become part of an enriched vision, a purgative, Frankensteinian animus: surgically molded into a quintessence of masculinity, the Byronic hero laid open to reveal that unregenerate egoism that lies beneath the romantic facade, he finds his brotherhood to Sade even – or most especially – as created through the innocence of Brontë's gaze.[71] Like the Sadeian libertine, he sees himself as the most consummate of realists, acting according to a precise and inviolable logic based on an ideology of necessary evil that takes nature as its justification and political and social power structures as its working models.[72] He enacts his violence according to a rigorous "justice" that accords perfectly with his sense that he is the most realistic of all the realists – the least sentimental, one of the few not co-opted by an official legal system that has capitulated to the cowardice of a fainthearted "morality." "Had I been born where laws are less strict and tastes less dainty," says Heathcliff, "I should treat myself to a slow vivisection of those two, as an evening's amusement"; Brontë could hardly be more explicit in her conflation of the analytic and the erotic into a cruel alliance, and implicit to the image is the cannibalistic greed of the sadist, whose "less dainty" tastes are piqued by the fantasy of consuming the opposition.[73] Consummately analytic, he boasts of his cool prudence and excels in the Sadeian refinement of "pulling out the nerves with red-hot pincers" (p. 143). Heathcliff's only available arousal is in sadism, which feeds itself on its own cerebrality; as Beauvoir says of Sade, "the male aggression of the sadist hero is never softened by the usual transformation of the body into flesh. He never for an instant loses himself in his animal nature; he remains so lucid, so cerebral, that philosophic discourse, far from dampening his ardor, acts as an aphrodisiac."[74] Heathcliff replaces his loss of Cathy with the arousal implicit in judgment, in the friction between conceptualizing transgression and repudiating it, but it is this very cerebral virtuosity that keeps from him the visitation he most desires. Brontë's is, as Bataille says, a "dream of a sacred violence," and she reifies her dream within the text in a ghost that may effect, all at once, Heathcliff's annihilation, his transfiguration, and his ecstasy.[75] Yet this holy ghost will not come to him until his eyes are fully opened – beyond Lockwoodian sightedness, beyond Sadeian judgment – although he cries, "Come in! come in! . . . do come. Oh do – *once* more! Oh! my heart's darling! hear me *this* time" (p. 33). Thus, perhaps, his wide-eyed gaze of exultation in death, the alternative rigor of a terrible and sacred visitation.

Heathcliff becomes, then, the sadist who recapitulates his own divestment by inflicting similar pain on others, by degrading women for being that part of himself that he most regrets having had excised, and by bringing everything within the bounds of his own corruption; he performs a parodic reduction of terms analogous to the realist's necessarily assimilative mode. Like Sade, who was obsessed with gathering up, counting, taking in, controlling, ingesting, he becomes purely acquisitive, taking the realist's notions of accounts payable and receivable to its extremity.[76] Heathcliff's consumption is compulsive: "avarice is growing with him a besetting sin," says Cathy soon after his reappearance (p. 90). He increases his stock in Earnshaw's house until it is his, and he assimilates the Grange and all its furnishings as well.[77] He appropriates his son, and Earnshaw's son. He confines Isabella; he steals Catherine Linton and locks her in. He systematically keeps others from even the things he has no use for himself, and he locks away his possessions compartmentally, with jealous care. The most notably pathological (and most explicitly Sadeian) extension of this compulsive ingestion of others' things is Heathcliff's necrophilia, his desire to possess the corpse of the woman he has both tormented and loved – "when I saw her face again – it is hers yet – he had hard work to stir me" from the grave, says Heathcliff (p. 228) – and with the explicit coprophilia of the sadist, Heathcliff reiterates his fantasy of joined coffins, where he will subsume the dissolution that was Cathy.[78] And as does the sadist, he "remains attached to the victim of his lust and to the individuality of that victim whose sufferings he would like to prolong 'beyond the bounds of eternity – if eternity has any.' "[79] Heathcliff imagines an ecstatic punishment for himself and his beloved that extends beyond death and thus continues retroactively to define present realities. He gets into everything, but he shares nothing; if one aperture is closed to him, he violates another (as does the sadist), coming in through windows when doors are shut against him. Endowed with the rapacity of the Sadeian hero, Heathcliff epitomizes Brontë's sense of the imperialistic/sadistic nature of a paternally driven, univocal realism.

Heathcliff, assimilating everything, is the consummate organizer, the plot-maker *par excellence*, the logothete, and that which hesitates to conform to his plan or to fulfill his agenda he whips into shape; conversely, and at the same time, he unveils the incipient madness in realism's purposefulness when that productivity is driven by some phantasm – Cathy – of the unnameable (Renfield epitomizes this condition, driven by a "Master" to enact the precise and internally reasonable tautology of his own coprophagic account-book). Like the realist, Heathcliff creates fictions explicitly and only to suit his purposes; as with the sadist, the pleasure he derives is in the fiction's power to suborn "good" (virtue, as defined by the status quo) by using the devices of realism with an explicitly manipulative intent to coerce.[80] And yet if his logical progressions, his sheer coercion of the word, affiliate him with the realist, he also, by his very extremity, simultaneously suborns that realism; Heathcliff is, in this, an embodiment of a reality unsaying itself into nihilism, and his physical undoing, a similar de-manifestation, ironically mirrors this.

His account of Isabella's elopement is evidence of his power to drive out alternative truths, even for the reader who knows his capacity for pragmatic or sadistic dissimulation, leaving nothing; this scene enacts, as well, yet another of realism's self-referentialities, devices that show a story deconstructing itself, as if to warn against any ingenuous trust in the reality at hand.[81] He creates for Nelly an elaborate story of Isabella's degradation, including the assertion most damning to her character: that the hanging of her spaniel excited her (this is true to the sadist's assumption that that which is abused asks to – "wants to" – be abused). "No brutality disgusted her – I suppose she has an innate admiration of it" (p. 127). The force of his "realistic," circumstantial account is such that Isabella's rebuttal, "Don't put faith in a single word he speaks. He's a lying fiend! a monster, and not a human being!" (p. 128), cannot be entirely effective; once more, the reader, implicated through the realist epistemologies of Nelly and Lockwood, is urged to equate Isabella's punishment with some necessary psychosexual crime and finally can believe neither one nor the other. Even after Heathcliff shows himself explicitly capable of using language as deceit as he orchestrates Linton Heathcliff's letters to the Grange, the force of his self-serving narrative about Isabella cannot be dismissed; the reader is suborned into a judgmental passivity that mimics Nelly's constant state of indignant impotence. Heathcliff wrenches language to his purposes with the same pleasure that marks the sadist's manipulation of his environment; he forces everything to work for his acquisitive agenda, to perform his particular reality. His entire narrative is predicated on the culpable and therefore punishable Lintons and Earnshaws, and he brings them both linguistically and physically to enact the terms of his realism. He degrades language, much as he degrades daughters, sons, and wives, by forcing it to yield only that which gives him the sadist's ratiocinative pleasure, and he reveals the nihilism lurking beneath one's unitary faith in the concept of the "real."

Working as she does in the nexus between realism and some unnameable other mode, Brontë implicates her readers in a bivalent world, with two guises of paternalism on one side and some other, inarticulable vision on the other – some sightedness whose metaphor has to reside within the text in a palpable but unspeaking ghost presence, one that refutes synthesis and sublation and finally brings the paternal force of retribution – Heathcliff's "moral teething" (p. 128) – to consume itself after long feeding off others' pain. Catherine feels herself torn between Edgar's kindness and Heathcliff's cruelty, and yet she sees them to be two sides of the same materialist coinage that is predicated on commensurability and use. She sees them both as sadists: "Your bliss lies . . . in inflicting misery" (p. 97). "You have killed me – and thriven on it" (p. 132). Killed off by them, subjected even after death to Heathcliff's necrophiliac fantasies, herself eaten up within a system that insists on a commodifiable transubstantiation based on the realities of profit and loss, Cathy may, after death, exact her own payment by merely standing before her lover. She does not *do* anything but manifest herself, and it is Heathcliff's own predisposition to have and get that destroys him. His masculine, Sadeian mind is the weapon Brontë sees as turning against him; the very idea of Cathy has, Heathcliff says, "devoured my existence. I am swallowed in the anticipation of its fulfillment" (p. 256). Brontë takes the fantasy of a system coprophagically consuming itself to its final extreme. The sadist's compulsion for acquisition finally includes his capacity to cannibalize himself: a "moral teething" indeed.[82]

That "realism" – as a genre or as a mode of thought – demands accountability and equivalence is a knowledge discovered firsthand by the mortally ill (or by the raped, the war-damaged, the holocaust survivor), who can no longer operate within the system because their reality exceeds its parameters; such knowledge is also sometimes visited on the artist, whose relationship to language or to materialities refutes the realist's necessary one-to-one contract. "I am dead," says the holocaust survivor, ironically aware of the displacement from commonality that has occurred. I am Dante returned from the underworld, Lazarus back from the grave, says Eliot. I am Cathy escaped from her coffin, says Brontë, and I am Heathcliff the demon. Brontë's rigor in exposing irreconcilable realities is so undeviating and fierce as to become (a) nearly unbearable (pleasure). It has been said that her vision has the barbarous candor of childhood, but it may, alternatively, or additionally, be argued that it is informed by a deep apprehension of a system that, bespeaking itself, perpetuates its own punitive desires. "Nonethical," says Van Ghent, "the book seizes, at the point where the soul feels itself cleft within and in cleavage from the universe, the first germs of philosophic thought, the thought of the duality of human and nonhuman existence, and the thought of the cognate duality of the psyche."[83] Brontë knows the terrorist potential of language (Calvinism must have provided for her a neat and obvious reminder[84]), but she refuses to become herself a terrorist, eliminating alternative dialogues. She refuses to count one realism as systemic even as she works within the mode of realism; she declines to use her Sadeian perceptions propagandistically by refusing to extrapolate her reality only from the power/punishment dynamic (this is an antisystematic tendency foreign to a masculinist epistemology).

Another way of putting it is that she apprehends and compassionates a weakness among the brotherhood that she refuses to exploit, that her work thus becomes a most potent subversion of the cruelties of a masculinist system whose pathology almost necessarily resides in sadomasochism, that her realism is a highly enriched version of the basic model emanating from within the brotherhood, as it *sees* a world of shared forms and prevailing forces through eyes less egoistic than the Lockwoodian norm. Sadomasochism, and necrophilia, incest, child abuse, coprophilia – Brontë seems to set out on an enumeration of all the 490 separate sins that can be designated within a system based on strict equivalences of cause and effect. Her gaze is unflinching as it lays bare the methods by which humans caught within a purely legalistic system may punish others and themselves, and in so doing find their most exquisite pleasures in punishment and in pain. Yet she conceives, without judgmental horror, of a muted Sadeian world – her world, *the* world, in all its pathos, as it accommodates itself to pain by learning to desire and to inflict pain. It might be said, with a certain inescapably painful irony, that she is capable, despite his every excess, of loving her brother(s)[85] – loving them, it must also be said, even knowing, as she must, that the brotherhood cannot exit the politics of friendship to embrace her in its turn.

Chapter Six

A Tropology of Realism in Hard Times

The following are facts which no man attempts to deny:—

1. Large numbers of honest and industrious people are badly fed, badly clothed, and badly housed.

2. Many thousands of people die every year from preventable diseases.

3. The average duration of life amongst the population is very short.

4. Very many people, after lives of toil, are obliged to seek refuge in the workhouse, where they die despised and neglected, branded with the shameful brand of pauperism.

5. It is an almost invariable rule that those who work hardest and longest in this country are the worst paid and the least respected.

6. The wealthiest men in our nation are men who never did a useful day's work.

7. Wealth and power are more prized and more honored than wisdom, or industry, or virtue.

8. Hundreds of thousands of men and women, willing to work, are unable to find employment.

9. While on the one hand wages are lowered on account of over-production of coal, of cotton, and of corn, on the other hand many of our working people are short of bread, of fuel, and of clothing.

10. Nearly all the land and property in this country are owned by a few idlers, and most of the laws are made in the interests of those few rich people.

11. The national agriculture is going rapidly to ruin to the great injury and peril of the State.

12. Through competition millions of men are employed in useless and undignified work, and all the industrial machinery of the nation

is thrown out of gear, so that one greedy rascal may overreach
another.

—Robert Blatchford, *Merrie England* (1894)

Hard Times

Just as the dream "is a (disguised) fulfillment of a (suppressed or repressed)
wish," so is Dickens's tropology in *Hard Times*[1] a condensation of the sterile
landscape of industrialism into a more enriched, less linearly inclined medium:[2] The daylight, paternal authority by which "realisms" are claimed
and displayed comes up against the venereal inclinations of language – hard
times, indeed. All those square-faced men insistent on flagellating their
daughters, their pupils, their constituents, and their very Hands with those
stinging, occlusive words, "Fact, fact, fact! . . . [and] Fact, fact, fact!" come
up against females who elude the program in one way or another – vixens
all, not one woman can be trained to speak the language.[3] No more will
Dickens bring language completely to a purely proprietous realism, to do
the father's service of instating a clear code between addressor and addressee
that holds no secrets *for its designated audience*, a "realism" in which, as is
both customary and necessary, the basic terms are agreed on beforehand.[4]
In the explicit gestures of plot, Gradgrind's resolute scourging of "fancy,"
his unreserved disapproval toward all carnival things, and his anxieties about
acrobatics and hostlership suggest that, for him, these compose a periphrasis
for sexuality and thus are felt as subversive of the realist's (and the father's)
socially oriented agenda, which is driven by a more sublimated form of
desire (these contorted bodies, simulacra of some ecstatic fit, these virile
horses and their handlers, are things no young girl, no daughter of his,
should see).[5] Gradgrindism's repression of every available outlet for the play
of fantasy – the not-real – generates within the story the extremisms of
both Tom's debauchery and Louisa's blank depression. Correlatively, Dickens's chosen setting within the most rigorous of anti-romantic red-brick
"realisms" generates his surreal tropology of madness and nihilism.

Hard Times reveals itself always at two competing levels, and if the Coketown mills spin out Dickens's political agenda, there is as well another

"factory." Dickens names himself within the text as "Time," that force which gradually weaves character into complexity, and whose factory is in a secret place, whose work is noiseless, and whose Hands are mutes (p. 87). "Time," the weaver-artist, complicates realism's reformist social program as it inevitably complicates the synchronous metonymies by which character is locked into the materialities of a limited time and space to enact its predetermined role.[6] Time reveals instead that the hidden and unspeakable – that which emerges in dreams and in poetry – is a potent alternative "reality" whose metonymies reciprocate to a transformative inner landscape. Yet Bounderby's power-looms do in truth weave a new kind of fate and spin a new kind of dream about which Dickens's realism must speak, despite the threat to the artist posed by this mechanically inclined world and the exponentially increasing obligation to address its problems. Dickens thus takes on, in *Hard Times*, an industrial-based reality that repudiates all that is fanciful, and he does so all the more effectively as he also implicitly problematizes the rigorously "realistic" and therefore fanciless mode this system demands of his artistry. *Hard Times*, with its serious moral intent and its condensed length, reacts with a surfeit of fancy, a density of absurdist language games, and a series of characters so conflictually denominated as to become a parade of correlatives for the artist's impasse between duty and pleasure. Dickens's instinct for the "unfathomable mystery" of human character and for the "secret place" in which art is made tells him that "realism" is, in every case, an epistemologically complex, overdetermined notion (pp. 64, 87), that character defined metonymically by the prescribed materialities of its circumstantial reality is character reduced to thesis and antithesis, and that language willfully held to the more overtly propagandistic agendas of realism turns on itself. His desire for what one might call "justice" and his awareness of his fully enfranchised place within a brotherhood that will understand him ensure that he will address the realities of the industrial state nonetheless.

The massive and extended Preston strike (over 20,000 people out of work, lasting from September 1853 through April 1854), whose exigencies demanded Dickens's attention, itself generated in the press a vision of hyperbole balanced against control. The fancy and bombastic rhetoric of Mortimer Grimshawe, Dickens's Gruffshaw, in the *Household Words* piece "On Strike," was played against the relative moderation of strike organizer

George Cowell's leadership. Cowell is described by Geoffrey Carnall in "Dickens, Mrs. Gaskell, and the Preston Strike" as "a most effective speaker, a master of Lancashire idiom, transparently sincere, resolute, exercising his authority with good-humored decisiveness."[7] Grimshawe, on the other hand, the "Thunderer of Lancashire," proposed radical social reorganization and spoke a language designed to move the strikers to a less reserved rebellion.[8] Grimshawe was not held, either by the press or by the workers, to be representative of the workers' position in the strike. According to Carnall, the press generally commented on the silent dignity and the control of the workers even as it manifested a significant ambivalence about the strike itself: The *Daily News* wrote that "there is something almost sublime . . . in the spectacle of so many thousands of human beings, actuated more or less by angry feelings, waiting quietly while their case was being decided.'"[9] This silence was, as Carnall implies, both reassuring – because it signaled the workers' rejection of violence as a programmatic response to their dilemma – and frightening, as it revealed the sense of unified power, where "the individual was merged in the mass, and that mass 'subjected to the action of a powerful external force.' "[10]

The multiple complexities (the ambivalence toward the workers, the fear of violent upheaval, etc.) that inform the prevailing journalistic images, and, indeed, that inform Carnall's own opposition of an idealized Cowell to a fairly discredited Grimshawe, must be bracketed here, leaving only the more generalized assertion that Dickens's novel plays itself out in a discursive field already explicitly oriented to questions of silence – empowered and impotent – and of speech – rhetorically controlled and responsibly effective and, on the other hand, demagogically powerful. As Carnall points out, it is significant at several levels that Dickens chooses to ignore Cowell's role in the Preston strike, that the one "representative" of the strike is Grimshawe translated into the loudmouthed Slackbridge. Yet setting aside the explicitly political implications of Dickens's gesture, one may see its bias as also mirroring the linguistic anxiety that permeates *Hard Times*, where muteness resonates against bombast, gentle reason against scandalous rhetoric. How *can* one speak, the novel seems to ask, in a way that is both productive and responsible?[11] *Hard Times* looks for that impossible thing – a rhetorical stance that perfectly balances the production of ameliorative action through beautiful or moving language against the need for "truth." Dickens seems to sense that in looking for a formal and semantic precision that is also aesthetically pleasing, one is likely to find catachresis, a language more chimerical than holistic in its shape and energies. Without belittling the political aspects, positive and negative, of Dickens's engagement with the Preston story, one could say that the political in this case dramatizes a personal anxiety within a novel that Dickens fills with multiple correlatives of himself. From Gradgrind and Bounderby to Sleary and Slackbridge, his fancy, interminable, unbearable, or compromised talkers are felt to be as self-castigatory as they are satiric.

Dickens wrote surrounded by evidence that "art" was up for grabs; its place in the world, its very definition, was being energetically and publicly explored as he wrote *Hard Times*. The London Art Union (1837–1911) was only the first, the most successful, and the most upright of a series of nineteenth-century art unions that were designed (some of them only putatively) to teach a population otherwise uneducated and disinterested about art. The London Art Union worked to make art available in the form of inexpensive prints and, through subscriptions, to hold raffles so that people of ordinary means could own original work.[12] The ongoing debate regarding that highly successful enterprise centered on a very real and insoluble dilemma – in a way, the dilemma of realism itself: Did the popularizing of art contribute, as it was meant to do, to the "humanizing" of its consumers, or did it only contribute to the degradation of art?[13] George Godwin, secretary of the society, takes a positive view of the proliferation of art unions: "every philanthropic spirit, who feels . . . that the cultivation of taste . . . softens men's manners and suffers them not to be brutal, must . . . be anxious to lend his utmost aid. . . . The influence of the fine arts in humanizing and refining, in purifying the thoughts and raising the sources of gratification in man, is so universally felt and admitted that it is hardly necessary now to urge it. . . . the mind is carried forward to higher aims, and becomes insensibly opened to a conviction of the force of moral worth and the harmony of virtue."[14] In the minutes from an 1842 meeting, one finds a larger claim: "To contemplate advantages arising to the whole nation from this association, may . . . seem extravagant . . . but . . . the elevation of one mind entails involuntarily the elevation of thousands."[15] It is utterly significant that the attacks on the London Art Union centered most frequently on its policy, one not typically shared by the other unions, of allowing the lottery winners to *choose* from among all the available paintings what they wanted to take home with them, the point of contention being, of course, both pedagogical and aesthetic. From the perspective of the London Art Union, the very success, financial and educative, of the venture depended on this choice, because "great additional interest in the subject is excited, personal examination and enquiry are induced, comparison between different works instituted."[16] For opponents of choice, the right to choose could only result in rewarding the worst artists by creating a market for their work, and in actual fraud as well.[17]

Dickens was well aware of the complexities of these issues, and at several levels (one can find in *Hard Times* his parodic version of Henry Cole's Department of Practical Art), for realism stands in precisely the relation to High Art embodied in the London Art Union's goals.[18] The committee's statement on the aims of art are spoken in realism's language: Art aims at "the development of the highest moral and intellectual elements, and their development with national modifications. . . . We would not even exclude the more homely scenes of common life, sensible that, provided they be combined with moral influences, they must always be a useful, as they are oftentimes the only intelligible mode in which Art can speak to a large portion of the community."[19] The questions raised by the art unions cannot, even now, be answered simply by anyone but unregenerate aesthetes and ideologues; one must feel in this confrontation between use and pleasure, between art as private and art as communal (the yearly art union displays of the prizewinners' pictures were immensely popular and constituted one of the few free art shows in London[20]) the genuine and ongoing dilemma of the artist who allows himself to think in terms of both public and private responsibilities. Dickens is himself caught between two imperatives that are more often than not in competition with one another; the "union" issue in *Hard Times* represents more than the most obvious questions of labor.

Hard Times, conscientiously intent on gazing at the most sterile and blackened of landscapes, becomes thus an enriched medium for the examination of fictional realism, which must itself seduce even as it protests; as art, it must, as Barthes says in *The Pleasure of the Text*, project between itself and the reader a mutual "site of bliss," even as it seeks, as realism, to "tell the truth" reportorially.[21] *Hard Times* consistently brings the reader to share in the deconstruction of its stated material "realism," whose utilitarian surface yields throughout to those alternative and ineffable truths produced by the artist's "mute Hands" that do not tell but only feel and make. Every character, every turn of the plot, every image has its doubled function as that which most precisely illustrates industrialism's ugly realities and as that which most thoroughly problematizes the notion of a fanciless realism; the word games that exploit doubled or tripled meanings perform the trick in small.[22]

Dickens cannot bear too much earnestness, even as he see the goodness in it; it is not insignificant that he drops Stephen Blackpool, spokesperson for all that is right, down a shaft where no one can hear his voice. Blackpool, the earnest man in love, reifies the dilemma of the artist who commits himself to two mistresses and impotently moans " 'tis a muddle"; bound to a language intrinsically "figurative," the artist who sees his responsibilities as moving inexorably toward realism's seriousness, with its fixed and moral intent and its responsibility to a fairly egalitarian representationalism, must see himself endangered. Irrevocably tied to an unregenerate sensualist, Blackpool yearns toward purity, toward good, productive action and is thus reduced to such impotence that he is canceled out as a character (which is why Dickens loses him on the road for so long). Neither the "whore," purely visceral, nor the "angel," all morality, is available to him, and it is highly significant that Blackpool's relationship reverses the more usual dynamic wherein the man is married to propriety and yearns after (sexual, ecstatic) "love." Blackpool is *wedded* to the embodiment of anarchy, anti-domestic and literally subversive of household, just as the nineteenth-century artist is wedded to a language that must exceed and subvert and enrich one's desire to utter only those exemplary "household words" used to promote a virtuous, domesticated realism. Thus, while Dickens's realism speaks with a seriousness of intent that itself putatively excludes fancy, his tropology supplies the lack even as it turns fancy to phantasms and madness. The realistic text may pretend to abnegate desire – it is not "romantic" – even as *Hard Times* specifically subverts or corrupts all marital and romantic desire within the story it displays, but the *body* of the text must arouse an alternative *aphrodisia*. If Dickens's image of the making of a woman/character/text suggests something of the seraglio – a secret place whose workers are muted so that no mysteries can be revealed – so, too, must the text hold its secret intuition of some alternative, non-rational energy.

The precise first-order realism of *Hard Times*, with its reformist focus on the material parameters of industrialization, is in fact infiltrated with language games in which the tacit, reassuring, and therefore unexciting, code between addressor and addressee is problematized and enriched.[23] By the terms of the novel, the fact-bound males are countered by females whose language, nonsensical, nihilistic, spiritual, or ingenuously humane, suggests that they hear differently from men and remain resistant to the realisms of their surroundings. One *hears*/reads always at two levels in this novel, and the most hackneyed clichés, the mundane realisms of speech mouthed by the essentially unimaginative, may transform themselves elementally. When Mrs. Gradgrind says, "if it was ever to reach your father's ears I should never hear the last of it" (p. 50), one first reacts to the statement's function as a botched cliché, uttered by a woman as free from linguistic fancy "as any human being not arrived at the perfection of an absolute idiot, ever was" (p. 17). Yet one also sees in this conflation an alternative, surreal vision of Mrs. Gradgrind as a contiguous extension of her husband, the ear of the other grafted to a man who is himself the "warehouse" of facts that is Coketown.[24] There is also in this a near-parodic reification of Dickens's doubled hearing: his ear for the (journalistic, political, masculine) "real" news versus his ear for the surreal, the anarchic, the desirous, the "feminine," the irrational. As stereotypical as the terms of this dichotomy are, they nonetheless define the doubleness of Dickens's own authorial voice, that balance between the generative and therefore unpredictable "female" and the retributive, backward-looking "male." Throughout the novel, one is meant to feel that paternal power is in part dependent on the daughter's ministrations; that Sissy carries always a salve – "The nine oils, Sir. To rub father with" – is only a most literal instating of the daughter's curative/ erotic powers (p. 24). Derrida, in "Otobiographies," makes this dichotomy explicit: "I have, I am, and I demand a keen ear, I am (the) both, (the) double, I sign double, my writings and I make two, I am the (masculine) dead the living (feminine) and I am destined to them, I come from the two of them, I address myself to them, and so on."[25] As long as Gradgrind remains only a man of facts – a "realist" – he deserves no more than his wife's pallid, worn-out head, with its diminished echoes. When he can at last hear his daughter, he has learned what the artist must always keep in mind, that one must listen to the multiple truths of any realism: To hear both the (masculine) pre-scribed and the "living (feminine)," to sign double, is to have an ear for the generative, the anti-programmatic, the desirous.

Yet desire is explicitly forbidden within Dickens's industrial state, which is, by its terms, sterile; and realism, too, is held to an obligation to channel itself toward productivity: it means to *get* someplace, to do some damage, to make some statement. Jakobson says, of realism, "following the path of contiguous relationships, the realistic author metonymically digresses from the plot to the atmosphere and from the characters to the setting in space and time."[26] The realist *follows the path* to its inevitable conclusion, led down it by the inexorable pull of contiguities; this is why Louisa's leaving the road to cross "a space of stunted grass and dry rubbish" for a glimpse of the circus is perceived by Gradgrind as such a serious infraction (p. 11). In *Hard Times*, the figures of Stephen Blackpool and Rachael literalize, in their enforced celibacy and their incorruptible and dogged goodness, realism's necessary withholding of passion and its vested interest in behavior that will best serve the interest of the (particularly defined realistic) state.[27] But Stephen's wife is the witch-like madwoman/whore who defies the sterile materiality of desire channeled into endless productivity or, as in the case of the antitheses to Bounderby and his lot, into endless virtuous action; she refutes the realist's systematic stereotypes as regards femality gone bad and productivity turned to profligacy, with her obstinate refusal to be killed off (the very figure of a text divorced from moral and domestic obligations, she is invincibly potent and damaging; she has become a "dead woman" replaced "by a demon in her shape," and Old Stephen cannot fathom why others die "while this abandoned woman live[s] on!" pp. 74–5). Yet if Dickens despises her, and only a willfully gynocentric reading can wrench her from her clear function as a homewrecking slattern, he nonetheless allows her to wander out of the picture alive and to reenter it at the end (p. 273). In this, Dickens refuses yet once again to fulfill unequivocally the realist's pact by which metonymy functions not only synchronously (the fallen woman's corruptive effect on her surroundings defines her) but also diachronously (her corrupt dissolution, in its extremity, should signal the immediate inevitability of her death).[28] Mrs. Blackpool is a marker, among the many markers, of Dickens's ambivalent regard for realism in its most reductively "responsible" mode, wherein character is not tolerated unless it can be made to yield a lesson, its synchronous metonymies predicting its diachronous, politically correct outcome.

Dickens problematizes his overt agenda with great subtlety, however, for the explicit energies of the story go toward furthering the earnest claim that human desire is withered by Coketown's oppressive power, that people are *made* by the ruthless contiguities of their environment into undifferentiated and therefore unsexed replicants: Mrs. Sparsit will forever keep her foot in the stirrup, but she will always be riding sidesaddle, Rachel will die a virgin, and Louisa will never find love nor bear children. Mrs. Gradgrind will always have a headache. Bounderby's refusal to help Stephen Blackpool obtain a divorce is the literalization of this forbidden state of desire among the workers, and James Harthouse's lassitude is its contingent effect among the aristocracy, and while their evocative names, Blackpool and Harthouse, defy the angular metonymies of their surroundings, their conditions are such that the black pool remains opaque and unstirred and the heart house remains empty. Within the acceptable realisms about the industrialist, it is implied that desire produces and is produced by the productivities of the factory; the closed circle shuts out Bounderby's mother as a locus for his desire as certainly as it does his wife – he gets up "out of the ditch" – and a man who does not need/want his mother and who seems utterly indifferent to the removal of his wife functions as a most literal contiguity of the "plant" as factory, not born but made, not desirous man but machine. This is a world, we are clearly meant to believe, that sublimates all its erotic energies into marketable productivity.

Dickens's realism, itself productively inclined, assumes (pretends?) that it can present discrete "Facts" within the syntagmatic relationship appropriate to its chosen subject, and it depends on the directional force of cause and effect to keep its ducks in a row; his surrealism puns on these ingenuous expectations. The Gradgrind children live with a "little conchological cabinet, and a little metallurgical cabinet, and a little mineralogical cabinet" that function as neat metonyms of their fragmented and insufficient selves; within the propaganda of Dickens's chosen realism, one knows a priori how this is to be read. There is no mystery in this metonymy: The children are themselves concretized fragments produced by a hard father formed from a hard system. Yet Dickens goes on to say that "the bits of stone and ore looked as though they might have been broken from the parent substances by those tremendously hard instruments their own names" (p. 9). Thus Gradgrind's "own metallurgical Louisa" is most literally a metonymic chip off the old block who lives in Stone Lodge, having been struck off

the parent with a piece of the thing that names her (p. 11); the implied
syntagmatic progression goes nicely from the obdurate industrialism embodied in Coketown's red-brick buildings to Stone Lodge to the wall- and
warehouse-like Mr. Gradgrind to his flinty offspring. Yet, as in the vision
of Mrs. Gradgrind hearing through her husband's ear, this image forces a
turn; it will not keep to the straight and narrow causeway at the end of
which one finds industrialism exposed and berated through its own realities.
To think of Louisa as broken by what she *is* − by her "own name" − is
to fracture the metonymic contiguity by which all cause emanates from the
single source of Coketown. This image signals Louisa's insular and impenetrable masochism, as it suggests that she has performed her own scoriations,
inflicted her own fragmentation in the name of the father. It inevitably
suggests the incestuous nature of Gradgrind's withholding of Louisa from
all pleasure and all love. This invitation to enter and participate in Louisa's
madness is, as Bounderby would say, another "kettle-of-fish" entirely from
Dickens's realist agenda, as it halts the code and breaks the syntagmatic
progression by virtue of its density (p. 15). Moreover, it alters the terms of
the novel to include a psychosexual subtext, an act that effectively questions
the primary construct of industrial realism by offering the possibility that
cause (industrialism) and effect (character) may in fact be reversed or even
obviated.

Oscillating between such doubled messages at every level of its discourse,
this novel about the hazards of productivity, whose own composition "used
up" Dickens to exhaustion, reflects in its tropes his anxiety about and his
resistance to the realistic mode.[29] Like Mrs. Gradgrind, who is always "dying out," "invariably stunned by some weighty piece of fact tumbling on
her," Dickens knows the danger of never hearing the last of the father's
authoritative voice (p. 14), of allowing one's artistic, spiritual, aesthetic, and
erotic imperatives to become diminished by the din of "realisms." His
apprehension of some alternative and unnameable energy brings his metonymies to challenge their own directional, propagandistic contiguities;
people, their characters formed in some secret place, seem as much to create
or to alter their surroundings as to be created or altered by them. If the
men of power in *Hard Times* have heads that are warehouse- and factory-
like, their "Hands" generate an erotic energy that forces Coketown to its
own exudant physiology: its black canal (like bile or excrement), its purple

river (like blood), its head (like an elephant's), its face (like a painted savage's), and, therefore, its savage, elephantine body. The artist has a vested interest in this metonymic reciprocity, of course, for without it there could be no "story," but only a preachment on the given deterministic text, but one cannot help but notice how Dickens goes out of his way to make characters refute their industrial identities with alternative fantasies; of them all, only Bitzer's albinism is pale enough to assure that he will take his character entirely from his surroundings. Even Mrs. Gradgrind retains a vague and urgent memory of love: "there is something . . . missed, or forgotten. . . . I shall never get its name now. . . . It makes me restless. I want to write to him, to find out for God's sake, what it is. Give me a pen, give me a pen" (p. 183). So while the writer's mind – his particularized vision of the Preston strike, his journalist's referentiality, his propagandistic intent – is set, that which comes from his Hand whips up an alternative set of fantasies ("Give me a pen, give me a pen"). Attuned to other imperatives (aesthetic pleasure, artistic amusement, "People mutht be amuthed . . . thomehow," p. 38), as well as to social responsibilities, Dickens thus consistently undermines the essential message of his particular realism: that humans must be made automatons – "people equally like one another" – in such an environment (p. 20). Contrariwise, as Tweedledee would say, machines must be brought to the blood's madness in such repression. Correlatively, the deictic pretensions of realism must be revealed as vulnerable, for what is manifested in *Hard Times* emerges as much through indirection and obliquity, through puns and word games, as in the syntagmatic precisions of logical discourse.

Hard Times is thus a most complex kind of realism, as its tropological venue is the nightmare and the fantasy, for the metonymies of such a place as Coketown must reflect the dual nature of its site as a locus of one form of productivity purchased at the danger of "using up" or perverting other desires; it is the paradigm both for industrialism and for an artistry committed to realism. The disguised fulfillments of repressed and suppressed wishes are condensed by the rigid parameters of Coketown's daylight reality, much as Dickens's typical methodologies are intensified by his conviction that, in conforming to the requisite number of parts for *Household Words*, "the difficulty of the space is CRUSHING."[30] The town sits within a landscape that enhances the sense that one is enclosed and locked in Pandemonium, as it is surrounded by a treacherous country "undermined by deserted coal-shafts, and spotted at night by fires and black shapes of stationary engines at pits' mouths" (p. 154). Dickens wants simultaneously to expose the logic of industrialism (of a programmatic realism? of parts publication produced explicitly to boost subscription sales?) as both flawless and quite mad, fueled by a monomania that, in its failure to account for necessary variables, becomes the profoundest unreason. At one level the very epitome of an enforced and fanciless order, Coketown sheds its linearities on the people defined within it. Yet Coketown, which looks like "the painted face of a savage," must also be seen as the very body of a madman, with its systemic physiology of black canal and purple river, and its sweat and steam and smoke (p. 20); it mimics the madman as it conducts itself so completely within a lockstep discourse on material productivity that it approximates the undeviating and rigorous precision of insanity.[31] All red and black, acrid, and panting, it constrains itself to its one allowable product; as with the madman, "this discourse, in its logic, commands the firmest belief in itself, it advances by judgments and reasonings which connect together; it is a kind of reason in action."[32] Dickens makes palpable the secret delirium residing underneath the "chaotic and manifest delirium" of Coketown's poisonous exudations, and it is in this secret delirium that we find "both what makes madness true (irrefutable logic, perfectly organized discourse, faultless connection in the transparency of a virtual language) and what makes it truly madness (its own nature, the special style of all its manifestations, and the internal structure of delirium)."[33]

Coketown, a strange town that is not a town, spontaneously generated all at once by the inhuman imperatives of mass production, signifies the fundamental distortions that must arise in a system of literary realism commited to representing the correlative distortions of industrialism. Such "realism" is a similar sort of town in that its ideological affiliation is all at one level, and its agenda fixed; all narrative movement, that which accounts for the past or generates the future, is pinned to one, present reality. "Coketown" begs the question of what "town" means, just as certainly as the term "realism" always begs the question of its particular limited reality. Thus the language that reveals character through metonymy in *Hard Times* must communicate Coketown's essential nature as a fabricated construct, its strangeness only masked by the conventional linearities of its architecture (again, Coketown also reifies Dickens's text production, with its "intense rushing," its "disjointed form of publication," its preexistent necessity as a boost for sales of *Household Words*[34]). In speaking of language, Wittgenstein uses this analogy: "Our language can be seen as an ancient city: a maze of little streets and squares, of old and new houses, and of houses with additions from various periods; and this is surrounded by a multitude of new boroughs with straight regular streets and uniform houses."[35] But Coketown is without a history; it has "several large streets all very like one another, and many small streets still more like one another, inhabited by people equally like one another, who all went in and out at the same hours, with the same sound upon the same pavements, to do the same work, and . . . every day was the same as yesterday and to-morrow, and every year the counterpart of the last and the next" (p. 20).[36] Its density all of the same red-brick material, with no buried layers of past discourses, it generates only one allowable meta-discourse, a purely syntagmatic progression, with everything leading to the factory, with all the Hands moving back and forth in lines to and from the work that names them. This is industrial Coketown's "realism," but language rebukes this merely reproductive linearity. Language is an ancient city, with an archeological opacity; it *turns* even when one tries to make it go straight, because it is by nature tropic. If the piston goes eternally up and down, caught in that line of "feeble agitation, without power or violence," that characterizes melancholia, the smoke serpents turn on themselves for ever and ever and never get uncoiled (p. 20).[37]

The steam engine's pistons, "all the melancholy mad elephants," drive the plant that drives the town, and indeed melancholia as the dominating sickness of Coketown serves Dickens well, to illustrate both the realist's dilemma and the industrialist's communicable madness (p. 63); melancholia is "madness at the limits of its powerlessness," a condition appropriate to the worker and to the worker-artist. ("I am so stunned with work, that I really am not able . . . to answer your questions." "I am three parts mad, and the fourth delirious, with perpetual rushing at Hard Times." "Why I found myself so 'used up' after Hard Times I scarcely know."[38]) That state in which one believes himself to be something else entirely, melancholia is a most vivid incarnation of metonymy consuming itself, of the imperatives of realism, which sees the world as one contiguous extension of its chosen "reality," taken to a logical conclusion. Among melancholics, "some think themselves to be beasts, whose voice and actions they imitate. Some think that they are vessels of glass, and for this reason recoil from passers-by, lest they break."[39] (This is, perhaps, a figure of the artist who calls himself a realist as the metonymous impact of his surroundings consumes his spiritual or aesthetic vision.) Coketown, a town, thinks itself a machine or a savage or a beast. Bounderby's vision suggests a similar mad logic; he is a "self-made man" and therefore, by the rigorous logic of such a construct, cannot have had a family. Capable of this delusion whereby he imagines himself as self-constructed, he may extend such autism to others: people work at machines with their hands; therefore they are Hands. To treat them as if they were otherwise would be to break the code, to give these Hands feet so that they would want to "be set up in a coach and six," to give them mouths so that they would eat "turtle soup and venison," and, most horrifically, to bring them to expect that they might be "fed [by other hands] . . . with a gold spoon" (p. 65).

The melancholic's derangement is metonymous characterization with a vengeance: One *becomes* one's very symbolic projection, thinking, metonymically, "I am as fragile and as frangible as that glass which seems my contiguous state; I am, therefore, made of glass." Bounderby, quintessential realist, mimics this paradigm as if its logic is irrefutable: "I am a self-made man, thus I am made from mud and dirt and water" – born in a watery ditch; "I am therefore unmothered," "kept . . . in an egg-box" as an unborn, commodified thing, left to hatch autonomously and accidentally into a "self-made" state. This free play of contiguities is a most material madness of things, one best suited to the industrial and to the realist's state. The tautology by which such "reasoning" proceeds is so enclosed as to seem incestuous, and indeed its products are monstrous (this circle is mirrored by the incestuous connotations in the Sissy Jupe/father – her own and Gradgrind – and the Louisa/father/brother pairings; incest, in fact, as one sees as well in *Wuthering Heights*, may well be a textual projection of the realist's intuition of the tautological enclosure essential to the project at hand). Thus the mad turns that Dickens brings to bear on language – Hands with feet and mouths, "mute Hands," people as pistons, therefore pistons as elephants – take the syntagmatic interdependence to its (il)logical extreme to reveal the surreality in reality.

In this mad, metonymically declined world, body parts necessarily prevail over the intact human form, and while Hands and legs are prominent synecdoches, it is most typically "addled heads" that dominate Dickens's toponymy.[40] Coketown, its weekday "reality" generated by the mad, plunging elephant-head piston, looking itself like the savage's painted face, is also a town of at least eighteen belfries filled with "barbarous jangling . . . bells" that drive "the sick and nervous mad" (p. 21); the bats in the belfries are, of course, clearly implied. (Time, in such hard times, takes on an imperative, gong-show force, with a banging presence that translates itself into Mrs. Gradgrind's perpetual headache; time shows up in Gradgrindian clocks that "knocked every second on the head as it was born," as if to literalize Giddens's assertion that in modernity there is an emptying of time into timepieces.[41]) Thus Coketown must be filled, by the closed logic of Dickens's metonymy, by humans similarly afflicted, and indeed it is jam-packed with people whose own heads are in danger of popping or falling off or rupturing. The knobs on Mr. Gradgrind's overstuffed head are "like the crust of a plum pie," a simile that defies the consistent metonymies whereby his forehead is a wall and his eyes take "cellarage in two dark caves," to suggest that those knobs might suppurate and ooze purple, like the ill-smelling purple river. Mrs. Gradgrind's poor head is continually wearing her out (p. 49). Tom fears for Sissy that "they'll bother her head off, . . . before they have done with her" (p. 46). Bounderby's head is stretched to grotesquery; he is "a man with a great puffed head and forehead, swelled veins in his temples, and such a strained skin to his face that it seemed to hold his eyes open, and lift his eyebrows up" (p. 13). This place, where all the people are imminently headless, overinflated balloons about to pop, suggests as an alternative to industrial or religious control a libidinal fantasy whereby the body could go amok, the mad elephant give in to musth. Their heads ruptured like so many balloons, the figures once so encased and concretized by their red-brick physiognomies would discover that, in matters of the id, "the head . . . is not any more than any old bit of skin."[42] One who "loses his head" becomes incapable of the flawless tautologies by which behavior is controlled and determined by one's perceptions of external contiguities (and it is not only the insane who impose on themselves such control); the "barbarous" church bells compete with the clanging piston to drive people beyond melancholia into frenzy, to a place where language is released from its obligations to contexture and combination, a place where desire rises up and presides over more utilitarian realisms.

Josiah Bounderby himself best embodies Dickens's dual impulses to bring language to his linear service and to yield to its dense and transformative pleasures; Bounderby's character, as dependent as it is on localized and temporalized metonymies for the substance by which it displays itself, resists the realistic program in *Hard Times* by refuting itself with its past. Bounderby is caught most literally in the realist's dilemma of needing to bring language to the univocal service of his present and manifest reality (p. 30). He works to create, retrospectively, the quintessential "realism" of the self-made man, and in attempting to work backward syntagmatically from his present reality, he is held to certain "truths" exclusive of, for example, a mother and father and a grandmother. His litanic repetition of the scenarios most likely to lead, realistically speaking, to his current state fails to contain his story, however. Like Louisa, he thwarts his metonymous identification as having been made from the crudest of Coketown materials even as he seems to fit the terms of Coketown most exactly. His utterly appropriate "metallic laugh," his "brassy speaking-trumpet of a voice," his makings "out of a coarse material" (p. 13), are revealed as fraudulent metaphors when we discover that he had had decent parents who had "loved him as dear as the best could" and had privileged him and sacrificed for him (p. 239). He had been "love[d] for love's own sake," which is to say that he has *not* been loved for the sake of the materialities he represents, and that this is not mere rhetoric is proved by his mother's actions and her genuine indignation when her son's honor is impugned (p. 240). He is *not* what he is because he was born in a ditch and kept in an egg-box; his character has nothing (that we can see) to do with his past and is not, therefore, explicable in the terms of his own current realism.

His words fill all the available space as he seeks to make himself consistent. When he is speaking his opinions among the circus people, Mr. E. W. B. Childers advises him to "give it mouth in your own building, will you. . . . Because this isn't a strong building, and too much of you might bring it down!" (p. 30). And indeed it can be said that Mr. Bounderby brings his own metonymous house down around his ears as it becomes apparent that there is too much of him – too much past, too much love, too many relationships – to fit the realism he now represents. Dickens signals this quite clearly from the beginning in the flamboyant hyperbole of Bounderby's tales of his past: "I passed the day in a ditch, and the night in a pigsty." "I was so ragged and dirty, that you wouldn't have touched me with a pair of tongs." "She kept a chandler's shop . . . and kept me in an egg-box." These are statements that declare Bounderby's fictionality at two levels simultaneously (his own fiction and Dickens's), for they are so artistically wrought as to amount to an authorial intrusion by which one's sense of fictionality is kept to the fore (pp. 14–15).[43] Mr. Bounderby professes to "call a spade a spade" (and having been born in a ditch, he should be able to do so), but Dickens uses him to imply that such resolutely utilitarian language most literally must distort "truth" – Bounderby is, in fact, a habitual liar – for the sake of a unilateral "realism." One could almost imagine that Bounderby is the parodic construct that reifies Dickens's own dilemma (if he is Blackpool in his desire to tell the truth and behave well, he is Bounderby in his addiction to the most outrageous of language games): the man who is so caught in the imperatives of his limited, programmatically ordained text that he reveals himself to be a "noodle," which is to say, among other things, to be flaccid and undesirable even to the likes of a hungry Mrs. Sparsit, for "the proceedings of a Noodle can only inspire contempt" (p. 271).

One must insist on thinking about *why* Dickens supplies Bounderby with the very past that most thoroughly subverts the novel's "realistic" assertion that a man's inhumane environment afflicts his character, the "realistic" assertion that, in the face of such determinism, mysteries of the spirit (evil and goodness) and mysteries of the flesh (desire and its concomitant states) may be explained in more gainful terms by the contiguities of one's material environment. Bounderby, with a fraudulent reality he has invented and endlessly rehearsed to aggrandize himself, is deployed by Dickens to be perceived by the reader simultaneously at several contradictory levels. Within terms familiar to both addressor and addressee as regards the party line on poverty and industrialization and their effects on character, he is bad because he has been misused, and he is ruthless because he has had to raise himself out of the ditch, but he is unregenerate because he has become the embodiment of the factory system. That one is clearly meant to recognize Dickens's prolepsis, to know all along the identity of the old woman who watches his house, brings one *at the same time* to exit the terms of this sociopolitical assumption as regards Bounderby, while not discarding the validity of the assumption itself. That Bounderby has lied does not negate the realism of the generalized pernicious effects of industrialization, even though his inexplicable badness brings to the fore Dickens's ambivalence about the social obligations of the realistic mode and, correlatively, his competing and oppositional ideologies about the very nature of character. In fact, Dickens does not ever halt the play of significance between his oppositional concepts of character – that it is determined by its surroundings and that it is immune to its surroundings – although he makes manifest in Bounderby how the reader may accommodate at once several levels of discourse on "reality."[44] But in supplying, as he so consistently does, two simultaneous possibilities for the assessment of character, and in giving Bounderby a dual function, he once again acknowledges that realism proper, while it serves a necessary purpose, is univocal and finally insufficient.

Dickens does not belittle, in *Hard Times*, the dark realities of the industrial state; yet one is constantly invited to exit Coketown's metonymies for others more appealing. Dickens *plays* with every one of his realist's obligations, freeing both language and character to act out, independently of their syntagmatic obligations. Like Louisa, "peeping with all her might through a hole in a deal board," and Tom, "abasing himself on the ground to catch but a hoof of the graceful equestrian Tyrolean flower-act," the reader is invited to get down to it. One has only to consider the sexual implications of a "graceful equestrian Tyrolean flower-act" (Zenobia, bareback) to see that there is an alternative agenda to industrial sterility in this "neutral ground upon the outskirts of the town, which was neither town nor country" (p.10). Apart from its industrialized constructs, and on the periphery of Coketown's realism, it is implied, is a place where language is freed from all political imperatives; existent in a "neutral" place, it may perform as it is inclined, rather than as it should. So, too, is "character" made a playful concept here, for when the circus comes to this neutral ground to play out its Rabelaisian fantasies, the Centaur, the Wild Huntsman, the Cupid, and the infant are all played by two men, convincingly enough (p. 27).

In this carnival world all the linear expectations based on discrete paradigms of identity and action merge:

There were two or three handsome young women among them, with their two or three husbands, and their two or three mothers, and their eight or nine little children, who did the fairy business when required. The father of one of the families was in the habit of balancing the father of another of the families on the top of a great pole; the father of a third family often made a pyramid of both those fathers, with Master Kidderminster for the apex, and himself for the base; all the fathers could dance upon rolling casks, stand upon bottles, catch knives and balls, twirl hand-basins, ride upon anything, jump over everything, and stick at nothing. (p. 32)

The conglomerated actors, "handsome young women," "husbands," "little children," "mothers," seem piled on one another in a dense and glorious heap, for when fathers pile up, so does everything else: "the father of one . . . was in the habit of balancing the father of another," "the father of a third . . . often made a pyramid of both those fathers." In the context of those ruthless metonymies that control all the heads in Dickens's industrial world, it is provocative to think here of Jakobson's discussion of "contiguity disorder," whereby syntactical rules give way to agrammaticism, causing the "degeneration of the sentence into a mere 'word heap.' "[45] Dickens might almost be said to fantasize the visual equivalent to this a-linearism in the jubilantly pyramidal world of the carnival, to give, as an antidote to the word bound and trussed syntagmatically, a sense of alternative energy. This is a place where propositions complete themselves with no regard for linguistic conventionalities – "Stand upon x" becomes "Stand upon bottles"; "Twirl x" becomes "Twirl hand-basins" – as if the sheer pleasure of the word prevails. The subtextual suggestion is of a remarkable sexual freedom and energy – the mothers performing "rapid acts on bare-backed steeds" and not "at all particular in respect of showing their legs," and the passel of indiscriminate children. This is a place where all the fathers can indeed "ride upon anything, jump over everything, and stick at nothing." Mr. Sleary, the benign father, presides over the circus world, and his very name and his very speech are meant to suggest that rigorous, hard-edged pronouncements may not be made here. He talks and talks (a luxury Dickens himself has lost to his preestablished compact format), and he urges others to "give . . . a Bethpeak" about that which is solely for amusement (p. 38). He holds a sexual mystery alternative to Coketown's garish frustrations (children here seem to emerge in great litters); his voice is "not eathy heard by them ath don't know me" because he represents a code oppositional to industrial realism's.

Although all of his characters may be found to subsidize their political functions with alternative complexities, it is in the enigmatic Louisa Gradgrind that Dickens most thoroughly tinctures his realism with intuitions of a counterproductive and seductive nihilism; if the parent (paternalistic) text is the scathing attack on the mad realities of industrialism, there is a daughter text that refutes antithesis and posits a retreat from the realistic mode. A character who is neither an embodiment of her surroundings nor one who brings her surroundings to embody her self, she is the speculum from which one might read one's own desires and the figure that predicts Dickens's instinct that "realism," narrowly defined, is insufficient to his desirous relationship with language. Louisa is described most consistently in terms of absences and vacancies; in her face "there was a light with nothing to rest upon, a fire with nothing to burn" (p. 11), and on that face was "no tear" (p. 12). Louisa's is "a blind face groping its way" (p. 11). In a landscape of house- and factory-like people, she exists outside the spatial metonymies of her surroundings; her habitual retreat is "an opening in a dark wood" (p. 155). She does not actively resist the metonymic identifications that mark the others, as Sissy instinctively resists when she furnishes her imagined space with flowered carpets, or as Blackpool's wife defiantly resists when she perpetually sells the furnishings out from under her placed and dogged husband; Louisa's vacancy is the profoundest emptiness, the nihilism of one who cannot even *imagine* the alternatives to nothingness and who has no terms for the nothingness she feels. (Harthouse must talk of nothingness for her.) In a fiction operating at one level with ferocious, journalistic realism, she is the void at the hard outside edges of material realities.

Defying metonymy, Louisa is a most potent blank space. She leaves no mark of where she has been: "From the mistress of the house, the visitor glanced to the house itself. There was no mute sign of a woman in the room. No graceful little adornment, no fanciful little device, however trivial, anywhere expressed her influence" (pp. 117–18). This absence from her husband's house has twofold significance, as it confirms Louisa's inability to touch or to be touched by any but the father/artist. Without any "graceful little adornment" or "fanciful little device," this red-brick house and all its contents are exclusively a periphrasis for Bounderby, just as is the repossessed country house from which Louisa habitually absents herself for a hole at the woods' edge. Her refusal to touch Bounderby's houses is mute testimony to her refusal to touch or be touched by her husband, and it is verification that she will never love him. Far from translating desire for Bounderby into hands placed lovingly upon metonymous artifacts of him, she pointedly refutes any libidinal attraction to him in her disdain for his things. There is no cathexis, no narcissistic transference onto her surroundings, but only vacancy. Thus, once again in this novel of turns, the diegetical geometry is skewed, as the indices for Louisa's inward state are revealed as empty, designating only that which she is not.[46]

Nor is Louisa physically declined by a landscape that confirms or disputes the metonymies of Coketown. She is not substantial – not a house, a wall, a warehouse. If she is "metallurgical," she is a state of metal without a named shape or function (p. 11). She is not, like Sissy, a girl "so dark-eyed and dark-haired that she seemed to receive a deeper and more lustrous colour from the sun, when it shone upon her," able to transubstantiate her surroundings. In fact, Louisa remains most extraordinarily vague in this landscape of people so vividly drawn: "She was pretty." "Her features were handsome." She is a "most remarkable girl" (pp. 11, 117). Harthouse, who is effete but acutely observant, is said diegetically by Dickens (who thus valorizes his perceptions by his own non-ironic tone) to see her as cold and proud/sensitively ashamed; constrained/careless; reserved/watchful; indifferent/uneasy (p. 117). Yet she is neither one nor the other in these oxymoronic extremes, for we are not meant to see her as capricious. Nor is she the sum of their resolutions, that comprehensible if otherwise inarticulable middle term within the oxymoronic pairing. She is quite literally what language cannot say; she is the embodiment of that which is inarticulable and therefore inaccessible to realism. She refutes syntagmatic relationships just as she rebuffs the standard plot lines of realism for women. She does not love beyond her brother, she does not descend Mrs. Sparsit's staircase to hell, she does not capitulate to desire, she does not recover in the end to become a wife, a mother, a happy person. And neither does she die. She is, in short, as subversive as her twin Estella, who brings Dickens to the exigency (unthinkable in realism) of a novel with two endings that negate each other. "I am here beside you," she says, "barefoot, unclothed, undistinguishable in darkness" (p. 174): She is what fiction must become – an erotic cipher – if it repudiates the externalities by which character is defined and delimited to the stereotypes imposed by (economic and therefore political) materialities.

Louisa exists between the poles of an industrial/fictional realism that forbids or attenuates desire and the phantasmagoric dreamscape this reality must generate in compensation. Louisa is an alternative to the other tropological fantasies within the text, a dream-symbol that replaces Dickens's dense industrial metonymies with an opening for the erotic fantasies of those who watch her: She "baffle[s] all penetration," a state that invites the effort, awakening dreams of penetration effected (p. 117). Her past is made of "plumbless depths" that arouse one to plumb them (p. 92). She is the antithesis to the willful positivism of literary realism, for she is the unsayable who may be displayed only in terms of what she is not. Louisa is the antithesis to the "useful," linguistically and economically, in this world of use, for her social class raises her above the productivity of the Hand, and her sex disqualifies her for managerial work. In *Dombey and Son*, Dombey thinks of his daughter in terms that make explicit the moneyed female's purely ornamental and domestic value within the world of the trader/realist: "But what was a girl to Dombey and Son! In the capital of the House's name and dignity, such a child was merely a piece of base coin that couldn't be invested – a bad boy – nothing more."[47] Her ornamental function disallowed in this place without fancy, Louisa is designated as the most irredeemable casualty of her surroundings, and she is also, *ex post facto*, immune to the "realisms" of her situation as a character. She is neither an angel (Rachael), nor a whore (Mrs. Blackpool). Nor is she, as is Sissy, that potent conflation of sensuality and innocence that makes up the domesticated "angel of the house."[48] She looks to the very depth of the fire she watches and can say "I don't see anything in it, . . . particularly" (p. 49), because she does not dream – has "never dreamed" – and she does not desire (p. 93).[49] She is not, in other words, a personality gradually destroyed by accretions from her industrial, fact-filled surroundings, for she has "never had a child's heart," "never dreamed a child's dream" (p. 93). Neither are we meant to believe that she is, like Bounderby, born insufficient, her vacancies intrinsic to her nature.

Louisa's is an alternative pathology, an alternative reality; she is a place both dense and empty, the embodiment of a father's fantasy of a daughter/ woman/text born utterly pure, utterly open, and utterly his. "You have dealt so wisely with me, father, from my cradle to this hour," she says to Gradgrind, "that I never had a child's belief or a child's fear" (p. 93). She is not formed by nature to be what she is, and she is not made what she is by her world; she is *made* by her father. It is her father who pronounces her sexually mature: "My dear Louisa, you are a woman!" (p. 86). It is her father, only, who holds her, only her father whom she touches, both hands on his shoulders, only her father's eyes into which she gazes fixedly (pp. 199–200). Louisa is the text of the father's deepest and unwritten desire; it is no accident, then, that her mother is made to be so completely inconsequential, "a weak transparency," a "feeble and dim" light (pp. 183–4). Mrs. Gradgrind is no competition at all, either for Louisa's affections or for Gradgrind's, and she inspires only mild exasperation in the reader, who is, after all, accustomed to Dickens's excising of the mother for the daughter. Nor is it an accident that Louisa's husband is a bumptious fool, nor that her brother is a selfish baby, nor that her lover is an effeminate, halfhearted nihilist. Even the ending – "Herself again a wife – a mother – lovingly watchful of her children. . . . Such a thing was never to be" – holds her apart. It is no accident that the *only* one in *Hard Times* who becomes worthy of this fantasy woman is, finally, her own father, who begins as "Gradgrind" and ends as Dickens.[50] If Bounderby lampoons the imperatives of realism in his retroactive justification of character, Louisa is the very figure of the artist's desire and fear. Lovely, untouched and untouching, she is the *poesis* of an eroticism that does not yield its secrets to the word. Yet she is also utterly dissociative, and if she defies the syntagmatic trap indispensable to realism, she also defies description.

Thus she is also utterly damaged – "tired," "tired a long time" (p. 12) – and has become what Catherine Clement calls the "indifferent hysteric," who signifies eros through every kind of anesthesia that will still her body, who turns all erotic stirrings into her own pain, who defies stimulation.[51] When, at age fifteen, she allows herself to show her revulsion at Bounderby's kiss – a first and a last – she rubs the kissed cheek until it is "burning red." "You'll rub a hole in your face," says Tom. "You may cut the piece out with your penknife if you like . . . I wouldn't cry," she responds (p. 19). Once she becomes Bounderby's wife, "there was no mute sign of woman in the room," says Dickens. Nobody home. "What does it matter?" is her refrain (p. 93). Her attraction to Harthouse is never brought to a state of pleasure; it does not go through the realist's romantic arc of resistance, capitulation (actual or imagined) to desire, and finally guilt. Rather, it circumvents the middle term with the ruthless economy of the hysteric and goes straight to pain: "If you ask me whether I have loved him, or do love him, I tell you plainly, father, that it may be so. I don't know," she cries just before becoming "an insensible heap" (p. 200).[52] Like her equally isolate sister Estella of *Great Expectations*, she is the one break in the reciprocal contiguities of place and person in *Hard Times*, and as such she is a most poignant monstrosity and a most perfect purity. She is the paradoxical figure of an art/woman that cannot comprehend or feel desire, and exiting that most singular and potent realism, she is thus at once both unimpeachable and utterly violable. Metonymy is subverted by such interiority: dream yields to dream.

It is, at the least, not sufficient to reduce Louisa Gradgrind to those psychosexual terms that might suggest something of Dickens's own libidinal fantasies and preoccupations.[53] I would suggest instead that she is a potent sign within the text of *Hard Times*, an embodiment of Dickens's resistance to realism's co-opting of language to its causes and a cautionary cripple, the paradox of a hysteria so attuned to desire as to find it intolerable. If the melancholiac is a figure for realism's exhausted metonymizing, the hysteric is the exact figure for a realism whose self-imposed control has induced selective amnesias and condensations; that unnameable, (un)forgotten manifold that provokes one's incessant attempts at recollection may well be felt to generate a correlative, hysterical denial, a refusal to look back into a past that if it will not yield the thing itself nonetheless threatens to yield up its quotient of forbidden desire.[54] Louisa is a form of broken desire, and as such she resists the language that can describe a woman/text only through the physicalities that limit that desire as they concretize it. However the metonymy for woman (desire) is chosen, whether the contiguity is as intimate as "Arms that are braceleted and white and bare / (But in the lamplight, downed with light brown hair!)" or as distant as the periphrastic elaborations of her by the surrounding landscape, it delimits. But Louisa, indefinable, is also necessarily a completely internalized figure, damaged. With no language to describe her state, she is made to embody an eroticism turned in on itself – the trope that winds itself into a tight, impenetrable coil.

One must not hope to resolve the antinomies by which *Hard Times* works, for, after all, one *understands* at every moment of reading it the necessity for, and the validity of, both truths; the real and the surreal coexist because they are interdependent. It is not just any reader who is disturbed by these seeming contradictions. It is the reader who returns to the text with her own prescribed realist's agenda, by which one *makes sense of*, orders, and reduces all the terms, who is disturbed. In retrospect, one searches for the novel's *telos*: What *are* "the limited options for and restrictive means towards the denouement"? What *is* the "plot allowed by the narrative given and by the genre to which it belongs"?[55] Viewed in these terms, *Hard Times* is a curious novel indeed, almost dissolute, as it seems perpetually distracted from its retributive sacrifice of Tom Gradgrind (about whom we care so little) and its martyring of Stephen Blackpool (whose implacable virtue makes us impatient). One's interest is not really in these two characters, nor is it in the action that surrounds them, and thus one finds that the *telos* of Dickens's realism is made to be virtually insignificant by the alternative densities within the novel. There is so much turning going on. Bounderby's history is reversed, and though we know all along that he is "the Bully of humility" who coerces and bullies humility into his service, the prolepsis of the old woman does not prepare us for the analepsis of his thoroughly mundane, healthy childhood. Mr. Gradgrind turns good, and while there are ample clues that he is not a bad man, his salvation at the expense of both Louisa and Tom is a significant generational irony and an unusual investment of authorial energy.[56] In one of the strangest elaborations of character in any novel, Mrs. Sparsit ends up behaving – one can hardly think of what to call it – like a combination of Sherlock Holmes and a jealously crazed husband; she awakens an entire, wonderful subtext as she stands streaming, in parti-colored stockings, with prickly things in her shoes and caterpillars festooning her dress (p. 195). And then there is Louisa, fainting at her father's feet like a proper heroine, not because she has gone the Clarissa route and not because she has taken the low road of desire, but because . . . well, one cannot say, exactly. These are all gestures subversive of a completely proprietous realism, and they are subsidized by a tropology that exposes the unreason in reason and the unreality in reality. But if the mimesis in *Hard Times* is meant to be comically slipshod, its semiosis is not. Dickens seems to say that one must acknowledge "realisms" even knowing that they are all prescribed by the systems they choose to attack or valorize, just as one must understand the essential barrierlessness of pure desire. Neither one nor the other, but both.

Chapter Seven

"Zenobia in Chains"

———

Zenobia was esteemed the most lovely as well as the most heroic of her sex. She was of a dark complexion. . . . Her teeth were of a pearly whiteness, and her large black eyes sparkled with uncommon fire, tempered by the most attractive sweetness. Her voice was strong and harmonious. Her manly understanding was strengthened and adorned by study. She was not ignorant of the Latin tongue, but possessed in equal perfection the Greek, the Syriac, and the Egyptian languages. She had drawn up for her own use an epitome of oriental history, and familiarly compared the beauties of Homer and Plato under the tuition of the sublime Longinus.

—Edward Gibbon, *The Decline and Fall of the Roman Empire*

Real Romance

Built on a series of what appear to be equally imperative contradictions, *The Blithedale Romance* seems to be purely dialectical in its energies,[1] both internally and in its relationship to the reader.[2] So endowed, it seems very much to be participating in what theorists of the romance define as a "communal conversation," that open-ended dialogue that is the antithesis to social, political, and linguistic single-mindedness. It seems to be, in fact, the romance that it calls itself, rather than a work operating within the more politically driven impulses of realism.[3] Richard H. Millington, in *Practicing Romance*, believes it to "aim . . . at a kind of joint apostasy, a salutary mutual rage" that by so implicating the reader invites her to join in the ongoing conversation. Such an act "might save us from the deeper guilt of Coverdale's perennial observership, his empty relation to himself and others," says Millington.[4] Its dialectical candor and its narrative humility seem to imply, with others of Hawthorne's works, that there is no (locatable) zero-order "truth" to which *The Blithedale Romance* aspires, but rather that it exists in that resonant space between oppositions where one may pursue but not claim the unnameable. Neither philosophy nor realism, romance is, says M. l'Aubepine, somewhere between transcendentalism above and "the great body of pen and ink men who address the intellect and sympathies of the multitude" down below; *The Blithedale Romance* is "essentially a day-dream, and yet a fact," a thing that resides in a place "between fiction and reality."[5] Located thus in an unannexed territory, the romance may be more siren than clarion, more seductive than coercive. Its function may be not to territorialize for order and legality but to de-center.

But in fact, *The Blithedale Romance*, rather than an ongoing negotiation among vital oppositions, is a capitulation, victim to its own ambivalence about romance and the competing mode of realism. Its possibilities for an enriched, multivocal reality are subverted in the end by a series of revelations that, by suborning the alternatives resident in the unnameable and the immemorial, retroactively valorize the very status quo its utopian vision would seek to question. Its vacillations hold open territories but fail to protect them; its narrative integrity is so dissolute that there are great gaps in the plot that leave the text vulnerable to the unchecked energy of a normalizing and leveling synthesis. *The Blithedale Romance* is triply overdetermined: Hawthorne, while seeking to exorcise his own self-named "feminine" predilections in art and life, is nonetheless working defensively within a genre hierarchy that locates the romance as feminine (passive, receptive, dreamy, ineffectual, etc.) and realism as masculine (aggressive, effectual, spatially and temporally precise, etc.); Zenobia, infused with Hawthorne's ambivalence, his anxiety, and his desire, is the predestined sacrifice of romance to an abortive realism, of the "feminine" to the "masculine," and of feminism to paternalism. Northrop Frye's formulation seems a good touchstone against which to test *The Blithedale Romance*:

The essential difference between novel and romance lies in the concept of characterization. The romancer does not attempt to create "real people" so much as stylized figures which expand into psychological archetypes. . . . That is why the romance so often radiates a glow of subjective intensity that the novel lacks, and why a suggestion of allegory is constantly creeping in around its fringes. Certain elements of character are released in the romance which make it naturally a more revolutionary form than the novel.[6]

Yet Hawthorne's novel bears the burden of his recent political history, his personal history relative to those friends who made up the Brook Farm community, and an aesthetic and intellectual history whose Enlightenment ideals preclude a man's allowing himself full license to "[radiate] a glow of subjective intensity." Endlessly inventive in its own self-deprecation (its narrator is only one of many such gestures), the text becomes an equilibration of "extremisms," linguistic, political, artistic, and erotic, into an essentially domestic order. *The Blithedale Romance* may stand as warning both to romance and to realism, for it, rather than the unapologetic realism Bersani sees as antithetical to desire, loses potency as it gains in vitriol.

This synthesis is epitomized for Hawthorne, as always, in marriage, but within this particular text he invests an unmarriageable female with all of the attributes, both gorgeous and questionable, of romance. She is from the beginning irredeemable, and if she is not to be saved, neither, then, is romance. It is as if by hypostatizing an otherwise unnameable force within the terms of a genre (romance) and a gender (female), he perverts its productively subversive energy. He dares himself here to face the logical and political implications of his self-perceived "feminine" powers of empathy – those insights that make him more fit for romance than for realism – and then makes a virtue of expediency when he is brought to abandon these insights to the imperialistic energy of an aggressive, unilateral realism; in this he merely recapitulates his own failed participation in Brook Farm. Hawthorne's stock in trade for the legitimizing of romance is redemption through marital love; this is a solution at once both morally palatable and artistically safe, as it disciplines and justifies the pure erotic pleasure of romance (writing) through the retroactive propriety of its conjugal outcome. But in *this* romance the dialectical stakes are set very high for a rigged game: Feminism proper is embodied and set forth to be, if not domesticated, then necessarily repudiated. Feminism's putative antithesis in

The Blithedale Romance is philanthropy, but while each is proved to be a vagary of the Promethean ego from which it springs, feminism is most thoroughly rebuked by domesticity. And feminism, the articulated equality of the female and the modes by which she proceeds, is here so inextricably bound to romance that one problematizes the other. In Hawthorne's world, a married feminist and a realistic romance are skewed oxymorons, for in marriage, as the old joke goes, "We are one and I am he"; neither romance nor feminism can surmount the paternal interdiction of such a "synthesis" as this. Hollingsworth's self-named "inflexible severity of purpose" (p. 43), his sermonizing (at the Pulpit/rock), and his apparent willingness to exploit Coverdale's illness and his weakened state with "the ulterior purpose of making [him] a proselyte" (p. 57) stand within the text as emblems of this subjugation of alternative voices to a particular, egoistically defined realism. Feminism is thus overmanned in *The Blithedale Romance*, and romance is infiltrated by the devices of realism, as Hawthorne first raises the stakes of his contest and then, in yielding to his own ideological and artistic ambivalence, invites colonization.[7] And when colonists come, the banner is carried by a white, Christian male leading men like himself, and their intransigence as regards otherness – women, African Americans, Native Americans, to name a few – is legend.[8]

The historical Zenobia, queen of Palmyra and "determined to make Palmyra mistress of the Roman Empire in the East," encodes within Hawthorne's Zenobia that feminist/feminine energy that itself threatens to colonize – if only to the service of anarchy and of romance – and that must be conquered and displayed in golden chains.[9] The battle royal is set between Zenobia and Hollingsworth; Hawthorne sees to it that there are no other powers equal to them within the text, and yet it is predetermined that Zenobia, the antithesis to order and the very embodiment of romance, must be brought to heel (Aurelian sets the eternal precedent). But that feminism she represents politically becomes the logically articulated justification of alternative voices implicit to romance as a genre, and thus Hawthorne, in repudiating feminism, is brought also to repudiate the more "feminine" form within which he works. One might, without any great leap in logic, argue that Hawthorne's demonized version of feminism as a freeing of uncontrollable power is another fantasy of the Thing – this one given teeth and claws. Woman as allegorical figure – displayed thus in

oppositional poses of rigor and receptivity – becomes monstrous and misshapen (witness Zenobia's corpse) when so invested. Zenobia, echoing Fuller's premise in "The Great Lawsuit," sees in man's degradation of woman
his own degradation and makes of the domestic and submissive Priscilla a
"type"; she "is the type of womanhood, such as man has spent centuries
in making. . . . He is never content, unless he can degrade himself by stoop-
ing towards what he loves. In denying us our rights, he betrays even more
blindness to his own interests, than profligate disregard of ours!" (p. 122).
This is the figure of Compromise – mere being, the Nietzschean "past,"
representative of all human "being" that is inauthentic and severed from
its own manifold. This cast-iron tautology of desire and degradation binds
Hawthorne to its terms, and needful of romance, he stoops, defensive and/
or apologetic, to the form he has himself enervated and reduced to passivity. Castigatory (obliquely, slyly) of feminism, *The Blithedale Romance*
deconstructs itself *as romance* in its compulsion to domesticate the erotic
and the political power of the female voice. Hawthorne, in his artistic
ambivalence, subverts himself. *The Blithedale Romance* is a failed one, and
when romance fails, realism does not merely replace it. Realism, whose
balance of social productivity and artistic play rests on a sublimated energy,
an intuition of "romance" or the ineffable, is not the mere product of
defaulted romance. Hypostatized as romance and then sacrificed by Hawthorne, this energy is vitiated, leaving realism to concede itself to its own
propagandistic impulses (an irony of the first order, since this confirms and
fulfills exactly Hawthorne's worst fears about his writing). A dichotomous
system of good versus not-good and an adversarial positioning relative to
the unnameable take over by fiat.

The conflicts in *The Blithedale Romance* between isolation and community, between feminism and submission to paternal authority, between
eroticism and duty, are reciprocal to Hawthorne's ambivalence about his
own artistic responsibilities as a man in the world of (political and economic) work, and this reciprocity is exacerbated by his having put himself
to the test in the two oppositional modes of Brook Farm and the Custom
House (that Hawthorne is moved to write about Brook Farm ten years
later is, I think, attributable to the antithetical extremism of that more
party-oriented and less morally ambiguous political experience of being
ousted from his appointment at the Custom House – the terms of the

dialectic emerge irresistibly). To be empathetic, introspective, erotic, and "feminine," or to be egoistically consolidative, politically active, virilely moderate, and "masculine" – that is the (loaded) question that his failures at both communal life and political life force him, in retrospect, to confront yet once again. But to articulate a choice between what he perceives as the feminine and the masculine modes is to give up the safety of his putatively apolitical vision; to *say* unequivocally that one supports the "feminine" as an equally legitimate epistemology is to modulate from a problematic empathy that is itself felt as womanish and thus arrive at feminism. Yet, of course, Hawthorne cannot (no more than can Coverdale) speak of feminism without a condescending smile: "What matter of ridicule do you find in this, Miles Coverdale? . . . That smile . . . makes me suspicious of a low tone of feeling, and shallow thought" (p. 120). It is one thing to appropriate "Woman" for that metaphorical richness that allows her, inherently contradictory herself, to represent and to embody a language at once so desirably both slut and queen. This is why Zenobia must be so gorgeous, when her historical prototype Margaret Fuller "had not the charm of womanhood," for she is no *mere* feminist, but also the feminine, the ineffable, erotic word, the fallen Eve who arouses taxonomy into metaphor.[10] Hawthorne, in love with the symbolic and disquieted by the real, has no desire to deal with such a woman as Zenobia politically and actually, but she is, irresistibly, romance bespeaking its own enticing degradation.

And so a feminist reader may find *The Blithedale Romance* a greater affront than usual, for it disguises its anti-feminist agenda and its fundamental membership in the boys' club quite beautifully. (Coverdale is *not* Hawthorne! Not entirely.) It is as if, angry at one bewildering and unattainable love, half desired and half despised (that man's world of politics, of action, of realism), Hawthorne has courted another, a beautiful rival set up, in fact, precisely to be sacrificed as dumb, as excessive, as irrational after her presence (re)awakens the regard of the first. It is no surprise that critics speak of the homoerotic implications of the Coverdale/Hollingsworth friendship, for it reifies exactly this classic American ambivalence about men getting out of the saddle or off the raft long enough to hear women. And beyond this Huck-honey motif lies the more general fantasy of virile homosexuality about which Derrida speaks in "The Politics of Friendship"; the love–hate relationship between Coverdale and Hollingsworth, for all its fitful petulance, has beneath it a bedrock of commonly shared assumptions.[11] Their membership in the brotherhood makes them more attuned to each other than either could ever be to Zenobia; their speechifying guarantees the "being-together that any allocution supposes, including a declaration of war," while Zenobia's similarly hortatory discourses are met with either condescension (Coverdale) or disgust (Hollingsworth).[12] Hawthorne's putative affiliation with romance ensures that Zenobia will be a monumentally erotic figure; his decision to politicize so explicitly her otherwise "ineffable" femaleness allows him to give her enough rope to hang herself.

With both romance and realism so overtly politicized, Hawthorne is able to hold the specter of feminism up as shield and as warning of what might happen if "female" energies find a voice. Yet Hawthorne's political experience had, after all, done much to recommend an alternative mode; so infuriated by his misadventures as a political pawn in the Custom House affair that "the lion was roused in him," he was brought to the salutary and bracing simplicity of manly outrage.[13] He toys, in *The Blithedale Romance*, with a clearly ironic fantasy of a woman-run country: "I should love dearly . . . to have all government devolve into the hands of women. I hate to be ruled by my own sex; it excites my jealousy and wounds my pride" (p. 121). Still smarting, Hawthorne brings the feminist issue of an equal political voice to the fore even as he unsays it by placing it in Coverdale's half-sentimental, half-ironic mouth. Yet Hawthorne has heard what Margaret Fuller has to say, and he knows that a true feminist agenda must threaten the status quo (of which he is a part) just as thoroughly as would a non-playful, undilettantish socialism. He thus yields, in *The Blithedale Romance*, to equivocation, appearing to valorize (almost) that which he intends to sacrifice, for while he is willing to allow the voluptuous Zenobia to spring full-blown from his head, it is only to drown her in the end. That he creates a feminist at all suggests that at some level he understands and wishes to confront both the emotional and the logical inconsistencies on which he predicates his romance – to force the argument with an unwholesome but beautiful mistress and get the affair over with. And to do Hawthorne justice, he sets himself against the richest of erotic fantasies in Zenobia, for unlike all the others, he brings her to possess what might be called a "self" (thus the controlling metonymy of her inescapable flower becomes essential in keeping her character firmly in hand).[14] One must speculate that Coverdale's long-withheld adoration of the childish and wifely Priscilla – the perfect medium – is the cathartic result of this resolution, especially given the evidence of his alternative attraction to Zenobia. Like Marlow, Hawthorne gives himself a choice of nightmares, and while he punishes Hollingsworth, he divests himself most particularly of Zenobia.

Hawthorne has, as early as "The May-Pole of Merrymount" (1836), explicitly articulated the geopolitical American landscape in which a necessary if unlovely paternal authority must supersede one's guilty complicity in a fertile, and thus anarchic, beauty; he has, too, signaled his capacity for self-abasement and for penance, much as Hester does when she puts aside fancy work for stitching paupers' clothing, by wrenching "The May-Pole" by main force from gaiety to sobriety. "History," after all, cannot be revised into romance, neither that of Mount Wollaston nor that of Brook Farm. Sophia writes in 1843 that her husband is "as free of prejudice and party and sectarian bias as the birds, and therefore wise with a large wisdom that is as impartial as God's winds and sunbeams," but this is even less true in 1851 than it was in 1843.[15] Hawthorne is never really free of his fathers' judgmental voices; this is why he always imposes on his fiction some rigorous frame, some history to balance the fantasy, so that he can discipline himself in advance of the erotic game of imagining. As he well knows, his Puritan fathers were not tolerant of deviance and demanded "a severe and masculine morality"; their rhetoric made it explicitly clear that anything less than an "iron masculinity" constituted reprehensible effeminacy.[16] And of course romance itself cannot be completely exonerated in this struggle, for if realism tends toward the reductionism necessary to effect its program, romance, as Hawthorne well knew, had voluptuous tendencies, lapsing frequently into gothicism, sentimentalism, and prurient sensualism. Thus, as is often the case in eroticism, his self-restraint prefigures the sadomasochistic dynamic through which discipline awakens pleasure (and vice versa) – the set piece at Merrymount does, after all, become the whipping post, and as is usual in these games, the female plays the most disposable part. Thus, inevitably perhaps, just as Merrymount gives way, by virtue of its own artistically enforced demotion from a scene of beauty to a scene of depravity, to the stern, gray paternalisms of Endicott's tribe, so, too, does *The Blithedale Romance* repudiate its own name. This is what Hawthorne is encoding in "The Masqueraders," which so inevitably brings Merrymount to mind, for this chapter becomes, as do so many others of the final chapters of *The Blithedale Romance*, a force of retroactive reclamation for Puritan/ paternal justice. The pagan masque, with its paradox of revelatory disguise, lays out the bacchanalian "truth" behind Blithedale's utopian pretensions, just as it also exposes the language of romance as clothed in mischief, and it presumes both the inevitability and the necessity of an Endicott (Hollingsworth) who will destroy the masque/fertility rite and restore order.[17]

Romance, ineffable and inner-directed, does not aspire to conform to mandates for social, political, and artistic reductionisms that would impose order and structure (if it did, it would be realism), and it can accommodate only so much ambivalence about its worthiness as a mode of thought and as a genre before capitulating to its own inherent capacities for excess. It is not a form employed by vigorous men: "The yeoman and the scholar – the yeoman and the man of finest moral culture, though not the man of sturdiest sense and integrity – are two distinct individuals, and can never be melted or welded into one substance," says Coverdale (p. 66). A man of sturdier sense and integrity – a writer of realism – might also be a yeoman, for, after all, the two forms of toiling are there not so different, but a romancer is more wedded to the erotic pleasure of the text than to a less profligate and dutiful mode.[18] *The Blithedale Romance*, about Hawthorne's failure to accommodate even the romantic environment of Brook Farm to his artistic habits, is thus the most deeply self-abasing of his books. It is one thing for Hawthorne to satirize his Custom House experience, divested as it is of all threatening erotic potential and of all moral ambiguity; exclusively a world of men, and dominated by foolish old men, explicitly commercial and indisputably politicized and corrupt, it allows him to caricature the memory of an appetitive past purged of sexuality. The "permanent Inspector," husband of three forgotten, dead wives and father of twenty forgotten, dead children, remembers only his culinary past, as if to caricature the sterile greed of the place. "The Custom-House" even affords Hawthorne a masculine form, satire, and it is so satisfyingly unimpeachable that he is content to leave it as it is in later editions. But it is another thing entirely to render into fiction a complex, erotically declined social experiment to which he feels he has failed to measure up, either politically or artistically. Hawthorne has evidence from the two antithetical environments of the Custom House and the farm that either he can write with the (phallic) instrument, investing it with erotic energy, or he can find, as Creon puts it so succinctly in *Antigone*, "other furrows for his plow." In both "The Custom-House" and *The Blithedale Romance* (and elsewhere) he asserts, rather defensively, that he lacks enough spunk to do both, and *The Blithedale Romance* is his most extended confession of this self-perceived effeminacy.

Mystery (romance) thus becomes degenerate in this novel, whose opening words describe a charlatan's opportunism in his display of the lady in white, a figure of compromised inspiration, her receptivity the trick of a mesmerist who could as easily bring her down to all fours to bark like a dog, instead of veiling her in diaphanous illusion.[19] The richly ambiguous play of science against supernaturalism that characterizes the Hawthornian territory of infinite possibility is reduced in these opening paragraphs to a sideshow; it is as if Hawthorne is making his *apologia* for the fallen nature of his romance through the metaphor of mesmerism. The complex diachrony of his vision reveals a deep-seated anxiety, both about the genre he has chosen and about his ability to effect it, as Coverdale characterizes the "present state" of mesmerism, as he writes (as compared with twelve or fifteen years earlier, when he saw the Veiled Lady), as having been purged of showmanship and brought to "[affect] the simplicity and openness of scientific experiment" (p. 5). Romance, in other words, has been coerced or cajoled by reality (and realism) into at least the guise of accountability: the Custom House informs the commune; marriage and a family inform the delightful premarital eroticism of the Sophia letters with postcoital and postpartum truths; the literary marketplace informs the illusion of artistic autonomy.[20] Coverdale, speaking from some fifteen years' distance, recalls his enthralled response to a show laid out (as is the romance) with "all the arts of mysterious arrangement, of picturesque disposition, and artistically contrasted light and shade, . . . made available in order to set the apparent miracle in the strongest attitude of opposition to ordinary facts" (p. 6). The effect is enhanced by the rumor that the Veiled Lady is a beautiful woman of family and fortune – in other words, that the theatrical mesmeric subject, a woman perhaps fallen, or of low class, or mentally deranged, or all three, has been replaced by some Una of purity and grace.[21] Here would be romance indeed, an erotic loveliness all unspoiled and respectable, a text at once both seductively appareled in "all the arts of . . . arrangement" and also rectified to purity.[22] No masquerade of loveliness, but the real thing.

Yet as Zenobia (Hawthorne) knows, this is merest fantasy, made such by the masculine fear that "so questionable a creature" as romance/woman might as easily conceal horrors as high-born purity beneath her veil: "the lips of a dead girl, or the jaws of a skeleton, or the grinning cavity of a monster's mouth" (p. 113), "the face of a corpse; . . . the head of a skeleton; . . . a monstrous visage, with snaky locks, like Medusa's, and one great red eye in the centre of the forehead" (p. 110). The urge to write romance might reveal itself as a necrophiliac desire for a dead form (the daylight world having proved itself fraught with anti-romance). Or, bringing romance to life through some Frankensteinian hubris, one leans in for a kiss and finds oneself in the "grinning cavity of a monster's mouth" (p. 113). This fantasy of being swallowed into an insatiable genital/oral abyss suggests that Hawthorne has indeed briefly lifted the veil between his fantasy of the feminine and the reality of feminism, between the vaguely debasing eroticisms of romance-writing and the actuality of women like Zenobia/Fuller who will indeed open their mouths. "There will be ten eloquent women, where there is now one eloquent man," predicts Zenobia (p. 120). "Thus far, no woman in the world has ever once spoken out her whole heart and her whole mind. . . . society throttles us, as with two gigantic hands at our throats!" (p. 120). Poor Hawthorne, receptive to the feminine, fears that he has had a hand in loosing the monster through the "feminine" voice of his romance, and she is all horrors combined.

But Coverdale claims of the Veiled Lady that "her pretensions . . . whether miraculous or otherwise, have little to do with the present narrative; except, indeed, that I had propounded, for the Veiled Lady's prophetic solution, a query as to the success of our Blithedale enterprise" (p. 6). Thus Hawthorne also, and more consciously, proclaims his sense of an unrecoverable vision, of his own mouth made undesirable, stripped of its erotic appeal. In this version of the nightmare, it becomes his mouth/voice, dead, unfleshed, or monstrous, or, like Westervelt's, fraudulent, snake-oilish. This loss of artistic potency is a fear that he reiterates soon after in Coverdale's sense that he cannot translate the heat of that first Blithedale fire because his heart no longer burns and his inspiration has become a mere "sigh" of its former self. What is left is "the merest phosphoric glim-mer," a "chill mockery of a fire" that gives only insufficient imaginary warmth (p. 9). The blazing fire at the center of his memory of Blithedale may have been "somewhat too abundant," proving by its prodigality that those around it were "no true farmers" given to New England economies. But "it made the men look so full of youth, warm blood, and hope, and the women . . . so very beautiful, that I would cheerfully have spent my last dollar to prolong the blaze," he says (pp. 23–24). Thus the "Sibylline" response the Veiled Lady makes to Coverdale's question suggests that Haw-thorne himself is left wondering whether or not his own "Blithedale en-terprise" will fail. Coverdale, equally willing to watch, whether the show represents "the birth of a new science, or the revival of an old humbug" (p. 5), becomes a most appropriate arbiter of the novel's fallen perspective as he also serves to proclaim Hawthorne's ambivalence about the writing of romance; he is himself but a "chill mockery" of the living author, an emblem of Hawthorne's sense of depleted vitality.

In *The Blithedale Romance* the precarious balance between imagination and actuality gives way before Hawthorne's cathexis to the memory of Brook Farm as an eroticized ideal (this remains a thing apart from his intellectual assessment of that adventure). He has seen in Brook Farm a living, politically based enactment of socialistic community, and he has witnessed Margaret Fuller as a prime mover in this new Eden. Brook Farm asked that Hawthorne actually *associate* with people, a task Sophia believed him to find wearisome: "Since I saw you at the farm," she writes, "I wish far more than ever to have a home for you to come to, after associating with men at the Farm all day. A sacred retreat you should have of all men. Most people would not like it, but notwithstanding your exquisite courtesy and conformableness and geniality there, I could see very plainly that you were not leading your ideal life."[23] The farm, unlike the Custom House, offered a model of the free play of dialogic possibility that underlies the romantic mode, and it was predicated on a relative barrierlessness in which character truly did exceed its definitional components to reside somewhere between oxymoronic oppositions: transcendentalist socialists, feminist Fou-rierists, intellectual farmers, a veritable wonderland of hydra-headed enthu-siasts. More particularly, through Fuller's involvement the experiment became more inevitably and explicitly sexualized: Coverdale's intentionally provocative references to Fourier's theory of an equivalent, necessary, and logical sexual freedom suggest the tincture to which that radical experiment was distilled for Hawthorne, and Hollingsworth's overwrought disgust gives some further insight into the depths to which he was moved by this possibility.[24] Yet the more problematized the actualities, the more profound Hawthorne's sense of having somehow fallen short of an Edenic marriage of fertility – social, agronomical, political, artistic – and purity. Itself a romance and "certainly, the most romantic episode of his own life" (p. 2), Brook Farm necessarily refutes a placid reductionism to "fancy-sketch" (p. 1).

Hawthorne's preface repudiates both realism and historicity as it denies that the novel records "the actual events of real lives" or that it "put[s] forward the slightest pretensions to illustrate a theory . . . in respect to Socialism" (pp. 1–2), and thus it locates itself by default within the potent residual affect that exceeds these particulars. With his usual self-deprecatory irony, he claims instead that *The Blithedale Romance* is a place "where the creatures of his brain may play their phantasmagorical antics" (p. 1). Forced, unlike his European counterparts, whose "Faery Land" is an established and accepted place, to arouse himself to the "strange enchantment" necessary to produce romance, he feels this auto-eroticism as at once both artificial and pleasurable (p. 2). The phantasmagoria is itself a double phenomenon, akin to the marriage of politics and art, a chimerical product of science and technology that facilitates mystery at the same time it suborns it.[25] It is also, as the name suggests, a troubling vision, its images fevered (it is no surprise to find the novel filled with fever imagery); in refuting the constrictions of any systematic evaluation of "actual events," he also relinquishes the safety of such a prescribed orientation for the more dangerous regions of his own psyche. At once both deprecatory and grandiose, Hawthorne's claimed phantasmagoria is one that gives rise to the most pleasurably fearful specter of the erotic Zenobia, the feminine, the romance, the unsayable, grown large and given a voice. As Hester unbound, Zenobia is the hyperbolic feminine, so untrammeled as to necessitate her eternal flower. If beneath the veil might lie skeletons, monsters, one-eyed Medusas, and dead girls, Zenobia, in wearing her sexuality on her head, and with her mind full of weeds, becomes a surrealist's dream of a speaking eroticism.

And thus, most particularly in *The Blithedale Romance*, where it could have proved otherwise, Hawthorne sees that one must eschew erotic (linguistic) pleasure for those domestic proprieties that keep women and texts in their places. Hawthorne translates theoretical socialism, with its class and gender barrierlessness, into the barrierlessness of erotic desire (Fourier's "consummated Paradise," p. 53), setting against it the hegemonies of the marital state. And marriage wins out, while romance is submerged, drowned. In love, says Kristeva, the "I" is "sovereign yet not individual. Divisible, lost, annihilated; but also, and through imaginary fusion with the loved one, equal to the infinite space of superhuman psychism";[26] in marriage, the erotic bond is formalized and becomes a definitive closure within a paternalistic system. All leftover women must be accounted for; it is generally best to kill them off, particularly since nunneries are distinctively un-American institutions (Hawthorne cannot take George Moore's unabashed step of turning his compromised woman into a Sister Teresa or James's gleefully reluctant one of consigning Madame de Cintre to Carmelite oblivion). Theoretically, there is no better way than marriage to keep a woman both circumscribed and sexually immanent in a nice sort of way, just as there is no more conclusive resolution of plot.

This legal pairing ensures that the paternalistic voice will prevail, for marriage is precisely that subordination of female to male. Pretending to be rounded, complex characters, Zenobia and Hollingsworth are bound within the rigorous typologies of their controlling humors; seeming to exceed stereotype through their respective densities of characterization, they fall back in the end, exhausted by their textual gymnastics, into the most stereotypical of forms. One senses that Hawthorne's capitulation is to more visceral imperatives than one finds in other similar teleological economies; his gestures of reconciliation are solemnized in a way that, for example, Chopin's drowning of her protagonist is not. It is as if, in the compulsion to confess his crime of romance before some McCarthyite body, he must also give up his characters to the exigencies of reform. Thus their value accrues or diminishes in proportion to their marriageability; extremisms like those embodied by Zenobia and Hollingsworth, and ironic detachment like that embodied by Coverdale, must all be leveled into domestic moderation by that black hole of fierce passivity that is Priscilla. Priscilla is a concealed nothingness, a lacuna to match those holes in the plot; she is an empty purse, looking for the commodification of marriage.

She is pure otherness frightened out of its wits so that it can approximate the decorous vacuity of wifeliness. One sees in her the genuine article, a vacancy that by comparison reveals Louisa Gradgrind's nihilism as tense, profoundly enriched resistance. Priscilla, the original, bridal "veiled lady," claimed as bride and as daughter simultaneously when Hollingsworth brings her to throw off the veil and take his hand (in marriage) (p. 203) – only marriage will make her, and when it does, she becomes the domestic succubus on whom the enfeebled Hollingsworth (like the others, now reduced to impotence) must lean. And as everyone knows, when marriage is the solution, romance goes out the door.

But Zenobia is a woman, not a girl, not bridal, but unbridled, the Medusa laughing: "What girl had ever laughed as Zenobia did?" (p. 47). Zenobia stands for otherness – explicitly, female otherness, but also, encoded in her historical source and in her dark beauty, the otherness of race and class,[27] – and she is, as such, the antitype of an individuation patterned explicitly on the masculine, white, Christian(izing) colonist prototype on which the ideal (of) American character is based;[28] too, she is romance, the antitype of the colonizing realism, propagandizing for one agenda or another, that springs from such resolute individuation. Possessed of an unnameable energy, she is "fair enough to tempt Satan with a force reciprocal to his own" (p. 214). She is a name, a "public name" that is meant to override both her baptismal and her patronymic names, removing her from a singular, locatable, and manageable womanhood to something much larger (p. 8). She is also that which strips manly "heroisms" of their trappings to show them for something more egoistic, less grand, and somehow foolish; "not exactly maidenlike," she laughs out loud and open-mouthed (p. 47). "The presence of Zenobia caused our heroic enterprise to show like an illusion, a masquerade, a pastoral, a counterfeit Arcadia," says Coverdale (p. 21); she simply *embodies* this potent subversion of grandiose "heroic enterprise," even as Hawthorne chastises this iconoclasm by bringing her to kneel before the virile Hollingsworth. She is equally the subversion of domesticity, a truth neatly encoded in her evil-tasting gruel – "Nature certainly never intended Zenobia for a cook," says Coverdale (p. 48) – and in her anti-maternal teasing of Priscilla. Coverdale impugns what he perceives as her inconsistencies – "her mind was full of weeds" – and finds her energies purely disruptive of the normal order: "she made no scruple of oversetting all human institutions, and scattering them as with a breeze from her fan" (p. 44). And "Oriental," she is also embodied romance, that which in the long-lived polarization between the novel and the romance holds within it the seductively grand proportions of the Gothic and the heroic, the anti-mundane and the extra-contemporaneous (p. 213) (this, of course, links her, as in so many other ways, to *Frankenstein*'s orientalism and the subtle yellow monster).[29] When *she* tells the Blithedale romance, as she in fact does in "Zenobia's Legend," she tells it "wildly and rapidly, hesitating at no extravagance, and dashing at absurdities" that the narrator/ author is "too timorous to repeat"; *she* gives it, as if she is the very source and fountain from which romance flows, "the varied emphasis of her in-imitable voice, . . . the freshest aroma of . . . thoughts, as they [come] bub-bling out of her mind" (p. 107). She brings her audience to breathless pleasure with language both interdicted (unrepeatable) and "inimitable," and she brings her victim, a wide-eyed paragon of female submission, near to a dead faint. She is to be both desired and feared, revered and repudiated, loved and hated, for she is all that threatens the status quo, a "Pandora" (p. 24), a "witch" (p. 45), an "enchantress" (p. 45). Romance incarnate, she is also the emblem of its failure, brought low by its own self-indulgent eroticism.

Coverdale/Hawthorne, who envisions Zenobia as erotically potent, an open flower, a naked and fallen Eve, castigates his own desire and repu-diates his ambivalence as regards femininity, feminism, and art in his pen-ultimate and final revelations of Zenobia's (Fuller's) death and his choice of the female type represented by Priscilla (Sophia).[30] While Hawthorne enacts his punishment of both Zenobia and Fuller in Zenobia's drowning and disfiguration and his approval of Priscilla's pallid but obstinate vision of herself as helpmeet in Coverdale's avowed love, he also, by virtue of the melodramatic conclusiveness of these gestures, erects the devices of a denatured realism in the place of "romance." By this, I mean that with her love-stricken suicide, he emphatically closes the dialogue as regards Zenobia's worth, and at the same time retroactively depreciates every word he has had her say; every generous gesture, every apparent transcendence of weak "femaleness" is assimilated after the fact and made to seem mere subterfuge. Hollingsworth, whatever his zealotry, is validated in his con-tempt for female altruism, an inherent contradiction that Coverdale also impugns. Moreover, by having Coverdale announce at the very end his long-enduring and heretofore unspoken love for Priscilla, Hawthorne guarantees that his own putative receptivities as regards feminist thought are similarly impugned; Coverdale is proved to have been no less besotted, no more objective or idealistic, than Zenobia. Hawthorne thus willfully refutes himself and his instincts for the inconclusiveness of the romance, for his narrator, already ironically conceived as a near-parodic version of the artist as impotent voyeur, is shown to be a sentimental fraud. All of those infinite possibilities within the human heart, that anti-reductionist empathy that elsewhere keeps Hawthorne's fiction apart, to some extent, from the habitual sexisms of his daily life, are reduced to the bathos of failed love. This is a hallmark of realism at its most rigorously ideological, this definitive resolution in favor of some important message (and one may take one's pick of the anti-feminist messages associated with Zenobia). In this case, however, Zenobia's bathetic end preaches a double message, and its extra-textual implications are damagingly anti-feminist.

Inescapably, Zenobia's suicide is an artistic elaboration on Margaret Fuller's own death by drowning – his version being the more satisfactory retribution for illicit love, as it says that a woman will be brought thereby not merely to death but to unsanctified and unheroic suicide. Hawthorne's elaboration of Fuller's death makes a clearer lesson of it than reality did, for though it may be posited (indeed, Hawthorne himself posits it) that God the Father in his infinite wisdom and mercy drowned Fuller and her lover and her child to obviate her sexual/political transgression, Hawthorne makes it clear that Fuller's own female weakness is more to the point.[31] Fuller's body was never found, but Hawthorne here forces one to view it as he fantasizes it to have been, brought to its knees in an agony of repentance and terror – and not only that, but he links her to a hapless village schoolmistress, whose suicide gave Hawthorne the unenviable but memorable opportunity to drag the pond for her body and to see the awful corpse: "her stiffened death-agony was an emblem of inflexible judgment pronounced upon her," he writes in his notebook.[32] Zenobia's kneeling posture and imploring hands are testimony to two equivalent guises of paternalism, for they image forth both a woman at the feet of an angry God ("her knees, too, were bent, and – thank God for it! – in the attitude of prayer," p. 235) and a woman brought, paralyzed, to her knees under the rigor of some Sadeian punishment. She becomes the gruesome metonymy for her own transgressiveness, that parodic contiguity of contorted flesh that shows outwardly the architecture of the (departed) spirit. Zenobia's gorgeous body betrays her: Coverdale speculates that she has imagined herself as a lithesome lady of the lake, her hair streaming behind, her face a pale water lily, thus further trivializing her suicide retroactively by placing it in the realm of female vanity, but Zenobia's body in its rigor lays her soul bare.[33] She becomes "the dead girl . . . the skeleton" Zenobia has had Theodore envision beneath veiled womanhood (p. 113). And what Hawthorne does to Zenobia's character, he does also to Fuller's; what he does to Zenobia's political postures, he does also to Fuller's feminism. Retroactively compromising Zenobia, he also compromises Fuller, and both calumnies are effected through subtle indirection and in the guise of sympathy.[34] It has been conjectured that Hawthorne attempts to dissociate Zenobia from Fuller; by having Coverdale see Fuller mirrored in Priscilla's face and having him receive a letter from Fuller, Hawthorne, it is speculated, strews the text with red herrings. But his disclaimers have the same effect as Magritte's faithfully representationalist painting of a pipe, above which is written, with calligraphic clarity, "Ceci n'est pas une pipe." The painting is not a pipe, and Zenobia is not Fuller, but they both *look* an awful lot like the things they are said not to be. And in case one is about to miss the connection between Zenobia and Fuller, Hawthorne brings it inescapably to mind by naming Fuller in the text. The gesture of investing Priscilla with this identification seems particularly cynical, since it guarantees, among those who knew Fuller, an immediate resistance. The timorous, yet stubbornly proprietous Priscilla cannot be meant as Fuller, one must think, thus more inevitably bringing one to locate Fuller's place in the text within Zenobia.

And yet further, in this lovingly grotesque portrait of the drowned Zenobia, Hawthorne bodies forth the textual agonies of a romance punished into realism: "Ah, that rigidity! It is impossible to bear the terror of it" (p. 235). He takes the erotic corpus, that which in *The Scarlet Letter* can live because it proclaims its own degradation, just as the beautiful Hester can live because she scourges her own desire through the *A*, and he cripples and disfigures it to make it speak its message[35] (the *A* that is the very emblem of Hawthorne's artistic dilemma, the letter that so beautifully and lovingly elaborates its own humiliation). The text of *The Blithedale Romance* is riddled with holes, and there can be no simple accident in this strange amnesia. The lacunae are noticeable only after the fact, much as the characters of Coverdale and Zenobia are fully compromised only retroactively; one returns to the text to discover what, exactly, was said at Eliot's pulpit between Zenobia and Hollingsworth, and one returns to look for confirmation of exactly how Priscilla falls back into Westervelt's hands, and one returns to search out the terms of Zenobia's relationship with Westervelt. One returns, too, to validate the narrative or symbolic function of the Veiled Lady plot, which can be integrated into the larger plot only by main force of critical will. But finally, one is not bewildered, because the syntagmatic momentum of a familiar paternalistic logic allows one to make the necessary leaps. The subtextual depletions of the Zenobia (feminism)/ romance energies free the text to proceed linearly; it is as if the dredging up of Zenobia's body from the depths is an emblem of Hawthorne's divestiture, as if Zenobia, pierced in the breast by Hollingsworth's hooked pole, has been prefigured in Hawthorne's betrayal of her (Aurelian, a kinder centurion than Hollingsworth, took his Zenobia home in chains).

There is a grammar intrinsic to this novel that supersedes the spontaneous complexities of character or the free play of dialogic energy, an inevitability conforming to the logic of realism which says that language is to be used precisely to make a point. In realism, character is at least superficially in the service of this point, which, while it is located exteriorly to individuals, is always contiguously bound by metonymy to them, bringing them to a kind of bond-servant duty to the larger text. Metonymy, with its evidential authority, links spirit with its tangible surroundings, making them interdependent; transcendence and mystery are thus hook-poled to material circumstance. Zenobia, hothouse and jeweled flower, Hollingsworth, penitentiary-pulpit – metonymies giving all one knows and all one needs to know in a place where the only alternative to their materialistically displayed identities is a "mystery," the Veiled Lady, perpetrated by a fraud. Their recalcitrance is all the more inescapable in the company of Priscilla and Coverdale: If Hollingsworth and Zenobia are carved in stone, predetermined and announced as such metonymously, it is equally significant that neither Priscilla nor Coverdale is given such an identifying device. Priscilla's lack of a metonymic code suggests that she is as yet undefined and simultaneously harmless, because without metonymy, she cannot be said to have any contiguous effect on her environment. Reciprocity between character and environment is not yet in place, for she is still trying to make out the voice that calls to her, and thus she is a puppet, quite literally sagging and drooping and sinking throughout.[36] Coverdale, removed from those urban contiguities that best express his character, is so protean as to defy metonymy.[37] But romance, in contrast to realism's virtual anatomizing of character through metonymy, is based on a significant interdiction, an awareness that one may speak *around* the ineffabilities of desire and the complexities of human character, and it is, in that way, antiprogrammatic and asyntagmatic. "The romancer deals with individuality," says Frye, "with characters *in vacuo* idealized by revery, and, however conservative he may be, something nihilistic and untameable is likely to keep breaking out of his pages."[38] The language of romance participates candidly in the irreducible density of poetry, where each word becomes "an unexpected object, a Pandora's box from which fly out all the potentialities of language," and its words rise above and thus thwart the forward-moving linearity of dialectically propelled argument (it is not insignificant that Coverdale is a failed poet).[39] Romance seduces one from duty to the pleasure of the text – unless, of course, it mistrusts itself. If it insists on peeking beneath the veil, if it "come[s] hither, not in holy faith, nor with a pure and generous purpose, but in scornful skepticism and idle curiosity," the lovely apparition vanishes (p. 113), and materialism takes its place. The lover gives way to the wife. It is no surprise, then, that *The Blithedale Romance* is quite thoroughly domesticated in its (linguistic) impulses: Cause and effect, subject and verb, metonymy and character, love and marriage – they all go together like a horse and carriage, the one pulling the other briskly along behind.

Thus Hawthorne leaves it: It is either Zenobia/hothouse flower or Hollingsworth/penitentiary-pulpit, or no one, who defines the terms. And Hawthorne betrays Zenobia/romance, and only Zenobia and romance, by giving his story over to Coverdale's enervated voice and by then leaving lacunae in the plot to be claimed by the more habitual and familiar narratives of realism.[40] When one is left to fill in such textual gaps, it is generally done with the syntagmatically precise economy inherent to plot summary (one thinks here of Lockwood's summation in a sentence or so,

of Nelly Dean's long story in *Wuthering Heights*); density yields to the grammar of a narrative superstructure in which one supplies the terms to fit the
pattern. Hollingsworth's story is invulnerable to such gaps; indeed, it thrives
on them, for as Hawthorne makes very clear, his "philanthropic theory"
is antithetical to the ambiguities afforded by "human wisdom, spiritual
insight, and imaginative beauty" (p. 54) and immune to exigencies of circumstance or emotion. His is a true syntagma, "a systematically arranged
treatise" utterly independent of the text into which he has been interpo-
lated. As text, Hollingsworth is a veritable *Helmet of Salvation*, which, even
damaged, with its cover knocked off, retains its propagandistic value; everything he does and says feeds back into the tautology of his pre-established
worth as a man. But Zenobia is a woman and thus is dependent on
circumstantialities to qualify her feminism and redeem her fallen state; she
is at risk when her character is filled in from externally prescribed narratives
about female predilections and behaviors. (We see this most unequivocally
when Hawthorne himself later works by extrapolation to explain Fuller's
attraction to Ossoli: "As for her toward him, I do not understand what
feeling there could have been, except it were purely sensual. . . . this rude
old potency bestirred itself and undid all her labor in the twinkling of an
eye."[41]) One has been given the ideological grounds for the final confrontation between Zenobia and Hollingsworth, but not the specifics of their
quarrel. However, Coverdale may enter at its conclusion and, without
having the details recapitulated, make the appropriate paternalistic assumptions; it is, after all, a case of the good daughter versus the bad one – quite
literally.[42] Without the complete story, we must assume with Coverdale
that it is the old story of a deeply principled if somewhat egocentric man
who chooses the devoted and virginal girl over the voluptuously corrupt
woman. The truth is, "it is the simplest thing in the world . . . to bring a
woman before your secret tribunals, and judge and condemn her, unheard,
and then tell her to go free without a sentence. . . . any verdict short of
acquittal is equivalent to a death-sentence" (p. 215). If Hollingsworth
wanted Zenobia's money, it only proves that he had no desire for her
carnal self. Given the code, one can proceed quite efficiently through the
syntagmatic inevitabilities of (sexual) cause and (punitive) effect; one merely
completes a sentence within the known proscriptive terms.

Or, again, one "knows" that Zenobia is sexually experienced because

her erotic potency must serve both to substantiate and to devalue her political claim to an Amazonian independence (and vice versa): If she wears
her heart on her sleeve as regards Hollingsworth, she displays her hothouse
ripeness metonymically in the moist flower nestling in her hair. It is, thus,
left to the reader to define her as once married to Westervelt or to imagine
an alternative means by which her "ripeness" has occurred. Hawthorne
understands that there is no necessity for any explicit answer to her past,
for one may proceed, unimpaired, without it: "It is clear that her 'antecedents' have been questionable. She has been no stranger, from her girl-
hood upwards, to what the French call Love," submits the *North British
Review* in 1853.[43] That old potency, bestirring itself. Reduced to univocacy
and without realism's full mechanism in play, the metonymy is in the
service of an ideological position (as contrasted to, for example, the irreducible *A*), and it locates her from the first moment of her appearance
within a relentlessly tautological system that will use it both to signify and
to condemn her erotic power. The flower is "actually a subtle expression
of Zenobia's character" (p. 45), and it says this at once: she is fallen into
knowledge, sexually and spiritually, and therefore she will die; her death
simultaneously proves her fallen state and validates itself by virtue of the
retroactive confirmation it supplies. The story that has produced her current
state is, quite simply, irrelevant. The flower is, thus, predictive of a plot
that we discover in retrospect to have been inexorably prejudicial to her.
Coverdale, in his delirium, cries out: "That flower in her hair is a talisman.
If you were to snatch it away she would vanish, or be transformed into
something else!" (p. 45); in this he is correct, for the flower is Hawthorne's
talisman, that which keeps Zenobia bound to his terms, for without it, no
longer circumscribed by its metonymy, she would indeed either vanish or
become "something else."

If the flower stands for Zenobia's opened hymen, it stands also to signal
another such cleft in the text; the erotic potency of romance is dependent
on just such knowledge and experience of desire as Zenobia's and is what
makes romance, for Hawthorne, at once both so attractive and so dubious.
What was said of Victorian novelists may be said in spades of Hawthorne:
Sex "is often a major motive . . . as it has been in all sorts of plots since
stories first began," but he "pat[s] the beast gingerly with fingers protected
by a thick glove of sentimental reverence, and then hastily pass[es] on."[44]

The flower is doubly degraded, first hothouse and then jeweled, both profoundly attractive and hyperbolically artificial, and its metonymic code
overrides all specific details of characterization by subsuming them into its
message. The flower ensures that Hawthorne can leave textual gaps that
will be filled in by extrapolation. And this, of course, presumes a reader
won over by or seduced into the logic of paternalism.[45] The text, after all,
depends on an *understanding*: that however equally balanced the competing
ideologies seem to be, however it mimics the appearance of a "heteroglossic
polylogue of ideological discourses,"[46] it is, underneath, fortified with the
Puritan spirit that sees the Blithedalers as "pilgrims" "whose present bi-
vouâc was considerably farther into the waste of chaos than any mortal
army of crusaders had ever marched before" (p. 52). And in this embattled
territory, such women as Zenobia are burned as witches; indeed, Coverdale
fantasizes her immolation at Pulpit Rock, where she stands condemned
before Hollingsworth: "Had a pile of faggots been heaped against the rock,
this hint of impending doom would have completed the suggestive picture"
(p. 214). Infiltrated by the devices of a programmatic realism, but without
realism's full working energy, *The Blithedale Romance* is as subverted and
compromised a romance as was the communal experiment that Hawthorne
used to invoke it, an experiment that, at least in Hawthorne's eyes, carried
the seeds of its own demise.[47] Thus Hawthorne, even knowing the exigencies to which paternal justice might resort in order to contain witchery,
leaves his text to be taken over by the iron Puritans who lurk always in
the peripheries of his own consciousness.

Zenobia, conceived as pure anti-paternalistic instinct, is not by Hawthorne's terms a failed feminist, for by his terms any "feminism" will by
its nature be incapable of sustaining a logical base and a coherent structure:
neither romance nor woman bears too much examination, and if it is
brought to testify before the brotherhood, it suborns itself. Unlike her
historical namesake, Zenobia is not conceived as a woman capable of effecting the terms of her political agenda; she is not, in fact, at all certain
of what that agenda should be. She is, rather, what the *American Whig
Review* called "a mere fierce, wild wind, blowing hither and thither, with
no fixity of purpose, and making us shrink closer every moment from the
contact."[48] This assessment of her character is not simply a misogynistic
attack on Zenobia's passionate nature (although it is that as well), for in its

claim that she has "no philosophy" by which she is guided, it inadvertently calls into question the very possibility of consistency in a female character who exists outside the domestic mother/whore model. It also calls into question the possibility of an acceptably formalized romance, dependable enough to satisfy the judicial authorities; the Endicotts who lurk around Blithedale, for example, will find Coverdale running from the masquers "like a mad poet hunted by chimaeras" (p. 211).

Classic assumptions about womanhood as inherently devoid of the capacity for objective logic negate the possibilities for a reasonable and consistent feminism (this is one reason why Hawthorne keeps Hester's ruminations tacit rather than articulated), and in Hawthorne's playing-out of this prejudice in the conflictual space of *The Blithedale Romance*, he reveals as well the kink in realism's logic, the rabbit hole into which it so invariably tumbles, for if "feminism" – perceived here as a political mode, a mode of being, and an essence – is intrinsically chaotic and anti-programmatic, subject to reversals and involutions, then a realism that shares this fantasy of women will necessarily be infected textually with the virus they carry. One may *not* characterize a woman within realism from the perspective of a conviction of her perpetual, unpredictable, mutational force. Only the most rigorous stereotype will hold her under this duress, and it is realism's curse and its pleasure to place character in the *world*, in an interactive relationship to the environment. It is not that Hawthorne fails to realize Zenobia as feminist – that would presume a standard from which she deviates – but that he proves such a creature to be as chimerical and anarchic as those masquers in the woods. At best, woman is ruled by "free, generous courtesy" and "the religious sentiment in its utmost depth and purity"; her spirit is "refined from that gross, intellectual alloy, with which every masculine theologist . . . has been prone to mingle it" (p. 121). At worst, she is "false, foolish, vain, destructive of her own best and holiest qualities, void of every good effect, and productive of intolerable mischiefs. . . . an almost impossible and hitherto imaginary monster – without man as her acknowledged principal" (pp. 122–3). Under the sway of such oppositional extremisms, both the text and the woman may careen at any moment off the straight and narrow path of realism's syntagmas.

Either governed by "free and generous sympathy" or, conversely, "void of every good effect, and productive of intolerable mischiefs" – in neither case is it possible for a woman to be just, for justice presumes consistency, and it presumes judgment, invariant and inflexible, based on that consistency.[49] Yet, as Zenobia proves, woman is herself all too real – she makes herself *felt*, in the heart, in the crotch, in the hand, in the pit of the stomach, even as she, by her nature, subverts the possibilities for an ordered reality and, by extension, for a naturally ordered realism (she forces realism toward totalitarian gestures, toward sadism). Outside of the brotherhood of friends who make and carry out the laws, she may be judged, but she cannot judge: Like the two Justines, Sade's and Shelley's, like Louisa Gradgrind, like Eustacia Vye, like Hetty Sorrel, like Edna Pontellier, all of whom suffer variously the effects of a masculine law, such a lovely woman/text as Zenobia proclaims her own deserving (in)violability, her simultaneous capacity to be both radically abused and untouchable. "Void of every good effect, and productive of intolerable mischief. . . . without man as her acknowledged principal," the text of *The Blithedale Romance* suffers from its author's self-fulfilling intuition of his own "manly" failure. Hawthorne's punitive energies, coupled with his ambivalence, create the essential paradox of a "romance" that cannot contain a realist's righteous indignations over the "real" conditions of his immediate environment. The real Custom House affair, the real utopian experiment of Brook Farm, the real feminist Margaret Fuller and the spawn of feminists she represents, the real tribe of women writing and writing while Hawthorne remains meticulously, chastely cautious – Zenobia, who is robust and politicized, who speaks and writes and has made a name for herself, stands for all these injurious realities. The wonderful irony here is, of course, that Hawthorne's Zenobia – man-made as surely as Frankenstein's monster is man-made – enacts a complete textual subversion with the very (wishfully conceived) anarchies Hawthorne accords to feminism and the feminine, but the victory is, as is usual in such cases, a Pyrrhic one.

Hawthorne, a failure at the socialism of Brook Farm and a failure at the commercialism of the Custom House, where his imprimatur marked commodities more material than romance, is guilty, in *The Blithedale Romance*, of the very thing he most fears; betrayal is an "unmanly" sin, and Hawthorne betrays Zenobia. And the betrayal of Zenobia is a betrayal of himself and of his own text, for Zenobia is not merely contemptible, but a fully enriched embodiment of his love and fear – she is romance, femaleness, beauty, eroticism. He proves himself here to be exactly that weak and inconstant creature prone to fancy, to moonlight, to shadows and clouds, he so often confesses himself to be; he proves himself as, indeed, unfit for the more stoic engagements of realism; he proves himself to be, through his effete narrator Coverdale, deserving precisely of Priscilla and unequal to Zenobia. Zenobia is also feminism, Margaret Fuller brought back to life for one last chance, and if feminism were to be proved viable, so, too, would romance be vindicated for Hawthorne, for feminism would fully legitimate his pursuing an alternative to his paternalistically defined and unilateral "realism" through a mode that he did not feel to be "effeminate" by virtue of its random energies. Feminism could provide the theoretical construct by which an alternative mode of thought and expression could be validated; it could wipe the smirk off Coverdale's face as he speaks of women's concerns, because its author would be freed of the homophilia that makes the "feminine" an embarrassing but irresistible joke among the brotherhood. But Hawthorne's courage fails, and his ambivalence makes him impotent; it is easier, after all, to believe Fuller "a great humbug."[50] He sets things up and then turns his back, leaving spaces to be claimed by the dominant ideologies, and this is the more unforgivable because he really does seem to see and understand that "secret tribunal" under which women are tried and condemned. He also admits, through Coverdale's confession, his own shameful complicity: "That cold tendency, between instinct and intellect, which made me pry with a speculative interest into people's passions and impulses, appeared to have gone far towards unhumanizing my heart" (p. 154). (But as George MacDonald says in *Lilith*, "self-loathing is not sorrow."[51])

The Blithedale Romance, by taking on the whole muddled Brook Farm affair considered in the light of Hawthorne's post–Custom House politicization, hypostatizes in Zenobia a "romance" beset by the imperatives of a flesh too solid to etherialize and an environment too real to transcend; it becomes, thus, a most revealing case by which one may study the delicate ecologies of realism and romance. The novel senses itself to be fraudulent as romance, and it signals its capitulations at multiple levels, from the enervated voice of its narrator to the sideshow quality of the Veiled Lady motif to the catachresis of a heroine both grandly proportioned and disfigured, both spiritually and, in the end, physically. In deciding to meet the ineffable squarely, head-on as woman/romance, and without modernism's license to aggrandize this unavailable Thing with Heideggerean nostalgia, Hawthorne is brought to reveal the double fantasy, but without the synthesis realism may afford: the immemorial, the unnameable, that excitation that goads one to get at it somehow, emerges in its dual guises, as the sublime and as the grotesque, as the sadistic and the masochistic – and Zenobia's body, alive and dead, could not be a more graphic inscribing of this duality. Romance fails in *The Blithedale Romance*, and because it is divided against itself, only the more opportunistic and ideological energies of realism may take its place. Hawthorne desublimates the excitation that produces his art. He does not then merely sacrifice this manifold to the proprieties – for placing a lovely thing on a scaffold may well increase its erotic potency, rather than vitiate it – but instead reduces it to a near embarrassment of bathos. Realism is thus caricatured in all its ideological univocacy, and romance is caricatured as hyperbolic, overblown, and irresponsible.

Coverdale fantasizes about Zenobia as art, and he wishes that he could see her sculpted, "because the cold decorum of the marble would consist with the utmost scantiness of drapery, so that the eye might chastely be gladdened with her material perfection, in its entireness" (p. 44). Hawthorne wishes for a way to present "womanliness incarnated" in all its erotic force, but with none of eroticism's corruptive powers – marble is, after all, impenetrable – for that would allow for a romance both powerfully seductive and unimpeachably pure. But Hawthorne is incapable himself of this impossible vision, for he can separate neither eroticism nor romance from degradation. Given Coverdale's fantasy of Zenobia in marble, and given Hawthorne's much later metaphor of Fuller as the inept sculptress of herself, one is left with two visions of womanliness incarnated in sculpture:[52] Hiram Powers's "The Greek Slave," the most famous statue produced by an American in the nineteenth century, and Harriet Hosmer's "Zenobia in Chains." "Zenobia in Chains" is fully clothed, crowned, and utterly regal. Powers's statue is naked, her virginal modesty assaulted by the viewer, whose pleasure is enhanced by the fantasy of her being held right before ravishment. She will be sold and she will be raped. This narrative, an old story, is clearly implicit for all to read (it would not need the subtext Powers supplies, perhaps unconsciously, in the phallic post on which she rests her hand).[53] If Hawthorne "found little of beauty or merit" in "The Greek Slave," he cannot but have had it in mind in his reveries on Zenobia as statuary.[54] But the later "Zenobia in Chains" is an anomaly, and as such it provides no ready narrative, for here is a woman, clothed but beautiful, chained but unhumiliated, captured but still crowned and regally empowered. For all of Hawthorne's immense imaginative resources, he cannot envision a woman thus. Neither a woman nor a text, in fact. And so romance must predicate itself on a humiliative eroticism, and the female voice must be, as in "The Greek Slave," silenced except through the language of a body whose erotic power is commensurate with its degradation. Realism is, in this environment, virtually stripped to a barebones aggression; it becomes the sheer physical ugliness of materiality in decay that Hawthorne fantasizes as beneath the gossamer veil of woman/romance – "the lips of a dead girl, or the jaws of a skeleton," or "the face of a corpse." If realism's precise forthrightness is built on necessary and willful amnesias, romance must scotomize the real in order to make its fantasies work. Hawthorne, too beleaguered by reality and by realism to effect the erasures of memory, of the past and of the present, necessary to romance, flays his own "feminine" text, and you will hardly believe how much it alters her person for the worse.

Chapter Eight

Dreams of Sleep

What indeed *does* man know about himself? Oh! that he could but once see himself complete, placed as it were in an illuminated glass case! Does not nature keep secret from him most things, even about his body, e.g., the convolutions of the intestines, the quick flow of the blood-currents, the intricate vibrations of the fibres, so as to banish and lock him up in proud, delusive knowledge? Nature threw away the key; and woe to the fateful curiosity which might be able for a moment to look out and down through a crevice in the chamber of consciousness and discover that man, indifferent to his own ignorance, is resting on the pitiless, the greedy, the insatiable, the murderous, and, as it were, hanging in dreams on the back of a tiger. Whence, in the wide world, with this state of affairs, arises the impulse to truth?

—Friedrich Nietzsche, "On Truth and Falsity in Their Ultramoral Sense"

Speaking in Tongues

Because Kate Chopin suffers and enjoys comparisons with the hard-core European realism of Zola and his party, *The Awakening* may do to preface a few last words on realism's behalf. To protest her sacrifice of Edna, L. scoffs lovingly in a letter to "My dear little Katie," "Why not let joy & triumph await those who dare defy the edicts of merciless custom – but all this would be foreign to the school of Realism & you are as realistic as Zola."[1] Yet *The Awakening* is a perfect reverie on the ambiguities of the real and on the ambivalence of one working within the realistic mode. *The Awakening*, from its title on, seems almost willfully to introduce the idealist's monkey wrench into the realist's machine. When Chopin changed her original title, *A Solitary Soul*, to its present declaration of Schopenhauerean ambiguity, she forcefully reminded her readership once again of realism's double-sided heritage of idealism and positivisim/empiricism. In fact, subsequent critics have failed to agree that it is Zola, exactly, or realism, exactly, that keeps this bird on the wing, and as if the book's own ambivalences were inevitably to be recapitulated in the phylogeny of the critical texts, these very terms have also generated their antitheses. When Cyrille Arnavon resurrected *The Awakening* in Paris in 1953, after his 1946 assessment of it as realism in the spirit of Dreiser and Norris, he took care to indict the novel's "dubious romanticism" and its "poetic" tendencies.[2] After Kenneth Eble posted a reminder of the "forgotten novel" in a 1956 *Western Humanities Review*, the variations on this theme of Chopin's generic schizophrenia became legion.

Yet clearly *The Awakening* shares in realism's premises, and like so many others who sense an obligation to the real, Chopin feels it as a mode that both cripples and releases her aesthetically. A double impulse to sink and swim, to perform realism's social and political duties and to evade those propagandas, infiltrates the text with visions of nullification; one need only think of the self-canceling motif of an eternal cycle of waking into sleep, or of the potently oxymoronic values inherent in the sinking swimmer or the crippled bird in flight. The whole novel performs a resistance too subtle and potent to find its way into any exegetical clarity; it awakens the terrifying sense that life slips like water through one's hands, that sleeping and waking are too close for comfort, that living within reality in the ways that a woman may be vouchsafed to live is the next thing to death, that one who leaps into consideration of the real (the realist author as well as the characters under consideration) is, in fact, not waving but drowning, stepping in for a brisk swim and ending up as sunken treasure.

Resting on the textual fathoms that lie beneath the realistic energies of *The Awakening* is the controlling oxymoron of Chopin's continued subversion, through indirect discourse, of Edna's power to speak, even as she claims to have gained, and is said by her creator to have gained, that power and the selfhood it implies. After making primary the theme of conscious, self-determining speech within and about the world, Chopin then simultaneously retracts this possibility for her characters by locating her story in an interstitial space between narrative and dialogue: "And the ladies . . . all declared that Mr. Pontellier was the best husband in the world. Mrs. Pontellier was forced to admit that she knew of none better." "They stood outside the window and the cook passed them their coffee. . . . Edna said it tasted good. She had not thought of coffee nor of anything. He told her he had often noticed that she lacked forethought." "How strange and awful it seemed to stand naked under the sky! how delicious! She felt like some new-born creature, opening its eyes in a familiar world that it had never known."[3]

The Awakening is woven of indirect discourse, as if to say, obliquely but irresistibly, that one may never escape from translation, that all of the language that feels (to the author, to the character) as if it emerges autonomously from the solitary soul in fact is made of antiphonal echoes. This gesture of parrotry may be seen to have a double significance in the context of realism, as it suggests that Edna's penchant for challenging directness, once she has found her tongue, is both depriving the author of a more poetic ambiguity and setting Edna herself up for a fall from which Chopin would protect her as long as possible; the Edna who speaks for herself is not a negotiator, and though she speaks at times in the full righteousness of a defensible position, she does not make herself heard in the ways she would wish. "You have been a very, very foolish boy, wasting your time dreaming of impossible things. . . . I give myself where I choose. If he were to say, 'Here, Robert, take her and be happy, she is yours,' I should laugh at you both."[4] Robert hears her and disappears like a scared rabbit. More globally, indirect discourse reminds one of realism's intuition of its own ventriloquistic throwing of a self-defined and limited "real" into the mouths of its characters. *The Awakening* performs at the level of process the drama Hawthorne puts on stage with the Veiled Lady and her mesmerist, for if Edna sleepwalks and sleeptalks her author's fantasies, the text gives us to feel almost palpably through its indirect discourse that Edna is a metonymy of Chopin herself, the contiguous automaton dreamed up by one who feels herself to be mesmerized as well.

The scene in Chapter 23 where Edna first discovers the champagne exhilaration of a storyteller's power over her audience might be used as emblematic of Chopin's seamless appropriation of dialogue into a near-paraphrase of speech and, through this, of her dreamlike elisions of what is said and what is thought (it should also be noted that Chopin's conflation here of erotic storytelling and intoxication – "the champagne was cold" – is an authorial confession to the pleasures of the text). In this gesture of assimilation she reveals realism's apprehension of its willful fabrications re-garding one's duty to and options for action within the world, and she also provides one of those self-referential moments that realism uses to comment on its own enterprise of documenting the real (the lovers in the boat have been mirrored by the Chênière Caminada chapter). Edna/Chopin tells a fiction – the story of runaway lovers – and "every glowing word seemed real" to her auditors: "She had one of her own to tell, of a woman who paddled away with her lover one night in a pirogue and never came back. . . . It was a pure invention. She said that Madame Antoine had related it to her. That, also, was an invention. Perhaps it was a dream she had had."[5] In this moment of linguistic triumph, Edna is mute; she might just as well be drowning. This intimate connection between the author and her char-acter, between the spoken and the thought, between the real and the dreamed, between the scare quote and the paraphrase, and between realism and the virtually surreal is only more palpably obvious here than in other texts. As if to prove all those integumental connections that realism feels as pulling against its syntagmatic obligations, Chopin locates herself be-tween the lines, and what she discovers is, I think, the vacancy of being neither here, in the real world, nor there, in the dubious safety of sleep.

There is, of course, in *The Awakening* a rather obvious other level of anxiety relative to realism besides that resident in the competing imperatives of tropological pleasure (Chênière Caminada dream language) and social duty (language wide awake), but the additional complexity of a gendered claiming of the "real" only shows an exacerbated version of the artist's dilemma. Chopin knows that the realist's question of "self-determination" versus assimilation is necessarily a second-order concern for one working within her sense of an already and perpetually embattled female autonomy. "Reality" plants a flag for reason and teleological inevitability, leaving to the subalterns, the women, the children, the visionaries, and the fools the

residue that cannot be fully controlled, and *The Awakening*, in fact, perpetually confronts this maddening capacity of the empowered discourse to
alter the world retroactively. From the very first conundrum of Raoul's
fever, to the hammock scene, to Edna's removal to the pigeon-house,
Chopin makes a claiming of the real contingent on power: Léonce may
renovate both his house and, for public view, his marriage, in one simple
gesture obviating the declarative and the constative, if not the performative,
terms of Edna's act of self-reliance; a brief announcement in the daily paper
of "sumptuous alterations," while perhaps suggestive of a piquant authorial
irony that intuits a more bounteous sensuality in the works, clinches the
deal.[6] Chopin makes it clear that she understands that one who defines
reality must have the power to make that narrative stick, and whatever her
stated objections to feminism, whatever her subsidies of an "intellectual
freedom" defined in standardly masculinist terms, she clearly communicates
her intuition of a contaminated thought supply in *The Awakening*. If Schopenhauer via Kolbenheyer permeates the conscious epistemological stance
with German idealism, it is nonetheless true that Emerson, resident American idealist, puts Edna to sleep.[7] It is true, too, that one feels the novel as
invaded by a virtual sleeping sickness, so that the question of Raoul's fever
becomes infectious. Chopin enacts what she cannot unequivocally assert:
that a woman who thinks or tries to act in this particular real world will
sense, as Edna clearly does, that she is sleepwalking on the precipice.

Chopin's novel reinforces realism's sense that the artist, regardless of
gender, must find "reality" an Alice in Wonderland proposition when it
makes its way into (fictional, artistic, tropologically energetic) language; the
woman artist, bringing into the aesthetic field her additional subversive
energy, may produce exactly that "realism" most bent on unsaying itself.
But *The Awakening* is only more thematically and formally attuned than
many other realist texts to the nihilism implicit in this double vision; its
sea changes, its sense of the always whispering Gulf, merely reify the gaps
and fissures in realism's syntagmatic program. Say what she might about
loving furniture polish and dress patterns, and about the "accidental" and
somewhat regrettable emergence in her text of fractious, erotically inclined
women, Chopin has her vengeance against realism's assimilative energies
as she spins a text subversive of its own projection of the real. She finds
that the paternally designated, bureaucratically encumbered space of the

ordinary real is paradoxically accommodative, for it sets up a system whereby vagaries and disputations are so many waves in the Gulf; when the "real" world is made definitionally obvious, then madness, hysteria, dreaming, irresponsibility, and sheer meanness are as easy to spot as to name. Then she creates a text that exceeds the terms that might pigeonhole it. *The Awakening*, a member of realism's underground, sustains a vertiginous balance between realism and realism's own self-canceling impulses, between forward, syntagmatic movement and the downward pull that thwarts teleological necessities by suggesting a kind of nihilistic hole beneath the text.

This, then, is the context in which Chopin's interweaving of indirect discourse with a dialogue shocking in its candor and energy takes place. Multiple other nullifications stand behind and validate Chopin's use of indirect discourse, but it is this impulse to assimilate Edna's speech back into the flow of the narrative that most clearly implies both the overt and the insidious dangers for realism of an entry into full ideological or erotic candor. As Edna learns language, she proves herself to be painfully outspoken and playfully irreverent; this energy is counterbalanced as she loses dialogue to Chopin's dense, "poetic" paraphrase. Edna cannot, in the beginning, speak for herself among men or mannish women like Mm. Reisz (she finds a private voice with Adèle); she is shy, about French novels, about all matters, like childbearing, obliquely erotic; she is diffident, about asserting her right to sleep undisturbed, about her conviction of her children's health, about her sufficiency as a mother, falling into tears rather than exploding with exasperated rage. That she cannot swim is a metonymous extension of that proclivity for sinking; it literalizes Edna's fear of speaking as a fear of drowning, as if to open her mouth is to risk having it filled so full she will choke. And so when she learns to swim, she learns to speak, totteringly at first in her querulous responses in "delicate note[s] of pathos" to Robert and then more assuredly in her commands and abrupt answers to Léonce: "Don't wait for me." "No; I am going to stay out here."[8] And, as if the two skills are inseparable (as indeed they are), she learns also to hear the paternal voice for what it is: "She wondered if her husband had ever spoken to her like that before, and if she had submitted to his command. Of course she had; she remembered that she had" (p. 32). Chopin clearly knows that one must learn to speak forthrightly to produce results in the real world. She knows as well that one must learn also to enforce the right to speak in order to discover the correlative right to silence – "Don't speak to me like that again; I shall not answer you"; these are crucially interdependent, for speech as uncontrolled spillage is often confessional and self-abasing. Here, then, in the famous swimming scene, are indeed the first words of her increased awareness and authority; her ability to speak and her consequent ability to choose silence over apology or confession are born here (witness the scorched fish scene in Chapter 17 for evidence of this dual power, p. 52).

And yet if Edna begins in triumph, she ends this scene in something worse than simple defeat. Prostrate, feeling her delicious, combative energy lapse into enervated feebleness, she is made here a virtually allegorical figure for realism's thematic and imagistic preoccupation with exhaustion, brain fever, fainting, and muted depression; it is as if Chopin projects into Edna the realist's simultaneous sense of a powerful and stimulating obligation to shape and alter the world – to swim, head up – and a commensurate awareness of how very futile that effort might be – to sink. She is overpowered not from without but from within, and this is the failure the book reifies through to the end and that it both predicts and resists through indirect discourse. Léonce has the last word of the scene, literally, but this is not the most deadly aspect of Chopin's intuition, for the cycle between Edna's exhilaration and her exhaustion is virtually autonomous. She moves from "a dream, a delicious, grotesque, impossible dream, to feel again the realities pressing into her soul" (p. 32), and it is this oppression of realities from without and within that allows her in the end to dive in for a swim and find in the middle of it that she is not equal to the energy it takes to stay afloat. The message is double, announcing both a textual angst and a spiritual angst: The realist writer moves from tropological fancies, delicious, grotesque, and impossible, to a responsibility to articulate the realities of the social, economic, and political environment; the woman waking to the real soon finds her energies draining away from inside. Edna, in the end, "tottered up the steps, clutching feebly at the post" (p. 33), enervated by her own unendurable power, which, recognized, must at all costs then be contained.

Chopin is, I think, convinced of the Nietzschean wisdom she puts into Mm. Reisz's mouth, that the artist (Edna, Chopin, the writer, the woman

NINETEENTH-CENTURY LITERARY REALISM

writer) must have a "courageous soul," a "soul that dares and defies" (p. 63), but she is also possessed of the realist's recognition that sublimity cannot be sustained within a venue filled with the infinite bits and pieces of an often-trivial materiality. Her sense of a necessarily willful and inevitably tidal power produces the authorial fantasy of a Chopin piece played with irresistible virtuosity; it invests in the Schopenhauerean theme of music's potency the correlative knowledge of an evanescent production that cannot sustain itself beyond its explosion into sound. But if Edna is any indication, Chopin is possessed by a sense of her own exhaustibility in a world and an artistic mode that demand that one stay the course. One senses Chopin's inclusion in that league of women who, operating under the duress of the "real," feel on occasion the pit yawning beneath their energetic efforts to save themselves through art, through politics, through this sheer effort of will. Her intuition of the inevitable failure of energetic defiance makes itself felt throughout the text, and that she deprives her creation of speech even as she empowers her to utter it serves a dual purpose. It signals, along with myriad other devices, this prophetic insight into the failure of the human will to defy for more than episodic moments; it shows with poignant clarity why realism cannot imagine and refuses to pretend to grand heroisms. And, in an act of solicitude, it works to save a female creature who cannot *be* saved, by virtue of its own textual affiliation to a realism that must drown its most beautiful and recalcitrant women as sacrifices of pleasure to duty, tropological fancy to syntagmatic force, figure to pedagogical effect.

One must not forget where, finally, Chopin's checks and balances lead: to the Gulf. She senses how the language of a particular realism will always fail to suffice, how the struggle to discover language and then the battle to speak with candor in a society given to sentimental euphemisms are in the end disappointments, failing to produce enough change within the real world of men and work to make any difference at all. She can, thus, allow Edna first to kiss Robert and then to speak to him candidly about his infantile fantasy of a transfer of ownership from Pontellier to himself. But she cannot create a realistic situation in which Edna's language, if it is to be candid, will cause Robert to stay. The terms are simple: if candor, then not love; if love, then not candor. The only role she can envision for a speaking woman is as Echo, standing behind Narcissus to confirm his own voice. "Oh, I was demented . . . recalling men who had set their wives free, we have heard of such things," says Robert. "Yes, we have heard of such things," says Edna (p. 106). Robert says: "I've been seeing the waves and the white beach of Grand Isle, . . . I've been working like a machine, and feeling like a lost soul. There was nothing interesting." And Edna responds, famously, in mirror speech (p. 99). There is a world of difference between Echo and Narcissus, for though they say the same things about reality and themselves, their meanings are vastly different. This particular Echo has immense potential, for humor, for irony, for creativity, for sensuality, for play, and all of this energy is implicit in her words that mirror and mock the men who speak them. But should she ever speak declaratively or seek to assert a constative that does not meet the approval of the status quo, her words will not be heard.

Kate Chopin was, as one of her typical male admirers said, "realistic almost to a fault, artistic – daring" (*Miscellany*, p. 136). And in fact *The Awakening* is a performance in which realism may be felt in all its considerable complexity. The realism Chopin pursues within the specific expectations of a definable mode is as usual enriched through the correlative reality of writing as a woman artist. She has intuited the double bind of realism: that in seeking to write artistically about how character is co-opted by circumstances grown too large to be fully controlled, one proves through language's erotic resistance to duty the very spirit of resistance feared to be lost. But she has gone beyond that intuition to something at once more complex and more irremediable, for in writing within realism's parameters, she recognizes that a woman, speaking, either will parrot the status quo or will not be heard productively. Edna tries to articulate her dilemma to Dr. Mandelet, but finds herself choking on what her autonomy will mean for her children in the cast-iron realism of her social and political world. "She felt that her speech was voicing the incoherency of her thoughts and stopped abruptly" – this is a world where clarity is inseparable from confusion when one sees precisely the inescapable trap of the double bind. The gaining of language in such a system is tantamount to confronting the foreclosure of possibility that pushes Edna into such deep water in the end. (To be rescued is not to be saved, and this, I think, Chopin must have known.)

Reason and Rule

Perhaps it will seem banal to say that realism, at least as I have articulated it here, comes as close as it is possible to come to communicating ordinariness – that it is indeed "realistic" in a perfectly commonsensical way. To say that it is ordinary, however, is by my terms to imply an immense, conflictual richness: a combination of mundanity, angst, triviality, and sublimity; a mixture of socially responsible, reformative willfulness and anarchic, subversive desire; the missionary position vying with more Sadeian gymnastics; a resolute gaze, fixed on things, assessing their effects, whether or not they work, whether they need to be fixed or thrown out or reorganized, with always the brief, over-the-shoulder glance at the immemorial.

There is a genuinely pragmatic energy within realism that accommodates the ineffable without yielding entirely to it, despite the Birnam Wood tenaciousness of the assault; but as is often pointed out, there is no "heroism," if heroism is to be defined conventionally in terms of the grand gesture. And heroism of the "romantic" type, or of the Nietzschean type, is a deeply seductive image, for it accords one an unimpeachable self (and the "self is such a dazzling object that if one looks *there* one may see nothing else").[9] Such a hero, as long as he *is* heroic, does not allow the real to make him, to finish him (off), to consume him with its sticky contiguities and spit him out a prosthetic man. He is not reduced to passivity. He (and I use the pronoun consciously, since this figure is textually produced) may be felt to recognize reality in its immediacy and with full unabashed awareness of his being within an autonomous dynamism that may, at any moment, enact both his sentence and his execution.[10] The hero in our fantasy will *feel* this cruelty as a joyful cruelty, for it enforces his only option, which is to be blithe (blithely resistant to what he knows he cannot control; blithely aggressive, blithely untouchable, even with the guillotine blade in descent). Heroic, he is immune to reality even in defeat, and at his best he gets the better of it. Such a figure in literature is, as Freud would say, a transmission of the writer's egoistic fantasies to the reader; he provides an *"incentive bonus,* or a *forepleasure . . .* which is offered to us so as to make possible the release of still greater pleasure arising from deeper psychical sources . . . enabling us thenceforward to enjoy our own daydreams without self-reproach or shame."[11] As we read, we all become, more or less,

Walter Mitty, and a good, virile hero provides the foreplay for better fantasies to come.

Realism, though, declassifies its prophets and sibyls and heroic warriors (when George Eliot claims to have given them up, she only means that she has located them at home), and it therefore deprives one of the full potency of one's fantasies of immunity. There is in realism's scope a systemic complexity, a sense of ecological balance, that forces one to recognize that the hero who grandstands, who takes the hill all by himself, must necessarily do so always at the expense of someone and something else (the model of response is familial rather than autonomous). What *this* form of participation calls for is humility instead of a striking heroism – and humility is, after all, rather an embarrassing word. (Say it to Nietzsche, for example, and he will call you a housewife or a governess or worse; say it to Deleuze and Guattari and see what they say.) It asks a more difficult thing than the simply heroic, because one runs the risk of looking bad – like a sentimentalist or a milquetoast or a collaborator – despite one's best intentions, and despite whatever private nihilisms and ironies and anarchies one entertains. It asks for a combination of watchfulness and caution that reveals the complex web in which one makes one's moves, and this watchfulness must be coupled with an active participation in the material world undertaken with a full awareness of how dreadfully wrong that participation may prove to have been in the diachronic long run. It calls for "attention" in the sense that both Iris Murdoch and Simone Weil speak of it, but it also calls for action undertaken despite one's conviction of "necessary fallibility."[12]

It is, after all, much more appealing to be an iconoclast, an anti-Oedipus who doesn't move in circles, a schizophrenic out for a walk instead of a neurotic on the couch, than to have to wrestle with the fragile contingency of one's choices in the world; one who recognizes the "real" as contingent must always perform the arbitrary rather than the metaphysically or heroically necessary action, and do so with a commensurate recognition that a given gesture may turn out to have been authoritarian rather than morally or ethically authoritative. Realism *performs* this intuition, almost despite whatever particular ideological or epistemological position it chooses to take relative to the real. Essentially liberal by definition of its reformative energies, realism at once reifies and defuses the impulse toward authoritarian correctives that an exasperation with elements of the status quo inevitably produces. Its Nazi teachers, its demagogues strutting and preening – these are the wry figures of its own fantasies of control, but even a relatively non-reflexive realism carries within it its own deconstructive energy, a restlessness that holds it from the linguistic terrorism of a language that silences other voices. It suggests a kind of heroism alternative to the spectacular variety, as it seems to recognize that giving up the chance to look heroic or to answer back or to clinch the deal is often a most potently subversive and seemingly inexplicable gesture.

Realism seems to presage Richard Rorty's formula for living as a liberal ironist within the postmodern condition, as it acts more or less as a public liberal in its reformative focus on character within environment and as a private ironist in its self-reflexive and tropological displacements of a more irremediable, less production-oriented energy.[13] It seems to recognize that, as Iris Murdoch says, "reasons are public reasons, rules are public rules. Reason and rule represent a sort of impersonal tyranny in relation to which . . . the personal will represents perfect freedom. The machinery is relentless, but until the moment of choice the agent is outside the machinery. Morality resides at the point of action."[14] To attempt to erect a system (or an anti-system) designed to reconcile a sustained freedom of personal will with productive action in the world is utopian, and as a utopian gesture it is in itself desirable and productive. To attempt to break the circle and divert the machinery may result in the breathtaking tour de force of, for example, an enterprise like *Anti-Oedipus*. To take the Nietzschean tack of celebrating a Saturnalia *within* the system is also exhilarating; to mount the scaffold only to be the one who "smashes it to pieces, throws it into confusion, and then puts it together ironically, pairing the strangest, separating the nearest items" is to imagine confronting and subverting the empty-husked tautology one cannot escape.[15] All these Zarathustran gestures, in fact, are so very seductive that one should perhaps attempt to approach them with irony intact; desire is, after all, always reciprocal to something, and the bigger they come, the harder they fall. Realism, if it lacks the sexy hyperboles of a more provocative mode of representation, at least may be said to leave one's hands free for other kinds of work.

From my point of view as a woman and as a feminist, realism's refusal to privilege extremisms seems a therapeutic gesture (with "therapeutic" taken as positive change rather than as a return to a dubiously defined, socially mandated "health" or "sanity"); realism, because it locates itself epistemologically within the impossible question of the "real," works both against an essentialist reading of character (and therefore of gender and race) and against the alternative determinisms of cultural, historical, and political power structures. It lays out a terrain and then discovers to the reader and to itself that in the telling of it the terms shift and metamorphose as if within the subtle increments of a dream reality. Looking to materialities for clues to the human soul, it discovers, as might be expected, that the assumption of reciprocity between things and people has more than merely the effect of revealing dead souls and living machines or living souls and dead machines, more, in other words, than any ideological or philosophical expectation can cover. This is not to say that the novel, and realism in particular, is intrinsically "humanistic," for the promotion of an unself-conscious and unproblematized humanism is hardly to be desired. Rather, it is to premise that realism lends itself to a sentimentalized humanism only superficially and with necessary skepticism, that its apprehension of an inescapable manifold running like a live current through the coercions and putative determinisms of the material environment destabilizes humanism's well-shaped "man" and opens the field of consideration.

This is not enough, not radical enough and not big enough to make much difference in the world. But when has art ever made a political difference at the level of policy? If art works at all to alter the terms (and I believe that it very often does), it does not work in ways that match the paradigms of philosophical and political systems: " 'and what are poets for in a destitute time?' " asks Heidegger, a time when, "at bottom, the essence of life is supposed to yield itself to technical production," when "the nature of technology is established in the objective character of its raw materials."[16] What are poets for in a world of materialities so overweening that machines begin to stamp their impress on the humans who are touched by them? For Heidegger, preoccupied with technology's invasive power throughout his inquiry on the poet, poets are to do what philosophers cannot do: piercing through objectification, they are to provide a dwelling place for all of us left homeless by the technological bulldozer ("poetic creation, which lets us dwell, is a kind of building").[17] Rorty, in a chapter balancing Proust's enterprise against the anti-metaphysical enterprises of Nietzsche and Heidegger, sees Nietzsche and Heidegger succumbing at last to a rigidifying code by virtue of their very heroic efforts to produce philosophies of Becoming and Being: "So the lesson I draw," he says, "from Proust's example is that novels are a safer medium than theory for expressing one's recognition of the relativity and contingency of authority figures."[18] Or as James says, "The house of fiction has . . . not one window, but a million," and "at each of them stands a figure with a pair of eyes, or at least with a field glass."[19] Realism *enacts* contingency and suggests that there are many ways of seeing, and thus subverts at one essential level the grand narratives it may at another level work to substantiate. The function of poetic language and of the artistic delineation of character in the world is to perform an uncertainty and a contingency that a theory of uncertainty and contingency by its very nature as theory undoes. The *idea*, "bony and hexahedral and permutable as a die," the desiccated "*residuum of a metaphor*," the metaphor's "evaporated product," may by virtue of its capacity for isolation from a text be used in the marketplace as a token of exchange – it may help purchase a full-blown theory – but the literary work is much harder to cash in.[20] The literary work may deconstruct, and indeed realism's systemic balance is built on a recognition of its own precariousness, but to some large extent it refutes the policy of exchange.

If realism's destabilizing effect is not seismic, neither is it negligible. Heidegger and Rorty aside, psychoanalysis teaches, and pedagogical experience teaches, and child-rearing teaches the hard lesson that one makes oneself heard (if at all) only through a system of endless, finely incremented negotiations. One makes oneself heard through repetition, through a recognition of what Donald Davidson calls the "passing theory," by which people within language adjust themselves at every moment to as many of the environmental and existential signals as they can recognize and accommodate. Within certain systems, Money talks, of course, and may be quite succinct and non-reflexive in its demands. But when people talk, no matter how crucial the issue, how "right" the cause, how necessary the agenda, even to the point of life or death, it is not the issue, the cause, or the agenda that will bring others to listen and respond; preaching is always, by definition of the crowd having already chosen to attend, preaching to the predisposed choir. Realism is a reminder that reality is a negotiation within an infinity of terms and that "justice" is entirely dependent on the outcome of one's serious and effective engagement within those terms.

The position relative to realism one finds in this book will seem to some readers merely sentimental and ingenuous; it will seem to others to be deeply cynical, indeed defeatist, about the possibilities for literary language to do more than hum and vibrate within political and social systems designed to assimilate and disperse all efforts at disruption. It actually lies somewhere in the middle (another of those damning words, of course), sharing the Habermasian optimism of an assumption that communicational competence is possible, with a commensurate sense that it is *only* by the smallest, most mundane-seeming gestures and only by the most minute gradations that literature can contribute to change in the world. Its deconstructionist intuitions suggest that one cannot know, by any certain or metaphysical means, that those changes one would like to see promoted are the "right" ones; indeed, those intuitions suggest that both realism's language and the critic's language are trudging dumbly in a circle from which there is no escape, theoretical or otherwise. One text may appear as a draft horse turning some central grindstone for production purposes, and another may seem one of those aery carousel affairs used to cool down racehorses, but the ring around the fixed point remains the same. Realism, by my reading, seems to intuit these perennial fears; the sense that one is dreaming, that one cannot know full wakefulness, that one may in fact be dreamed up entirely in another's head permeates realism at every level.

Realism communicates its intuition that whatever agreed-upon reality is currently down on the books will make itself felt at the social, political, judicial, domestic, and erotic levels, and it signals that it is willing to compromise with the status quo, within reason (using its language, representing its totems and icons and shibboleths, realism maintains a certain obligation to the environment it seeks to correct). This overt willingness to negotiate is what has made realism rather an embarrassment in a cultural environment that has put its money on modernism and the avant-garde. It is also what makes realism a mode rather than a genre, for realism adapts itself so variously that its texts differ vastly from one another and have, as individual texts, a certain chimerical quality that is thoroughly confusing to the taxonomist. So in the end one must always return to specific novels with specific questions regarding the real under consideration. One must take realism's invitation to participate both in the realistic text's syntagmatic logic and in its density and, as the individual novels prove, to recognize that in each instance this equation is, by virtue of its construction within the metamorphic "real," newly made and laid out over new (more or less archeologically enriched) terrain. The given text's performative encroachments on the reader's complacency and the critic's complacency may be considerable, as it enacts the double bind of necessary action carried out from within ambivalence and, at the deepest level, uncertainty regarding the "real." And finally, the critics of realism must acknowledge a necessary and inevitable complicity with the mode they seek to understand. If realism itself disallows heroism and the grand gesture, it ensures that its analogues within the critical discourse must be similarly diffident, similarly bereft of grand illusions or globalizing truths.

Notes

INTRODUCTION

1. I shall be violating a number of rules in my discussion of realism, the most immediately obvious violations being my generalizations across time (the nineteenth century) and space (the British Commonwealth and the United States). This is not to deny the usefulness of a more finely calibrated approach, but only to destabilize the terms of the discourse in the hope of producing an additional perspective. I am trying to negotiate between analysis of literary realism as a mode of text production particular to time and place and analysis of literary realism as evidence of an epistemological positioning that exceeds the circumstantialities of time and place. I am also attempting to avoid the implication that there is some relatively unimpeachable continuity of discourse to be discovered through the meticulous tautology of definition and taxonomy. Scrupulous attention to the specifics of each text would obviate any possibility for more generalized assertions; rather than take that road of continual and necessary qualification, I shall be rather willfully blithe.

2. Henry James, *Literary Criticism: Essays on Literature, American Writers, English Writers*, ed. Leon Edel (New York: Library of America, 1984), 63.

3. George Eliot, "The Natural History of German Life: Riehl," in *Essays and Leaves from a Note-book* (Edinburgh: William Blackwood & Sons, 1884), 268.

4. William Dean Howells, *Criticism and Fiction and Other Essays*, ed. Clara Marburg Kirk & Rudolf Kirk (New York University Press, 1959), 37.

5. Eliot, *Essays*, 232–4.

6. Eliot, *Essays,* 236.

7. Eliot, *Essays*, 232.

8. Roland Barthes, *S/Z*, trans. Richard Miller (New York: Hill & Wang, 1974), 167.

9. George Eliot, *Adam Bede*, ed. Stephen Gill (New York: Penguin, 1985), 532.

10. See Michel Foucault, "The Discourse on Language," in *The Archaeology of*

Knowledge and The Discourse on Language, trans. A. M. Sheridan Smith & Rupert Sawyer (New York: Harper & Row, 1972), 225–6, on "fellowships of discourse."

11. Samuel Beckett, *Proust* (London: John Calder, 1975), 25. George Levine, *The Realistic Imagination: English Fiction from Frankenstein to Lady Chatterley* (University of Chicago Press, 1981), 4, says that the Victorians wrote "with the awareness of the possibilities of indeterminate meaning and of solipsism" even as "they wrote *against* the very indeterminacy they intended to reveal."

12. Donald Davidson, *Inquiries into Truth and Interpretation* (Oxford: Clarendon Press, 1991), 137: ". . . disagreement and agreement alike are intelligible only against a background of massive agreement. Applied to language, this principle reads: the more sentences we conspire to accept or reject (whether or not through a medium of interpretation), the better we understand the rest, whether or not we agree about them." See, too, N. L. Wilson, "Substances without Substrata," *Review of Metaphysics*, vol. 12, no. 4, issue 48 (June 1959), 521–39, for Wilson's use of the term "principle of charity." This essay is interesting in the context of literary realism, not least because it examines the question of what constitutes an Individual.

13. D. H. Lawrence, *Women in Love* (New York: Penguin, 1989), 579. All further page references to *Women in Love* will be cited parenthetically.

14. See Davidson, *Inquiries into Truth and Interpretation*, 193: We decide that "a sentence or theory fits our sensory promptings, successfully faces the tribunal of experience, predicts future experience, or copes with the pattern of our surface irritations, provided it is borne out by the evidence," based on the metaphysical assumption of a commensurability with some ideal body of independently existent forms. Davidson argues that "the simple concept of being true" is better served by locating it within the tautology of Tarski's Convention T. This sentence is true: " 'Snow is White' is true if and only if snow is white." In English, it is, according to Davidson, upon this foundation that the concept of truth is built. See, for example, "On the Very Idea of a Conceptual Scheme," in *Inquiries into Truth and Interpretation*, 194.

15. See Hilary Putnam, "The Craving for Objectivity," *New Literary History*, vol. 15, no. 2 (Winter 1984), 229–39. Putnam argues that Austin's "enough is enough, enough isn't everything" "applies to interpretation as much as to justification," 230.

16. Wilhelm von Humboldt, "On the Historian's Task," *History and Theory: Studies in the Philosophy of History*, vol. 6, no. 1 (1967), 58–9.

17. Eliot, *Adam Bede*, 222–3.

18. Eliot, *Adam Bede*, 223.

19. Eliot, *Adam Bede*.

20. Roland Barthes, "The Discourse of History," trans. Stephen Bann, in *Com-*

parative Criticism: A Yearbook, ed. E. S. Shaffer (Cambridge University Press, 1981), 14.

21. Barthes, "The Discourse of History," 14. See, for example, Pierre Macherey, *A Theory of Literary Production*, trans. Geoffrey Wall (London: Routledge, 1978). Realism is to be read for what it represses rather than for what it says; it is the model of a neurotic text that speaks a truth unavailable to itself but recoverable through analytic intervention.

22. Eliot, *Adam Bede*, 23.

23. G. W. F. Hegel, *Lectures on the Philosophy of World History*, trans. H. B. Nisbet (Cambridge University Press, 1975), 12.

24. See Michael Riffaterre, *Fictional Truth* (Baltimore: Johns Hopkins University Press, 1990), xiii–xiv: "Truth in fiction rests on verisimilitude, a system of representations that seems to reflect a reality external to the text, but only because it conforms to a grammar. Narrative truth is an idea of truth created in accordance with the rules of that grammar."

25. See Raymond Tallis, *In Defense of Realism* (London: Edward Arnold, 1988), 75–6, 107, 154, as he discusses the critic's condescension toward the "ordinary reader."

26. See Jean-François Lyotard, *The Differend: Phrases in Dispute*, trans. George Van Den Abbeele (Minneapolis: University of Minnesota Press, 1988), for a reading of what constitutes a "victim."

27. Nineteenth-century attitudes toward physicians are also interesting in this context of arbitrated truth. Consider Gaskell's *Wives and Daughters*, with Mr. Gibson's medical perceptions providing another layer of complexity as regards character. The novel is filled with people who may or may not be mortally ill – the lines separating physical, mental, and spiritual forms of malaise are shown to be painfully ambiguous, with doctors of various sorts making diagnoses that in effect change how character is perceived and how it is "treated."

28. See Eric Sundquist, *American Realism: New Essays* (Baltimore: Johns Hopkins University Press, 1982), introduction.

29. See Simone de Beauvoir, "Must We Burn Sade?" trans. Annette Michelson, in Marquis de Sade, *The 120 Days of Sodom and Other Writings*, trans. and compiled Austryn Wainhouse & Richard Seaver (New York: Grove Weidenfeld, 1966), 3–64. She speaks of Sade's gluttony and his coprophilia, along with his inheritance scams, in terms of obsessional accumulation, 25–6.

30. As Donald Davidson says in *Inquiries into Truth and Interpretation*, 194, "the totality of sensory evidence is what we want provided it is all the evidence there is; and all the evidence there is is just what it takes to make our sentences or theories true. Nothing, however, no *thing*, makes sentences and theories true: not experience, not surface irritations, not the world, can make a sentence true. *That* experience takes a certain course, that our skin is warmed or punc-

tured, that the universe is finite, these facts, if we like to talk that way, make sentences and theories true. But this point is put better without mention of facts. The sentence 'My skin is warm' is true if and only if my skin is warm. Here there is no reference to a fact, a world, an experience, or a piece of evidence."

31. See Walter Benn Michaels, "*Sister Carrie*'s Popular Economy," *Critical Inquiry* (Winter 1980), 373–90.

32. Anthony Giddens, *The Consequences of Modernity* (Stanford University Press, 1990), 18.

33. Eliot, *Essays*, 268–9.

34. Giddens, *Consequences*, 18.

35. U. C. Knoepflmacher, *Emily Brontë: Wuthering Heights* (Cambridge University Press, 1989), 32.

36. Michael Riffaterre, "Cronotopes in Diegesis." Unpublished manuscript.

37. It is Michael Riffaterre's argument in *Fictional Truth*, xiv, that narrative truth works because "any verbal given will seem to be true when it generates tautological derivations that repeat it in successive synonymous forms. This is because the entire narrative sequence becomes saturated with these synonyms and functions consequently like a paradigm of references to the unchanging semantic structure of the given." My addition relative to realism would assert that the author's self-perceived responsibilities to keep both tropological fancy and ideological preoccupation subordinate to pedagogical effectiveness enrich this process considerably.

38. Donald Davidson, "Locating Literary Language," in *Literary Theory after Davidson*, ed. Reed Way Dasenbrock (University Park: Pennsylvania State University Press, 1993), 303.

39. Davidson, "Locating Literary Language," 304.

40. Jean-François Lyotard, *The Postmodern Condition: A Report on Knowledge, Theory and History of Literature*, trans. Geoffrey Bennington & Brian Massumi (Minneapolis: University of Minnesota Press, 1984), 73–5.

41. Jean-François Lyotard, *The Inhuman: Reflections on Time*, trans. Geoffrey Bennington & Rachel Bowlby (Stanford University Press, 1991), 78.

42. Davidson, *Inquiries into Truth and Interpretation*, 197.

43. Davidson discusses the Gricean circle in "A Nice Derangement of Epitaphs," in *Philosophical Grounds of Rationality: Intentions, Categories, Ends*, ed. Richard E. Grandy & Richard Warner (Oxford: Clarendon Press, 1986), 164: "A speaker cannot, intend to mean something by what he says unless he believes his audience will interpret his words as he intends."

44. Elias Canetti, *The Conscience of Words*, trans. Joachim Neugroschel (New York: Continuum, Seabury Press, 1979), 34.

45. In Tallis, *In Defense of Realism*, 20.

46. Beckett, *Proust*, 17.

47. Henry James, "The Art of Fiction," in *Literary Criticism*, 56: "One writes the novel, one paints the picture, of one's language and of one's time, and calling it modern English will not, alas! make the difficult task any easier. No more, unfortunately, will calling this or that work of one's fellow-artist a romance – unless it be, of course, simply for the pleasantness of the thing, as for instance when Hawthorne gave this heading to his story of *Blithedale*."
48. Charles Percy Sanger's much-anthologized 1926 monograph, "The Structure of *Wuthering Heights*," in *Wuthering Heights*, ed. William M. Sale, Jr. (New York: Norton, 1963), 286–98, makes Brontë's command of detail quite clear, demonstrates the novel's immaculate internal chronology, and reveals Brontë's knowledge of entailment, all of which align *Wuthering Heights* with accepted premises of realism.
49. Howells, *Criticism and Fiction*, 32.
50. Howells, *Criticism and Fiction*, 36, 38.
51. Howells, *Criticism and Fiction*, 32, 38.
52. David Musselwhite, *Partings Welded Together: Politics and Desire in the Nineteenth-Century English Novel* (London: Methuen, 1987), 22.
53. Musselwhite, *Partings Welded Together*, 22–3.
54. Immanuel Kant, *The Critique of Judgment*, trans. James Creed Meredith (Oxford: Clarendon Press, 1991), 57.
55. Kant, *Critique of Judgment*, 58.
56. Eliot, *Adam Bede*, 531–2.
57. Eliot, *Adam Bede*, 30.
58. Eliot, *Adam Bede*, 14, 13.

1: REAL REALISM

1. Frank Norris's definition of the "real Realism" is as good a place to start as any: "Observe the methods employed by the novelists who profess and call themselves 'realists' – Mr. Howells, for instance. Howells's characters live across the street from us, they are 'on our block.' We know all about them, about their affairs, and the story of their lives. One can go even further. We ourselves are Mr. Howells's characters, so long as we are well behaved and ordinary and *bourgeois*, so long as we are not adventurous or not rich or not unconventional. If we are otherwise, if things commence to happen to us, if we kill a man or two, or get mixed up in a tragic affair, or do something on a large scale, such as the amassing of enormous wealth or power or fame, Mr. Howells cuts our acquaintance at once. He will none of us if we are out of the usual.

  "This is the real Realism. It is the smaller details of every-day life, things that are likely to happen between lunch and supper, small passions, restricted emotions, dramas of the reception-room, tragedies of an afternoon call, crises involving cups of tea." Frank Norris, "Zola as a Romantic Writer," in *The*

Literary Criticism of Frank Norris, ed. Donald Pizer (Austin: University of Texas Press, 1964), 71. This essay appeared in *Wave*, June 27, 1896.

2. As James writes to Howells, "I regard you as the great American naturalist. I don't think you go far enough, and you are haunted with romantic phantoms and a tendency to factitious glosses; but you are on the right path and I wish you repeated triumphs." William D. Howells, *Criticism and Fiction and Other Essays*, ed. Clara Marburg Kirk & Rudolf Kirk (New York University Press, 1959), 96.

3. Leo Bersani speaks of "the realistic novelist's poignant effort to provide his society with some image of a viable and morally decent order"; begging the question of what constitutes viability and what constitutes a "morally decent order," this reformist impulse is, I would maintain, at the heart of realism. Bersani, *A Future for Astyanax: Character and Desire in Literature* (New York: Columbia University Press 1984), 61.

4. See, for example, George J. Becker's introduction in *Documents of Modern Literary Realism* (Princeton University Press, 1963), 15, for his placement of British realism relative to its continental counterpart: Although there was "a strong indigenous tendency toward realism among English writers in the last half of the nineteenth century . . . it was a narrow, sectarian realism, always watched over by the clergy. Up to a certain point the English writers had exploited the ordinary, the down-to-earth, rather more consistently than had their continental colleagues."

5. Becker, for example, in *Documents of Modern Literary Realism*, 16–19, sees American realism as less proscriptively censored in its energies and its representations than British realism, although he also asserts that the publisher's withdrawal of Dreiser's *Sister Carrie* is evidence, among other incidents, that realists had to, as Dreiser put it, "write about [life] as somebody else thought it was – the ministers and farmers and dullards of the home." American realism, however late in flowering, "escaped some of the mechanical rigor of naturalist determinism," because that society was fluid enough to relieve the artist of the sense that people are inexorably ground down by external forces. Howells, in *Criticism and Fiction*, 60, makes an extended distinction between British and U.S. fiction, to the detriment of the British, "whose thumb-fingered apprehension requires something gross and palpable for its assurance of reality." James, on the other hand, in 1904, in *The American Scene*, sees America as fundamentally different, lacking in those complexities that produce realism.

6. See George Levine, "By Knowledge Possessed: Darwin, Nature, and Victorian Narrative," *New Literary History*, vol. 24 (1993), 371–6, on Comte and positivism. His articulation of the dilemma of positivism, as a discipline that necessitates the suspension of all of the intellect's interventionist activities in the act of observation, is informative in this context. The positivist ideal of a complete suspension of the self infiltrates language with a "model of death and

of ultimate self-affirmation or resurrection," a paradox to mirror the idealism/ empiricism valences of realism. Howells, whose confidence in science as an analogue for the critic's task (like a naturalist or a botanist, he classifies; he sees "the laws of evolution in art and society") and whose interest in Comte would seem to place him on the empiricism end of the spectrum, is also given to rather Platonic visions: The artist can transmute ordinary detail into something of value and interest. "Why? Simply because the artist has made us see the idea that resides in it. Let not the novelists, then, endeavor to add anything to reality, to turn it and twist it, to restrict it." Howells, *Criticism and Fiction*, 9, 38. Howells's double duty as artist and critic makes his statements more than usually interesting, especially as he professes himself uncomfortable with criticism, but also burdened "by the guilty conscience of the novelist" who fears that novel-reading is a waste of time (p. 45).

7. See George Levine's discussion of realism's Aristotelian and Scholastic origins, *The Realistic Imagination: English Fiction from Frankenstein to Lady Chatterley* (Chicago University Press, 1981), 8–9, and his assessment of the effects of the shift from seeing realism as the reification of the ideal, with things as merely contingent realities, to seeing realism as it shifts to seeing ideas as empirically contingent on things.

Words often contain the etymological and historical means for their own undoing into self-contradiction. Freud felt this doubleness so powerfully that in "The Antithetical Meaning of Primal Words" he advanced a theory that each word originally meant a thing and its opposite. I am particularly interested in this tendency toward circularity in words like "realism" and "hysteria," the etymological bias of which throws definitions of "male hysteria" into, and for, a loop.

8. Manuscript, colloquium presentation, School of Criticism and Theory, Dartmouth College, Hanover, NH, 1993.

9. C. Hugh Holman, "Realism," in *A Handbook to Literature* (Indianapolis: Bobbs-Merrill, 1972).

10. See, for example, Catherine Belsey, *Critical Practice* (London: Methuen, 1980), Pierre Macherey, *A Theory of Literary Production*, trans. Geoffrey Wall (London: Routledge, 1978), and David Musselwhite, *Partings Welded Together: Politics and Desire in the Nineteenth-Century English Novel* (London: Methuen, 1987). For an energetic disputing of the assertion that realism is co-optive, see Raymond Tallis, *In Defense of Realism* (London: Edward Arnold, 1988).

11. Macherey, *A Theory of Literary Production*, viii.

12. Macherey, *A Theory of Literary Production*, vii.

13. Michel Foucault, "The Discourse on Language," in *The Archeology of Knowledge and the Discourse on Language*, trans. A. M. Sheridan Smith (New York: Colophon, 1972), 221.

14. Foucault, "The Discourse on Language," 221.

15. Levine, *The Realistic Imagination*, 23. Bersani, *A Future for Astyanax*, 311, says that "once criticism stops fishing for the truth in art, it can engage in the only activity which demonstrates both its own specificity and its affinities with art. That is, criticism can openly assume its status as an interpretive fiction, and yet demonstrate that its particular brand of interpretation consists in the elucidation of the sense-making procedures in art." Within the context of Bersani's argument that realistic fiction, through a "formal and psychological reticence" (p. 62), is an exercise in the containment of desire, the equilibrating effect of even such a critical approach to realism as he describes and enacts becomes evidence of his thesis: The critical reduction of a "realism" that is in fact dispersed among highly disparate and irreducibly differentiated texts may be said to reify this impulse for containment. As Bersani points out, criticism may, in reifying the texts under consideration, engage in subversive play, to some extent perpetuating whatever fragmentary and discontinuous energies the texts themselves contain, but "to a certain extent [criticism] will always undermine an art of the fragmentary and the discontinuous" (p. 312). *A Future for Astyanax* is itself a wonderfully ambivalent and enriched text, as it uses realism to argue for the possibility of a reinstatement of "a heterogeneity of our desiring impulses," "an Arcadia of polymorphous perversity" (p. 7), even as it concludes with readings of sadomasochistic texts that bring him to suggest that "there may be something we wish to resist in this seductive retraining of the self" (p. 310). I see no contradiction here that Bersani himself does not examine, but only wish to underscore the paradox implicit in his own textual articulation and performance of desire.

16. See D. A. Williams, "The Practice of Realism," in *The Monster in the Mirror*, ed. D. A. Williams (Oxford University Press, 1978), 264, for his comments on the realist's dilemma of recognizing the necessity and the power of aesthetic interventions while also maintaining a commitment to reproducing a sense of things as they are in the world—disorderly, chaotic, and so forth.

17. Levine, *The Realistic Imagination*, 3.

18. There is, too, the question of narrative raised by philosophers like Lyotard. See *The Postmodern Condition: A Report on Knowledge, Theory and History of Literature*, trans. Geoffrey Bennington & Brian Massumi (Minneapolis: University of Minnesota Press, 1984) for Lyotard's discussion of narrativity relative to other modes whose legitimation goes unquestioned.

19. Bersani, *A Future for Astyanax*, 310–11.

20. One might argue that postmodern assertions regarding language's affiliations with displacement, slippage, and erotic play provide, before the fact, the impetus for reconsiderations of realism's ambivalence. Eric Sundquist, in *American Realism: New Essays* (Baltimore: Johns Hopkins University Press, 1982), vii, says that "we live in a critical age that has grown remarkably attentive to (some

might say obsessed with) the ways in which literary texts restructure or subvert
the 'real' social structures they claim to represent, and in doing so call attention
to the fictions that the fabric of reality contains and depends on for its apparent
order." But a survey of the critical responses to realism over the past many
years will document a tendency toward qualification.

21. I would agree with Bersani, *A Future for Astyanax*, 62, that the realist author
"disguises a narrative performance of desiring fantasy which might have con-
tested that organization of desire into coherent personalities," but I would
argue against the first half of his sentence, that "in general he is anxious to
make us forget his own presence in his work." As I discuss later, as well,
authors within the realistic mode often encode their texts with markers of not
only a self-conscious fictionality but also an irony regarding their projects that
is, I would maintain, meant to be discovered.

22. As the following chapters will illustrate, the realistic writer has an entire rep-
ertoire of what seem to be internally deconstructive devices. Michael Riffaterre, in *Fictional Truth* (Baltimore: Johns Hopkins University Press, 1990), xv,
21, argues that "fiction emphasizes the fact of the fictionality of a story at the
same time it states that the story is true" through seemingly disruptive devices
and that this is a way to "point to narrative truth by seeming to flout it."
"Narrative verisimilitude tends to flaunt rather than mask its fictitious nature."
It is worth considering that, just as the fiction protects the authority of its
fictionality through calling attention to itself, the critic who exploits a similar
device does not breach the illusion of a sufficient critical discourse, but in fact
enhances it.

23. George Eliot, *Adam Bede*, ed. Stephen Gill (New York: Penguin 1985), 222
(chapter 17).

24. See Riffaterre, *Fictional Truth*, chapter 2.

25. See Becker's collection of these authorial statements in *Documents of Modern Literary Realism*. As even a cursory survey of eighteenth-century novels proves, self-
conscious references to matters of textual truth and to matters of construction are
very common. Authors seek to justify and explain their novels variously: Field-
ing claims to be writing "a comic epic in prose" in order to escape the full opprobrium of fiction writing, and Defoe, following Cervantes, claims to be a
historian reproducing documents. Modernist novelists like Woolf and Lawrence
are endlessly self-referential and are, as well, active critics of others' work. But
realism, according to standard definitions like that found in Holman's *A Handbook to Literature*, makes the reactive choice to replace falseness with a true re-
flection of life, and to do this by avoiding such things as artistic symmetries and
intricately exact plots; in other words, it is said to equate useful service as regards
the real world with a rigorously diminished artificiality. Realism's interpolations
and prefaces are, in this context, interestingly contradictory artifacts.

26. Henry James, *Literary Criticism: Essays on Literature, American Writers, English Writers*, ed. Leon Edel (New York: Library of America, 1984), 46.

27. Edith Wharton's "Author's Introduction" to *Ethan Frome* (New York: Signet, 1992) (the first such introduction in any of her books, p. xxii) enforces the contiguity between the author and the figure within the novel, the engineer, who brings the 24-year-old story back out into the open, and between the author and the story she conceives. She wishes, she says, to treat the subject of her *"granite outcroppings"* "as starkly and as summarily as life had always presented itself to [these] protagonists" (p. xx), and she knows what it is to be lured into a more ornamented and luxuriant approach: "Every novelist has been visited by the insinuating wraiths of false 'good situations,' siren-subjects luring his cockle-shell to the rocks; their voice is oftenest heard, and their mirage-sea beheld, as he traverses the waterless desert which awaits him half-way through whatever work is actually in hand. I knew well enough what song those siren [*sic*] sang, and had often tied myself to my dull job until they were out of hearing – perhaps carrying a lost masterpiece in their rainbow veils. But I had no such fear of them in the case of Ethan Frome" (p. xx). There are several things worth noting here, but I shall mention only the most salient. She emphasizes in this introduction the structural details of the novel, claiming that it is only the "construction" that is of significant interest (p. xix); she has, in this, both reified and justified after the fact her enactment of a story through the eyes of an *engineer*, whose task within the novel has to do with the delayed construction of a "big power-house" (p. 6). Another potent infiltration of the novelistic text and the critical one resides in the imagery of *"granite outcroppings;* but half-emerged from the soil,"* and of "siren-subjects luring [a] cockle-shell to the rocks." The "mirage-sea" confusion is repeated in the imagery of the final sledding scene, where "the last clearness from the upper sky is merged with the rising night in a blur that disguises landmarks and falsifies distances" (p. 119), and, of course, another cockleshell is lured to the rocks as the sled sails into the elm tree; the granite outcropping becomes an image of both internal character and its external consequence.

28. After reading nineteenth-century authors' explanations of their choices of narrative orientation, one cannot fail to see that the standard apologia for realistic techniques and preoccupations is a consciously moral one. They argue for a generous humanism, as Eliot says, "a deep human sympathy." The Goncourts claim for the novel that it is "becoming contemporary Moral History"; Howells argues for the representing of "what is unpretentious and what is true" as a means of reaching the "beautiful and the good." Howells sees it as the novelist's "privilege, his high duty" to interpret human nature. And as novels like Austen's *Northanger Abbey* or Peacock's *Nightmare Abbey* prove, the sense that fiction may contaminate character is very strong.

29. Howells, *Criticism and Fiction*, 46.

30. Eliot, *Adam Bede*, 222.
31. Eliot, *Adam Bede*, 223.
32. Quoted in the introduction, Eliot, *Adam Bede*, 14.
33. See Shakespeare, *Henry IV, Part I*, act II, scene iv, lines 124–5, for a reference to psalm-singing weavers.
34. George Eliot, *Silas Marner* (New York: Signet, 1981), 22.
35. Becker, *Documents of Modern Literary Realism*, 24.
36. Eliot, *Adam Bede*, 222.
37. Tallis, *In Defense of Realism*, 94.
38. Eliot, *Adam Bede*, 222.
39. Becker, *Documents of Modern Literary Realism*, 24.
40. Wharton, *Ethan Frome*, xx.
41. Howells, *Criticism and Fiction*, 37.
42. Becker, *Documents of Modern Literary Realism*, 7, points out what probably are the earliest uses in England of the literary terms "realism" and the "realist school," the first appearing in 1853 in the *Westminster Review*, the second in 1852 in *Fraser's Magazine*, where it was used but not defined. Clearly, the use of the term as specifically related to a literary mode was in the air earlier than 1851 (it needed no defining in *Fraser's*), but it is the less self-conscious use of "real" that reminds one of its double heritage of idealism and particularity, as when Hobbes, in *Leviathan* (1651), says "that some such apparitions were not Imaginary, but Reall," or when Addison, in *Spectator*, 275, says that "Homer tells us that the Blood of the Gods is not real Blood, but only something like it," or when the *Encyclopaedia Britannica*, vol. 18 (1797), speaks of "numberless absurdities, such as that . . . forms or sensible qualities are real things independent of their subject and the sentient beings who perceive them." Philosophically, Francis Bacon, the British empiricists of the seventeenth and eighteenth centuries, and the positivists of the nineteenth century were all in the business of discovering the "real," in reaction to those who located the term nonempirically. The *Oxford English Dictionary* entries on *real, realism, realist, realistic,* and *reality* are lengthy and informative. The entry from Bradley's *Appearance and Reality* (1893) is interesting in the foregoing context: "The more that anything is spiritual, so much the more is it veritably real."
43. Sigmund Freud, "Negation," in *The Complete Psychological Works of Sigmund Freud*, ed. James Strachey (London: Hogarth Press, 1961). Freud's essay is also compelling in the context of realism, as it relates the capacity for negation, which is a way of speaking repressed material without confronting it as such, with the capacity for judgment.
44. Sundquist, *American Realism*, 8.
45. Sundquist, *American Realism*, 3.
46. Sundquist, *American Realism*, vii, 3–5.
47. One means of making a clear distinction between realism and romanticism,

and thus of clarifying other assumptions of crossbreeding, is to assert, as does George Becker in the introduction to his *Documents of Modern Literary Realism*, 6, that the two schools hold "sharply different philosophical positions" and that realism as a movement was unified in its rejection of an idealist metaphysics and in its embrace of the basic tenets of scientific and positivist thinking. I would claim, on the evidence of their novels, that even when writers professed to positivism, and by no means did they all, their artistic engagement with the "real" inevitably produced epistemological ambivalence. I would also claim that positivism and idealism share a metaphysical territory that links them inextricably.

48. Sundquist, *American Realism*, 4.

49. James's story, says Blackmur, and the realist's story, says Sundquist, and the critic's story, says Kearns, is a fable of the writer " 'who struggles desperately to make society his prey, but fails because he cannot help remaining the harmless, the isolated monarch of his extreme imaginative ardent self.' "

50. Sundquist, *American Realism*, 4: "While it is not my intention to extend this view in detail—or to promote it as the greatest distinguishing feature of American fiction—I do want to suggest that it is within the framework of these widely accepted terms [romance and realism] that the significance of American realism must initially be considered."

51. Levine, *The Realistic Imagination*, 4: David Musselwhite's *Partings Welded Together* is another work that candidly bears out the formal and tonal complicities of the critical text with the attitude toward realism that it brings to the reader. Musselwhite, whose title reflects his own strategies, as well as a thematic continuity within his argument, provides an elaborate structure of what he calls three introductions (pp. 4–5), the first of which is "simple," and the second and third of which, consigned to appendixes, perform alternative functions, the one an introduction to the work of Deleuze and Guattari, the other a critique of Fredric Jameson's *The Political Unconscious: Narrative as a Socially Symbolic Act* (Ithaca, NY: Cornell University Press, 1981).

52. Levine, *The Realistic Imagination*, 329.

53. Levine, *The Realistic Imagination*, 4.

54. Levine, *The Realistic Imagination*, 4.

55. Levine, *The Realistic Imagination*, 4.

56. Levine, *The Realistic Imagination*, 4.

57. Clearly, I am ignoring the few extremists among both novelists and critics, those who at a conscious level exhibit no doubt whatever that their reality is the only one (it is another matter, perhaps, that their language betrays them nonetheless). Nineteenth-century British and American realism, and accounts of nineteenth-century realism generally, tend toward the prudential, the modest, and the provisional. A genre like socialist realism, or criticism like that of Lukács on realism, becomes another question entirely.

58. Macherey, *A Theory of Literary Production*, 7.
59. Macherey, *A Theory of Literary Production*, 7.
60. Sundquist, *American Realism*, 20.
61. This is not say that material realities, economic and otherwise, *are* necessarily alterable, but only that realism's doubleness refutes a purely deterministic reading of things.
62. See G. W. F. Hegel, *Reason in History*, trans. Robert S. Hartman (New York: Macmillan, 1953), xxi, 9–20. The connections between Hegel's imperative to "proceed historically, empirically" (p. 12) and the realist's commitment to close attention to and faithful rendering of detail in the service of a narrative that exits the premises of standard, grand teleological schemes are obvious. For an interesting conflation of novelistic and historiographic methodologies, see George Eliot, *Essays and Leaves from a Note-book* (Edinburgh: William Blackwood & Sons, 1884), 238–9; this entire essay, "The Natural History of German Life: Riehl," is pertinent to the assertion that there is a fluid movement between the assumptions of realism and those of an empirically based historiography.
63. Friedrich Nietzsche, *The Use and Abuse of History*, trans. Adrian Collins (Indianapolis: Bobbs-Merrill, 1957), 49.
64. Dominick LaCapra, "History and Psychoanalysis," in *The Trials of Psychoanalysis*, ed. Françoise Meltzer (University of Chicago Press, 1988), 12.
65. Nietzsche, *The Use and Abuse of History*, 39.
66. Hayden White, *Tropics of Discourse: Essays in Cultural Criticism* (Baltimore: Johns Hopkins University Press, 1978), 124.
67. Hayden White, *The Content of the Form: Narrative Discourse and Historical Representation* (Baltimore: Johns Hopkins University Press, 1987), 20.
68. Wilhelm von Humboldt, "On the Historian's Task," *History and Theory: Studies in the Philosophy of History*, vol. 6, no. 1 (1967), 57.
69. Stephen Bann, "The Historian as Taxidermist: Ranke Barante Waterton," in *Comparative Criticism: A Yearbook*, ed. E. S. Shaffer (Cambridge University Press, 1981), 30–1.
70. These assumptions exude themselves at several levels in conventional statements regarding historiographic practice, but two easily documentable themes are (1) that history is to be distinguished from fictional narrative because it deals with truth and speaks truth and (2) that historiography is superior to fiction as regards its truth value because it, unlike fiction, works by means of a clean, virtually transparent, metaphor-free narrative. For a representative statement of each, see Jacques Barzun, *Clio and the Doctors: Psycho-History, Quanto-History, and History* (University of Chicago Press, 1974), 47, ". . . metaphor is a recognized means of communication. . . . But it does not follow that metaphor as such is trustworthy," for metaphorical language "does not promote straight thinking." Language must avoid its affiliation with both figura-

tive and technical language, for "in order to be of use to the historian . . . technical terms must first fall into the public domain. It has always been so" (p. 73). See, too, Barzun's sections "How to Tell History from Other Works of the Mind" and "Interesting, But Is It True?" (pp. 92–7).

71. See, for example, Barzun, *Clio and the Doctors*, Marc Bloch, *The Historian's Craft*, trans. Peter Putnam (New York: Vintage, 1953), Edward H. Carr, *What Is History?* (New York: Knopf, 1962), R. G. Collingwood, *The Idea of History*, rev. ed., ed. Jan Van Der Dussen (Oxford: Clarendon Press, 1993), G. R. Elton, *Return to Essentials: Some Reflections on the Present State of Historical Studies* (Cambridge University Press, 1991), and Peter Gay, *Freud for Historians* (Oxford University Press, 1986).

72. See Marc Bloch's opening words in *The Historian's Craft*.

73. Chris Baldick, *In Frankenstein's Shadow: Myth, Monstrosity, and Nineteenth-Century Writing* (Oxford: Clarendon Press, 1987).

74. See Eileen Yeo and E. P. Thompson, *The Unknown Mayhew* (New York: Pantheon, 1971).

75. Riffaterre, *Fictional Truth*, xvi.

76. Henry James, *Literary Criticism*, 110.

77. Oliver Goldsmith, *The Vicar of Wakefield* (New York: Dutton, 1965), 64–5.

2: TALKING ABOUT THINGS

1. Donald Spoto, *The Art of Alfred Hitchcock: Fifty Years of His Motion Pictures* (New York: Anchor, 1992), xi.

2. I am purposely using vague, "poetic" terms like "ineffable" to talk about this perception of some overage beyond the accountability of material detail and circumstantial language. I do not wish to imply that I believe such a surplus to exist such that it can be tracked down and named (maybe so, maybe not). Instead, I wish to proceed on the assumption that the inability to discard completely such a notion—a "superstition," if you will, or a throwback to Platonism, or a theocratic impulse—is something of a commonalty, whether or not the age or the writer is enthralled by positivist enthusiasms. In fact, the seventeenth- and eighteenth-century schools of British empiricism in England and the Poor Richard pragmatism relative to the material world in the United States might be gathered to have produced an equivalent dis-ease regarding what they must give up in order to effect their programs. At the very least this must be true for the novelist, whose province of fiction and whose business of language thwart the illusion of absolute precision. See Richard Rorty, in the opening chapter of *Contingency, Irony, and Solidarity* (Cambridge University Press, 1989), 21–2. One may have a conscious philosophy that excludes the possibility of a "prelinguistic consciousness to which language needs to be

adequate" and still enact one's projects with an inalienable "disposition to use the language of our ancestors, to worship the corpses of their metaphors."

3. Charles Dickens, *Hard Times: For These Times* (New York: Holt, Rinehart & Winston, 1958), 182. Page numbers for this and the following novels will be cited parenthetically in the text. Emily Brontë, *Wuthering Heights*, ed. William M. Sale, Jr. (New York: Norton, 1972); Kate Chopin, *The Awakening*, in *The Complete Works of Kate Chopin*, ed. Per Seyersted (Baton Rouge: Louisiana State University Press, 1969); Nathaniel Hawthorne, *The Blithedale Romance*, ed. Seymour Gross & Rosalie Murphy (New York: Norton, 1978); Mary Shelley, *Frankenstein* (New York: Bantam, 1981); Bram Stoker, *Dracula* (Oxford University Press, 1983).

4. I shall speak later in detail of *The Blithedale Romance* as Hawthorne's ambivalent engagement in a place between the modes of realism and romance. With a reasonably clear sense of the realism/romance discourse in literary criticism and of Hawthorne's place within that discourse, I shall nonetheless blur his affiliation to romance. I shall do this not to argue that he is a "realist" but to carry out my reading of realism as always in an unstable ratio to exactly that energy Hawthorne names as Romance. See Eric Sundquist, "The Country of the Blue," in *American Realism: New Essays* (Baltimore: Johns Hopkins University Press, 1982), 3–24, for a discussion of Hawthorne relative to American realism. See, too, Marshall Brown, "The Logic of Realism: A Hegelian Approach," *Proceedings of the Modern Language Association*, vol. 96, no. 2 (March 1981), 226–8, for a discussion of the continuity between realism and romanticism.

5. I am choosing not to make incremental distinctions among the various "stages" of realism, attempting instead to see the realistic mode as always, and by definition of its implicit self-consciousness, in an unstable ratio to other impulses, literary, spiritual, and political. This refusal to privilege the historical "rise and fall" of the genre (indeed, my reluctance to call it a genre) is not to deny the value of such readings but only to attempt to reveal each novel as genuinely idiosyncratic, always in some very essential ways outside of any grand narrative. Nor am I discriminating among types of realism, as cataloged by Brown, "The Logic of Realism," 224: "Watt's formal and psychological realisms; C. S. Lewis' realisms of presentation and of content; Jakobson's five types of realism; Preisendanz' ten theses; realism as a transhistorical mode; realism as a general standard of value (as in Marxist critics) or a general term of opprobrium (as in Northrop Frye's writings); bourgeois, programmatic, and socialist realism; poetic and consistent realism; naturalistic and impressionist realism; *verismo, chosisme*, and the *Dinggedicht*." Brown's overview of the critical field (pp. 225–6) is helpful.

6. George Levine, *The Realistic Imagination: English Fiction from Frankenstein to Lady Chatterley* (University of Chigago Press, 1981), 5.

7. Jean-François Lyotard, *Heidegger and 'the jews'*, trans. Andreas Michel & Mark Roberts (Minneapolis: University of Minnesota Press, 1990), 33.
8. Samuel Beckett, *Proust* (London: John Calder, 1975), 76.
9. Frank Norris, *The Literary Criticism of Frank Norris*, ed. Donald Pizer (Austin: University of Texas Press, 1964), 78.
10. See Leo Bersani, *A Future for Astyanax: Character and Desire in Literature* (New York: Columbia University Press, 1984), for the argument that realistic fiction, in subduing desire for the sake of order, "makes for a secret complicity between the novelist and his society's illusions about its own order" (pp. 62–3). Realism's enforcement of a unified vision of character/self, according to Bersani, is dependent on "an impoverishment of desire"; "psychic coherence involves a serious crippling of desire" (p. 6). Realism's reformist agendas regarding society "are qualified by a form which provides this society with a reassuring myth about itself" (p. 60). Bersani's argument is a delicately balanced and subtle one that far exceeds the sum of his explicit judgments regarding realism's relationship to desire. I shall only say here that my own argument proceeds from the suspicion that the more violently desirous, less accommodative forms that Bersani sees as antithetical to realism's assimilative and leveling force are no more suggestive of, and perhaps are less productive of (at the level of pedagogical and performative effect), an intuition that the self is fragmented, discontinuous, and desirous than is realism. And after all, Bersani's own argument is an explicitly ethical one that is in realism's tradition of amelioration between extremes; he argues that "an imagination of the deconstructed, perhaps even demolished, self is the necessary point of departure for an authentically civilizing skepticism about the nature of our desires and the nature of our being" (p. 313), that "it is . . . only by allowing itself to be penetrated by logical argument that the theatricalized self can be saved from its own potential for a terroristic mode of desire" (pp. 310–11).
11. Clement Rosset, *Joyful Cruelty: Toward a Philosophy of the Real*, trans. David F. Bell (Oxford University Press, 1993), 77, 80.
12. Donald Davidson, "Locating Literary Language," in *Literary Theory after Davidson*, ed. Reed Way Dasenbrock (University Park: Pennsylvania State University Press, 1993), 303.
13. See, for example, David Musselwhite, *Partings Welded Together: Politics and Desire in the Nineteenth-Century English Novel* (London: Methuen, 1987), especially his chapters on Austen and Dickens.
14. Georg Lukács, *Essays on Realism*, trans. David Fernbach (Cambridge: Massachusetts Institute of Technology Press, 1980), 21. See, too, Theodor W. Adorno, "Extorted Reconciliation: on Georg Lukács' *Realism in Our Time*," in *Notes to Literature*, vol. 2, trans. Shierry Weber Nicholsen (New York: Columbia University Press, 1991), 216–40. Adorno states a forceful defense of modernism and avant-gardism, formalism and self-reflexiveness, as against Lu-

kács's post-1920s advocacy of socialist realism and his attacks on the degeneracies and decadence of other modes (these two Titans battle using the opposing poles of the realism I am describing). My position here as regards realism is, clearly, one of admiration, and it is an admiration predicated on realism's willingness to subordinate its aesthetic and psychic anxieties to a more socially oriented, communicative purpose. But while my approach includes a pedagogically activated comparison of realism's "humility" and social purposefulness with modernism's comparatively more focused narcissisms, it reads realism as dependent on and inextricably related to those impulses that Lukács argues to be "decadent." It is precisely this destabilizing energy that allows realism its earnestness while also activating its effectiveness.

15. *A Future for Astyanax*, 61. Bersani sees this imposition of form as a compelling unification; I see it as a gesture whose self-consciousness promotes its deconstruction; it is a way of seeing and unseeing order at once.

16. Musselwhite, *Partings Welded Together*, 143–226.

17. Musselwhite, *Partings Welded Together*, 165.

18. Lyotard, *Heidegger*, 12.

19. See, for example, Margaret Scanlan, "Terrorism and the Realistic Novel: Henry James and *The Princess Casamassima*," *Texas Studies in Language and Literature*, vol. 34, no. 3 (Fall 1992), 380–402.

20. Quoted in *A Hazard of New Fortunes*, ed. Tony Tanner (Oxford University Press, 1965), xviii. Haymarket Square was the site of a bombing that killed eight policemen; as Tanner puts it, "eight known anarchists were arrested, regardless of alibis, and in an atmosphere of brutal mob hysteria, one subsequently committed suicide and four were hanged" (p. ix).

21. Bersani, *A Future for Astyanax*, 62–3.

22. Jacques Derrida, *The Margins of Philosophy*, trans. Alan Bass (University of Chicago Press, 1982), 114.

23. See Walter Benn Michaels, "*Sister Carrie*'s Popular Economy," *Critical Inquiry* (Winter 1990), 373–90, for his reading of *The Rise of Silas Lapham* against *Sister Carrie*. Michaels's essay argues that realism may seem to subsidize the capitalist status quo, as in *The Rise of Silas Lapham*, while in fact enacting a formidable opposition: Howells's aesthetic "is by definition hostile to capitalism not because it necessarily exposes the miserable conditions that a capitalist economy creates . . . but because it is identified with a fundamentally agrarian, anticapitalist vision of the world" (p. 381). *Sister Carrie*, on the other hand, while overtly antagonistic to capitalism's degrading force, "is not anticapitalist at all and is, in fact, structured by an economy in which excess is seen to generate the power of both capitalism and the novel" (p. 390).

24. Scanlan, "Terrorism and the Realistic Novel," 381, argues for making distinctions among realistic novels: "For surely a realistic novel that articulates the fear that even those who resist the dominant ideology risk doing its work

is different from a realistic novel whose author appears to have been an unwitting conscript in the thought police of some anonymous power." I would go further and argue for realism's inevitable generation of an anti-totalitarian energy. One way or another, either through self-reflexive irony or through making itself felt as "an unwitting conscript," realism always produces a doubled sense of affiliation.

25. *Hard Times*, ed. George Ford & Sylvère Monod (New York: Norton, 1966), 287. The controversy stirred up by *Hard Times* and by Dickens's further commentary in *Household Words* is provocative in this context. Harriet Martineau, in the Ford/Monod volume, sees him as a rabble-rouser of the first order, his words highly incendiary, stirring resistance against "the great class of manufacturers – unsurpassed for intelligence, public spirit, and beneficence," 304.

26. See, for example, Bersani, *A Future for Astyanax*, 60: "The novel makes esthetic sense out of social anarchy. And the society being judged subtly profits from this novelistic order, even though the order includes a great deal of social criticism."

27. Realism, with its attentiveness to the physical world, seems even more than ordinarily to use terrain as a correlative for the topographies of text production, and there are references to this kind of contiguity throughout my readings of realism. But the notion of dropping a character down a hole is a standard joke among the fiction writers of my acquaintance, who use it to speak of plot devices that rid the text of troublesome or nonfunctional characters. Lee Smith, in *Family Linen*, creates an entire novel around the possibility that there is a corpse in the well, and if this is in response to "real" life in that her inspiration came from a news article, it is also a self-irony, a gesture toward precisely that novelist's exigency.

28. For a sustained analysis of realism and painting, see Elizabeth Deeds Ermarth, *Realism and Consensus in the English Novel* (Princeton University Press, 1983), and Michael Fried, *Realism, Writing, Disfiguration: On Thomas Eakins and Stephen Crane* (University of Chicago Press, 1985).

29. D. H. Lawrence, *Phoenix: The Posthumous Papers* (London: William Heinemann, 1936), 226.

30. One is tempted to think that those who shoulder the burden of producing a realism perceived as corrective might more painfully feel their impotence within the vast, inertial movements they force themselves to regard. Howells's "Black Time" is recounted by Edwin H. Cady, *The Realist at War: The Mature Years 1885–1920* (Syracuse University Press, 1958). Howells writes to Twain: "You always rather bewildered me by your veracity, and I fancy you may tell the truth about yourself. But *all* of it? The black truth, which we all know of ourselves in our hearts, or only the whitey-brown truth of the pericardium, or the nice, whitened truth of the shirtfront? Even *you* wont tell the black

heart's truth. The man who could do it would be famed to the last day the sun shone on." Quoted in *A Hazard of New Fortunes*, xxxii.

31. Clement Rosset, *Joyful Cruelty*.

32. Michel Foucault, *Madness and Civilization: A History of Insanity in the Age of Reason*, trans. Richard Howard (New York: Vintage, 1988). See, too, Elin Diamond's argument in "Realism and Hysteria," *Discourse*, vol. 13, no. 1 (Fall–Winter 1990–91), 61, that realism, as she defines it, is a form of hysteria, with a "fetishistic attachment to the true referent."

33. See Bersani, *A Future for Astyanax*, in the notes to his chapter 2, for his comment on Richard Chase's attempt to exonerate certain texts from "the immobilizing containment of anarchic impulse" (p. 67) by calling them romances; even these, says Bersani, "eventually submit to the pressures that belong to the realistic novel."

34. Amy Kaplan, *The Social Construction of American Realism* (University of Chicago Press, 1988), 8–9. See, too, Brown, "The Logic of Realism," 233–6, for his reading of how the idealistic philosophy of realism "grounded the polemics that set one realism off against another."

35. Levine, *The Realistic Imagination*, 12, 21. Realism has, as Levine's assertion clearly implies, often been cataloged as simple, unreflexive, and naive. J. P. Stern, for example, in *On Realism* (London: Routledge, 1973), 54, says that "of the fact that reality changes realism is more fully, more intelligently aware than any other literary mode: what it implicitly denies is that in this world there is more than one reality, and that this denial is in need of proof."

36. Marianne Moore, "Poetry." Poetry won't exist "till the poets among us can be / 'literalists of / the imagination' – above / insolence and triviality and can present / for inspection, 'imaginary gardens with real toads in them. . . . ' " See William Dean Howells, *Criticism and Fiction and other Essays*, ed. Clara Marburg Kirk & Rudolf Kirk (New York University Press, 1959), 13. As the Preface to Sundquist's collection, *American Realism*, points out, Ambrose Bierce's definition of realism in *The Devil's Dictionary* is "Realism, n. The art of depicting nature as it is seen by toads. The charm suffusing a landscape painted by a mole, or a story written by a measuring-worm." My assessment is closer to Moore's of poetry than to Bierce's of realism.

37. Nathaniel Hawthorne, *The Scarlet Letter*, in *The Portable Hawthorne*, ed. Malcolm Cowley (New York: Viking, 1974), 318.

38. See Sacvan Bercovitch, *The Office of The Scarlet Letter* (Baltimore: Johns Hopkins University Press, 1991).

39. Beckett, *Proust*, 24.

40. Beckett, *Proust*, 14.

41. See, for example, Virginia Woolf, "Mr. Bennett and Mrs. Brown," in *The Captain's Death Bed and Other Essays* (New York: Harcourt, Brace & Co.,

1950). Howells, in 1903, writes that "a whole order of literature has arisen, calling itself psychological, as realism called itself scientific, and dealing with life on its mystical side . . . we have indeed, in our best fiction, gone back to mysticism, if indeed we were not always there in our best fiction, and the riddle of the painful earth is again engaging us with the old fascination." Quoted in *A Hazard of New Fortunes,* xxviii.

42. Edith Wharton, *The House of Mirth* (New York: Penguin, 1985), 104.

43. See Ermarth, *Realism and Consensus,* 33–7, on realism's juridical exclusions of detail and on its predication of objects as in a system of relations.

44. Bounderby, about whom I speak later at length, is a very provocative figure read in the context of Musselwhite, *Partings Welded Together,* 143–226. Musselwhite's chapter on Dickens, and his discussion of the "Autobiographical Fragment" as Dickens's packaging and production of a humble authorial history, would support my sense that Bounderby is a self-ironic projection of "Dickens." He represents as well what Musselwhite says is "that popular middle-class pastime of proving one's working-class roots" (p. 154).

45. George Eliot, *The Mill on the Floss* (New York: Riverside, 1912).

46. Virginia Woolf, *Mrs. Dalloway* (New York: Harcourt Brace Jovanovich, 1981), IX.

47. William D. Howells, *Annie Kilburn* (New York: Harper & Brothers, 1891), 62–3.

48. Levine, *The Realistic Imagination,* 12, speaks of realism's impulse to name, for moral purposes, a reality that seems increasingly unnameable; beyond this philosophic and linguistic sophistication is, I think, another refinement of concern arising from the anxieties of a literary influence that had begun, with the appearance of the novel form as both result and cause, to privilege character, introspection, and a concomitant anxiety.

49. Bersani, *A Future for Astyanax,* 65. Bersani makes this statement in connection with a discussion of *Middlemarch* in which he argues that Eliot has communicated that Dorothea and Lydgate should be taken to task for "their solipsistic notions of structural harmonies in life" and then has undone her own ironic distance by indulging in "an ideally unified novelistic structure" that "may make us view with irony *her* irony about her heroes' early views of their relation to the social medium in which they must live." I would say that this is exactly the point: that the text itself destabilizes response, and that this gesture is never entirely ingenuous.

50. Catherine Belsey, *Critical Practice* (London: Methuen, 1980), 75.

51. Brown, "The Logic of Realism," 229, says, using Dickens's "moralizing *deus ex machina* conclusions" as an example, that "arbitrary interference with causal probability is an antirealistic trait." Later, however, he speaks of the commonly used nullifications within realism, devices like pretending to give a real proper

name for a person or place by leaving the space blank, so that, he says, realism "has a specificity and eats it too" (p. 232).

52. Quoted in *A Hazard of New Fortunes*, xx. The passage goes on: "Perhaps we can only suffer into the truth, and live along, in doubt whether it was worth the suffering. It may be an illusion, as so many things are (maybe all things); but I sometimes feel that the only peace is in giving up on one's own will."

53. See Roman Jakobson and Morris Halle, *Fundamentals of Language* (The Hague: Mouton, 1956), for a germinal statement of the association between realism and metonymy.

54. Umberto Eco, "Metaphor, Dictionary, and Encyclopedia," *New Literary History*, vol. 15, no. 2 (Winter 1984), 270.

55. Martin Heidegger, "The Thing," in *Poetry, Language, Thought*, trans. Albert Hofstadter (New York: Harper & Row, 1971), 165–82.

56. See Sundquist, *American Realism*, 12–13: "The realistic novel often depends upon translating a sufficiency, even a superfluity, of detail into determined hierarchical but mutually dependent orders – not only in order to correspond to the complicated fabric of contemporary life but also to make of such staggering detail its own ordering technique, one in which the value and scope of the self (and of value itself) is measurable and in which, as a result, the distinction between aspects of the self and its implemented devices becomes increasingly obscure." Sundquist goes on to speak of the "concomitant exhilaration and fear" this sense promotes.

57. See Brown, "The Logic of Realism," 236.

58. Kaplan, *The Social Construction of American Realism*, 3, argues that Richard V. Chase's thesis regarding romance in *The American Novel and Its Tradition* (Garden City, NY: Doubleday, 1957) is formative rather than reactive: "the romance thesis – like the texts it privileges – seems to grow full-blown out of the American soil to define the exceptional nature of American culture, [but] in fact it emerges victorious from an implicit political attack on alternative forms of fiction and criticism." The realism/romance dichotomy, which, as Kaplan points out, is in the service of a position regarding what constitutes character and value, is used and always has been used just as opportunistically as most other definitional terms. Frank Norris, for example, uses the terms in a way that reveals how they must remain artificial impositions in the service of one's position: "Naturalism is a form of romanticism, not an inner circle of realism." See *The Literary Criticism of Frank Norris*, 72.

59. "Now, Mrs. Sparsit was not a poetical woman; but she took an idea in the nature of an allegorical fancy, into her head. . . . She erected in her mind a mighty Staircase, with a dark pit of shame and ruin at the bottom; and down those stairs, from day to day and hour to hour, she saw Louisa coming" (p. 185).

60. Howells, *Annie Kilburn*, 67–8. I would like to point out here the Alice in Wonderland touch of having a fictional character cite a fellow character as "the only philanthropist whom she had really ever known."
61. *Hard Times* (1958 ed.), 312.
62. Lawrence, *Phoenix*, 517.
63. Beckett, *Proust*, 76.
64. Norris, *The Literary Criticism of Frank Norris*, 78.
65. Virginia Woolf, *To the Lighthouse* (New York: Harcourt Brace Jovanovitch, 1989), 178.
66. See Martin Heidegger, "The Letter on Humanism," trans. Frank A. Cappuzi in collaboration with J. Glenn Gray, in *Basic Writings*, ed. David Farrell Krell (New York: Harper, 1977), 193–242, esp. 217–21.
67. I would agree with Bersani, *A Future for Astyanax*, 69–70, on his reading of the heroes of realistic fiction, up to but not including his analysis of effect. Bersani argues for a list of anarchic characters, among them Heathcliff and Zenobia, who support novelistic structures that will guarantee their "expulsion from the viable structures of fiction and of life. The novelist glamorizes a figure who exposes the factitious nature of the social and esthetic orders in the name of which the novelist will sacrifice that figure." I would argue that neither Heathcliff nor Zenobia is sacrificed, any more than Edna Pontellier is sacrificed as she walks into the sea, since the performative effects of their pervasive presences supersede and extend beyond their "life" in the story.
68. The historical Zenobia was led through Rome in golden chains.
69. Sigmund Freud, *New Introductory Lectures on Psychoanalysis*, trans. James Strachey (New York: Norton, 1965), 100.

3: DOMESTIC VIOLENCE

1. See Raymond Williams, *Writing in Society* (London: Verso, 1983), 166–74. Critics use various metaphors to articulate this doubleness. D. A. Williams says that "the Realist recognizes that the individual is a pearl-like product of the secretions of society," but "also cling[s] to a belief in a core identity – the grain of sand around which the pearl is formed." In D. A. Williams, ed., *The Monster in the Mirror* (Oxford University Press, 1978), 273–4.
2. George Moore's sister novels, *Evelyn Innes* and *Sister Teresa*, become emblematic in this context, as they dichotomize character through the diptych of the two novels and through the contrasting orientations of Evelyn Innes as sensualist and as singer of Wagner, in the first work, and Evelyn Innes, under her nun's name of Sister Teresa, voiceless, spiritualized, isolated, in the second work. One senses a fatigue that grows from the artist's struggle to manage

character in the world (a fatigue shared by Evelyn Innes and Moore himself) and that generates a reciprocal withdrawal into the realm of the spiritual.

3. Walter Benn Michaels, "*Sister Carrie*'s Popular Economy," *Critical Inquiry* (Winter 1980), 378–9.

4. It is interesting to consider *Sons and Lovers*, with its impulses both fictional and explicitly and unabashedly autobiographical, in the context of realism. It has, relative to Lawrence's other work, a nearly deadpan, chronological fidelity to the facts of his life as he perceived them at the time; yet it is strikingly not an updated version of the nineteenth-century English *Bildungsroman*. Realism's complex ambivalence about character in the world is supplanted here by a narcissism so profound that externalities either lose their alternative power or are co-opted into objective correlatives. Lawrence claimed, after Frieda, with her knowledge of Freud, had read the text, that he had represented an Oedipal situation that might be considered common to others, but this seems to have dawned on him after the fact.

5. Raymond Tallis, *In Defense of Realism* (London: Edward Arnold, 1988), 211.

6. See George Levine, *The Realistic Imagination: English Fiction from Frankenstein to Lady Chatterley* (University of Chicago Press, 1981), 33–5, on the passive hero in realism.

7. See Lawrence's *Psychoanalysis and the Unconscious, and Fantasia of the Unconscious* (New York: Viking, 1967), 125–36, or his *Assorted Articles* (Freeport: Books for Libraries, 1968).

8. Again, see *Fantasia of the Unconscious*. See, too, Elin Diamond, "Realism and Hysteria," *Discourse*, vol. 13, no. 1 (Fall–Winter 1990–91), 61. Her essay on late nineteenth-century drama argues that "Realism is more than an interpretation of reality; it *produces* 'reality' by positioning its spectator to recognize and verify its truths," and thus, she argues, the constant reiterations of the Oedipal family in "Ibsenist" drama reify and perpetuate among its viewers a sexist ideology. This is, I think, a tough call to make, either for drama, which is more explicitly "performative," or, by extension, for realist fiction. My interrogation of this plausible assertion would ask whether the intrinsic melodrama, the tacit recognition by both audience and author of the standard codes for which realistic detail is enlisted as costumery, does not better serve the cause of gender skepticism than does a less apparently "realistic" but far more compellingly complex model of characterization. See Marshall Brown, "The Logic of Realism: A Hegelian Approach," *Proceedings of the Modern Language Association*, vol. 96, no. 2 (March 1981), 230, for his discussion of the close and self-conscious affiliation of nineteenth-century realism with drama.

9. One might also productively (and with a certain inescapable malice) juxtapose both the discussion of art in *Women in Love*, as it manifests itself in analyzing Loerke's representation of a horse (pp. 525–7), and Lawrence's use of the horse

as aesthetic example in *Fantasia of the Unconscious*, 125–6, with Sissy's encounter with Gradgrind over the same subject in *Hard Times*.

10. Elizabeth Gaskell, *Wives and Daughters* (New York: Oxford University Press, 1987), 32.

11. Per Seyersted and Emily Toth, eds., *A Kate Chopin Miscellany* (Natchitoches: Northwestern State University of Louisiana Press, 1979), 137.

12. See Robert Bernasconi, "Deconstruction and the Possibility of Ethics," in *Deconstruction and Philosophy: The Texts of Jacques Derrida*, ed. John Sallis (Chicago: University of Chicago Press, 19): 122–39. Bernasconi (p. 130) discusses Derrida's sense of the difference between *systematic* incoherence and systematic *incoherence*: a *systematic* incoherence "would in the end amount to a *coherent* incoherence."

13. If, as Leo Bersani argues in *A Future for Astyanax: Character and Desire in Literature* (New York: Columbia University Press, 1984), 5–14, realism is aware of the threat of desire and thus provides strategies for containment, it does not successfully purge itself of the knowledge, the experience, and the expression of this desire. The question becomes whether this "containment," which is undeniable, is less subversive than more openly anarchic modes; I would argue that it is not.

14. See Jacques Derrida, "The Politics of Friendship," *The Philosophical Forum*, vol. 85, 632–44.

15. Bersani, in *A Future for Astyanax*, argues for a version of self that, rather than valorizing the intact and coherent, celebrates the fragmented, the scenic, the peripheral, the discontinuous. This alternative is imagined as a freeing of those desires necessarily constricted within the rationally ordered, socially integrated subject, and Bersani premises, as against realism, a literature that would perform this liberation. I would agree that a reductive humanism could profitably be replaced with such a reading of self, as Bersani describes and accords to such texts as Gilles Deleuze and Félix Guattari's *Anti-Oedipus: Capitalism and Schizophrenia*, trans. Robert Hurley, Mark Seem, & Helen R. Lane (Minneapolis: University of Minnesota Press, 1983). I am, however, inclined to believe that subversion comes in more secret forms than the theatrics of a radically deterritorialized vision of self. And as Bersani points out in his final chapter, "Persons in Pieces," "at the limit, the enjoyment of sexual *and* literary fantasies requires the annihilation of all humanity" (p. 288), in effect, producing a reduction from complexity to a theory of humors once again, with character driven solely by desire.

16. See Freud, "Negation," in *The Collected Psychological Works of Sigmund Freud*, trans. James Strachey (London: Hogarth Press, 1964), 235–9.

17. Edith Wharton, *Ethan Frome* (New York: Signet, 1992), 6.

18. See, for a reading of typical nineteenth-century attitudes toward mesmerism, Simon Schaffer, "Self Evidence," *Critical Inquiry*, vol. 18, no. 2 (Winter 1992),

349–62. One thinks naturally in this context of Lily Bart's final "dream" of a child on her arm, as she sinks gradually from a kind to sleep to death. This scene, which reproduces exactly (and with an authority that compels full belief in Wharton's knowledge of it) that state of drugged exhaustion so potent that it is "as though some cruel stimulant had been forced into her veins" (p. 322), records as well the culmination of a textual anxiety that has permeated the novel. Lily feels from the child "a gentle penetrating thrill of warmth and pleasure" as she falls into sleep, but then she is torn by "a dark flush of loneliness and terror" (p. 323). Childless, but protecting a child (she tries "to keep awake on account of the baby") (p. 323), drugged but jolted into terror, Lily is a figure for the (female) novelist whose textual imperatives for reconciliation and resistance are equal and opposite forces.

19. Jean-François Lyotard, *The Postmodern Condition: A Report on Knowledge, Theory and History of Literature*, trans. Geoffrey Bennington & Brian Massumi (Minneapolis: University of Minnesota Press, 1984), 75.

20. See my note 39 on legs in Chapter 6 on *Hard Times*.

21. Each of these figures is an essence of mutability balanced against a nightmarish permanence and solidity: Cathy's ghost is ephemeral yet enduring, while her corpse is unchanging but, like Dracula himself, just before sudden, total decay. The monster is huge, heavy, utterly material, and, as the film versions underscore with their vision of a stitched-together giant, also in peril of disintegration, like some clay figure weak in the joints and too heavy to bear its own weight. Dracula, undead, is both immortal and ready to decompose. And thus when Zenobia changes her living tropical flower, emblem of a beauty premised on overripeness, for a diamond flower, we sense an immense significance in Hawthorne's gesture.

22. Paul Ricoeur, "The Metaphorical Process as Cognition, Imagination, and Feeling," *Critical Inquiry*, vol. 5, no. 1 (Autumn 1978), 144.

23. Robert Frost, *Selected Letters*, ed. Lawrance Thompson (New York: Holt, Rinehart & Winston, 1964), 466.

24. See David Musselwhite, *Partings Welded Together: Politics and Desire in the Nineteenth-Century English Novel* (London: Methuen, 1987), 17–42, for assertions about realism's dictatorial obsession with family structures.

25. Jane Austen, *Mansfield Park* (New York: Bantam, 1983), 33–4.

26. See Musselwhite, *Partings Welded Together*, 17–42, for his own and multiple other readings of Austen's use of *Lovers' Vows*.

27. Kate Chopin, *The Awakening*, ed. Margaret Culley (New York: Norton, 1976), 66.

28. The way marriage is treated in fiction is, I think, deeply significant, as it reifies larger cultural assumptions. I do not mean here to underplay the literal status of the institution, the literal issues, of concern to feminists then and now, of a woman's place within the institution; nor do I mean to elide the considerable

political anxieties that may find their way into the domestic field. Undine Spragg is, among other things, quite clearly an emblem of the social climber, whose acquisition of wealth, through marriage or through other markets, suggests as well a *failure* of transcendence as "bad" character prevails.

29. See Northrop Frye, *Anatomy of Criticism: Four Essays* (Princeton University Press, 1957), 353, for his comments on the Oedipus complex as evidence of Freud's considerable abilities as a reader of literary texts.

30. See Gregory L. Lucente, *The Narrative of Realism and Myth: Verga, Faulkner, Pavese* (Baltimore: Johns Hopkins University Press, 1981), 14: "In contrast to Hegelian idealism and Platonic realism, early and middle nineteenth-century realists did not regard artistic language as problematical or deceptive so much as functional, the key moment of communicable transition between the world of the senses and that of the intellect."

31. See Dale M. Bauer, *Feminist Dialogics: A Theory of Failed Community* (Albany: State University of New York Press, 1988), 182.

32. Michaels, "*Sister Carrie*'s Popular Economy," 377. The fact that *Sister Carrie* is so often relegated to the underclass of naturalism (with its determinisms and brute physicalities) is interesting in this context, as it suggests something of the tautology necessary to maintain a Howellsian vision of realism as productive and ethical in both method and effect: if such evident infidelity and such overt promiscuity, then not realism.

33. See Brown, "The Logic of Realism: A Hegelian Approach," 236.

34. George Levine, in "By Knowledge Possessed: Darwin, Nature, and Victorian Narrative" *New Literary History*, vol. 24 (1993), 375–6, quotes Darwin's *Autobiography*: Early on, he writes that "my mind . . . seems to have become a kind of machine for grinding general laws out of large collections of facts." Toward the end he says that "I have attempted . . . to write the following account of myself, as if I were a dead man in another world looking back at my own life. Nor have I found this difficult, for life is nearly over with me. I have taken no pains about my style of writing." This metonymizing is a stunning example of the potent deadness of the character whose very strength – his grinding machine of a brain – is also a kind of anesthesia.

35. Quoted from *L'Art brut*, in Gilles Deleuze and Félix Guattari, *Anti-Oedipus: Capitalism and Schizophrenia*, trans. Robert Hurley, Mark Seem, & Helen R. Lane (Minneapolis: University of Minnesota Press, 1989), 17.

36. Jean-François Lyotard, *The Inhuman: Reflections on Time*, trans. Geoffrey Bennington & Rachel Bowlby (Stanford University Press, 1991), 18–20.

37. Levine, "By Knowledge Possessed," 369.

38. Levine, "By Knowledge Possessed," 369.

39. Samuel Butler, *Erewhon and Erewhon Revisited* (New York: Modern Library, 1955), 223, 224, 234.

40. Butler, *Erewhon*, 256.

41. Among the learned gentleman's predictions and assessments are the following: Machines, having shown already a remarkable capacity for evolution, may become conscious entities (p. 224); animal life has certain mechanistic affiliations, and plant life displays a kind of consciousness (pp. 224–7); humans may be more physiologically determined than endowed with "temperament" (p. 227); machines may learn to hear and to speak (p. 229); machines are "supplementary limbs" (p. 256).

42. Harriet Martineau, "The Factory Legislation: A Warning against Meddling Legislation" (Manchester, 1855), in *Hard Times*, ed. George Ford & Sylvére Monod (New York: Norton, 1966), 304.

43. See Deleuze and Guattari, *Anti-Oedipus*, 1–50, on "desiring-machines," "the body without organs," and the "subject."

44. See "Realism," in C. Hugh Holman, *A Handbook to Literature*, 3rd ed. (Indianapolis: Bobbs-Merrill, 1960).

45. See Arnold Habegger, *Gender, Fantasy, and Realism in American Literature* (New York: Columbia University Press, 1982), for ruminations on realism and "sissy" writers.

46. Levine, *The Realistic Imagination*, 27.

47. Gilles Deleuze, *Masochism: Coldness and Cruelty* (New York: Zone Books, 1991), 9–23. Deleuze is, of course, arguing here for the separability of the two phenomena.

48. Charles Dickens, *David Copperfield* (Boston: Riverside, 1958), 44, 97, 54.

49. Lyotard, *The Postmodern Condition*, 77.

50. Immanuel Kant, *The Critique of Judgment*, trans. James Creed Meredith (Oxford: Clarendon Press, 1991), 106. It seems to me that for Kant, the pleasure, while dependent on the pain, prevails and is in fact an accordance of full dignity to the human subject able to participate in the sublime.

51. Edmund Burke, *On the Sublime and Beautiful* (New York: P. F. Collier & Son, 1909), 36 (Part I, Section 7).

52. See Levine's chapter "The Landscape of Reality," in *The Realistic Imagination*, 204–26, on the sublime in English fiction.

53. Stephen Knapp, *Personification and the Sublime* (Cambridge: Harvard University Press, 1985), 67.

54. See Martin Heidegger, *Poetry, Language, Thought*, trans. Albert Hofstadter (New York: Harper & Row, 1971), in "What Are Poets For?" 92.

55. See Ian Watt, *The Rise of the Novel* (Berkeley: University of California Press, 1967).

4: THE INHUMAN

1. John Locke, *An Essay Concerning Human Understanding*, ed. Peter H. Nidditch (Oxford: Clarendon Press, 1990), 572. This passage is also quoted by Paul de

Man, "The Epistemology of Metaphor," *Critical Inquiry*, vol. 5, no. 1 (Autumn 1978), 13-30.

2. Flannery O'Connor, *The Complete Stories* (New York: Farrar, Straus & Giroux, 1990), 124-5.

3. Charles Dickens, *Little Dorrit*, ed. John Holloway (New York: Penguin, 1967), 43.

4. David Musselwhite's efforts in *Partings Welded Together: Politics and Desire in the Nineteenth-Century English Novel* (London: Methuen, 1987) are notable in this regard, for the book is quite explicitly provoked by Musselwhite's antipathy to Thatcher, his sense of the relentless reduction of everything to a banal sameness. Acute, irascible, thoroughly self-conscious, ironical about the difficulties of escaping the Oedipalized environment he sees as pulling stories always back to a marriage and the family version of Hegelian synthesis and sublation, Musselwhite constructs his book and sustains his tone in ways meant to subvert the tendencies of the critical text to fall into the habits of its object texts. A wonderful book, it cannot, nonetheless, be said to have evaded complicity in all kinds of normative procedures.

5. Ludwig Wittgenstein, *Philosophical Investigations*, trans. G. E. M. Anscombe (New York: Macmillan, 1958), 223.

6. Donald Davidson, *Inquiries into Truth and Interpretation* (Oxford: Clarendon Press, 1990), 126.

7. Hilary Putnam, "The Craving for Objectivity," *New Literary History*, vol. 15, no. 2 (Winter 1984), 229-39.

8. Jacques Derrida, "The Politics of Friendship," *The Philosophical Forum*, vol. 85, 633. Richard Rorty's seminar discussion of Derrida's essay during the 1992 School of Criticism and Theory began my thinking about women and friendship.

9. Derrida, "Politics of Friendship," 642. See Michel Foucault, *The Use of Pleasure: The History of Sexuality*, vol. 2, trans. Robert Hurley (New York: Pantheon, 1985), for his definitions of "virile moderation" and "virile homosexuality."

10. See K. J. Dover, *Greek Homosexuality* (Cambridge: Harvard University Press, 1978), for photographs of the vase paintings in which this posture occurs; see, too, Foucault, *The Use of Pleasure*, 196.

11. Derrida, "Politics of Friendship," 642. See Michel de Montaigne, "On Friendship," in *Selected Essays*, ed. Blanchard Bates (New York: Modern Library, 1949), 63: "Moreover, to say the truth, the ordinary talent of women is not such as is sufficient to maintain that converse and fellowship which is the nurse of this sacred tie; nor do they appear to be endued with firmness of mind to endure the strain of so hard and durable a knot. . . . This sex in no instance has ever yet been able to reach [friendship], and by the common agreement of the ancient schools is excluded from it."

12. This essay will use the terms "man" and "woman" as if there were no gender trouble afoot. This is not because I deny the problematizing of such terms, but instead because I see them as having been virtually emptied of all but allegorical significance *in the context of this particular argument.* There are too many feminisms, too many increments along what may or may not be a continuum between "male" and "female" to allow for anything other than a symbolizing of these terms as they apply to my discussion of realism here.

13. It is, of course, many things besides. Ellen Moers's section in *Literary Women* (New York: Doubleday, 1976) on the novel as Shelley's translation of birth and death anxieties into textual matter is by now a standard but no less convincing and provocative reading. See, too, *The Endurance of Frankenstein: Essays on Mary Shelley's Novel,* ed. George Levine & U. C. Knoepflmacher (Berkeley: University of California Press, 1979). See, too, Gary Kelly, *Women, Writing, and the Revolution, 1790–1827* (Oxford: Clarendon Press, 1993). This book refers only in passing to Shelley, and focuses on Helen Maria Williams, Mary Hays, and Elizabeth Hamilton.

14. See Simon Schama, *Citizens: A Chronicle of the French Revolution* (New York: Vintage, 1989), 497–8, for a brief discussion of the paradox of a totalizing concept of human rights that remained explicitly exclusive of women and other "supplicants for citizenship" and of Olympe de Gouges's document, "sneered at then and since," "A Declaration of the Rights of Women and Citizenesses." See, too, Jürgen Habermas, "Citizenship and National Identity: Some Reflections on the Future of Europe," *Praxis International,* vol. 12, no. 1 (April 1992), 1–19, for an exploration of the more recent enactments of this paradox. He himself uses as evidence for citizenship's assumption of a core of universal human rights the example of Article Four of the Revolutionary Constitution of 1793, which gave to *"every* adult foreigner who lived for one year in France . . . the active rights of a citizen" (p. 13). He does not comment on the exclusion of women from full participation in and enactment of these rights. See, too, Chris Baldick, *In Frankenstein's Shadow: Myth, Monstrosity, and Nineteenth-Century Writing* (Oxford: Clarendon Press, 1987), for historical background related to Shelley's perceptions within the novel regarding the revolution.

15. See Susan Winnett, "Coming Unstrung: Women, Men, Narrative, and Principles of Pleasure," *Proceedings of the Modern Language Association,* vol. 105, no. 3 (May 1990), 507, on homoaesthetic reading. Mary Shelley, *Frankenstein* (New York: Bantam, 1981), xxii. All further page references will be cited parenthetically in the text.

16. See Jürgen Habermas, "Discourse Ethics: Notes on a Program of Philosophical Justification," in *Moral Consciousness and Communicative Action,* trans. Christian Lenhardt & Shierry Weber Nicholsen (Cambridge: Massachusetts Institute of Technology Press, 1990), 44. See Paul Youngquist, "The Mother, the Daugh-

ter, and the Monster," *Philological Quarterly*, vol. 70, no. 3 (Summer 1991), 339–59, for an argument that Shelley's novel repudiates Wollstonecraft's vision of the universality of reason and her androgynous utopia and looks instead to bodily and, specifically, sexual imperatives. One might say instead that Shelley's holistic vision of a gendered (i.e., sexual) but fully human (i.e., rational) subject is what is at risk here.

17. Schama, *Citizens*, 502.
18. If, as Joseph W. Lew argues in "The Deceptive Other: Mary Shelley's Critique of Orientalism in *Frankenstein*," *Studies in Romanticism*, vol. 30, no. 2 (Summer 1990), 255–83, "Shelley encounters herself" at the very heart of the novel in the story of Safie's mother, dead, this only further substantiates the self-referential nature of her discourse.
19. Habermas, "Discourse Ethics," 46.
20. Habermas, "Discourse Ethics," 46.
21. Nathaniel Hawthorne, *The Blithedale Romance* (New York: Norton, 1978), 105.
22. As Moers, *Literary Women*, 97, points out, Shelley was actively reading her mother's work around the time of her writing of *Frankenstein*.
23. See Diana Fuss, "Fashion and the Homospectatorial Look," *Critical Inquiry*, vol. 18, no. 4 (Summer 1992), 713–37, for a discussion of the fragmented and dispersed body images in fashion photography that recall Lacan's discussion of the "images of the fragmented body": "images of castration, mutilation, dismemberment, dislocation, evisceration, devouring, bursting open of the body" (p. 718).
24. For a further twist on this, see the extremely violent film *Frankenstein Unbound* (1990), in which Elizabeth, literally ripped open by the monster from throat to crotch, is restitched by Frankenstein to be the monster's bride. The permutations are seemingly endless.
25. See Jacqueline Lichtenstein, "Making Up Representation: The Risks of Femininity," trans. Katharine Streip, in *Misogyny, Misandry, and Misanthropy*, ed. R. Howard Bloch & Frances Ferguson (Berkeley: University of California Press, 1989), 77–87, on the connection between corrupt rhetorical decorativeness and the female and her form.
26. Lew, "The Deceptive Other," argues that "Orientalism" is a primary anxiety and inescapable fascination within the novel. Leo Bersani, *A Future for Astyanax: Character and Desire in Literature* (New York: Columbia University Press, 1984), 63–6, argues that realism inevitably undermines its own illusion of reality as fragmented, discontinuous, and essentially scenic, rather than narrative, by imposing on its details on overarching *telos* that reasserts stillness, legibility, and order. I would argue otherwise. As I have suggested is the case in many novels whose basic premises are realistic, *Frankenstein*, with its concentricities, undoes itself. There is no center at the center of this book.

27. See Jacques Derrida, "Structure, Sign and Play in the Discourse of the Human Science," in *Writing and Difference*, trans. Alan Bass (University of Chicago Press, 1978), 278–93, for an examination of the notion of the center and of the effects of a loss of faith in that center.

28. See Michel Foucault, *Madness and Civilization: A History of Insanity in the Age of Reason*, trans. Richard Howard (New York: Vintage, 1988), 136–50, for the locus of hysteria in female softness and permeability: "if internal space is dense, organized, and solidly heterogeneous in its different regions, the symptoms of hysteria are rare and its effects will remain simple" (p. 149). ˙

29. See Gayatri Spivak, "Translator's Preface," in Jacques Derrida, *Of Grammatology* (Baltimore: Johns Hopkins University Press, 1976). Her meditation on the function of the author's preface provides a gloss for Percy Shelley's Frankensteinian patchwork. "The preface is a necessary gesture of homage and parricide, for the book (the father) makes a claim of authority or origin which is both true and false" (p. xi), says Spivak; one can see, then, the very problematizing of origin that marks the monster's own generation.

30. Derrida, "Politics of Friendship," 633–4.

31. See Chantal Mouffe, "Feminism, Citizenship, and Radical Democratic Politics," in *Feminists Theorize the Political*, ed. Judith Butler & Joan Scott (New York: Routledge, 1992), for her discussions of citizenship.

32. Habermas, "Discourse Ethics," 47, 50; "Strawson's phenomenology of the moral is relevant because it shows that the world of moral phenomena can be grasped only in the performative attitude of participants in interaction, that resentment and personal emotional responses in general point to suprapersonal standards for judging norms and commands, and that the moral-practical justification of a mode of action aims at an aspect different from the feeling-neutral assessment of means–ends relations, even when such assessment is made from the point of view of general welfare."

33. Derrida, "Politics of Friendship," 644.

34. Derrida, "Politics of Friendship," 638.

35. See, as well, Peter Brooks, " 'Godlike Science/Unhallowed Arts': Language, Nature, and Monstrosity," in *The Endurance of Frankenstein: Essays on Mary Shelley's Novel*, ed. George Levine & U. C. Knoepflmacher (Berkeley: University of California Press, 1979), 205–20.

36. de Man, "Epistemology of Metaphor," 21.

37. Jacques Derrida, "White Mythology," in *The Margins of Philosophy*, trans. Alan Bass (University of Chicago Press, 1982), 248.

38. See Paul Ricoeur, "The Metaphorical Process as Cognition, Imagination, and Feeling," *Critical Inquiry*, vol. 5, no. 1 (Autumn 1978), 146.

39. de Man, "Epistemology of Metaphor," 21.

40. See James R. Kincaid, " 'Words Cannot Express': *Frankenstein* Tripping on

the Tongue," *Novel*, vol. 24, no. 1 (Fall 1990), 26–47, for his analysis of the characters' reiteration of the assertion that words fail adequately to represent what they hope to be able to communicate.

41. Derrida, "Politics of Friendship," 633.

42. Ricoeur, "The Metaphorical Process," 144.

43. Ricoeur, "The Metaphorical Process," 147–58. See Liliane Papin, "This Is Not a Universe: Metaphor, Language, and Representation," *Proceedings of the Modern Language Association*, vol. 107, no. 5 (October 1992), 1253–65, for its reading of how the Western predisposition to link thinking with seeing, and thus with inevitable metaphorization, persists, even as physics' "new emerging reality" thoroughly undermines the adequacy and accuracy of standard vision.

44. See Mary A. Favret, "A Woman Writes the Fiction of Science: The Body in *Frankenstein*," *Genders*, no. 14 (Fall 1992), 50–65.

45. Jean-François Lyotard, *The Inhuman: Reflections on Time*, trans. Geoffrey Bennington & Rachel Bowlby (Stanford University Press, 1991), 2.

46. See Richard Rorty, "Foucault, Dewey, Nietzsche," *Raritan*, vol. 9, no. 4 (Spring 1990), 2–5, for the argument that one can think the "inhuman thoughts" necessary to become a "knight of autonomy" while enacting in the public sphere his "moral identity as a citizen." See, too, Rorty, *Contingency, Irony, and Solidarity* (Cambridge University Press, 1989).

47. Luce Irigaray, *Speculum of the Other Woman*, trans. Gillian C. Gill (Ithaca, NY: Cornell University Press, 1985), 261–2. The entirety of "Plato's Hystera" is compelling in the light of *Frankenstein*.

48. Montaigne, "On Friendship," 67.

49. Montaigne, "On Friendship," 71.

50. Irigaray, *Speculum*.

51. Davidson, *Inquiries into Truth and Interpretation*, 247.

52. See Friedrich Nietzsche, *The Will to Power*, trans. Walter Kauffman (New York: Random House, 1967), sec. 522, p. 283; consider, too, Fredric Jameson's *The Prison-House of Language: A Critical Account of Structuralism and Russian Formalism* (Princeton University Press, 1972).

53. Derrida, "Politics of Friendship," 637.

54. Habermas, "Discourse Ethics," 46. One is brought here to think as well of Godwin's *Caleb Williams* and the ambiguities of the final trial scene.

55. The monster equates himself with Adam at points throughout the text, but at a less explicit level Shelley equates him with Eve; see page 85, where Frankenstein, with Adam-like ill-temper, curses the hands that formed the monster and got him into so much misery.

56. Gary Larson, *The Prehistory of the Far Side* (New York: Andrews & McMeel, 1989), 230. I am indebted to a response made by Eve Sedgewick in a 1992 colloquium at the School of Theory and Criticism for this reference.

57. The optimism of *The Postmodern Condition: A Report on Knowledge*, trans. Geoffrey Bennington & Brian Massumi (Minneapolis: University of Minnesota Press, 1984), is muted in *The Inhuman*, where Lyotard says that his belief that the system, consolidated under the name of development, could be used to express the "infinitely secret [inhumanness] of which the soul is hostage" was mistaken; "the system rather has the consequence of causing the forgetting of what escapes it" (p. 2).

58. See Locke, *An Essay Concerning Human Understanding*, bk. IV, ch. 4, 569–73, for his discussion of monsters and changelings: "But I am not so unacquainted with the Zeal of some Men, which enables them to spin Consequences, and to see Religion threatened, whenever any one ventures to quit their Forms of Speaking, as not to foresee, what Names such a Proposition as this is likely to be charged with: And without doubt it will be asked, If *Changelings* are something between Man and Beast, what will become of them in the other World? To which I answer, I. It concerns me not to know or enquire."

59. Davidson, "On the Very Idea of a Conceptual Scheme," in *Inquiries into Truth and Interpretation*, 185.

60. See Davidson, "On the Very Idea of a Conceptual Scheme," 251–2, 186.

61. Friedrich Nietzsche, *Ecce Homo*, trans. Walter Kaufmann (New York: Random House, 1969), 266.

62. Donald Davidson, "A Nice Derangement of Epitaphs," in *Philosophical Grounds of Rationality: Intentions, Categories, Ends*, ed. Richard E. Grandy & Richard Warner (Oxford: Clarendon Press, 1986), 194.

63. Davidson, *Inquiries into Truth and Interpretation*, 195.

64. Davidson, "A Nice Derangement of Epitaphs," 168–9.

65. Davidson, "A Nice Derangement of Epitaphs," 168.

66. Davidson, "A Nice Derangement of Epitaphs," 167.

67. Thus Judith Butler, in *Gender Trouble* (New York: Routledge, 1990), argues convincingly that the only avenue to equality is in the blurring of gender distinctions, which are in any event artificial; cross-dressing, as her final solution, may seem to some a long run for a short slide (or is it the other way round?), but in fact it would obviate the problem altogether by producing a genuine "human."

68. Derrida, "Politics of Friendship," 637.

69. Umberto Eco, "Metaphor, Dictionary, and Encyclopedia," *New Literary History*, vol. 15. no. 2 (Winter 1984), 270.

70. It is meaningful in the context of my overall argument to quote Kincaid, " 'Words Cannot Express,' " 29, in his assessment of Shelley's language: "Waiving as inadmissible, crude, and certainly unpublishable the possibility that Mary Shelley simply didn't have many words at her disposal and was thus stymied, we hasten to the failure of language itself. . . . " One does not need

to know Grice on implicatures to recognize in this coy pastiche of legal metaphor and lip service to "political correctness" a suggestion that the poor girl hadn't a clue as to what she was up to.

71. Derrida, "Structure, Sign and Play," 122.

72. Lewis Carroll, *Alice's Adventures in Wonderland & Through the Looking Glass* (New York: Clarkson N. Potter, Inc., 1960), 101.

5: BRONTË'S VARIATIONS ON A THEME BY SADE

1. Emily Brontë, *Wuthering Heights*, ed. William M. Sale, Jr. (New York: Norton, 1972), 72. All further references to the pages of the novel will be cited parenthetically.

2. Realism's intuition that the "real" is a matter of negotiation and adjudication generates what might be called, for short, a kind of paranoia – the sense that one may see, experience, or think things that either will be perceived as madness or *are* madness. In this system, a text may be given the Schreber treatment, whereby the madman's story (in Schreber's case, *Memoirs of My Nervous Illness*) is true only in translation: What he asserts to be the case is not really the case, but what his text *is* supplies an unequivocal etiology, a representative symptomatology. To some extent literary criticism always performs as if it is necessary translation; Emily Brontë, however, seems to have prophesied the standard reception of her book as fey, beginning with Charlotte Brontë's "Biographical Notice," in which she takes on the task of becoming her sister's interpreter. See U. C. Knoepflmacher, *Emily Brontë: Wuthering Heights* (Cambridge University Press, 1989), 2–10.

3. Georges Bataille, *Literature and Evil*, trans. Alastair Hamilton (New York: Marion Boyars, 1985), 22.

4. Jean-François Lyotard, *The Lyotard Reader*, trans. Andrew Benjamin (New York: Basil Blackwell, 1989), 20. See Brontë's poem about dreaming, dated 13 April 1843, in *Wuthering Heights and Poems*, ed. Philip Henderson, intro. Margaret Drabble (London: J. M. Dent & Sons, 1978), 332–3.

5. Lyotard, *Reader*, 19.

6. Lyotard, *Reader*, 19. See Leo Bersani, *A Future for Astyanax: Character and Desire in Literature* (New York: Columbia University Press, 1984), 66: "Desire is a threat to the form of realistic fiction. Desire can subvert social order; it can also disrupt novelistic order. The nineteenth-century novel is haunted by the possibility of these subversive moments, and it suppresses them with a brutality both shocking and eminently logical."

7. See Iris Murdoch, *The Sovereignty of Good* (New York: Ark, 1985), 93, for her reading on the search for the Good as conducted through a selfless apprehension of reality.

8. Throughout this essay, whose orientation necessitates my use of the term in its most general sense, "sadomasochism" will hold its fairly typical meaning of an erotic pathology in which one takes pleasure from both giving and receiving pain. Gilles Deleuze, in *Coldness and Cruelty* (New York: Zone Books, 1991), disputes the inextricability of sadism and masochism through a reading of Leopold von Sacher-Masoch, and any extended and refined analysis of the term itself would need to consider his argument. Richard von Krafft-Ebing, *Psychopathia Sexualis*, 12th ed. (New York: Pioneer, n.d.,) 213, asserts that "the perfect counterpart of masochism is sadism" and that "lust in the infliction of pain and lust in inflicted pain appear but as two different sides of the same psychical process, of which the primary and essential thing is the consciousness of active or passive subjection" (p. 215). Freud, of course, posits great refinements in causality and definition, while maintaining the inextricability of these pathologies. See, for example, "The Economic Problem of Masochism," in *The Complete Psychological Works of Sigmund Freud*, vol. 19, trans., ed. James Strachey (London: Hogarth Press, 1961), 159–70. For my purposes, however, I shall rely on Krafft-Ebing as the source from which our general sense of the term is derived. I have focused on Sade's work as a vast repository of evidence for this pathology and, more particularly, as a place in which linguistic and sexual concerns are, for the author-subject himself, inextricable. I do not imagine Brontë to have known Sade's work.

9. For the details of Sade's various incarcerations and for her assertions that Sade's ecstatic excesses of imagination increase proportionately to his enforced repression, see Simone de Beauvoir, "Must We Burn Sade?" trans. Annette Michelson, in Marquis de Sade, *The 120 Days of Sodom and Other Writings*, trans. and compiled Austryn Wainhouse & Richard Seaver (New York: Grove Weidenfeld, 1966), 3–33. Beauvoir says that "it was not murder that fulfilled Sade's erotic nature: it was literature" (p. 33).

10. Sade's Château of Silling is the inviolable, isolated place to which his libertines take their entourage to enact the escalating criminalities of *The 120 Days of Sodom*. Of course, I do not mean to imply here that Brontë was herself untouched by outside influences, historical and textual. Knoepflmacher, in *Emily Brontë: Wuthering Heights*, speaks to the issue of Brontë's textual sources (pp. 28–38), as does the early book by Florence Swinton, *The Sources of "Wuthering Heights"* (Cambridge: W. Heffer & Sons, 1937). And as Chris Baldick's *In Frankenstein's Shadow: Myth, Monstrosity, and Nineteenth-Century Writing* (Oxford: Clarendon Press, 1987) makes clear, nineteenth-century literature works within a discursive field much preoccupied by monstrosity as a metaphor, an analogy, an actuality; from political rhetoric and through assimilations and reproductions, specifically of Shelley's vision in *Frankenstein*, the apprehension of character as potentially monstrous is not far beneath the surface.

11. Brontë, *Wuthering Heights and Poems*, 342.
12. Dorothy Van Ghent, "On *Wuthering Heights*," in *Emily Brontë's Wuthering Heights*, ed. Harold Bloom (New York: Chelsea House, 1987), 12.
13. Bloom, *Emily Brontë's Wuthering Heights*, 9.
14. Bersani, *A Future for Astyanax*, argues that realism is defined precisely by its *inability* to accommodate desire.
15. See Margaret Homans, "Repression and Sublimation of Nature in *Wuthering Heights*," in *Emily Brontë's Wuthering Heights*, ed. Harold Bloom (New York: Chelsea House, 1987), 61–78, for her reading of nature's absences in the novel.
16. See Roland Barthes, *Sade, Fourier, Loyola*, trans. Richard Miller (New York: Hill & Wang, 1976), on Sade's pleasure in inventing machineries, 152–4; Heathcliff's ingenious device for the starvation of the hatchlings suggests, relative to Hareton's clumsy hanging of pups from the chairback, a certain precocious aptitude for sadism.
17. A. C. Swinburne, *Miscellanies* (New York: Worthington Co., 1886), 269–70.
18. This dynamic – as knowledge increases, so, too, does control and therefore power – informs the *Bildungsroman*, a notably masculine genre that increasingly refines itself through a series of nineteenth-century novels. For an anarchic vision of "character" that disputes this assimilative model, see Gilles Deleuze and Félix Guattari, *Anti-Oedipus: Capitalism and Schizophrenia*, trans. Robert Hurley, Mark Seem, & Helen R. Lane (Minnesota: University of Minnesota Press, 1989): "A schizophrenic out for a walk is a better model than a neurotic lying on the analyst's couch" (p. 2).
19. See Sade, *The 120 Days of Sodom*, 106–7.
20. See Angela Carter, *The Sadeian Woman and the Ideology of Pornography* (New York: Pantheon, 1978), especially her chapter "The Blonde as Clown," for a reading on Isabella's type of inviting bruisability.
21. See Murdoch, *The Sovereignty of Good*, 93–5, for her discussion of an apprehension based on humility, an attempt to see the "unself." See, too, David J. Gordon, "Iris Murdoch's Comedies of Unselfing," *Twentieth Century Literature*, vol. 36, no. 2 (Summer 1990), 115–36.
22. Carter, *The Sadeian Woman*, 27. Note that Carter does not argue that in a Sadeian world a free woman will seem monstrous, but that she will "be a monster," thus emphasizing the corruptive effects of an intensely repressive environment, in her sense that one excess necessarily breeds another. Brontë eludes corruption by, in effect, escaping the terms of the dialectic.
23. Two parodic extremes of marital behavior typify the Heights. The enforced Cathy Linton – Linton Heathcliff union takes the economic and sexual coercions of marriage to parodic excess in a Sadeian mockery of the sanctified pretenses of that institution, whereas Hindley Earnshaw's love epitomizes the alternative "romantic" version of marriage that excludes all society but that of the loved and possessed (owned) object.

24. See Jacques Derrida, *The Ear of the Other*, trans. Peggy Kamuf & Avital Ronell (New York: Schocken Books, 1985), 16, for a discussion of language in relation to paternalism and maternalism. See Jean-François Lyotard, *The Postmodern Condition: A Report on Knowledge*, trans. Geoffrey Bennington & Brian Massumi (Minneapolis: University of Minnesota Press, 1988), 63: "By terror I mean the efficiency gained by eliminating, or threatening to eliminate, a player from the language game one shares with him."

25. Michel Foucault, *The Archaeology of Knowledge and The Discourse on Language*, trans. A. M. Sheridan Smith & Rupert Sawyer (New York: Harper & Row, 1972), 216.

26. See Lyotard, *The Postmodern Condition*, 73–9, for his discussion of realism. See, too, Bersani, *A Future for Astyanax*, particularly his chapter "Realism and the Fear of Desire."

27. Jon Stratten, *The Virgin Text: Fiction, Sexuality, and Ideology* (Norman: University of Oklahoma Press, 1987), 60. Bersani, *A Future for Astyanax*, 67, asserts that realism "depends, for its very existence, on the annihilation or, at the very least, the immobilizing containment of anarchic impulse."

28. See Roman Jakobson and Morris Halle, *Fundamentals of Language* (The Hague: Mouton, 1956), especially chapter 5 of "Two Aspects of Language and Two Types of Aphasic Disturbances," for a discussion of realism and metonymy. See, too, J. Hillis Miller, "The Fiction of Realism: *Sketches by Boz, Oliver Twist*, and Cruikshank's Illustrations," in *Dickens Centennial Essays*, ed. Ada Nisbet & Blake Nevius (Berkeley: University of California Press, 1971), 85–153, for a discussion of metonymy.

29. See Sade, *The 120 Days of Sodom*, 111, as Sade talks, in "Reflections on the Novel," of verisimilitude: "But in counseling you to embellish, I forbid you to stray from verisimilitude," "we do not ask that you be true, but only that you be convincing and credible," etc. Yet he clarifies the relationship between sightedness and "verisimilitude" as his astigmatic vision, exacerbated by suppression, renders a grotesquely giantized and disproportionate "reality."

30. Brontë, *Wuthering Heights and Poems*, 345.

31. See Lyotard, *The Postmodern Condition*, 78, on the sublime. The attraction of the sublime lies in its stimulation of a feeling inextricably made up of self-aggrandizement and humiliation; in the pleasurable pain it affords, it is, according to Lyotard, a form of masochism.

32. Bloom, *Emily Brontë's Wuthering Heights*, 11.

33. "There are three men and one woman living at the Heights, one old (Jacob), one middle-aged (Heathcliff), and one the same age as the woman (Hareton). An unmarried young woman does not live in a house of men, therefore she is married to one of them. The old one is too old and a servant, the young one is of ambiguous status but appears to be a servant, therefore she is married

to Heathcliff." Sade, among other things a list-maker, maliciously refines this obsession with logical permutations. See "Florville and Courval," in which Sade invents an intricately logical scenario in which the unfortunate virtuous woman discovers herself all unwittingly to have slept with her brother, to have killed her son by her brother, to have been the instrument of her mother's death. In *The 120 Days of Sodom* 133–90. One could imagine one of Sade's ménages given as a problem on the LSAT.

34. Bersani, *A Future for Astyanax*, 307.

35. See Patricia Yeager, "Violence in the Sitting Room: *Wuthering Heights* and the Woman's Novel," *Genre*, vol. 21 (Summer 1988), 203–29, for her discussion of Brontë's comedic sense.

36. Lockwood is a cautionary figure for theories of communicational competence, whether Habermasian or Davidsonian, since his extreme complacency guarantees that translation will not be multivalent. In other words, his social position and class relative to the teller, Nelly, and his self-absorbed temperament bring him to a "translation" carried out with no sensitivity to any idiom other than his own. It is a case of Putnam's "Enough is enough, enough isn't everything," where the hearer is perfectly satisfied that he has enough on the basis of his own faulty listening apparatus.

37. See Lyotard, *The Postmodern Condition*, 5, 47: "Since 'reality' is what provides the evidence used as proof in scientific argumentation, and also provides prescriptions and promises of a juridical, ethical, and political nature with results, one can master all of these games by mastering 'reality.' That is precisely what technology can do" (p. 47). Lockwood's methods are predictive of this quantitative system of value.

38. See Miller, "The Fiction of Realism," 94–103, for his discussion of exteriorities and their metonymic value in defining character.

39. See Jakobson and Halle's discussion of contexture-deficient aphasia, or contiguity disorder, *Fundamental of Language*, 71–82, a condition in which metonymic connections fail.

40. One sees in Sade a similar sense of disposable sequences, for which the sexual play leading up to orgasm is the paradigm; the prompt post-coital amnesia about the object of one's desire is magnified, so that often, in Sade, the partner is quite literally disposed of at the moment of climax, as if the act of simultaneous disposals intensifies the orgasm by clearing the way for the next. See Bersani's chapter on sadomasochism, "Persons in Pieces," *A Future for Astyanax*, 286–315, for a reading on "the masturbator's murderous intolerance of whatever spoils his exciting sexual invention," which is provocative in the context of Lockwood's appropriative eyes and ears.

41. See Barthes, *Sade, Fourier, Loyola*, 27.

42. For an extended and provocative discussion of sightedness in the novel, see Beth Newman, " 'The Situation of the Looker-on': Gender, Narration, and

Gaze in *Wuthering Heights*," *Proceedings of the Modern Language Association*, vol. 105 (October 1990), 1029–41.

43. *The Marquis de Sade: Selections from His Writings*, ed. Paul Dinnage (New York: Grove Press, 1953), 179: "Let us never lose sight of the fact that the woman who most tries to charm us is certainly concealing faults that would most certainly disgust us if we did but know them. Let us imagine them, suspect them, guess at them – these details; and this first process, at the very moment love is born, will perhaps extinguish it. If she is a maiden, be assured she will reek of some unhealthy odor, if not at one period, then at another: is it really worthwhile going into raptures over a cloaca?"

44. Barthes, *Sade, Fourier, Loyola*, 27.

45. Sade, *The 120 Days of Sodom*, 212–14. There is in this similarity between Sadeian and Petrarchan simile a certain piquant irony when one considers the theory that the "Laura" of Petrarch's sonnets was married, in 1325, to Paul de Sade, ancestor of the Divine Marquis. See Jean Paulhan, "The Marquis de Sade and His Accomplice," in *Justice, Philosophy in the Bedroom and Other Writings*, compiled and trans. Richard Seaver & Austryn Wainhouse (New York: Grove Weidenfeld, 1966), 23.

46. The corrupt duenna is, of course, a standard accomplice within Sade's fictions.

47. She is a less privileged sister to Charlotte Brontë's Mrs. Fairfax. Whereas Jane Eyre has a second language, French, that allows her to "understand" Adèle Varens and, simultaneously, to pity Adèle's aloneness and to scorn her French capriciousness and inherent triviality, Nelly, like Mrs. Fairfax, does not even possess the language by which a figure like Adele could be analyzed.

48. See Walter Benn Michaels, "*Sister Carrie*'s Popular Economy," *Critical Inquiry* (Winter 1980), 378.

49. Foucault, "Discourse on Language," in *The Archaeology of Knowledge*, 216.

50. See Bersani, *A Future for Astyanax*, 53–61, on the assimilative force of realism.

51. Brontë, *Wuthering Heights and Poems*, 346.

52. See, in *The 120 Days of Sodom*, 241–50, Sade's "Statutes" for behavior in the château, especially those pertaining to the wives. For example, "The least display of mirth, or the least evidence given of disrespect or lack of submission during the debauch activities, shall be esteemed one of the gravest of faults and shall be one of the most cruelly punished" (p. 248).

53. One cannot help but notice how thoroughly dogs, mainly bitches and pups, pervade this text. See Thomas Laqueur, "Orgasm, Generation, and the Politics of Reproductive Biology," in *The Making of the Modern Body: Sexuality and Society in the Nineteenth Century*, ed. Catherine Gallagher & Thomas Laqueur (Berkeley: University of California Press, 1987), 3, as he discusses theories of ovulation in the 1840s. Since it had become clear that in dogs, ovulation could occur without coition, "it was immediately postulated that the human female, like the canine bitch, was a 'spontaneous ovulator.' "

54. Linton Heathcliff's arrested sexuality, his deferred gender, seems significant in the context of Brontë's own often-noted resistance to perceiving herself in stereotypically "feminine" terms. See, for example, Stevie Davies, *Emily Brontë: The Artist as a Free Woman* (Manchester: Carcanet, 1983), 29–31.

55. See Julia Kristeva, *Black Sun: Depression and Melancholia*, trans. Leon S. Roudiez (New York: Columbia University Press, 1989), 27–8.

56. Sade makes some of his most vicious fantasies about matricide. See the story of Eugénie de Mistival in *Philosophy in the Bedroom*. Eugénie empowers herself sexually by raping her mother, having her raped by a syphilitic, and then sewing her genital orifice shut to ensure that the syphilis will do its slow and deadly work. Carter's discussions of motherhood, in *The Sadeian Woman*, 104–36 are interesting in the context of matricide and empowerment.

57. See, for essays on this "maternal ethic," Sara Ruddick, "Maternal Thinking," *Feminist Studies*, vol. 6 (1980), 342–67; Margaret Urban Walker, "Moral Understandings: Alternative 'Epistemology' for a Feminist Ethics," *Hypatia*, vol. 4, no. 2 (1989), 15–28; Paul Lauritzen, "A Feminist Ethic and the New Romanticism – Mothering as a Model of Moral Relations," *Hypatia*, vol. 4, no. 4 (1989), 29–44.

58. Murdoch, *The Sovereignty of Good*, 32–40.

59. See Thomas Laqueur, *Making Sex: Body and Gender from the Greeks to Freud* (Cambridge: Harvard University Press, 1990), for a detailed discussion of the one-sex and the two-sex models of physiology, both of which predicate "correct" form on the male model. See, too, Barthes, *Sade, Fourier, Loyola*, 123–4.

60. See Luce Irigaray, *Speculum of the Other Woman*, trans. Gillian C. Gill (Ithaca, NY: Cornell University Press, 1985), 55–80, for a discussion of Freud's assertions about "penis envy."

61. Krafft-Ebing, *Psychopathia Sexualis*, offers only two cases of sadism in women that have been scientifically documented. For sadism in males, see particularly case studies 14–47. Pages 80–217 deal with sadism, masochism, and sadism/masochism.

62. See Deleuze, *Coldness and Cruelty*, 18–19, as he discusses Sade's affiliation with rigorous reasoning. The Sadeian libertine may pretend to be interested in the persuasion or "education" of his victims, but in fact "nothing is more alien to the sadist than the wish to convince, to persuade, in short, to educate." "He is interested in something quite different, namely to demonstrate that reasoning itself is a form of violence, and that he is on the side of violence, however calm and logical he may be. He is not even attempting to prove anything to anyone, but to perform a demonstration related essentially to the solitude and omnipotence of its author."

63. Sade takes this commensurability between humans and surroundings to its logical extreme in his fantasies of naked, living bodies used as articles of furniture.

64. See Barthes, *Sade, Fourier, Loyola*, 137–8: In incest, "the crime consists in

transgressing the semantic rule, in creating homonymy: the act *contra naturam* is exhausted in an utterance of counter-language, the family is no more than a lexical area . . . to transgress is *to name outside the lexical division* (the basis of society, for the same reason as class division)."

65. One cannot escape the homoerotic implications of Heathcliff's response to Hareton (p. 255) in the context of the sadist's rabid misogyny.

66. This vision of a domestic artifact layered over with sides of meat and guarded by a "liver-coloured bitch" cannot seem completely benign or natural within Brontë's sadistically inclined world. See Carter's discussion, in *The Sadeian Woman*, 137–50, of flesh and meat. Lockwood's circumstantial description of this meat-hung cupboard, which cannot be dissociated from the cupboard bed in which he sleeps and dreams of butchery, is consequential to his reductionist perceptions of the female gaze.

67. See N. M. Jacobs, "Gendered and Layered Narrative in *Wuthering Heights* and *The Tenant of Wildfell Hall*," *The Journal of Narrative Technique*, vol. 16, no. 3 (Fall 1986), 204–5, on Brontë's resentment of gender stereotypes. See, too, Kristeva, *Black Sun*, 28–30, on the necessity of recovering the lost object – the mother – as the erotic object.

68. Bloom, *Emily Brontë's Wuthering Heights*, 2.

69. Swinburne, *Miscellanies*, 264. Whatever one's theoretical position on the "author," the recurring critical sense of Emily Brontë as inextricable from her single novel speaks to the ways in which we continue realism's search for the means by which boundaries may be discovered and set.

70. See Margaret Homans, *Women Writers and Poetic Identity* (Princeton University Press, 1980), 104–6.

71. See Bloom, *Emily Brontë's Wuthering Heights*, 19. Van Ghent traces the archetype of the daemonic, which has "had, in modern mythology, constantly a status in ethical thought. The exception is Heathcliff. Heathcliff is no more ethically relevant than is flood or earthquake or whirlwind."

72. See Seaver and Wainhouse, eds., *Justine*, 608. Clement, the libertine priest, admonishes Justine to understand the essentially egoistic basis of all action, and concludes with a Sadeian homily: "Ask the lamb, and you will find he does not understand why the wolf is allowed to devour him; ask the wolf what the lamb is for: to feed me, he will reply. . . . the strong who immolate the weak, the weak victims of the strong: there you have Nature, there you have her intentions, there you have her scheme." Heathcliff, too, tends to speak disdainfully of the "lambs": "Cathy, this lamb of yours threatens like a bull! . . . It is in danger of splitting its skull against my knuckles" (p. 99).

73. Jacques Blondel has commented on Heathcliff's statement in the context of the executioner's assertion in *Justine*, ed. Seaver & Wainhouse. See Bataille, *Literature and Evil*, 20–1. Sade's own taste for vivisection is, of course, unabashed. See *The 120 Days of Sodom*, for example: "His first passion was to sever

a finger; his second is to pluck up some flesh with a pair of red-hot tongs, to cut off the flesh with a pair of scissors, then to burn the wound. He is quite apt to spend as long as four or five days whittling away a girl's body piecemeal, and she ordinarily dies while the cruel operation is still advancing" (p. 647). See Carter, *The Sadeian Woman*, 138–42, on cannibalism.

74. Beauvoir, in *The 120 Days of Sodom*, 32. See, too, Paulhan, in *Justine*, 16–17, on Sade's encyclopedist tendencies.

75. Bataille, *Literature and Evil*, 24.

76. Beauvoir, in *The 120 Days of Sodom*, 25–6.

77. Sade is explicitly anti-neighborly, as is Heathcliff. Obsessed with bringing low the two families against which he has measured himself, Heathcliff makes it his chief pleasure to reduce them, by a process of self-defined and highly logical "justice," so that their misery might aggrandize his power. His sadistic version of "love thy neighbor" fits explicitly within the Sadeian system that enhances the libertine's own power by degrading his neighbor's. See Pierre Klossowski, "Nature as Destructive Principle," in *The 120 Days of Sodom*, 69, as he discusses the Sadeian bad-neighbor policy.

78. See Krafft-Ebing, *Psychopathia Sexualis*, 88–105, for case studies on necrophilia and coprophagia. In reading these accounts, one sees reiterated the sadist's lust for blood: Leger "tore out her heart, ate of it, drank the blood, and buried the remains" (p. 94). "The abrasions of the skin on Motta's thighs were produced by his teeth, whilst sucking her blood in most intense lustful pleasure" (p. 67). Heathcliff's own vampirish qualities are considerable: Isabella says he's "not a human being." Said by Cathy to have killed her "and thriven on it" (p. 132), he himself asserts of Edgar that "the moment her regard ceased, I would have torn his heart out, and drank his blood!" (p. 125).

79. Klossowski, in *The 120 Days of Sodom*, 70.

80. As Sade does in arguing so "rationally," Heathcliff uses the "moral" expectations of his hearers to dupe them. Sade, as Deleuze points out in *Coldness and Cruelty*, 20, uses a "naturalistic and mechanistic approach imbued with the mathematical spirit," which accounts for "the endless repetitions, the reiterated quantitative process of multiplying illustrations and adding victim upon victim, again and again retracing the thousand circles of an irreducibly solitary argument." Yet the anima released by this method – like the indecipherable totality that is Heathcliff – exceeds and mockingly rebukes a social "realism"; the logothetical audit reveals an alternative economy.

81. Bounderby's story being undone by his mother; Dickens's double endings of *Great Expectations*, his nullification in *Hard Times* of Louisa's story in his "neither this nor not this" conclusion; Coverdale's deconstruction of his authority in the final, unconvincing admission of his love of Priscilla, etc.

82. See Krafft-Ebing, *Psychopathia Sexualis*, 88–99, for studies of anthropophagy.

83. Bloom, *Emily Brontë's Wuthering Heights*, 25.

84. By most accounts, Aunt Branwell, from whom Joseph is said to be modeled, was extremely rigorous in her religious tutelage of the Brontë children. See, for example, Davies, *Emily Brontë: The Artist as a Free Woman*, 10–12.

85. Branwell's excesses are well known; he may be said to stand, here, most intimately for that disabled part of oneself and others – that masculine pathology that is taught to enact its power so destructively, its despair so grandiosely – with which one must, nonetheless, come to terms.

6: *A TROPOLOGY OF REALISM IN* HARD TIMES

1. This chapter is a revised and lengthened version of an essay that originally appeared as "A Tropology of Realism in *Hard Times*," *ELH*, vol. 59 (1992), 857–81.

2. Quoted from Freud's *The Interpretation of Dreams*, in Jean-François Lyotard, *The Lyotard Reader*, ed. Andrew Benjamin (Cambridge: Basil Blackwell, 1989), 21. Lyotard's "The Tensor" and "The dream-work does not think," 1–55, discuss metonymy and metaphor in the context of the dream, evaluating Jakobson's formula regarding metonymy and narrative, found in Roman Jakobson and Morris Halle, *Fundamentals of Language* (The Hague: Mouton, 1956), 81.

3. Charles Dickens, *Hard Times: For These Times* (Holt, Rinehart & Winston, 1958), 6. All further page references to the novel will be cited parenthetically in the text. It is of interest that Robert Blatchford, in the 1894 socialist text *Merrie England* (New York: Humboldt Publishing Co., n.d.), which is also a refutation of Manchester School political economy, plays throughout on the repetition of the word "fact." Blatchford refers occasionally to Dickens and explicitly to *Hard Times* through references to Gradgrind. See John Holloway, "*Hard Times*: A History and a Criticism," in *Dickens in the Twentieth Century*, ed. John Gross & Gabriel Pearson (Toronto: University of Toronto Press, 1962), 159–74, for his location of Dickens's examination of utilitarianism within the specific context of the Manchester School.

   It is profitable to think of the uniformly recalcitrant, if variable, female characters with which this novel is filled: Sissy, Louisa, Mrs. Gradgrind, Mrs. Sparsit, Mrs. Blackpool, and Rachael all undermine the paternalistic systems of industry, education, and domesticity in which they exist – Rachael with her spirituality no less than Mrs. Blackpool with her physicality. See Lynda Zwinger, "The Fear of the Father: Dombey and Daughter," *Nineteenth Century Fiction*, vol. 39 (1985), 420–40. Zwinger reads Florence's relationship to her father in terms that are informative in the context of my argument.

4. See Jean-François Lyotard, *The Postmodern Condition: A Report on Knowledge, Theory and History of Literature,* trans. Geoffrey Bennington & Brian Massumi (Minneapolis: University of Minnesota Press, 1988), 73–9. Lyotard speaks of

the "therapeutic uses" to which realism is put, as it stabilizes the referent, arranging it "according to a point of view which endows it with a recognizable meaning, to reproduce the syntax and vocabulary which enable the addressee to decipher images and sequences quickly, and so to arrive easily at the consciousness of his own identity as well as the approval which he thereby receives from others" (p. 74). See Michael Riffaterre, *Fictional Truth* (Baltimore: Johns Hopkins University Press, 1990), for a discussion of the agreement, equally implicit but less ideologically oriented, that the reader makes with fiction to accept simultaneously that the story is both fictional and true.

5. See Blatchford, *Merrie England*, 125, as he uses "Gradgrind" as a generic term.
6. See J. Hillis Miller, "The Fiction of Realism: *Sketches by Boz, Oliver Twist*, and Cruikshank's Illustrations," in *Dickens Centennial Essays*, ed. Ada Nisbet & Blake Nevius (Berkeley: University of California Press, 1971), 98–103, for a discussion of the relationship between synchronous metonymies and diachronous events: "the predominance of metonymy reinforces that deterministic vision of man's life which is often said to be an essential aspect of realistic fiction" · (p. 101).
7. Geoffrey Carnall, "Dickens, Mrs. Gaskell, and the Preston Strike," *Victorian Studies*, vol. 8, no. 1 (September 1964), 36.
8. Carnall, "Preston Strike," 39–41.
9. Carnall, "Preston Strike," 34–5. See, too, Harold Perkins, *The Origins of Modern English Society* (London: Routledge & Kegan Paul, 1969), 398–9. Perkins's brief description strikes the same tone and uses this same quotation from *The Daily News*.
10. Carnall, "Preston Strike," 36.
11. Carnall's reading of Dickens relative to Mrs. Gaskell is that Dickens enjoys the "lies" of fiction-making in a way that Mrs. Gaskell does not, and while this makes his novel less effective than Gaskell's as regards industrial issues, this enjoyment makes for a better novel overall than Gaskell's *North and South*. David Musselwhite's *Partings Welded Together: Politics and Desire in the Nineteenth-Century English Novel* (London: Methuen, 1987) is informative in the context of Gaskell's treatment of workers in her fiction.
12. Anthony King, "George Godwin and the Art Union of London, 1837–1911," *Victorian Studies*, vol. 8, no. 2 (December 1964), 104. Membership was one guinea per year. "The Society's purpose was to purchase works in oil, water-colour, and sculpture, which, with medals and engravings commissioned by the Committee, were to be distributed among the members by means of a ballot. The members would decide the proportion of the subscriptions to be allotted for prizes and this sum was then to be divided into a number of smaller amounts which the subscribers would win. They were then entitled to choose a painting, to the value of their cash-prize, from one of the five leading galleries" (p. 104).

13. John Ruskin's *Fors Clavigera* (1871), a series of letters to workmen designed to introduce them to art, is an interesting variation on this motif.
14. King, "George Godwin and the Art Union of London," 107.
15. King, "George Godwin and the Art Union of London," 112.
16. King, "George Godwin and the Art Union of London," 120.
17. King, "George Godwin and the Art Union of London," 111.
18. Henry Cole's relationship, adversarial, to the art unions is explored by Carnall, "Preston Strike." See, too, Quentin Bell, *The Schools of Design* (London: Routledge & Kegan Paul, 1963).
19. King, "George Godwin and the Art Union of London," 118.
20. King, "George Godwin and the Art Union of London," 111.
21. Roland Barthes, *The Pleasure of the Text*, trans. Richard Miller (New York: Hill & Wang, 1975), 4. See Stephen J. Spector, "Monsters of Metonymy: *Hard Times* and Knowing the Working Class," in *Charles Dickens*, ed. Harold Bloom (New York: Chelsea House, 1987), 230, for his assertion that, while realism is difficult to define, "one can say that realistic texts, like realistic paintings and photographs, intend to tell the truth: what they report they intend to be verifiable." John P. McGowan, in "*David Copperfield*: The Trial of Realism," *Nineteenth Century Fiction*, vol. 34 (1979), 8–9, gives a more explicitly detailed definition. Like Spector, I offer no elaborate definition of "realism." *Hard Times* is not, and clearly was not meant to be, a realistic novel, if by that one means that its overriding purpose is to persuade the reader that it is committed to verisimilitude. Dickens problematizes realism generally (he is said by McGowan to have made an "absolute abandonment of realism in the celebration of 'Fancy' in the 1850's," p. 8), and in *Hard Times* he intensifies his ambivalence. In his patronymics, in the humor that signals his amused and ironic distance from his actors at their play, and in his omniscience he seems to claim "truth" while undermining an illusion of realism. See Riffaterre, *Fictional Truth*, 29–52.
22. In fact, Dickens's industrial landscape is a thin covering over the carnival spectacle of language turning people's mouths against them. The most fanciless realists find themselves in the coils of their own language, their syllogisms turned as absurd as if they had blundered through the looking glass. The third gentleman undertakes to teach a lesson about the difference between realism and aestheticism: "you are not to have, in any object of use or ornament, what would be a contradiction in fact. . . . This is the new discovery. This is fact. This is taste" (pp. 6–7). This is a parody of utilitarianism in all its arrogance, and yet still Sissy would have representational flowers on her carpet, because, "if you please, sir, I am very fond of flowers," she says. And the third gentleman then plays his trump card in this language game: "And is that why you would put tables and chairs upon them, and have people walking over them with heavy boots?" he crows (p. 6). Like Alice, the third gentleman

starts out with a baby in his arms and ends up holding a pig (p. 6). Dickens has Sissy make the crucial distinction between words, things, and representations that the fact-man cannot see. She knows that these "flowers" are representations and not "realities": "They wouldn't crush and wither. . . . they would be the pictures of what was very pretty and pleasant" (p. 6). Dickens clearly intuits the surrealistic comedy that must arise when language imagines itself as representative of "reality." What Magritte paints much later in his precise representation of a pipe, entitled "This is not a pipe," Dickens has Sissy say: "This [word or picture] is not a flower." Thus Dickens suggests again that "realism" will be assaulted by language the moment it is articulated. See Michel Foucault, *This Is Not a Pipe*, trans. and ed. James Harkness (Berkeley: University of California Press, 1982), for a meditation on this painting. See, too, McGowan's argument, in "The Trial of Realism," on Dickens's changing apprehension of the function of the word in its relationship to "reality." One must, in fairness, read Holloway's defense of the third gentleman as a spokesperson for the Board of Trade's "Department of Practical Art," in *"Hard Times*: A History and a Criticism," 163–4.

23. This is not to say that the reader is baffled or confused by what Dickens is doing, but only that Dickens reverses, retards, and even accelerates the movements toward decipherment with a tropology that introduces madness – unreason and anti-reality – as a subtext.

24. See Jakobson and Halle, *Fundamentals of Language*, 78, on the connection between surrealism and metaphor, as opposed to cubism and metonymy.

25. Jacques Derrida, "Otobiographies," in *The Ear of the Other*, ed. Christie McDonald, trans. Avital Ronell (New York: Schocken Books, 1985), 21.

26. Jakobson and Halle, *Fundamentals of Language*, 78.

27. *Merrie England* makes it clear that socialism, no less than this realism, argues against the excesses to which *aphrodisia* is prone: "My ideal is frugality of body and opulence of mind," 12.

28. See Miller, "The Fiction of Realism," 103: "the diachronic sequence has the same irresistible coercion as the synchronic law which says that between a man and his door knocker there will inevitably be some degree of resemblance and sympathy." For an alternative perspective as regards this woman's behavior, see Xavier Gauthier, "Why Witches?" in *New French Feminisms*, ed. Elaine Marks & Isabelle de Courtivron (New York: Schocken Books, 1981), 199–203.

29. See Charles Dickens, *Hard Times*, ed. George Ford & Sylvère Monod (New York: Norton, 1966), 277, for Dickens's comments on his exhaustion on finishing *Hard Times*.

30. Ford and Monod, *Hard Times*, 274.

31. Michel Foucault, *Madness and Civilization: A History of Insanity in the Age of Reason*, trans. Richard Howard (New York: Random House, 1988), 96.

32. Foucault, *Madness*, 97.
33. Foucault, *Madness*, 97.
34. Ford and Monod, *Hard Times*, vii.
35. Ludwig Wittgenstein, *Philosophical Investigations*, trans. G. E. M. Anscombe (New York: Macmillan, 1968), 8e.
36. Spector examines the problems this passage raises from a different angle in "Monsters of Metonymy."
37. Foucault, *Madness*, 122.
38. Ford and Monod, *Hard Times*, 276–7.
39. Foucault, *Madness*, 117.
40. Legs become a significant synecdoche throughout the novel: the teachers turned like identical table legs, 7; the church on its "florid wooden legs," 21; Merrylegs, the dog, 25; Mr. E. W. B. Childers, the circus star, whose legs are "very robust, but shorter than legs of good proportions should have been," 27; Mr. Childers and Master Kidderminster, "with their legs wider apart than the general run of men, and with a very knowing assumption of being stiff in the knees," 31; the leg of pork to be raffled off, 61; the leg riddle, 256–7; the circus ladies "so demonstrative of leg," 258; Lady Scadgers, with her "mysterious leg," etc.
41. Anthony Giddens, *The Consequences of Modernity* (Stanford University Press, 1990).
42. See Lyotard, *Reader*, 12–17. Lyotard is, of course, speaking in the context of Daniel Paul Schreber, whose condition I have referred to elsewhere and whose text, *Memoirs of My Nervous Illness*, trans. & ed. Ida Macalpin & Richard Hunter (London: Dawson & Sons, 1955), may be taken as emblematic of the multiple levels at which "truth" may be deciphered.
43. The balanced, metrically sophisticated line, "I passed the day in a ditch, and the night in a pigsty," the vaudeville ring of "I was so dirty that . . . ," and the double-duty of "kept" in "She kept a chandler's shop . . . and kept me in an egg-box," are all meant to draw explicit attention to Dickens's comic virtuosity.
44. Raymond Williams, *Writing in Society* (London: Verso, 1983), 169. Williams points out that to attack one's material surroundings as corruptive of the humans within it is to take a relatively modern view of character as influenced, if not determined, by environment and to suggest that one promotes a realism of material cause and effect. To suggest, as Dickens does so clearly with Bounderby, Sissy Jupe, Rachael, and Stephen Blackpool, that "some virtues and vices are original and both triumph over and in some cases can change any environment" is to take a less modern, more spiritually oriented view and to suggest that what is "real" about human character is predetermined and unalterable; therefore it is immune to all propagandas and programs of reform (p. 169). See Williams's chapter, "The Reader in *Hard Times*," 166–74.

45. Jakobson and Halle, *Fundamentals of Language*, 71. See, too, Mikhail Bakhtin, *Rabelais and His World* (New York: Midland Books, 1984), for the anti-totalitarian implications of the carnival.
46. See Riffaterre, *Fictional Truth*, 14.
47. Charles Dickens, *Dombey and Son* (London: Collins, 1954), 23. One will think, too, of Mrs. Pocket in *Great Expectations* (New York: Holt, Rinehart & Winston, 1972), 181, who has been raised to be "highly ornamental, but perfectly helpless and useless."
48. For elaborations on these categories, see Nina Auerbach, *Woman and the Demon: The Life of a Victorian Myth* (Cambridge: Harvard University Press, 1982).
49. That Louisa so often stares into the fire seems another of Dickens's subversions of standard expectations, for by the inescapable symbolisms of fire and passion, one expects that sooner or later Louisa's fire will be unbanked, her flames awakened. See Gaston Bachelard, *The Psychoanalysis of Fire*, trans. Alan C. M. Ross (Boston: Beacon Press, 1964), for a reading on the symbolisms of fire.
50. Which is to say that he begins as a flat, ideologically declined puppet and ends up as a man. See, among the many discussions of fathers in the work of Dickens, Leonard F. Manheim, "The Law as Father," *American Imago*, vol. 12 (1955), 17–23. See, too, Zwinger's feminist essay, "The Fear of the Father." This intimate and problematic association between daughters and fathers at the expense of the living and present mother has received a great deal of critical attention as regards its psychosexual implications. Yet the pattern is so frequent in the nineteenth-century novel as to suggest something beyond the preoccupations of men regarding their daughters and the equivalent Oedipal attraction of daughters to their fathers. One need only look at Jane Austen or George Eliot to find female novelists who create utterly ineffectual and foolish mothers, against whom powerful father/daughter liaisons are formed. As in *Hard Times*, this pattern suggests as much about stereotypes of authorship – that rigorous ordering that must be subsidized by "paternal" authority – as about psychosexual "realisms."
51. Helen Cixous and Catherine Clement, *The Newly Born Woman*, trans. Betsy Wing (Minneapolis: University of Minnesota Press, 1986), 39.
52. See Josef Breuer and Sigmund Freud, *Studies in Hysteria*, trans. James Strachey (New York: Basic Books, 1957), for case studies that illustrate this phenomenon whereby eroticism is channeled directly into pain.
53. See Zwinger, "The Fear of the Father," 428–31, and Robert Clark, "Riddling the Family Firm: The Sexual Economy in *Dombey and Son*," *Journal of English Literary History*, vol. 51 (Spring 1954), 69–84, for a psychosexual reading.
54. See Elin Diamond, "Realism and Hysteria," *Discourse*, vol. 13, no. 1 (Fall–Winter 1990–91), 60–92, for a discussion of late nineteenth-century realist drama and hysteria.
55. Riffaterre, *Fictional Truth*, 131–2.

56. See Fredric Jameson, *The Prison-House of Language: A Critical Account of Structuralism and Russian Formalism* (Princeton University Press, 1972), 167–8, for a brief reading of *Hard Times* suggesting that "the novel is primarily the education of the educator, the conversion of Mr. Gradgrind from his inhuman system to the opposing one. It is thus a series of lessons administered to Mr. Gradgrind."

7: "ZENOBIA IN CHAINS"

1. The title of the 1859 statue by Harriet Hosmer is "Zenobia in Chains." Hawthorne was acquainted with the community of female artists in Rome where Hosmer lived and worked. See Rozsika Parker and Griselda Pollock, *Old Mistresses: Women, Art, and Ideology* (New York: Pantheon, 1981), 101–3.
2. Feminism/anti-feminism, communality/individuality, aestheticism/pragmatism, realism/romance, etc.
3. See Emily Miller Budick, "Sacvan Bercovitch, Stanley Cavell, and the Romance Theory of American Fiction," *Proceedings of the Modern Language Association*, vol. 107, no. 1 (January 1992), 78–91.
4. Richard H. Millington, *Practicing Romance: Narrative Form and Cultural Engagement in Hawthorne's Fiction* (Princeton University Press, 1992), 175–6.
5. All quotations are from *The Centenary Edition of the Works of Nathaniel Hawthorne. Volume III: The Blithedale Romance and Fanshawe*, ed. William Charvat & Roy Harvey Pearce (Columbus: Ohio State University Press, 1964), 2.
6. Northrop Frye, *Anatomy of Criticism: Four Essays* (Princeton University Press, 1957), 305.
7. As Eric Sundquist, *American Realism: New Essays* (Baltimore: Johns Hopkins University Press, 1982), 3–24, Frye, *Anatomy of Criticism*, 304–12, and Henry James, "The Art of Fiction," in *Literary Criticism: Essays on Literature, American Writers, English Writers*, ed. Leon Edel (New York: Library of America, 1984), among others, quite reasonably argue, it is impossible to separate the two entirely, but Hawthorne's very self-consciousness about the form to which he is drawn enforces the distinctions between realism and romance and thus endangers a holistic interaction of the two modes.
8. See John P. McWilliams, Jr., *Hawthorne and Melville, and the American Character: A Looking-glass Business* (Cambridge University Press, 1984), 1–20, for the sources of the vision of the "Young American." See, too, Sundquist, *American Realism*, 3–24, for a discussion of American realism in relation to romance and to Hawthorne in particular. While Sundquist suggests that Hawthorne resists the "intrusion of the real into the territory of the romance" (p. 8), he also makes a series of interesting connections between Hawthorne and realism.
9. "Zenobia," *Encylopaedia Britannica*, 11th ed., 1910–11: "the Palmyrenes occupied Egypt in A.D. 270, not without a struggle, under the pretext of re-

storing it to Rome," and Zenobia was called queen. When Aurelian became emperor of Rome in 270, he retook Egypt for the empire and captured Zenobia on the bank of the Euphrates; she was led through Rome in golden chains in Aurelian's triumphal return. For an full description of Zenobia, see Edward Gibbon, *The Decline and Fall of the Roman Empire*, vol. 1 (New York: Modern Library, n.d.), 262–70.

10. See the text of Hawthorne's diatribe against Margaret Fuller for a description of her physical and spiritual shortcomings. In *The Portable Hawthorne*, ed. Malcolm Cowley (New York: Viking, 1974), 657–9. I shall operate on the premise that just as Coverdale is both Hawthorne and not-Hawthorne, so, too, is Zenobia Fuller and not-Fuller. However, it is my strong feeling that both are very deeply imbued, intentionally so, with the perceived attributes of the real persons.

11. One could go a step further than I have taken my argument; if this step seems a large one, it may also prove to be productive. Zenobia's body figures (in) the text of *The Blithedale Romance* so powerfully that it becomes, to say the least, a dominant motif. One sees this kind of preoccupation in another kind of narrative as well, on a theme shared by Daniel Schreber, in *Memoirs of My Nervous Illness*, John Addington Symonds, in his *Memoirs*, and an anonymous Hungarian physician, contributing to the second edition of Krafft-Ebing's *Psychopathia Sexualis*. These men share a fantasy, spoken of in remarkably similar terms, of becoming a woman: The (male) body is felt as metamorphic, becoming female in a state of complicity with other women's bodies. Hawthorne's preoccupation, including his sadism in dredging up Zenobia's contorted remains, may have some affinities with these narratives, which are also, *by definition* of what they are and say, committed both to the "real" and to the romantic, or cabalistic, or magical. On Symonds and the Hungarian physician, see Ed Cohen, "The Double Lives of Man: Narration and Identification in the Late Nineteenth-Century Representation of Eccentric Masculinities," *Victorian Studies*, vol. 36, no. 3 (Spring 1993), 353–76.

12. Jacques Derrida, "The Politics of Friendship," *The Philosophical Forum*, vol. 85, 636.

13. Rose Hawthorne Lathrop, *Memories of Hawthorne* (London: Kegan Paul, Trench, Trubner & Co., 1897), 96–7, 195–214; Sophia Hawthorne describes Hawthorne's fury at the calumny of having been charged, in a document signed by thirty men, of having been "in the habit of writing political articles."

14. Millington, *Practicing Romance*, 163–4, argues that Zenobia is "in full possession of her body," a genuine presence.

15. Lathrop, *Memories of Hawthorne*, 55.

16. See McWilliams, *Hawthorne and Melville*, 30.

17. See Dale M. Bauer, *Feminist Dialogics: A Theory of Failed Community* (Albany: State University of New York Press, 1988), 38–50, for a reading of the mas-

querade in terms of Bakhtin's theory of carnival. See, too, Gilles Deleuze and Félix Guattari, *Anti-Oedipus: Capitalism and Schizophrenia*, trans. Robert Hurley, Mark Seem, & Helen R. Lane (Minneapolis: University of Minnesota Press, 1989), 30-1, on group fantasy: "(The great socialist utopias of the nineteenth century function, for example, not as ideal models but as group fantasies—that is, as agents of the real productivity of desire, making it possible to disinvest the current social field, to 'deinstitutionalize' it, to further the revolutionary institution of desire itself.)"

18. See D. H. Lawrence, "Hawthorne's *Blithedale Romance*," in *Studies in Classic American Literature* (New York: Penguin, 1961), 112-15, on what he sees as the farce of Hawthorne's trying to idealize labor.

19. See Simon Schaffer, "Self Evidence," *Critical Inquiry*, vol. 18, no. 2 (Winter 1992), 349-62, for his discussion of the political response in France to mesmerism; in 1784, Benjamin Franklin served on a Paris commission to investigate the phenomenon. The Franklin report states that "the imagination is that active and terrible power by which are operated the astonishing effects that have excited so much attention to the public process" (p. 357). Franklin's commission located the principle of the imagination in the eyes and the uterus, whose "empire and extensive influence . . . over the animal economy is well known" (p. 357), thus locating both imagination and mesmeric sensitivity within the female, and the "female" aspects of susceptible men.

20. Of the relationship of the Sophia correspondence to Hawthorne's other writing much has been written; see, for example, Leland S. Person, Jr., "Hawthorne's Love Letters: Writing and Relationship," *American Literature*, vol. 59, no. 2 (May 1987), 211-27; this essay is also interesting for what it has to say about Hawthorne's investing of his own literary power in fully embodied female others. Discussions of Hawthorne's changing relationship to the literary marketplace in the late 1840s and early 1850s are also provocative in this context; see, for example, Richard H. Brodhead, "Veiled Ladies: Toward a History of Antebellum Entertainment," *American Literary History*, vol. 1, no. 2 (Summer 1989), 273-94. See, too, Jane Tompkins, *Sensational Designs: The Cultural Work of American Fiction, 1790-1860* (Oxford University Press, 1985), 3-39.

21. See Schaffer, "Self Evidence," 351-5, on the investigators' suspicions of mesmerism as linked to the quackery of Parisian street artists and on their detailing of the "astoundingly erotic orientation of mesmeric bodies."

22. See Jacqueline Lichtenstein, "Making Up Representation: The Risks of Femininity," trans. Katharine Streip, in *Misogyny, Misandry, and Misanthropy*, ed. R. Howard Bloch & Frances Ferguson (Berkeley: University of California Press, 1989), 77-87.

23. In Lathrop, *Memories of Hawthorne*, 46.

24. Julian Hawthorne, *Nathaniel Hawthorne and His Wife: A Biography* (Boston: Houghton Mifflin, 1891), 227, gives Hawthorne's journal entry for July 28,

1851, in which he writes of having received the loan of "three or four volumes of Fourier's works, which I wished to borrow with a view to my next romance." See Bauer, *Feminist Dialogics*, 182, for a synopsis of Fourier's plan: "Fourier's theory of group formation embodied a dialectic that took the isolated, frustrated ego of bourgeois society, passed it through a moment of uninhibited lust, and finally, when the bourgeois could at last recognize and accept his own desires, which were normally unconscious, permitted the coming together of people in full spiritual and sensual love relations." See, too, Taylor Stoehr, "Art vs. Utopia: The Case of Nathaniel Hawthorne and Brook Farm," *Antioch Review*, vol. 36 (1978), 89–102, for a more explicit discussion of the Fourierist base of Brook Farm.

25. Hawthorne would have been aware of the coining of this term in 1802 for a show, in London, of optical illusions produced mainly through a magic lantern. In keeping with his active interest in that crux between magic and science represented by daguerreotyping and mesmerism, his use of this word is fraught with dual significance. For him to use this term as regards the "creatures of his brain" that produce the romance is to suggest his doubled sense of the fraudulent and the powerful elements of his craft. The text mirrors this fear of fraudulent mystery in Westervelt's exploitation of mesmerism. See the *Oxford English Dictionary* for a more complete history of the term.

26. Julia Kristeva, *Tales of Love*, trans. Leon S. Roudiez (New York: Columbia University Press, 1987), 5.

27. Zenobia Septima Bathzabbai was eastern or "oriental" (thus imbuing, through the stereotype of the oriental, Hawthorne's Zenobia with further connotations of a voluptuous, potentially cruel intelligence), and among the traditions relating to her is her interest in religions and her treating of the Jews in Palmyra with favor: the Talmud mentions her as protecting Jewish rabbis. See *Encyclopaedia Britannica*.

28. See McWilliams, *Melville and Hawthorne*, 25–36.

29. See George Dekker, "Once More: Hawthorne and the Genealogy of American Romance," *ESQ*, vol. 35 (1st quarter 1989), 71.

30. Julian Hawthorne, *Nathaniel Hawthorne and His Wife*, 15, reproduces a letter from Hawthorne to Sophia: Sophia is, Hawthorne says, his "sinless Eve." Just as Coverdale is a compromised version of Hawthorne, Priscilla may be felt as a straw figure as compared with the warm and intelligent Sophia who lives in her letters: Priscilla is Sophia's "wifeliness" distilled.

31. Cowley, ed., *The Portable Hawthorne*, 658: "Providence was, after all, kind in putting her, and her clownish husband, and their child on board that fated ship."

32. See *The American Notebooks*, ed. Claude M. Simpson (Columbus: Ohio State University Press, 1972), 261–67.

33. One must wonder if Hawthorne has also in mind the other historical Zenobia,

wife of Rhadamistus. Pursued by his enemies, Rhadamistus threw Zenobia into the Araxis to save her from capture and defilement. She was pulled from the river by shepherds and resuscitated. There is an 1850 painting (which Hawthorne probably would not have seen) by William Bouguereau, "Zenobia found on the Banks of the Araxis," in which Zenobia languishes, monumental, revealed at full length, and draped in wet clothes, her breasts naked, in the arms of the shepherds.

34. Lathrop, *Memories of Hawthorne*, 187: Fuller writes to Sophia, "if ever I saw a man who combined delicate tenderness to understand the heart of a woman, with quiet depth and manliness enough to satisfy her, it is Mr. Hawthorne."

35. See Lichtenstein, "Making Up Representation," 78-9, on "Asiatic" rhetorical strategies. Zenobia's oriental or Asiatic beauty represents a rhetorical paradigm, placing against Attic simplicity an ornamental excess defined by classical tastes as "enervated," "emasculated," and "almost effeminate." "The innumerable critics of rhetoric . . . have generally condemned such Asiatic stylistic figures [hyperbole, metaphor, too-frequent tropes of any kind] in a vocabulary borrowed from the lexicon of the prostituted body. . . . as if every manifestation of an excessive taste for images could only be thought through the aesthetic-moral category of perversity, of a culpable seduction that originates in a certain femininity."

36. See Schaffer, "Self Evidence," 352-3, on the common assertion that mesmerism turned people into "puppets."

37. See George Levine, *The Realistic Imagination: English Fiction from Frankenstein to Lady Chatterley* (Chicago University Press, 1981), 33-4, on the realistic hero's necessary passivity. Coverdale's long illness is a hallmark of the realistic hero who must fall helplessly ill because he cannot, by virtue of his position within a realistic novel, do heroically grand and definitive things. Brought to passivity through illness, to some extent he escapes the embarrassment of his necessarily effete role.

38. Frye, *Anatomy of Criticism*, 305.

39. Roland Barthes, *Writing Degree Zero*, trans. Annette Lavers & Colin Smith (Boston: Beacon, 1970), 48.

40. This is not, as can be argued is the case in *The Marble Faun*, because Hawthorne is confronted with the unsayable. He says, in *Blithedale*, "if the vision have been worth the having it is certain never to be consummated otherwise than by a failure" (pp. 10-11). Instead, he seems confident that the narrative will complete itself correctly without his filling in the details. See T. Walter Herbert, Jr., "The Erotics of Purity: *The Marble Faun* and the Victorian Construction of Sexuality," *Representations*, vol. 36 (Fall 1991), 128-9, as he discusses the Palazzo Cenci section. During Hilda's disappearance into the castle, the energy of her purity is sustained, paradoxically, by the reader's pornographic imaginings of what might be happening to her despite her resistance; when

she emerges unviolated, there can be no "formal explanation" of how her purity has remained intact. The lacuna is filled here, but the fantasy of rape it provokes as explanation, which is subsidized by the Beatrice Cenci allusion, is proved incorrect. Thus the ineffability of the romance asserts itself.

41. Cowley, ed., *The Portable Hawthorne*, 657-9.

42. See T. Walter Herbert, Jr., "Nathaniel Hawthorne, Una Hawthorne, and *The Scarlet Letter:* Interactive Selfhoods and the Cultural Construction of Gender," *Proceedings of the Modern Language Association*, vol. 103, no. 3 (May 1988), 285-97, for an argument that discusses Hawthorne's anxieties about his daughter Una, who he feels is "continually doing unbeautiful things." The Una/Duessa split (Una, Spenser's maiden of purity, vs. Duessa, the shape-shifting monster) is provocative in the context of Priscilla/Zenobia.

43. *The Blithedale Romance*, ed. Seymour Gross & Rosalie Murphy (New York: Norton, 1978), 277.

44. Cecil David, *Early Victorian Novelists: Essays in Reevaluation* (Indianapolis: Bobbs-Merrill, 1935), 19.

45. Budick, "The Romance Theory of American Fiction," 82, sees the romance writers as "express[ing] their commitment, not to a process which ends in closure, but to free and uncircumscribed individual speaking." There is, in this non-zero-sum game, an infinity of possibilities; the imperialistic appropriation of a place and people to a particular point of view is thus thwarted, at least in theory. If the female voice is not explicitly validated, neither is it co-opted or delegitimatized.

46. Bauer, *Feminist Dialogics*, 18.

47. Hawthorne is relatively dismissive of *The Blithedale Romance*. See *The English Notebooks* (New York: Russell & Russell, 1962), 383. Julian Hawthorne, *Nathaniel Hawthorne and His Wife*, 431, 200, also devalues Brook Farm and, implicitly, devalues the novel: "The subject of this community has been so exhaustively and exhaustingly canvassed of late, and it seems to be intrinsically so barren of interest and edification . . . that the present writer has pleasure in passing over it without further remark."

48. J. Donald Crowley, ed., *Hawthorne: The Critical Heritage* (New York: Barnes & Noble, 1970), 270.

49. See Susan Moller Okin, "Thinking Like a Woman," in *Theoretical Perspective on Sexual Difference*, ed. Deborah L. Rhode (New Haven: Yale University Press, 1990), 145-59, as she traces this classical assertion that women are not equipped for higher ethical and judicial thought.

50. Cowley, ed., *The Portable Hawthorne*, 658.

51. George MacDonald, *Lilith* (Grand Rapids: Wm. B. Eerdmans, 1981), 203.

52. Cowley, ed., *The Portable Hawthorne*, 659. Hawthorne says of Fuller: "She set to work on her strange, heavy, unpliable, and in many respects, defective and evil nature, and adorned it with a mosaic of admirable qualities. . . . She took

credit to herself for having been her own Redeemer, if not her own Creator; and, indeed, she was far more a work of art than any of Mr. Mozier's statues. But she was not working on an inanimate substance, like marble or clay; there was something within her that she could not possibly come at, to re-create and refine it; and, by and by, this rude old potency bestirred itself, and undid all her labor in the twinkling of an eye."

53. See Herbert, "The Erotics of Purity," 124.
54. See Herbert, "The Erotics of Purity," 126, on the Powers statue and the Hawthornes. See, too, *The English Notebooks*, 392, and Parker and Pollock, *Old Mistresses*, in which plates of both statues appear. Powers's statue toured America in 1848–50 and was much discussed and written about. Hosmer's statue, which appeared in 1858, must also have become familiar to Hawthorne, post-*Blithedale*, for he spent time, when in Italy, at the commune of women artists, among whom was Harriet Hosmer.

8: DREAMS OF SLEEP

1. *A Kate Chopin Miscellany*, ed. Per Seyersted & Emily Toth (Natchitoches: Northwestern State University of Louisiana Press, 1979), 135.
2. *Miscellany*, 169, 177.
3. Kate Chopin, *The Awakening*, ed. Margaret Culley (New York: Norton, 1976), 9, 33, 113.
4. Chopin, *The Awakening*, 106–7.
5. Chopin, *The Awakening*, 70.
6. Chopin, *The Awakening*, 93.
7. Chopin, *The Awakening*, 73. See Katherine Kearns, "The Nullification of Edna Pontellier," *American Literature*, vol. 63, no. 1 (March 1991), 62–88, for my discussion of Chopin's projection of epistemological/philosophical ambivalence onto her character.
8. Chopin, *The Awakening*, 30–2.
9. Iris Murdoch, *The Sovereignty of Good* (New York: Ark, 1986), 31.
10. See Clement Rosset, *Joyful Cruelty: Toward a Philosophy of the Real*, trans. David F. Bell (Oxford University Press, 1993); see "The Cruelty Principle."
11. Sigmund Freud, *The Complete Psychological Works of Sigmund Freud*, vol. 9, ed. James Strachey (London: Hogarth Press, 1961).
12. Murdoch, *The Sovereignty of Good*, 34, 22.
13. I should acknowledge here a response by Richard Rorty in 1992 to what I would like to remember as my devil's-advocate assertion that his "liberal ironist" was a banal solution to a complex problem: he thanked me for the compliment. I suspect that interchange is what began my thinking about realism, which has culminated in my own sense that a certain enriched "banality" (for that is how it necessarily appears when all the wickedly entertaining stuff

has been internalized) is also the best defense against the aggrandizements and extremisms – philosophical, political, and social – that work so covertly to sustain the status quo by keeping its parameters clearly in place.

14. Murdoch, *The Sovereignty of Good*, 16.
15. Friedrich Nietzsche, "On Truth and Falsity in Their Ultramoral Sense," trans. M. A. Mügge, in *Early Greek Philosophy and Other Essays. vol. 2: The Complete Works of Friedrich Nietzsche*, ed. Oscar Levy (New York: Russell & Russell, 1964), 190.
16. Martin Heidegger, *Poetry, Language, Thought*, trans. Albert Hofstadter (New York: Harper & Row, 1971), 112.
17. Heidegger, *Poetry, Language, Thought*, 215.
18. Richard Rorty, *Contingency, Irony, and Solidarity* (Cambridge University Press, 1989), 107.
19. Henry James, *Literary Criticism: Essays on Literature, American Writers, English Writers*, ed. Leon Edel (New York: Library of America, 1984), 1075.
20. Nietzsche, "On Truth and Falsity in Their Ultramoral Sense," 182.

Index